Essential Readers in
Contemporary Media and Culture

This series is designed to collect and publish the best scholarly writing on various aspects of television, film, the Internet, and other media of today. Along with providing original insights and explorations of critical themes, the series is intended to provide readers with the best available resources for an in-depth understanding of the fundamental issues in contemporary media and cultural studies. Topics in the series may include, but are not limited to, critical-cultural examinations of creators, content, institutions, and audiences associated with the media industry. Written in a clear and accessible style, books in the series include both single-author works and edited collections.

Series Editor
Gary R. Edgerton, Old Dominion University

THE ESSENTIAL
CULT TV READER

THE ESSENTIAL CULT TV READER

Edited by
David Lavery

THE UNIVERSITY PRESS OF KENTUCKY

Copyright © 2010 by The University Press of Kentucky

Scholarly publisher for the Commonwealth,
serving Bellarmine University, Berea College, Centre College of Kentucky, Eastern Kentucky University, The Filson Historical Society, Georgetown College, Kentucky Historical Society, Kentucky State University, Morehead State University, Murray State University, Northern Kentucky University, Transylvania University, University of Kentucky, University of Louisville, and Western Kentucky University.
All rights reserved.

Editorial and Sales Offices: The University Press of Kentucky
663 South Limestone Street, Lexington, Kentucky 40508-4008
www.kentuckypress.com

14 13 12 11 10   5 4 3 2 1

Unless otherwise noted, images are provided by Jerry Ohlinger's Movie Material Store.

Library of Congress Cataloging-in-Publication Data

The essential cult tv reader / edited by David Lavery.
   p. cm. — (Essential readers in contemporary media)
  Includes bibliographical references and index.
  ISBN 978-0-8131-2568-8 (hardcover : alk. paper)
  1. Television series—United States. 2. Television viewers—United States. 3. Television series—Great Britain. 4. Television viewers—Great Britain. I. Lavery, David, 1949–
 PN1992.8.S4E87 2010
 791.45'6—dc22   2009035878

This book is printed on acid-free recycled paper meeting the requirements of the American National Standard for Permanence in Paper for Printed Library Materials.

Manufactured in the United States of America.

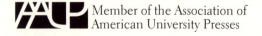

Member of the Association of American University Presses

Contents

Acknowledgments   vii

Introduction: How Cult TV Became Mainstream   David Lavery   1
Absolutely Fabulous   Angelina I. Karpovich   7
The Adventures of Brisco County, Jr.   Bartley Porter and Lynnette Porter   15
Alias   Henrik Örnebring   22
Angel   Joyce Millman   28
The Avengers   Angelina I. Karpovich   36
Battlestar Galactica   Ian Maull and David Lavery   44
Blake's 7   Steven Duckworth   51
Buffy the Vampire Slayer   Milly Williamson   60
The Comeback   Joanne Morreale   68
The Daily Show and *The Colbert Report*   Sam Ford   77
Dark Shadows   Jonathan Malcolm Lampley   84
Dexter   Michele Byers   90
Doctor Who   Matt Hills   97
Farscape   Jes Battis   104
Firefly   J. P. Telotte   111
Freaks and Geeks   Jonathan Gray   120
Heroes   Nikki Stafford   127
The League of Gentlemen   Leon Hunt   134
Life on Mars   Robin Nelson   142
Lost   Marc Dolan   149

Miami Vice   Jon Stratton   159

Monty Python's Flying Circus   Marcia Landy   166

My So-Called Life   Michele Byers   174

Mystery Science Theater 3000   Robert Holtzclaw   181

The Prisoner   Douglas L. Howard   189

Quantum Leap   Lynnette Porter   201

Red Dwarf   Dee Amy-Chinn   208

Roswell   Stan Beeler   214

The Simpsons   Jonathan Gray   221

South Park   Jason Jacobs   229

Stargate SG-1   Angela Ndalianis   237

The *Star Trek* Franchise   Rhonda V. Wilcox   244

Supernatural   Alison Peirse   260

This Life   Stephen Lacey   268

Torchwood   Matt Hills   275

24   Steven Peacock   282

The Twilight Zone   Jonathan Malcolm Lampley   291

Twin Peaks   David Bianculli   299

Ultraviolet   Stacey Abbott   307

Veronica Mars   Sue Turnbull   314

Wonderfalls   Stan Beeler   322

Xena: Warrior Princess   Carolyn Skelton   329

The X-Files   Mikel J. Koven   337

Appendix: Series by Genre and Nationality   345

TV and Filmography   349

Works Cited   359

List of Contributors   381

Index   387

Acknowledgments

As an experienced editor of collections, it is impossible for me to imagine having a better ensemble than the American, British, Canadian, New Zealander, and Australian contributors to this book. My sincere thanks to Stacey Abbott, Dee Amy-Chinn, Jes Battis, Stan Beeler, David Bianculli, Michele Byers, Marc Dolan, Steve Duckworth, Sam Ford, Jonathan Gray, Matt Hills, Robert Holtzclaw, Doug Howard, Leon Hunt, Jason Jacobs, Angelina Karpovich, Mikel Koven, Stephen Lacey, Jonathan Lampley, Marcia Landy, Ian Maull, Joyce Millman, Joanne Morreale, Angela Ndalianis, Robin Nelson, Henrik Örnebring, Steven Peacock, Alison Peirse, Bart Porter, Lynnette Porter, Carolyn Skelton, Nikki Stafford, Jon Stratton, J. P. Telotte, Sue Turnbull, Rhonda Wilcox, and Milly Williamson for their timely and brilliant contributions. A special thanks to Jonathan Lampley, Ian, and Angelina, who came through at the last minute and went beyond the call of duty. Special thanks, too, to Angelina, Stacey, and Simon Brown and to the amazing Janet and Kim for many hours of conversation about television.

This book began at the University Press of Kentucky under the guidance of Leila Salisbury, and I want to express my appreciation to her, her successor Anne Dean Watkins, copy editor Linda Lotz, and series editor Gary Edgerton for all their guidance and support.

I did most of the work on this book in a London flat from which I could see, behind the mosque across the street, the original BBC broadcasting tower at Alexandria Palace—the one the Doctor climbs at the end of "The Idiot's Lantern" (*Doctor Who*, 2.7). It seemed like a perfect spot to be thinking about television and especially about a book like this, concerned as it is with both American and British shows. Even on the other side of the Atlantic, I needed and felt the support of the wonderful women in my family: my wife Joyce and my daughters Rachel and Sarah. Thanks to them—again.

Introduction

How Cult TV Became Mainstream

David Lavery

On Friday the thirteenth of February 2009, only five days after the manuscript of this book was delivered to the publisher, a new series called *Dollhouse* debuted on FOX. It aired after *Terminator: The Sarah Connor Chronicles* (*T: SCC*), a series (based on the successful movie franchise) that was already midway through its second season and in jeopardy due to weak ratings in its former Monday night time slot. *Dollhouse* had originally been slated to air on Monday as well, with the long-running (and probably on its last legs) *24* as its lead-in, but the executives at FOX decided to pair the two shows together at week's end. Friday night was rife with history for the network: It was on Friday that *The X-Files* had overcome a poor start to become a cultural phenomenon and cash cow in the mid-1990s. A decade later, Friday had spelled disaster for *Firefly*, which met an untimely end there after idiotic micromanagement by a "desperate network" (Carter) that was dissatisfied with the series' narrative structure.

Joss Whedon, *Dollhouse*'s creator, had been the man behind *Firefly* as well, so the show's relegation to this traditional TV graveyard seemed like déjà vu to Whedon's fans, but FOX tried to spin its new Friday lineup positively. Lower ratings on Friday would be more easily overlooked, we were told, and the pairing of *T: SCC* and *Dollhouse* would be a natural match, for both shows were likely to appeal to cult audiences. Both *T: SCC* and *Dollhouse* came on the scene too late to be included in this volume, but three other Whedon series—*Buffy the Vampire Slayer* and *Angel*, as well as *Firefly*—have entries here.

Elsewhere—on a night ruled by the expectation of high ratings and on another network—ABC was attempting a similar move. It paired *Lost* and the struggling-for-an-audience American version of *Life on Mars* back to back on Wednesday night. (See the chapters on *Lost* and the British version of *Life on Mars* in this volume.)

How did FOX's cult TV Friday work out? By the time you read this, we will all know. What about ABC's experiment? (In the first few weeks, *Life on Mars* lost a sizable share of the *Lost* audience.) The answer will tell us much, as will this book, about the state of cult television at the end of the "noughties." Does cult television need to be ghettoized to succeed? Can it be mainstreamed? What exactly is cult television anyway?

When this collection was in development, ABC's *Grey's Anatomy*, the popular hospital melodrama, was on my original list of series worthy of inclusion. This provoked a strong objection from an eventual contributor to these pages. How on earth could I suggest that *Grey's*, a mainstream entertainment that, beginning in the fall of 2007, had been brazenly positioned to go up against ratings champion *CSI*, deserved coverage in a book such as this? Arguing that *Grey's* conformed to the basic cult media litmus test established by Matt Hills—that is, it attracted "passionate, enduring, and socially organized fan audiences" ("Media Fandom" 73)—I defended my position. (Note that *Grey's* did not make the final cut.)

This tiff was pertinent to the current debate about cult media, including television, in the early twenty-first century. Cult and mainstream, obscure and popular, esoteric and exoteric—the boundaries have blurred. At the end of the last century, movie studios tried to cultivate the genius behind increasingly successful independent filmmaking by institutionalizing it, setting up their own in-house "independent" nurseries. In a less noticed but comparable development, an American television network rolled the dice on a new series codeveloped by that most cultish of directors David Lynch (*Eraserhead*, *Blue Velvet*). The result was *Twin Peaks*. After momentarily capturing the public's almost undivided attention, it flamed out (see David Bianculli's chapter in this volume), but the precedent had been set. Individuals with cultish sensibilities—Judd Apatow (*Freaks and Geeks*); Chris Carter (*The X-Files*); J. J. Abrams (*Alias*, *Lost*); Joss Whedon (*Buffy the Vampire Slayer*, *Angel*, *Firefly*); Carlton Cuse (*The Adventures of Brisco County, Jr.*; *Lost*); Eric Kripke (*Supernatural*); Matt Groening (*The Simpsons*); Rob Thomas (*Veronica Mars*); Matt Stone and Trey Parker (*South Park*); Bryan Fuller

(*Wonderfalls*); Jon Stewart and Stephen Colbert (*The Daily Show* and *The Colbert Report*); James Manos Jr. (*Dexter*); Damon Lindelof (*Lost*); Ronald D. Moore and David Eick (*Battlestar Galactica*); Tim Kring (*Heroes*); Rockne O'Bannon (*Farscape*); Jeremy Dyson, Mark Gatiss, Steve Pemberton, and Reece Shearsmith (*League of Gentlemen*); Rob Tapert (*Xena: Warrior Princess*); Joe Ahearne (*Ultraviolet*); and Russell T. Davies (*Absolutely Fabulous, Doctor Who, Torchwood*)—began contributing to television in the United Kingdom and the United States, giving us much of the essential cult television this book covers.

The Essential Cult TV Reader also examines a number of older, "classic" cult programs that were created and originally broadcast before cult TV had become quite so self-conscious: *The Avengers, Blake's 7, Dark Shadows, Miami Vice, Monty Python's Flying Circus, Mystery Science Theater 3000, The Prisoner, Quantum Leap, Red Dwarf, Star Trek*, and *The Twilight Zone*. Also included are a number of more recent series that have come to be considered cultish, whether they intended to be or not.

No doubt every reader of this book will be inclined to contest some of its content, dubious about the inclusion of this or that show, upset that a particular favorite has been omitted. That is as it should be, for cult television will always be, as Steven Peacock notes in these pages, "notoriously slippery." In the chapters that follow, you will find a wide variety of justifications for cult membership. The Gwenllian-Jones–Pearson establishment clause—"Cult television's imaginary universes support an *inexhaustible range of narrative possibilities*, inviting, supporting and rewarding close textual analysis, interpretation, and inventive reformulations"—is often cited or evoked in these pages. Equally important is their observation that cult TV has evolved into "a meta-genre that caters to intense, interpretive audience practices," affording "fans enormous scope for further interpretation, speculation and invention" ("Introduction" xii, xvi).

Not surprisingly, the important investigations of Matt Hills, himself a contributor to this book, are often referenced, especially his contention that cult television is distinguished by its "hyperdiegesis": "the creation of a vast and detailed narrative space, only a fraction of which is ever directly seen or encountered within the text" (*Fan Cultures* 137). Another important stance taken by Hills is that, rather than simply "celebrating cult texts for their supposed uniqueness," we should focus on "analyzing and defining cult TV as a part of broader patterns within changing TV industries" ("Defining Cult TV" 522).

For all the sophistication of the debate that informs these pages, we should not forget what might be called the commonsense or public understanding of cult television. As noted by Robert Holtzclaw (in his chapter on *Mystery Science Theater 3000*), cult TV is most readily identifiable by "the fervency of a program's audience support, the degree to which its language and catchphrases enter its audience's vocabulary, fans' determination to amass collectibles and memorabilia, and conventions at which like-minded souls can congregate and share their passion." This is what underpins more theoretical considerations.

In their investigations into particular cult works, the contributors to this volume offer a number of probing, perhaps enduring, questions:

Can a dip in a show's quality actually enhance its cult appeal? (We're looking at you, *24*.)
Are the makers of cult series obligated to answer the fans' clamor for greater involvement?
Does the presence of a star with cult status or a cult of personality guarantee the cult status of a series?
What is the relationship between camp and cult-ivation? Between badness—"the sheer crappiness of the series and the crappiness it attributes to the universe" (Hanks, quoted by Steven Duckworth in his chapter on *Blake's 7*)—and cult TV?
What are the specific connections between genre hybridity or genre bending and cult status?
Does "Brilliant but Cancelled" status (the name of a Web site on the subject) actually enhance culthood?
Why is the fantastic—the "left of real" (J. J. Abrams's term)—such fertile ground for cult shows?
How does the strategic use of the cameo enhance the possibilities of cult?
Is it possible for a television show to gain cult status largely through nostalgia?
Would the current conversation about cult television have transpired without the validation of TV on DVD?
Are "B.Y.O. [bring your own] subtext" shows (Joss Whedon's phrase) ipso facto cult shows? What role do intertextuality, metatextuality, and serialization play in the growth of cult television?
Is cult TV always countercultural? (Is the reverse true?)
Has Showtime consciously positioned itself (against its "not TV" rival HBO) as a cult TV venue?

Does cult television exhibit a unique approach to character investment?

Is it still true that standard-issue television cult work, in keeping with tradition, "represents a disruptive rather than a conservative force" (Kawin 19)?

How does cult television differ—in subject matter, audience, marketing, narrative—from cult film?

Do cult shows by their very nature record seismic shifts in the evolution of television programming?

How will the emergence of multiple platforms for television programming change the nature of cult television?

Are there narrative forms unique to cult television? If so, how have they influenced all of series television?

What is the place of the "conspiracy theory" in fostering or sustaining cult TV?

Are the traditional youth demographics of cult television changing?

To what degree has cult television created transnational languages and viewing practices and furthered globalization?

The answers to these questions—tentative, of course, because the state of cult television is in constant flux—can be found in the chapters that follow, sometimes in the form of more questions.

Of the series covered in this book, fewer than half are still on the air or "alive" in some shape or form at the time of this writing. After a year's layoff due to the writers' strike, the seventh day (aka season) of *24* has played out, but the Bush administration is over and the "tortures" of Jack Bauer may well have lost their appeal. FOX is about to transplant *Absolutely Fabulous* to American shores. The stories of *Angel* and *Buffy* have been reborn in comic book form (*Angel: After the Fall* and *Buffy the Vampire Slayer: Season Eight*). The last season of a grimmer-than-ever *Battlestar Galactica* is over, both human and Cylon have made it to a devastated Earth, and the final Cylon was revealed to be . . . Ellen Tigh? After gorging on the satiric feast of the 2008 presidential election, *The Daily Show* and *The Colbert Report* are learning to cope with the Obama era. *Dexter* recently completed a third season, which saw our favorite serial killer getting married, anticipating fatherhood, and perhaps preparing to "jump the shark." *Doctor Who* is in a period of huge transition, with the mastermind behind the series' regeneration, Russell T. Davies, about to be replaced by one of its most brilliant writers (Steven Moffat), and the Tenth Doctor (David Tennant) about to regenerate into a twenty-something Eleventh. By general consensus, *Heroes* had a terrible, strike-shortened sophomore season (creator Tim Kring even issued an apology) and continued to gravely disappoint its audience, both mainstream and cult, in season 3. After crossing the Atlantic, *Life on Mars* dropped Sam Tyler into 1973 New York, but the series had a difficult time adjusting to the longevity demands of American television. Five episodes into its penultimate season, *Lost* (which has a predetermined end date) boldly came out of the cult closet and declared itself to be a mind-bending sci-fi series more complex and challenging than any in the history of the medium. Like *Absolutely Fabulous* and *Life on Mars*, *The Prisoner* is coming to America (on basic cable's American Movie Classics), although it is being filmed in Africa. *The Simpsons* has completed a record-setting twentieth season (and more than 440 episodes) and still retains much of its worldwide appeal. The controversial and profane *South Park* is far behind *The Simpsons* in longevity (fourteen seasons and only 181 episodes, but already signed for a fifteenth), but it continues to push the taste envelope as its satirizes both Right and Left (a dream sequence in "The China Problem" has George Lucas and Steven Spielberg raping Indiana Jones). *Star Trek* is no longer on the small screen, but cult TV maestro J. J. Abrams's origin movie is about to relaunch the franchise in the multiplexes. The universe of *Stargate SG-1* is still alive, though barely perpetuated in a series of straight-to-DVD movies. With Dean rescued from hell by an angel, the Winchester boys are now battling with divine minions from both above and below in anticipation of a coming apocalypse on *Supernatural*, which exhibits its cult allegiances in stand-alone episodes such as "Monster Movie," with a murderous shape-shifter taking the form of 1930s movie monsters from Dracula to the Mummy. *Torchwood*'s future is somewhat in doubt, but the United Kingdom's finest alien-monster squad will return in a spring 2009 miniseries. *The X-Files* was briefly reincarnated, for the second time, in 2008 in a pedestrian, forgettable movie, *The X-Files: I Want to Believe*, reminding us yet again (as had *Buffy*, *League of Gentlemen*, *Star Trek*, *The Twilight Zone*, *Stargate*, and *Doctor Who* before it) that some cult universes are indigenous to television. For updates on current cult television covered in this book, links, and additional entries on cult programs from around the world, visit the *Essential Cult TV Reader* Web site: http://davidlavery.net/Cult_TV/.

Absolutely Fabulous

Angelina I. Karpovich

Absolutely Fabulous was, on the surface, a fairly traditional BBC sitcom about the shallowness and superficiality of the fashion and public relations (PR) industries. Its creator, Jennifer Saunders, was the less prolific half of the BBC comedy sketch show *French and Saunders* (an early precursor to one of the central relationships on *Absolutely Fabulous* appeared in a *French and Saunders* sketch titled "Modern Mother and Daughter"). Her comedy partner Dawn French enjoyed a high-profile career, acting in the theater, creating two successful BBC comedy series (*Murder . . . Most Horrid* and *The Vicar of Dibley*), and having her own fashion line. Saunders, in contrast, appeared to do little outside of the partnership with French until 1992. Indeed, within the creative partnership itself, Saunders mostly played the straight woman to French's frequently over-the-top, farcical characters. Even in the wake of the show's success, Saunders insisted that she had reluctantly created *Absolutely Fabulous* on her own only because French was unavailable (Aitkenhead). Thus, even to an audience familiar with Jennifer Saunders as a comedy performer, *Absolutely Fabulous* was initially an unknown entity.

Absolutely Fabulous centers on Edina Monsoon (played by Saunders), the forty-something owner of a London PR agency. Despite the apparent incompetence of Edina and her employees (most notably her entirely clueless assistant Bubble, played by Jane Horrocks), Edina enjoys a lifestyle of luxury, invariably in the company of her longtime best friend, the hedonistic Patsy Stone (Joanna Lumley). Later episodes suggest that Edina's wealth comes from maintenance payments from her two ex-husbands rather than from her business. Edina shares her house with her sensible and disapproving daughter Saffy (Julia Sawalha) and, later on, her mother, Mrs. Monsoon (June Whitfield).

While the early episodes offer bold brushstrokes in characterization designed to produce maximal comic effect, nuances in the characters' personalities emerge over the course of the series. Edina is apparently considered a professional success, despite her lack of organization and generally poor interpersonal skills. She earns the recognition of her peers and is nominated for awards within the PR industry. Yet she longs for approval, most frequently from Patsy but also from the men who appear intermittently in her life and, though she is loath to admit it, from Saffy.

Patsy, in turn, is extraordinarily callous and often downright cruel, particularly to Saffy. Yet she experiences brief flashes of insecurity and seems slightly afraid of Mrs. Monsoon, instantly reverting to her teenage self in interactions with Edina's mother. The mutual antagonism between Patsy and Saffy is another of the show's constant narrative refrains. Patsy takes advantage of every opportunity to abuse Saffy, verbally and sometimes even physically, yet she inexplicably tries to help her in other situations ("Sex" and "The Last Shout, Part 2").

The show initially presents Saffy as the sober and sensible alternative to the hedonistic Edina and Patsy. The conflict between mother and daughter is a popular theme in the early seasons, with the comedy derived from the reversal of their expected roles. Saffy eventually takes on a more significant role within the overall text of the show. She is the only major character whose life undergoes substantial changes during the course of *Absolutely Fabulous*. She first appears as a teenager, moves on to university, leaves home, graduates, travels the world, and finally starts a family of her own. The other major characters' circumstances stay relatively static throughout the course of the show (despite Edina's temporary financial struggle in "Poor" and Patsy's slight change of occupation in "Gay"). Thus, the central "situation" of this situation comedy remains unchanged. It is not Edina's latest fashion outfits or the occasional topical references that suggest the passage of time in the *Absolutely Fabulous* universe; rather, it is Saffy's evolution from a downtrodden teenager into a confident and (despite her mother's best efforts) well-adjusted adult.

Mrs. Monsoon and Bubble initially appear as secondary characters who are even more one-dimensional than the leads, yet they too gain prominence and complexity as the show develops. Mrs. Monsoon injects enough shrewd remarks into her interactions with Edina and Patsy to suggest that she may be exaggerating her disorientation and forgetfulness, possibly to distract attention from her kleptomania, which is subtly but persistently referred to throughout the show. Here, the comedy is derived from the juxtaposition between Mrs. Monsoon's morally dubious actions and her thoroughly prim appearance: in a way, she combines some of Edina's and Saffy's personality traits, serving as a conceptual bridge between the two characters.

Bubble, too, develops as the show progresses. Initially, she is little more than a caricature, notable only for her supreme incompetence and for a dress sense that is not just over the top but completely incongruous and erratic. Both these characteristics help to establish Edina as a successful and relatively competent professional in comparison to Bubble. Yet Bubble may not be as airheaded as she appears. Like Mrs. Monsoon, her inanity is punctuated with sharp and precise put-downs, usually directed at Patsy. In what is ultimately a satisfying paradox, a show about shallowness and superficiality subtly presents even its secondary characters as relatively complex and multilayered.

Edina's relationship with Patsy is the center of the show. Although neither woman seems to know the meaning of the words *loyalty* and *respect*, they are the only constants in each other's chaotic lives. Edina's relationships with her daughter and mother are far more distant and transitory, and her two husbands and son have left (escaped?) her. But Patsy is invariably there, often jealously driving away anyone else who wants to get close to Edina. She directs most of her venom at Saffy, who arguably doesn't want to be near Edina in the first place. Most of the time, Patsy's relationship to Edina seems to be one-sided and parasitic: she is always borrowing from Edina (her car, money, other belongings), turning up at Edina's house uninvited and wanting a favor, or persuading Edina to go on a holiday, shopping, or to lunch with no intention of paying her share. Yet as the season 2 episode "New Best Friend" shows, Edina would not be better off without Patsy. Their attempts to find new best friends stall because neither of them is capable of relating to other people, and as the end of the episode shows, Edina can be just as selfish and callous as Patsy. The status quo is restored at the end, and despite some arguments between the two characters, it is never seriously challenged again for the rest of the series.

Although both Edina's persistent but entirely superficial interest in all forms of New Age spirituality and well-being and her ex-husband

Marshall's reliance on self-help guides are early precursors of any number of postmillennial fads (from the popularity of organic food to the celebrity following of Kabbalah), the show is rooted in the 1980s, with materialism and consumerism the main targets of its satire. The association with the 1980s was further underscored by the 1994 release of a single titled "Absolutely Fabulous" by the quintessentially 1980s band the Pet Shop Boys. The song, which contained samples of dialogue from the show, was released as part of the annual Comic Relief charity event; it reflected the popularity of Edina and Patsy and ultimately reached number 6 on the U.K. singles chart.

With its focus on the more outlandish aspects of the world of high fashion and its unusually prominent (for an early 1990s prime-time BBC show) and positive references to homosexuality—Edina's second husband and son are gay, she relishes the possibility that Saffy may be a lesbian, and Patsy once spent a year living as a man—*Absolutely Fabulous* quickly gained cult status among fans of camp. Indeed, the show's very title deliberately invokes precisely the kind of hyperbole identified by Sontag as one of the defining characteristics of the camp aesthetic. At the same time, Patsy's iconic beehive hairdo and devil-may-care attitude made the character a favorite with drag impersonators, a real-life audience reaction that was subsequently incorporated into the show.

As a sitcom, *Absolutely Fabulous* is notable for employing a large amount of slapstick physical comedy. Many of the episodes delight in Edina or Patsy falling out of taxis, over hedges, and down stairs while drunk, high, or hung over. Most episodes also extract comedic value out of Edina's chaotic dress sense and supposed fatness. Thus, the show provides a sophisticated combination of verbal, physical, and situational humor, along with social commentary and the occasional foray into camp.

In retrospect, *Absolutely Fabulous* can be seen as an early reaction to the "laddism" phenomenon that dominated British popular culture in the 1990s. Largely based on hedonism and the pleasures of alcohol, sex, and, to a lesser extent, camaraderie, laddism was in some ways the opposite of the "new man" social construct (Edwards, *Cultures*). In television, the epitome of laddism is the sitcom *Men Behaving Badly*, whose male protagonists' lifestyles are the embodiment of hedonistic, infantile irresponsibility. If we discount the fashion industry, in many ways, the pursuits and preoccupations of the main protagonists of *Absolutely Fabulous* and *Men Behaving Badly* are strikingly similar. Curiously, *Absolutely*

Fabulous was never used as a point of reference when the term *ladette* emerged in the United Kingdom in the late 1990s to describe young women whose behavior was boisterous and fueled by alcohol. Perhaps, despite all their crudeness and frequent pratfalls, Edina and Patsy were still more refined than the ladettes who would follow them. More likely, the show was popularly perceived as a hyperbole, and Edina and particularly Patsy were seen as characters who were both over the top and larger than life, which made it difficult to imagine them as antecedents to real-life social phenomena. Nevertheless, *Absolutely Fabulous* was, in some ways, an unprecedented representation of women in a mainstream television show that would turn out to be ahead of its time.

On another level, *Absolutely Fabulous* can be interpreted as a satirical and largely negative comment on postmodernism and its values. Edina and Patsy are obsessed with appearance, with labels, with the latest trends. One of their most consistent driving impulses is consumption, and another is a quest for fame (though they are seemingly happy with achieving proximity to celebrities rather than seeking fame for themselves). Their shallowness is matched and exceeded by that of their peers. Moreover, *Absolutely Fabulous* is quite cynical about the possibility of any kind of redemption for these two women. Although they are frequently faced with the consequences of their shallowness and irresponsibility, neither character ever learns her lesson. This lack of moralizing is arguably one of the key elements of the show's appeal. Indeed, Saffy's portrayal tends to become unsympathetic whenever her disapproval of Edina and Patsy leads her into holier-than-thou territory, suggesting that the show's lack of an overt moral message is quite intentional.

Unusual for a British sitcom, *Absolutely Fabulous* is very international in its outlook. Significant story lines repeatedly take the characters and the action abroad, to France, the United States, and Morocco. Although the comedy in these episodes is generally derived from the clash of cultures and, more specifically, from Edina's and Patsy's insensitivity and their inability to function independently, the foreign-location episodes are more notable for conceptual and industrial reasons. Conceptually, the international scope of *Absolutely Fabulous* is symptomatic of Saunders's commitment to verisimilitude in the midst of the show's hyperbole and occasional surrealism. Because the focus is on apparently successful and well-paid fashion and PR professionals, it is necessary to break with the BBC's established tradition of studio-based sitcoms to represent the jet-setting aspect of their lifestyles. This departure from the norm is even more significant in institutional terms, signaling the BBC's commitment to a significantly higher than usual production budget for a show of its genre. At the same time, *Absolutely Fabulous*'s overseas trips promoted its success outside the United Kingdom, particularly in the United States, where the show became a hit on Comedy Central and Saunders and Lumley subsequently guest-starred as Edina and Patsy in a 1996 episode of *Roseanne*. Roseanne Barr had been a vocal fan of *Absolutely Fabulous* and had even acquired the rights to a U.S. remake, though this was never produced ("Roseanne Plans").

Another unusual feature is the show's frequent use of dream sequences and flashbacks. Edina's and Patsy's loose grip on reality, unreliable memories, and almost constant inebriation all prompt vivid and lovingly re-created sequences that recall their pasts (sometimes through a psychedelic haze), imagine alternative realities, or suggest their and other characters' futures. The show's frequent and varied departures from its main setting, both geographically and temporally, are one of the most significant features distinguishing it from other U.K. sitcoms of the same period. These departures are used quite deliberately, either to introduce new elements to the characters or the plot (as in the episodes "France" and "Morocco," in which Edina and Patsy show unexpected sides of their characters when they are forced to cope with unfamiliar surroundings) or to showcase some of the many celebrity cameos—most memorably, when Edina encounters God, played by 1960s music and fashion icon Marianne Faithful, once during a near-death experience ("The Last Shout, Part 1") and once in a dream ("Donkey").

The early *Absolutely Fabulous* series was a critical and commercial success. The show received a spate of award nominations in the United Kingdom and abroad, winning the British Academy of Film and Television Award for Best Comedy Series in 1993 and an International Emmy in 1994. Saunders won a Best Comedy award for her writing from the Writers Guild of Great Britain in 1993, and the show was nominated as Most Popular Comedy in the 1996 National Television Awards in the United Kingdom—notable because these awards are voted for by the viewing public.

However, the show's history is fractured. The first three seasons ran between 1992 and 1995, with the final episode of season 3 billed as the last-ever episode and titled "The End." The episode ends with a flashforward, twenty-five years into the future, that shows Edina and Patsy as pensioners who are still happily overindulging in alcohol, cigarettes, and clubbing—a fitting conclusion. Yet eighteen months later, two additional special episodes were broadcast, also billed as the last ever in the show and entitled "The Last Shout, Parts 1 and 2." In 2001 the series returned yet again for another two seasons and two specials, completing its run in 2004 and returning for a (supposedly final) Comic Relief special in 2005. Although the first three seasons garnered almost universal critical praise, the later seasons and specials were met with much less enthusiasm and a diminishing number of viewers. Perhaps the audience began to tire of a show that kept announcing its end and then returning. Perhaps, having been significantly ahead of its time in the early to mid-1990s, and having predicted and preempted some of the most prominent postmillennial pop cultural developments and trends, *Absolutely Fabulous* had finally lost its cutting-edge originality. Perhaps, in a twenty-first-century world apparently obsessed with the likes of Paris Hilton (seemingly a less bright version of Bubble), *Absolutely Fabulous* could no longer successfully satirize the fashion and PR industries, whose real-life excesses were now greater and far more visible than the hyperboles imagined by Jennifer Saunders in the early 1990s.

Nevertheless, *Absolutely Fabulous* remains a cult moment in television, with the 1992–1995 seasons as the pinnacle of the show's freshness and originality and the subsequent episodes as additions to the *Absolutely Fabulous* canon. Though the show's cultural impact may not be immediately obvious, it has had a substantial influence on the television industry, particularly in comedy. Saunders's subsequent show, *Mirrorball*, which employed the main cast of *Absolutely Fabulous* in entirely new roles and situations, was an interesting though ultimately unsuccessful experiment. Some of Edina and Patsy's relationship dynamic, as well as a toned-down version of Patsy's personality, was echoed in the U.S. sitcom *Cybill*. More significantly, Patsy and Edina's intense friendship, together with their love of designer labels and their desire to participate in glamorous social events, can be seen as clear influences on some of the central preoccupations of the characters of *Sex and the City*, with its focus on female friendship, cocktails, parties, and designer shoes. At the same time, the more over-the-top and outrageous aspects of Patsy's personality seem to have directly informed the character of caustic socialite Karen Walker in *Will and Grace*. Parallels between the characters range from the almost continuous alcohol consumption and often tenuous grip on reality to the vicious put-downs and both characters' colorful pasts and highly ambiguous sexual identities. To a lesser extent, echoes of some of the prominent stylistic and narrative elements of *Absolutely Fabulous* can be noted in shows as diverse as *Ally McBeal* and *Arrested Development*. Thus, despite its flawed later seasons, *Absolutely Fabulous* is significant in a variety of ways: as a show whose creative influence continues to be felt internationally, as one of the BBC's most unusual yet most successful prime-time programs, and, finally, as a perhaps unwitting piece of social commentary that predicted many of the excesses of twenty-first-century celebrity culture.

The Adventures of Brisco County, Jr.

Bartley Porter and Lynnette Porter

Long before *Survivor*'s "outwit, outplay, outlast" motto, Brisco County Jr. uttered these words: "I can outshoot, outride, outspit, outfight, outthink John Bly or any one of his gang. . . . That's all I've got to say on the subject." In many ways, Brisco is the ultimate survivor of a once popular but nearly dead genre: the television Western. Brisco, however, has survived even TV cancellation to gain cult status by anticipating, in its first episode, "the coming thing": "It's 1893. We're only seven years away from a new century, the 20th century. Don't you sense it? The coming thing. It's right out there on the horizon. It's just around the corner. . . . If I knew exactly what it was, it wouldn't be coming. It would already be here." *The Adventures of Brisco County, Jr.* blended familiar elements from the Western, detective–murder mystery, science fiction, and buddy–road-trip genres; threw in some father issues for psychological development (so common these days on *Lost*, *Heroes*, and other 2000-era favorites); and cast in the lead role Bruce Campbell, a cult movie actor and master of the sly delivery. As the first series created and often scripted by Jeffrey Boam and Carlton Cuse (later of *Nash Bridges* and *Lost* fame), *Brisco*'s scripts often presented "the coming thing" to television audiences about a decade ahead of its time.

Brisco himself defies not only the murderous John Bly gang but also conventions of stock TV Western heroes. In the pilot episode, Jonah Collier—a *San Francisco Gazette* columnist who has also interviewed the famous lawman Brisco Sr.—describes Junior as a "Harvard-educated lawyer, a scholar, by all accounts a man of refinement, elegance, and polish." In contrast, audiences first see Brisco Jr. as a dusty cowboy about to be hanged by banditos who accuse him of cheating at cards. Brisco protests his innocence shortly before he is caught in the crossfire between rival gangs. A stray bullet bisects the rope, and Brisco rides away on Comet, his faithful horse. Clearly, appearances can be deceiving; Brisco is more than he initially seems. He is constantly in a jam but always manages to escape, often assisted by fate. He is a rogue but also a skilled lawyer; a bounty hunter who wants more than money; a forward thinker who looks forward to "the coming thing" but accepts that it will bring new problems; a son determined to punish his father's killer (Bly), but a man not hell-bent on revenge; a ladies' man who respects women, especially sometimes-flame Dixie, as equals. Brisco often reflects 1993 ideas and morals within the series' 1893 setting.

One definition of cult TV requires a series to challenge viewers' perceptions of how the world operates. Perhaps that's why science fiction and fantasy series most often top the lists of cult television programs; they operate on worlds or in dimensions atypical from audiences' experience. Cult TV inspires loyal fans to continue their enjoyment and promotion of their favorite series long after its cancellation. These fans not only understand the mythology on which episodes are based but often continue to develop it beyond canon. *Brisco* clearly meets these criteria.

Brisco flirts with science fiction, especially through its mythology of a mysterious object known as the Orb and time traveler–turned–outlaw John Bly, but its setting and characters come straight from the Old West playbook. Its mixture of genres helps ensure its status as a cult series. Plus, *Brisco* is well written and acted. In addition to Campbell, the cast includes Julius Carey (frequent guest on, among others, *Murphy Brown, The District, JAG, The Unit*), Kelly Rutherford (*Melrose Place, Threat Matrix, Gossip Girl*), Christian Clemenson (most recently an Emmy winner for his role on *Boston Legal*), and recurring guest star John Astin (probably best known from *The Addams Family*).

Although *Brisco*'s ratings didn't justify its renewal after one season, it quickly developed a devoted following who liked FOX's Friday night lineup of *Brisco* as the lead-in to the more popular (and cult TV exemplar) *X-Files*. When the series was relegated to Saturday mornings, fans followed. Even today, when Campbell makes convention appearances, he is just as likely to be asked about his role as Brisco County Jr. as Ash from the *Evil Dead* movies and video games or Autolycus, Prince of Thieves, who appeared first in *Hercules: The Legendary Journeys* and then in *Xena: Warrior Princess*, two other cult series. Fans still maintain *Brisco*-devoted Web sites.[1]

When the series finally debuted on DVD in 2006, fans and critics joyfully welcomed it like an old friend, and reviews praised not only the series but also star Campbell. The *Hollywood News* review exalted Campbell as "fandom king, the hero that millions of fans worship," and it acknowledged that the DVD collection easily shows the series' "charm and cult status" (Heath). An even more enthusiastic review was published by *Blogcritics Magazine*, which found the series worthwhile simply because of Campbell: "Part of his popularity can be attributed to his chin,[2] some more to his fantastic onscreen charisma, but there is something else. That something else is fun, he just seems like a fun guy, and it comes through in his roles" (Beaumont).

Campbell isn't the only reason to catch up on the DVD episodes for those who missed the original. Peter Brown of *iF Magazine* summed up the series' original performance: *"The Adventures of Brisco County Jr.* is one of these shows never to be given a chance in hell of succeeding despite having a large, devoted fan base—and it sure didn't help it was on the quick draw FOX network either. Part Western, part science-fiction, all hilarity [the series is] anchored by the B-movie maven himself in the lead role" ("DVD Review"). It's no surprise that Brown gave the DVD set an A.

The Adventures of Brisco County, Jr. continues to thrive in the twenty-first century, while remaining true to its nineteenth- and twentieth-century roots. Its continuing popularity is based on the following: "in jokes" for faithful viewers; a time-bending, science-inspired Western mythology; and the cult of Bruce Campbell.

"In Jokes" and Repetition

Repeated events, images, and catchphrases provide inside jokes for faithful viewers. One member of the Bly gang, Pete Hutter, defies logic by being killed multiple times throughout the series (similar to the running joke of Kenny's multiple deaths on *South Park*). Pete is killed by a fellow gang member during a shoot-out with Brisco ("The Adventures of Brisco County, Jr.," 1.1), dissected by Chinese stars ("And Baby Makes Three," 1.24), and stabbed by a pitchfork ("High Treason, Part 2," 1.27); each time, he returns with a lame excuse for cheating death. Pete also has a fondness for his weapon, and jokes about "Pete's piece"—and who can

From left: bounty hunters Colonel March (Terry Bradshaw) and Mason "Cowboy" Dixon (Jim Harbaugh); our heroes Lord Bowler (Julius Carry) and Brisco County Jr. (Bruce Campbell); Grissle Wallens (Carl Banks); and Aldo Buttuchi (Ken Norton Jr.) in the series' finale, "High Treason."

and can't touch it—constitute a running gag in several episodes. Multiple jokes also refer to the cowboys' stylish hats, from Bly gang member Big Smith's huge hat with money sewn into the band, reflecting the "price on his head," to Lord Bowler's bowler, which prompts many an outlaw insult.

References to popular culture from the twentieth century provide humorous anachronisms in the nineteenth-century stories. Dixie Cousins, Brisco's love interest, is less Miss Kitty (*Gunsmoke*) than Mae West, with her double entendre–laden dialogue and sultry delivery. Even episode titles flirt with being more adult than family viewing: "Deep in the Heart of Dixie" (1.11), despite its title, is a rather innocent tale of Brisco and Dixie on the run from killers. An Elvis impersonator, Aaron Viva (a tribute to *Viva Las Vegas*), is the sheriff of Hard Rock ("Hard Rock," 1.18)—a name appropriate for both a desolate western town and a chain of music memorabilia restaurants. Sly winks to popular culture or inexplicable plot devices that mock the serious nature of many Westerns from the 1950s and 1960s endear *Brisco* to its faithful fans.

A Science- and Science Fiction–Inspired Mythology

Brisco's interest in "the coming thing" leads him to work with Professor Wickwire in some of his adventures. During "High Treason, Part 2" (1.27), the professor reveals "the mother of all inventions," an airship (dirigible) that Brisco later rides out of town. After their adventure, Wickwire confides to Brisco that he intends to take his invention to potential buyer Count von Zeppelin in Germany. Fan historians who are aware of Germany's dirigibles in the early 1900s (e.g., the infamous *Hindenburg*) find Wickwire's comments not only humorous but also historically relevant. Wickwire's other inventions, including rubber bullets (which save Brisco and Bowler from certain death in "High Treason, Part 2"), an underwater suit with a bellows to maintain airflow ("Socrates' Sister," 1.5), and motorcycles ("Steel Horses," 1.13), also foreshadow later real-world inventions. In fact, *Brisco*'s fiction is often based in reality; by 1894—one year after Brisco's 1893 adventures—Hildebrand & Wolfmueller became the first company to patent a two-wheeled motorcycle, which it produced for customer purchase ("Invention of the Motorcycle").

Brisco's writers are also aware of the power of fiction. In "Brisco for the Defense" (1.9), lawyer Brisco quotes Mark Twain's *Pudd'nhead Wilson*, published by *Century Magazine* in 1893. Brisco's discussion of the story's "antediluvian world" is echoed in Bly's comments about his desire to rule such a world ("Fountain of Youth," 1.17). Brisco, like the series' writers, is clearly familiar with Twain's story, which becomes an ancestor text for the series. (The existence of numerous ancestor texts is a trait of Cuse's series, reaching epic proportions in *Lost*.)

The most memorable story arc, however, involves the Orb, a device stolen from the future by time traveler–turned–outlaw John Bly. In the pilot episode, Brisco learns that Chinese railroad workers have freed themselves using the power of a mysterious Orb they unearthed. When Brisco later finds the Orb on a train, he uses it to protect himself from being shot by villain Big Smith ("The Adventures of Brisco County, Jr.," 1.1). Professor Ogden Coles, an Orb scholar, claims that he has studied the Orb all his life and tells Brisco about several other orbs ("The Orb

Scholar," 1.2). Coles warns Brisco of the Orb's power, which is "wonderful, but in the wrong hands there is incomprehensible danger." When, later in that episode, Brisco is shot point-blank, Coles convinces him to take a rod from the Orb to heal himself. The rod glows blue, Brisco is told to have faith in the Orb (faith is a recurring theme in Cuse's series), and he is healed.

The Orb's story continues in other episodes ("Senior Spirit," 1.8; "AKA Kansas," 1.15; "Fountain of Youth," 1.17). In a classic battle between good (Brisco) and evil (Bly), the Orb's power can determine the fate of humanity not only in *Brisco's* 1890s but also in the future. The saga ends when a woman from 5502, tracking Bly and the Orb, tells Brisco that Bly is a villain who wants to rule the world and has escaped through time by using the Orb's power. Brisco becomes even more determined to bring time traveler Bly to justice, not only for his father's murder but also for the future of humanity. Brisco himself uses the Orb and takes a quick trip to the future to advise his buddy Bowler to avoid a bullet ("Bye Bly," 1.20); once present-time Brisco knows that Bowler is safe, he stabs and kills Bly with a rod from the Orb.

This continuing story infuses *Brisco* with time-travel stories that allow fantastic plot devices, such as Bly being transformed into a screaming tornado and pulled into the Orb, where he becomes trapped for a time ("Fountain of Youth," 1.17). Although *Brisco's* episodes provide a fond look at science, its sci-fi Orb arc gains the most attention from fans.

The Cult of Bruce Campbell

Bruce Campbell's career is a practical guide to becoming a cult idol. His collaboration with childhood friend Sam Raimi includes *The Evil Dead* and *Evil Dead II: Dead by Dawn*.[3] These low-budget 1980s horror films star Campbell as bored S-Mart worker Ash, who accidentally travels to an undisclosed medieval time (with his car), finds the Necronomicon, and fights (you guessed it) the evil dead. The best version of similarly plotted films is the more commercially successful *Army of Darkness*, a glossier film that Roger Ebert praised: "The special effects in *Army of Darkness* are ingenious and a lot of fun. The makeup is state of the art. So are the severed limbs, geysers of blood, etc." Campbell also received a compliment as "a square-jawed, muscular comic book hero." With these films, Campbell was well on his way to becoming a cult hero. By the time he became Brisco, he had a legion of devoted fans who appreciated his droll delivery. Following *Brisco's* untimely demise, Campbell achieved even greater sci-fi cult fame through a recurring role in Raimi's and Rob Tappert's *Hercules* and *Xena* series and brief but hilarious cameos in the *Spider-Man* movies.

Even after twenty-five years, the evil dead won't leave Campbell alone. As the voice of Ash in the video games *Evil Dead: Hail to the King, Evil Dead: Fistful of Broomstick,* and *Evil Dead: Regeneration,* Campbell keeps the franchise alive. But Brisco is the character who gives him humanity and his widest fan appeal. At a 2000 Vulkon fan convention in Orlando, Florida, Campbell commented that he wished he could be as good a man as Brisco. This is clearly one of his favorite roles, not only for the mainstream fame and continued fandom it inspires but also because the character is genuinely likable and honorable. Although *The Adventures of Brisco County, Jr.* has moseyed into TV history, Brisco's and Campbell's fans make sure that their favorite cowboy-detective-lawyer will never ride into the sunset.

Notes

1. The Ultimate *Adventures of Brisco County, Jr.* Guidebook (www.theoasis.com/brisco) and the Brisco Fans Unite site (paul.rutgers.edu/~cwm/Brisco-County-Jr/) are two of the best.

2. Campbell's 2002 autobiography is entitled *If Chins Could Kill: Confessions of a B Movie Actor.*

3. Campbell's friendship with the Raimi brothers Sam and Ted goes back to their Michigan youth. Sam Raimi and Campbell have teamed for many other films, including the *Spider-Man* series, in which Campbell has had a series of small but interesting roles. For his fans, "spot Bruce" has become a game played within the context of Raimi films. Ted Raimi and Campbell also had recurring roles in *Hercules* and *Xena.*

Alias

Henrik Örnebring

With the following words, the lead character of *Alias* introduced the rather complex premise of the first season and a half of the ABC show:

> My name is Sydney Bristow. Seven years ago I was recruited by a secret branch of the CIA called SD-6. I was sworn to secrecy, but I couldn't keep it from my fiancé. And when the head of SD-6 found out, he had him killed. That's when I learned the truth: SD-6 is not part of the CIA. I've been working for the very people I thought I was fighting against. So, I went to the only place that could help me take them down. Now I'm a double agent for the CIA, where my handler is a man named Michael Vaughn. Only one other person knows the truth about what I do, another double agent inside SD-6. Someone I hardly know—my father.

Although this premise famously changed halfway through season 2, Sydney's monologue still highlights the themes and tropes that remained central throughout the show's run: high-octane spy action and complex conspiracies played out against a backdrop of family drama—or, as viewers quickly came to realize, family drama played out against a backdrop of conspiratorial spy action.

Before becoming the creator-auteur of *Alias*, J. J. Abrams had accumulated a number of screenwriting credits and produced another TV show, *Felicity*, a romantic drama about a college coed. Whereas Abrams's interest in love and family relationships was at the core of *Felicity*, it was the more specific theme of love and family relationships in the face of outlandish circumstances that became the core of *Alias*. Abrams is a self-confessed genre fan, and many of his screenplays contain fantastic or cultish elements: amnesia in *Regarding Henry* (1991), cryogenics in *Forever Young* (1992), and, of course, a massive asteroid about to kill all life on Earth in *Armageddon* (1998). According to Abrams, *Alias* sprang from a specific desire to tell stories with more fantastic, cult-type characteristics—Abrams himself uses the phrases "left of real" or "hyper-real" (see Dilmore 24 and Gross 36, respectively) to describe his preferred mode of storytelling.

In *Alias*, the theme of family is merged with science fiction and cult elements through the so-called Rambaldi mythology—a detailed backstory centered around fictional Renaissance inventor and visionary Milo Rambaldi, an eerily prescient figure who invented the science of genetics and a functioning mobile phone (among other things) in the 1500s and whose puzzle-like devices and prophecies of everlasting life continue to affect the present day. The Bristow family circle is particularly involved in this Rambaldi mythology—Sydney is central to Rambaldi's prophecies, as is her half sister Nadia Santos (introduced in season 3). Others with a stake in Rambaldi's prophecies are Irina Derevko and Arvin Sloane. Derevko, a Russian spy, is Sydney's mother; she married Sydney's father Jack as part of her mission to infiltrate the CIA. Sloane is Nadia's father, Jack's former best friend, and Sydney's archnemesis and evil father figure. It is these intersections between the Rambaldi mythology and the Bristow family backstory that provide much of the narrative drive of the show (see Brown and Abbott, "Can't Live with 'Em").

Lead actress Jennifer Garner had a *Felicity* connection, having starred in three episodes in the first season and thereby gaining the notice of Abrams, who offered her an audition for the lead when he was developing *Alias* (Wills). Others involved in the production of *Felicity* reappeared in *Alias* as well: actor Greg Grunberg (playing CIA agent Eric Weiss), director-producer Lawrence Trilling, and cinematographer Michael Bonvillain. Other key cast members included Ron Rifkin (series villain Arvin Sloane), Michael Vartan (Sydney's CIA handler and love interest Michael Vaughn), Carl Lumbly (Sydney's colleague Marcus Dixon), Victor Garber (a veteran of Broadway, playing Sydney's estranged father Jack), and Lena Olin (Sydney's even more estranged mother Irina). The series' cult status was further ensured by numerous fan-favorite cameos throughout the series: Quentin Tarantino, Roger Moore, Faye Dunaway, Richard Roundtree, Rutger Hauer, David Cronenberg, and Ricky Gervais, to mention just a few. Some cameos were more obscure than others, such as the appearance of B-horror icon Angus Scrimm as CIA interrogation specialist Calvin McCullough.

When the show opened, it immediately became not just a spy show but a "post-9/11" spy show: the first episode was broadcast on September 30, 2001. It was not the only show launched in the 2001–2002 season to use a spy–secret agent theme and to feature international terrorists as prominent villains: *The Agency* is all but forgotten today, but *24* went on to become a TV mainstay. Although these two shows lacked the supernatural elements of *Alias* and could therefore be considered more "realistic," it can be argued that *Alias* did a better job of portraying post-9/11 insecurities, despite the fact that its villains and plotlines had more in common with James Bond (more on this later) than with al-Qaeda. In *Alias*, good and evil are ambiguous, and alliances constantly shift: the enemy of today can be an ally tomorrow. Sydney has to work alongside Arvin Sloane, the man responsible for the death of her fiancé and countless others. Sydney's mother is sometimes an enemy, sometimes an ally. A key feature of recurring villain Julian Sark (played by David Anders) is his "flexible loyalties" (a description used by the character himself); Sark is always ready to betray his masters if it gives him an advantage. In the world of *Alias*, moral coherence is difficult to maintain: Sydney is always reluctant to let the ends justify the means, whereas her father Jack offers a more pragmatic and *24*-like perspective: sometimes you have to do evil in the name of good (Sutherland and Swan 132).

The combination of family drama, spy action, and a backstory with strong science fiction elements proved to be a critical hit. In its first season *Alias* got eleven Emmy nominations (it won two) and would garner an additional twenty-five Emmy nominations throughout its run. Jennifer Garner was nominated for Best Actress in four of the five seasons of *Alias* but never won, although she did win a Best TV Actress Golden Globe in 2002 for her performance in the first season. The critical acclaim never translated into mainstream success: the show quickly gained a loyal fan base but never ranked higher than 65 out of 191 and never had more than an average audience of 9.7 million (Brown and Abbott, "Introduction" 2)—respectable numbers, but ultimately not enough to sustain a high-concept, high-cost show.

The lack of mainstream success was likely due to the fact that *Alias* positioned itself as a cult show from its inception (Brown and Abbott, "Introduction" 3). The mix of science fiction and supernatural elements with spy conspiracies and a complex family backstory created a world eminently suited for fan speculation. This involved the deliberate creation of syntagmatic gaps and areas for narrative exploration outside the "main" text, a phenomenon termed *hyperdiegesis*—"the creation of a vast and detailed narrative space, only a fraction of which is ever directly seen or encountered within the text" (Hills, *Fan Cultures* 137). In this regard, *Alias* was very much a part of an ongoing development in serial TV production: from the 1990s onward, many TV series have been created, marketed, and maintained using modes of address and textual strategies designed to invite fannish readings and to create conditions conducive to the growth of a fan culture (Gwenllian Jones, "Web Wars" 166; see also Harris and Alexander; Hills, *Fan Cultures*).

The most important direct antecedents of *Alias* were probably *The X-Files* and *Buffy the Vampire Slayer*. *The X-Files* used a similar backstory, mixing supernatural and personal elements, and likewise had a "suspended enigma" narrative structure in which resolution of the show's central mysteries was forever put off and closure denied. Like *Alias*, *Buffy* featured a "woman warrior" lead character drawn into an age-old supernatural conflict, and she constantly felt the toll taken by her "job" (as slayer) on those close to her. As noted earlier, the personal cost of Sydney's dangerous job is made evident in the first episode of *Alias*, when Sydney's fiancé Danny is killed by her superiors because she has revealed to him that she is a spy.

As already indicated, the complexity and cult nature of the show quickly became a problem. During its first season and a half, *Alias* had a very dense narrative structure, often juggling five, six, or sometimes even seven or eight subplots within the same episode (not counting the "mission" narrative that was commonly resolved within the space of a single episode). It frequently employed narrative devices such as cliffhangers and in medias res openings (for a more in-depth discussion of the narrative structure of *Alias*, see Örnebring, "Show Must Go On"). The viewer of *Alias* was frequently put in the position of puzzle solver, as the Rambaldi devices sought by the protagonists and antagonists often took the form of riddles and codes. Since *Alias* was not performing as well in the ratings as had been expected, the pressure was on to simplify the show: it was too complex for its own good. On the DVD audio commentary for "Phase One" (2.13), the episode that "rebooted" the original premise of the show, Abrams notes: *Alias* "was a show about good guys working for the bad guys who had to pretend that they were bad good guys, some of the bad guys didn't know they were bad guys and other bad guys pretended they were good guys. . . . Getting rid of SD-6 [the main antagonist organization of season 1 and half of season 2] was more about trying to maintain the things we loved about the show, the relationships, the characters, and actually get rid of the stuff that made it hard for certain people to understand what the show was about." The narrative complexity decreased further in season 4, when the seasonal story arc was largely abandoned in favor of single-story episodes. According to writer Jesse Alexander, that was "one of the mandates we had gotten from the network," which had become "really concerned with the serialized nature of the show" and was convinced "the way that we told stories . . . was off-putting to a general audience" (DVD audio commentary for "Nocturne"). Typically, the decision to "de-cultify" *Alias* by decreasing its complexity and focusing less on backstory did not draw in the general audience; instead, it alienated the loyal fans who enjoyed precisely those elements that were toned down (Brown and Abbott, "Introduction" 3).

In terms of aesthetics and visual style, *Alias* aimed to be a "James Bond for the twenty-first century" from the get-go. The trademark exotic locales, elaborate action set pieces, and eye-catching Bondish gadgetry were all adapted for television and became defining characteristics of *Alias* as well. The gadgetry was even provided by Q-like comic-relief figure Marshall Flinkman (Kevin Weisman)—in the series' own vernacular, an "op-tech specialist"—emphasizing the show's Bond heritage. The action sequences in particular often transcended the limits (budgetary and visual) of the TV medium, and many of them (e.g., "Truth Be Told" [1.1], for which cinematographer Michael Bonvillain won an Emmy, and "Double Agent" [2.14], for which he was nominated) would not have looked out of place in a Hollywood action blockbuster. Locales from Sienna to Mongolia were re-created on Burbank back lots, often requiring a certain amount of visual and dramatic sleight of hand to remain convincing. In the audio commentary to "Full Disclosure" (3.13), producer Lawrence Trilling, writer Jesse Alexander, and production designer Scott Chambliss jokingly discuss the need to trick viewers so they don't realize that the production team can't afford to build expensive sets and film at exotic locations. Another signature feature of *Alias* was the portrayal of Sydney as a master of disguise, adding to the cult viewing pleasure. During the show's run, Sydney appeared as everything from a Russian maid (1.2) to a Swedish bikini babe (1.15) and Japanese geisha (2.7), and as a rule, her outfits were striking and risqué in a very nonspy fashion. *Alias* had a particular obsession with exotic nightclubs (extended nightclub scenes were featured in episodes 1.11, 2.17, 3.2, 3.6, 4.11, and 4.13, to mention just a few), where Sydney would usually appear in one of her fetishistic outfits or even, on one occasion, as the in-house crooner (1.21). Nightclub visits became so frequent over the course of the series that the one of the characters quipped, "What is it with these guys and nightclubs?" (Marshall Flinkman in 4.11).

The themes, backstory, and visuals all contributed to the distinct world of *Alias*—a world that quickly extended beyond the TV series itself. One of the marketing ploys for the first and second seasons was the creation of an alternative reality game (ARG), an Internet-based game based on an interactive narrative that allowed viewers to use clues provided in the TV episodes to unlock online riddles and progress through a narrative that further developed the fictional world of *Alias* (see Örnebring, "Alternate Reality Gaming," for an in-depth discussion of the *Alias* ARGs). Many TV series have since used ARGs or ARG-like features in their marketing (e.g., *ReGenesis, Lost, Heroes*), but *Alias* was an early adopter of the ARG format and the first TV series to use it. The ARG narratives followed the TV narratives closely, likely because some of the writers on the show were directly involved in scripting and producing the *Alias* ARGs (Deaddrop). *Alias* also spawned a series of successful novels that continued publication even after the cancellation of the series—most of them prequels to the series and focusing on either Sydney's or Vaughn's life before they met each other. Other multimedia tie-ins include a magazine, video game, comic book, and trading cards—all par for the course in contemporary TV production and marketing (Medina)—marking *Alias* as a cult show whose life continues well beyond the life span of the TV series itself.

Angel

Joyce Millman

If a cult television series is, by definition, a show that only a select slice of the viewing public cares deeply about, then *Angel* is one of the cultiest cults ever. Created by Joss Whedon and David Greenwalt, *Angel* was spun off from *Buffy the Vampire Slayer* and continued the stories of its supporting characters. This velvet-rope admissions policy—only die-hard *Buffy* fans could get in—ensured that *Angel* never climbed out of the ratings cellar. However, *Angel* was a success in one important area: it enriched the mythology for those who had fallen in love with all things *Buffy* and the Whedon way of storytelling. It resonated beyond the viewing.

When it premiered on October 5, 1999, *Angel* took the 9 P.M. time slot following *Buffy*, creating a Tuesday night programming block that helped establish the fledgling WB as destination television for teen and young-adult viewers (especially female). This double-header allowed for sweeps-period crossover episodes, such as the two-part "Pangs" (*Buffy*, 4.8) and "I Will Remember You" (*Angel*, 1.8) that aired on November 23, 1999, and featured Sarah Michelle Gellar (Buffy) and David Boreanaz (Angel) guest-starring on each other's shows. However, *Angel* was no *Joanie Loves Chachi*–type coattail rider. *Angel* adhered to the *Buffy* formula of mashing up pop genres (horror, comedy, mystery, romance, fantasy, soap opera) and drew from its predecessor's pool of writers. But, as I wrote elsewhere, "*Angel* is decisively its own show; although it shares themes with *Buffy*, it approaches them from a darker, more plaintive place" (Millman, "Death of Buffy's Mom").

We first meet the brooding, hunky Angel on *Buffy*, where he is the boyfriend of the slayer's dreams with one nightmarish imperfection: he is a vampire, her sworn enemy. But Angel is no ordinary vampire. Yes, he is 240 years old, immortal, and has enjoyed a centuries-long reign of terror with his lover, the elegantly cruel Darla. But after a Romanian rampage in 1898, evil "Angelus" was hit by a gypsy curse that caused him to regain his human soul. And from then on, he has been tortured by remorse for his past sins. He gave up feeding on human blood. Repulsed, Darla left him. The vampire with a soul is profoundly alone.

Flash forward to 1997 Sunnydale. Angel (as he is now known) becomes Buffy's ally, protector, and squeeze. But when he tenderly deflowers the slayer on her seventeenth birthday and experiences a moment of "perfect happiness," part two of the old gypsy curse kicks in (*Buffy*, "Innocence," 2.14). Angel's soul vanishes, and he reverts to the depraved Angelus. Buffy has to stick a magical sword into Angel's guts and dispatch him into a hell dimension (*Buffy*, "Becoming, Part 2," 2.22), where he suffers the equivalent of 100 years of torment before returning re-ensouled (and delightfully naked) early in the next season (*Buffy*, "Beauty and the Beasts," 3.4). But these star-crossed lovers are not meant to be. Angel realizes that Buffy, upon whose slender shoulders rests the weight of the world, deserves a boyfriend who can take her for a walk in the sunshine without bursting into flames. So the noble (or is that commitment phobic?) vampire leaves Sunnydale after Buffy's high school graduation (*Buffy*, "Graduation Day, Part 2," 3.22). And that's where *Angel* begins.

Angel seems like an odd character around which to build a spin-off. What can you do with a tongue-tied slab of beefcake who avoids sex (lest he lose his soul again), hides from daylight, and morphs into an ugly being with fangs? Whedon and Greenwalt found an imaginative solution. They "astutely placed Angel at the intersection of the two genres in which his wounded, night-crawling loner mystique makes the most sense—film noir and the superhero graphic novel" (Millman, "City of Angel"). Angel has come to Los Angeles to get over Buffy. Determined to atone for his sins by fighting evil, he hangs out his shingle as a supernatural private eye. With a nod to Raymond Chandler, the city of *Angel* is dazzling on the outside but rotten to the core. It's a town of vampires and soul suckers, but the real A-listers of evil are the slick attorneys of Wolfram and Hart, a powerful law firm that has been the devil's mouthpiece since the world was born. The firm's mysterious, unseen Senior Partners make corrupting or killing Angel the firm's number-one task.

Whedon and Greenwalt build sympathy for their vampire by emphasizing the humorous aspects of Angel's status as neither of this world nor out of it. Angel often wears the dazed look of a lost lamb. He's bewildered by modern life, and he's as penurious and cranky as you'd expect a 240-year-old (celibate) man to be. Yet he tries endearingly to fit in with humans; his halting attempts at small talk look more like he's pleading for mercy, and he's the worst dancer in the world. But for all the fun the show pokes at Angel's unhipness, the overall tone is melancholic. Angel wants forgiveness but knows he doesn't deserve it. He longs to be human again, but he's resigned to his eternal fate. He is an exquisitely tragic hero, part dark avenger, part world-weary gumshoe. Angel may hunt malevolent creatures, but the monster he fears most is the one inside himself.

The pilot episode, "City of," introduces the iconic opening credits: a shot of Angel walking down a dark alley, his long black coat flapping behind him. The letters of the title are ambiguously half-formed—they're in the process of either falling apart or being created, which is a beautiful metaphor for Angel himself. As Whedon describes the show in the "*Angel* 100 Featurette" on the season 5 DVD, "*Angel* is about how an adult faces what they've done with their life, goes forward with it, overcomes it." And, as an adult, Angel is a work in progress, a deeply flawed, lonely soul struggling to redeem himself. But redemption is hard work. There is pain and backsliding. Says producer Kelly A. Manners on the first season DVD set, "We have an alcoholic metaphor. Angel is one drink away from going back to his evil roots." As a vampire in recovery, Angel has sworn off human blood and subsists on pig's blood (chilled, straight up) procured from a butcher shop. But when battling tooth and claw with enemies in the show's hallmark gladiatorial fight scenes, he reveals the savagery lurking behind his laconic exterior.

What keeps Angel walking the straight and narrow? Like most twelve-steppers, he has given himself over to a higher power. In the pilot episode, Angel is befriended by Doyle (the late Glenn Quinn), the benign half-demon, half-human emissary of the mysterious Powers That Be. Doyle tells Angel that the Powers want to give him a chance to earn redemption by becoming a full-time champion for good in the fight against evil. But Doyle stipulates that Angel must learn to connect emotionally with the innocent folks he's helping: "It's not just about saving lives, it's about saving souls. Possibly yours in the process."

Angel discovers another reason to keep fighting in the first-season finale, "To Shanshu in L.A." (1.22): an ancient prophecy reveals that a vampire with a soul will play an important part in the coming Apocalypse and, as a reward, become human. As the series develops, the Shanshu prophecy's authenticity is questioned. But Angel, to his enemies' (and his own) surprise, keeps fighting, not for personal gain but for the good of humanity. Choices are what matter on *Angel*, not predestination, and Angel chooses to identify himself as "a man with a demon inside, not the other way around" ("There's No Place Like Plrtz Glrb," 2.22). Indeed, he has more of a conscience than the human yuppies of Wolfram and Hart, who sold their souls to the Senior Partners and never looked back.

On *Angel*, no one is simply good or evil. Doyle is a guardian angel, but he is tainted by past cowardice ("Hero," 1.9). Wolfram and Hart sharks Lilah Morgan (Stephanie Romanov) and Lindsey McDonald (Christian Kane) are unscrupulous backstabbers, but they occasionally help Angel. Good and evil are complex notions, interconnected. In "Reprise" (2.15), Wolfram and Hart managing partner Holland Manners (Sam Anderson) tells Angel, "Our firm has always been here, in one form or another. We're in the hearts and minds of every single living being. . . . The world doesn't work in spite of evil, Angel. It works *with* us, *because* of us."

In such a bleak universe, family is the one saving grace. Buffy has her Scooby gang; Angel has the team at Angel Investigations ("We help the helpless"). At various times during the series' run, Angel's team includes Doyle, who receives head-aching visions from the Powers That Be depicting the people Angel is supposed to help; ex-*Buffy* characters Cordelia Chase (Charisma Carpenter), the former queen bitch of Sunnydale High and now a humbled failed actress, and Wesley Wyndam-Price (Alexis Denisof), a watcher in disgrace; homeboy vampire hunter Charles Gunn (J. August Richards); campy, green, demon lounge singer Lorne (Andy Hallett); eccentric physicist Winifred "Fred" Burkle (Amy Acker), who was rescued by Angel after being sucked into a medieval, misogynistic alternative universe; and Angel's punky antagonist from *Buffy*, Spike (James Marsters) — the other vampire with a soul. Like their leader, the members of Angel's team are seeking redemption and wrestling with personal demons (both literal and metaphoric). They all harbor some shame, guilt, or trauma that has left them alienated from society and from their better selves. And in the land of Hollywood endings, they are seeking to start life over.

Through the often painful bonds of family, the lone wolf Angel reconnects with his own humanity and learns that "people who don't care about anything will never understand the people who do" ("Not Fade Away," 5.22). Like all families, Angel's suffers ripples of discord; the show's individual seasons revolve around the team breaking apart and finding its way back together again. Angel is the patriarch of his little tribe, and Cordelia, who evolves into a wise, goddess-like being, is the mother. Family tableaux recur. At the end of season 1, for example, Angel, Cordelia, and Wesley—the nucleus of the team—sit down to lunch and Cordelia tells Angel not to be embarrassed about drinking his glass of blood in front of them because "we're family" (1.22). A more disconcerting family portrait occurs midway through season 2. Darla (Julie Benz) has tracked down Angel, and he fears that his sexual attraction to her will cause him to relapse into Angelus. He tries to protect the team from himself by firing them without explanation. At the end of "The Thin Dead Line" (2.14), Angel pines for his lost family, watching from afar as Cordy and Gunn keep vigil at the wounded Wesley's bedside. The bad daddy has been cast out.

The family metaphors become reality in season 3 when Darla gives birth to Angel's son ("Lullaby," 3.9). She sacrifices herself to bring Connor into the world (driving a stake through her own heart as he's born), leaving Angel a single dad. (In a loving nod to nontraditional families, it takes a village—Angel's team—to care for the baby.) The episodes following Connor's birth constitute a heart-rending, fast-forward depiction of the emotional truths of parenthood. As a miracle child, Connor is besieged by kidnappers and would-be assassins—which can be read as an exaggeration of the terror new parents feel about keeping their child safe. In the episode "Sleep Tight" (3.16), Angel has to save Connor's life by allowing the demented time-traveling vampire hunter Holtz (Keith Szarabajka) to take the baby as a replacement for his son, whom Angelus killed. Three episodes later ("The Price," 3.19), baby Connor returns from Holtz's time-bending dimension as a sullen teenager; he's an angry mirror of the youthful Angel we have previously seen in flashbacks clashing with his own father.

Indeed, the Oedipal impulses in Angel's own past—upon rising as a vampire, he kills his father and sleeps with Darla, who is, in effect, his vampire mother—are repeated during Connor's lightning-speed adolescence. Connor (Vincent Kartheiser) has been taught by Holtz to hate Angel; in the third season finale, Connor tries to kill his father by binding him in a coffin and sinking him at sea ("Tomorrow," 3.22). And Connor breaks Angel's heart when he does the oedipal nasty with his pseudo-mom Cordelia, for whose affections he and Angel compete ("Habeas Corpses," 4.8).[1]

Family, redemption, redefinition—these are the big themes of *Angel*. But, like *Buffy*, *Angel* uses the anything-goes freedom of the fantasy genre to address hot topics and social issues. For instance, "Are You Now or Have You Ever Been?" (2.2) journeys back to Angel's life in Los Angeles during the 1950s, with references to communist witch hunts and discrimination against African Americans. The episode links Angel, who can be described as "different," to persecuted minorities (he tries to protect a young black woman from an angry mob) in an effective comment on the prejudice and the fear of "others" running through our national history. Other episodes deal metaphorically with AIDS (a parasitic demon preys on singles-bar pickups in "Lonely Hearts," 1.2), ethnic cleansing (genocide against half-breed demons in "Hero," 1.9), and the racial divide that widened with the beating of Rodney King by Los Angeles police officers (zombie cops terrorize Gunn's old ghetto neighborhood in "The Thin Dead Line," 2.14). The use of evil lawyers as the series' "big bad" serves nicely, in hindsight, as an allegory for the murky legal machinations that put George W. Bush in the White House in 2000 and defined his administration.

Yet all this richness and ingenuity couldn't insulate *Angel* from the fallout of *Buffy* leaving the WB in 2001, after a licensing fee dispute between the network and series producer Twentieth Century FOX Television. (FOX took *Buffy* to the rival youth network UPN, where it ran for two more seasons.) *Buffy*'s departure robbed *Angel*, then entering its third season, of its lead-in audience and crossovers.[2] During the next two years, the WB changed *Angel*'s time slot three times, frustrating fans without significantly improving ratings. The otherwise supportive *Entertainment Weekly* pronounced the show all but dead near the end of season 4, calling it a "marginal player for The WB" (Jensen and Rice). Surprisingly, though, *Angel* was renewed for a fifth season.

Whedon (who had been busy wrapping up *Buffy* and launching his FOX series *Firefly*) returned his attention to *Angel*, proposing a wild change of premise: Angel takes over as head of Wolfram and Hart and naïvely attempts to fight evil from within the system. With Wolfram and Hart's unlimited resources at their command (and powerful, evil clients to placate), Angel's team wrestles with temptation and settles for Pyrrhic victories. The fifth season is the ultimate redefinition, and it includes two of the finest episodes of the series.

The first, "Smile Time" (5.14), ambitiously stretches storytelling boundaries, much like *Buffy*'s musical episode "Once More with Feeling" (6.7) had done. Written by Whedon and Ben Edlund, the hilarious, surreal "Smile Time" finds Angel magically transformed into a scowling Muppet, mirroring his despondent view of himself as the Senior Partners' puppet. One week later came the shattering "A Hole in the World" (5.15), written and directed by Whedon, in which Wesley and Fred finally act on their romantic feelings for each other. Their joy is short-lived, however; Fred is poisoned by the ancient god Illyria, and even the team's heroic efforts can't save her. Wesley tenderly nurses Fred on her deathbed until she expires with a plaintive, "Why can't I stay?" on her lips. Her body turns into a blue carapace, and Illyria rises, wearing Fred as her earthly form. For the remainder of the series, Wesley (the show's Byronic antihero) becomes mad with grief and is obsessively attached to Illyria.

Ironically, *Angel*'s creative high coincided with its cancellation, which was announced by the WB on February 13, 2004. Whedon, caught off guard, posted his reaction on the Internet: "I've never made mainstream TV very well. I like surprises, and TV isn't about surprises, unless the surprise is who gets voted off something," he wrote. "I've been lucky to sneak this strange, strange show over the airwaves for as long as I have. . . . Remember the words of the poet: Two roads diverged in the wood, and I took the road less traveled by, and they CANCELLED MY FRIKKIN' SHOW" (Whedon posting to BronzeBeta).

Whedon cowrote (with Jeffrey Bell) the series finale, "Not Fade Away" (5.22), in which the team mounts a seemingly suicidal mission to destroy Wolfram and Hart and the root of evil on Earth. In the series' final scene, surviving team members Angel, Spike, Gunn, and Illyria make their last stand in an alley in the rain, as thunder rumbles and screeching hell-beasts (there's even a flying dragon) gather. "Personally, I always wanted to slay a dragon," Angel tells his motley troops. "Let's go to work!" He confidently raises his sword, and the screen abruptly goes to credits. In an interview with *The Onion A.V. Club* at the San Diego Comic-Con in August 2007, Whedon said of that open-ended final scene, "Redemption is something you fight for every day. So I wanted him to go out fighting" (Whedon, "Joss Whedon").[3]

The stirring, bittersweet finale, as much a beginning as an ending, was the perfect culmination of Angel's lessons in being human: we fall from grace and get back up again, forever moving toward that glimmer of forgiving light.

Notes

1. Cordelia's function as a maternal figure is made plain in the episode "Provider" (3.12), which ends with a family tableau of Angel and Cordelia falling asleep together (fully clothed) with baby Connor between them on the bed.

2. Although *Angel* and *Buffy* could no longer be linked via crossover episodes, the WB allowed David Boreanaz to appear in the *Buffy* series finale on UPN ("Chosen," 7.22).

3. At San Diego Comic-Con 2007, Whedon announced the launch of a new twelve-part comic book series, *Angel: After the Fall*, which continues Angel's story where the TV series left off. The first issue was released by IDW Publishing in November 2007.

The Avengers

Angelina I. Karpovich

Among the dozens of spy adventure series that emerged in the United Kingdom and the United States in the 1960s, *The Avengers* is perhaps the most memorable. Though it had significant characteristics in common with other hit shows of the genre—for example, it shared some elements of surrealism with *The Prisoner*, a playful lightheartedness with *The Man from U.N.C.L.E.*, and a particular representation of Englishness with *The Saint*—*The Avengers* had a unique identity rooted in its pioneering representation of women, its complex hybridization of genres, and its commitment to postmodern visual iconography.

The origins of *The Avengers* lay in a 1960 ITV show called *Police Surgeon*, which starred Ian Hendry as the eponymous Dr. Geoffrey Brent. Although the series itself enjoyed a lackluster reception, Hendry was popular with fans. He was brought back to ITV in 1961 in a new series as another investigative medic, Dr. David Keel. That series, produced by the Associated British Corporation for ITV, was created by Sydney Newman, though it would go on to have several producers. Among them was Brian Clemens, writer for *The Invisible Man* and *Danger Man*. Clemens would leave the most prominent mark as the writer of the show's most popular and memorable episodes and as its script editor and producer during its most successful phases.

In the first episode of the new show, called *The Avengers*, Keel investigates the murder of his fiancée Peggy by a drug gang, assisted by a mysterious stranger named John Steed, played by Patrick Macnee. Though initially a secondary character, Steed becomes more prominent during the show's first season, but visually and conceptually, he is still not quite the Steed of later episodes: at this point, his sartorial style is contemporary and run-of-the-mill, his allegiances are not entirely clear (though there are hints that he works for British Intelligence), and the overall character is much less refined than the neo-Edwardian wisecracking dandy of later episodes.

When Hendry left to concentrate on his film career, Macnee became the show's star. Unfilmed scripts that were to have featured David Keel were rewritten to accommodate Steed's new partners: Dr. Martin King (Jon Rollason) appears in three episodes of the first season before Dr. Cathy Gale (Honor Blackman) appears in the first episode of the second season and ultimately prompts the visual style and character dynamic the show is most remembered for.

Six of the episodes during this transitional phase also feature nightclub singer Venus Smith (Julie Stevens). Smith is nowhere near as competent and self-assured as Steed's later female partners, but her presence introduces a much lighter touch, including musical interludes and the possibility of romance. The success of the Cathy Gale character, however, led to Venus Smith being phased out. From the third season onward, the show's central dynamic is the partnership between John Steed and a single competent female agent.

Cathy Gale is an attractive young widow, a well-traveled anthropologist, a professional photographer, and a martial arts expert who is more than capable of disposing of the show's male villains in hand-to-hand combat without disturbing her glamorous hairdo. She famously wears leather suits and boots, which, combined with her sometimes stern manner and the pain she inflicts on the show's villains, essentially make her television's first dominatrix.

It is impossible to overstate the extent of Gale's departure from previous popular representations of femininity and womanhood. In the United Kingdom, women had had the right to vote for less than thirty-five years, and although the head of state was a woman, other women were absent from the upper echelons of public life. In popular culture, Wonder Woman and a number of other female comic characters had appeared in the 1940s, but their powers and, consequently, their realm of influence were entirely supernatural. Cathy Gale was based not on these fictional representations but on real-life contemporary female pioneers, such as anthropologist Margaret Mead and photographer Margaret Bourke-White (Miller, *Avengers* 67). It is significant that her power and success are firmly rooted in the real world, making her perhaps the first strong female character in popular culture who was genuinely accessible as a role model. Cathy Gale predates Modesty Blaise and any number of subsequent female crime fighters as a representation of a woman who combines intelligence, independence, and professional success.

Gale's popularity was immense; to capitalize on it, Blackman and Macnee even released a novelty single called "Kinky Boots," titled after Gale's signature high-heeled leather footwear. At the same time, Steed went through stylistic and conceptual changes, replacing his contemporary and unremarkable trench coat with classic English tailored suits, a bowler hat, and an umbrella (the latter two sometimes used as props in fight sequences) and acquiring a backstory that gave him aristocratic roots and an appreciation of luxury (from now on, Steed would seldom be far away from a bottle of champagne).

Limited production values influenced the look of the early episodes. Studio-bound and with access to only a small number of props, *The Avengers* was transmitted live or so close to live that small errors (such as camera wobbles or actors forgetting their lines) couldn't be corrected. As in other series of the period, long takes with little camera movement and a limited variety of shots led to a naturalistic style that was at odds with both the subject matter and the show's emerging preoccupation with irony and satire. Ultimately, the naturalistic camera work and editing became one of the show's strengths, with the majority of the later episodes beginning in ordinary, everyday settings only to reveal subversion behind a facade of normality. For instance, "a hospital doubles as a high-technology manufacturing plant, an abandoned mill hides an alternative universe, there are subterranean takeovers of Britain" (Miller, *Avengers* 130).

Like Ian Hendry before her, Honor Blackman was lured away from *The Avengers* in 1964 by the promise of a successful film career. Her appearance as Pussy Galore in *Goldfinger* both capitalized on the popularity of Cathy Gale and highlighted the Bond series' role as the big-screen forerunner of 1960s spy adventure television shows.

Steed's new partner was Mrs. Emma Peel, played by Diana Rigg. Like Gale, Peel was an attractive young widow (her adventurer husband, presumed dead, would reappear to explain her exit from the show in 1968), a scientist, and a martial arts expert with an eye-catching, soon to be iconic dress sense. Unlike Gale, Peel's relationship with Steed was distinctly lighthearted and flirtatious. The arrival of Diana Rigg coincided with the show's sale to U.S. television, and the deal resulted in higher production budgets. Videotape was abandoned in favor of 35mm

The playful relationship between Emma Peel (Diana Rigg) and John Steed (Patrick Macnee) was one of *The Avengers*' defining characteristics.

film, allowing much greater flexibility in editing, location shooting, and, ultimately, the kind of stories the show could tell. From the second Mrs. Peel season (1967) onward, the show was filmed in color, allowing the producers to add innovative set designs. Many episodes from this season, such as "Escape in Time," "Epic," "Death's Door," and "Dead Man's Treasure," used the show's increased budget and the greater production values offered by 35mm color film to create elaborate and spectacular set pieces to illustrate the scale of the villains' murderous ambitions. At the same time, the writers used the larger budgets to introduce more playfully self-aware intertextual references: the episode "The Living Dead" features a villain's underground lair that recalls the design of Fritz Lang's *Metropolis* (1927), while "Epic" and "The Superlative Seven" (the first set in a film studio, the second featuring an array of famous actors as guest stars) strive to include as many visual references to genre film conventions as possible.

Steed and Mrs. Peel achieved huge popularity on both sides of the Atlantic and around the world. *The Avengers* was the first British show to appear on prime-time network television in the United States (Chapman, *Saints* 52), and by 1968 it had even been sold behind the Iron Curtain to Hungary, Romania, Czechoslovakia, and Poland (Miller, *Avengers* 104). By the late 1960s the show had around 30 million viewers (Chapman, *Saints* 52), and with sales to 120 countries, it is reportedly the highest grossing British television export of all time (Miller, *Avengers* 5). Buxton speculates that international audiences would have missed most of the show's fairly prominent references to class and social relations, and the appeal of *The Avengers* for non-British viewers lay instead in the "quaint British charm" of "its juxtaposition of the traditional . . . and the modern" (107).

Despite these successes, Diana Rigg left *The Avengers* after the first episode of the 1968 season, eventually to follow in Honor Blackman's footsteps in a Bond film, playing the only woman James Bond ever married in *On Her Majesty's Secret Service* (1969). Mrs. Peel was replaced by Tara King (Linda Thorson), a young trainee in Steed's organization. Her relationship to Steed is markedly less equal and more reverential than that of Dr. Gale and Mrs. Peel, and it is also more obviously romantic. In some ways, Tara King is a return to the more "traditional" female representation, reminiscent of Venus Smith. Despite this, Tara is competent and self-sufficient, and the differences between her and Steed's two previous companions can be explained by her youth and relative inexperience rather than the producers' decision to return to a less radical representation of female characters.

The Avengers continued to be popular in the United Kingdom and Europe, but the show's popularity in the United States waned, and its broadcast on ABC was canceled. Without American financial backing, the show could not maintain the same technical and narrative standards, and the series ended in May 1969. Steed's and his companions' continuing popularity in continental Europe and Canada led to a two-season revival, *The New Avengers*, starring Patrick Macnee and costarring Gareth Hunt as Mike Gambit and Joanna Lumley as Purdey, in 1976.

The legacy of *The Avengers* was extended through authorized novels (two of them cowritten by Macnee), a 1971 stage play written by Brian Clemens and starring three of the show's previous guest stars, a series of radio plays broadcast in South Africa in the early 1970s, and a 1998 film adaptation directed by Jeremiah S. Chechik and starring Ralph Fiennes as Steed and Uma Thurman as Mrs. Peel (with a cameo by Macnee), which received almost universal critical derision for its lack of faithfulness to the original series.

Looking back on the show's success twenty-five years later, Linda Thorson explained its popularity as the general appeal of the 1960s: "a mythic time when fashion, music, color and pleasure worked together to transcend the given stuff of life" (Miller, *Avengers* 130). But the appeal of *The Avengers* is arguably greater than just 1960s nostalgia, particularly for viewers who instantly recognize it as cult viewing even if they were not yet born when the show was first broadcast. Rather, contemporary and subsequent viewers recognize in *The Avengers* a range and complexity of narrative and stylistic elements that distinguish it from, and make it more culturally significant than, most other television shows of its genre and period.

At its peak, the show was remarkable for its representation of a man and a woman as true equals in their workplace. Indeed, Steed is sometimes presented as inferior to his female partners in areas that are traditionally imagined as the "masculine" domain. For instance, he defers to Mrs. Peel on scientific matters, and an entire episode ("The Master Minds") centers on Steed having a substantially lower IQ than Mrs. Peel. Steed is fully aware of these inferiorities and doesn't challenge them. Physically, the women are presented as matches for the men, and in several episodes (most notably "A Touch of Brimstone"), it is the female partner, not Steed, who disposes of the main villain in a fight. Most crucially, in a perilous situation, the woman doesn't revert to a damsel in distress but is perfectly capable of rescuing herself ("The House that Jack Built").

At the same time, the relationship between Steed and his partners is both close and full of the kind of ambiguity that gives viewers an additional reason to watch the show: "Sexual tension suffuses a relationship that is neither fully collegial nor straightforwardly amicable. They are not quite lovers and not quite co-workers" (Miller, *Avengers* 66). Subsequently, several successful television shows used the formula established in *The Avengers: Remington Steele, Moonlighting,* and, perhaps most famously, *The X-Files* all used a perceptible but unresolved sexual tension between the central characters to add a layer of narrative complexity. Moreover, the presence of a female partner in a crime-fighting spy show arguably gave *The Avengers* a dimension that was absent from other shows of the genre: whereas the likes of *Mission: Impossible* and the Bond series relied on increasingly sophisticated weapons and gadgets, Steed and his partners relied primarily on their wits and their bare hands. As Miller points out, "*The Avengers* stands out from its . . .

counterparts of the time because it eschews conventional weaponry in favor of the extended and controlled body—the women and their martial arts—and the extended and controlled gentleman—Steed and his stick" (*Avengers* 94).

Indeed, technology is usually presented as a foe rather than a friend, with the exception of the cars driven by the characters, which function to reflect their personalities as much as to get them from point A to point B (Steed's vehicles are large, sturdy, and very traditional, while Emma's and Tara's cars are small, fast, elegantly sporty, and hypermodern). Many of the plots are ultimately about technology, with the villains portrayed as either "diehard reactionaries" who oppose the march of progress or "lunatic scientists who want to extend machine principles to human beings" (Buxton 101). The show's most famous antagonists, returning again and again despite being vanquished, are the Cybernauts, deadly humanoid robots without reason or obvious vulnerabilities. This 1960s preoccupation with the potential threat of technology (the "lunatic scientist" villain appears repeatedly in most spy series of the era and, of course, in several of the Bond films) returned to television in the 1990s, most prominently in *The X-Files*. According to Buxton, *The Avengers* resolves this anxiety about the conflict between tradition and progress by pointing to "the median ground between the two extremes, personified in the pure friendship between Steed and Emma Peel . . . the proof that traditional and modern values can coexist in a pure complicity" (101).

Notably, the series' treatment of these complex issues is not heavy-handed. Indeed, among the spy series of the 1960s, *The Avengers* is perhaps the least overtly ideological. While *The Man from U.N.C.L.E.*'s positive portrayal of an Iron Curtain protagonist is conditional on him being "on the same side" as his American and British superiors, *The Avengers* is notable for balanced portrayals of the Russians, who are still unmistakably Steed's opponents and the West's enemies. As Miller notes, "when Steed categorizes Russian voices as 'the other side' or 'our worthy opponents' in 'The Charmers,' he does so with affection and warmth. Warren Mitchell's characterization of Ambassador Brodny in 'The See-Through Man' is slapstick comedy; he is Steed's friend as much as his enemy" (*Avengers* 104).

Ultimately, Steed personifies *The Avengers*' portrayal of Britishness—or, more correctly, Englishness (references to the country outside London are scarce, and although Steed seems to revel in a Scottish heritage in "Castle De'ath," it's impossible to know whether to take him seriously).

As Buxton notes, this portrayal makes the series all the more appealing to international viewers. Fairness, humor in the face of adversity, ingenuity rather than brute force, and a traditionalism combined with robustness allow Steed to persist in the modern world without becoming an anachronism (the latter typified by Steed's steel-lined bowler hat, combining traditional gentleman's attire with the ability to stop a bullet—an ingenious and indispensable item for the modern spy-about-town). It is, of course, an entirely artificial construct, but a very attractive one. As a character, Steed is perhaps even more fictitious, but he is also more humane and more likable than any other spy of the period.

Finally, the show's unique appeal lies in its seemingly effortless mix of a variety of generic conventions. Besides the deliberately parodic episodes such as "Epic" and "The Superlative Seven," the show routinely combines elements of adventure, spy stories, and science fiction. And although the fantastical elements ultimately have a perfectly ordinary explanation, this doesn't detract from the impression that, if necessary, Steed and his companion can defeat supernatural foes with the same style and ease with which they dispose of everyday villains.

The Avengers lives on in syndication and on DVD; in a productive and dedicated fan community; in fan-organized, themed tours of "Avengerland" filming locations in southeast England (Miller, *Avengers* 3); in its continuing influence on contemporary television; and, perhaps most significantly, through its legacy as a pioneering representation of male-female relationships in Western popular culture.

Battlestar Galactica

Ian Maull and David Lavery

In 1977 the first *Star Wars* movie was released; a year later *Battlestar Galactica* appeared on ABC. The two were almost assuredly linked. The success of *Star Wars* had shown that there was a market for space battles, quasi-religious sentiments, and good old-fashioned heroism. Though *Battlestar* would last for only one season, it achieved a modicum of cult success that survived more than twenty-five years.

During this time, attempts were made to resurrect the show. Richard Hatch, who had played Apollo, spearheaded the campaign for a continuation of the story line. His efforts failed, although he may have succeeded in demonstrating a desire among fans for a return to the universe of *Battlestar Galactica*. In 2001 Bryan Singer and Tom DeSanto were announced as the creators of a new *Battlestar Galactica* series to be produced by the Sci-Fi Channel. Scheduling conflicts in the wake of the 9/11 attacks, however, meant that Singer became unavailable, and the project ground to a halt.

Eventually, the concept was handed over to David Eick and Ronald D. Moore, with the former agreeing to take part only if he had the freedom to scrap Singer and DeSanto's work and start over. With that concession, Eick and Moore set about creating not just a continuation of the 1970s series or a simple remake but a wholesale reimagining—an attempt to make *Battlestar Galactica* relevant and, indeed, important television for a twenty-first-century audience. They succeeded.

In December 2003 the miniseries that would serve as a backdoor pilot for the show aired on the Sci-Fi Channel. It proved to be a ratings success, earning Sci-Fi the third most watched broadcast in its history. The miniseries introduced viewers to the world of *BSG*. In an undisclosed time, in an unnamed region of space, humanity has settled the Twelve Colonies—twelve states under a single government. It is a time of relative peace. Forty years earlier, however, a terrible war had been waged between the Colonials and the Cylons, robotic servants created for hard labor and warfare. And, like most artificial intelligence in science fiction, the Cylons rebelled, turning against their masters and fighting a twelve-year war before signing an armistice and retreating into deep space. The Cylons are back, however, and this time they can appear human. Their agents have infiltrated the Colonies and sabotaged several defense systems, leaving the humans utterly vulnerable to a devastating sneak attack. Almost all life is wiped out in the Colonies, and the miniseries follows the efforts of the *Galactica* and the civilian fleet it has rescued as they attempt to flee known space in a bid for survival.

Airing as it did just over two years after the 9/11 attacks, it would be naïve not to recognize the significance of a surprise attack in a television series. Though the nuclear attacks on the Colonies are larger in scale than the attacks on the World Trade Center and the Pentagon, the sense of shock and disbelief among the people who witness them is the same. As news about the attacks gradually filters through the fleet, crew members of the *Galactica* are forced to wonder whether any of their family and friends are still alive, and what they did to deserve this in the first place.

Through the miniseries, we are introduced to the seven characters who appear as regulars in the show. Commander Adama, played by Edward James Olmos, is the paternal figure who holds everything together; though a decorated soldier, he is not a member of the admiralty nor the commanding officer of a particularly glamorous vessel. The *Galactica* is antiquated by modern standards, and Adama's insistence that it contain no networked computers (which had proved vulnerable to Cylon attack in the past) has perhaps contributed to the ship's planned decommissioning. The *Galactica* is to be turned into a museum. Like his vessel, we get the impression that Adama is somewhat weary and ready for retirement. The return to a war footing, however, seems to reinvigorate him as he sets out on the seemingly suicidal mission to drive the Cylons out of the Colonies. Adama is talked out of this course of action by Laura Roslin (Mary McDonnell), the former secretary of education who finds herself thrust into the role of president after the other forty-two government officials preceding her in the line of succession are killed in the attacks. McDonnell plays the matriarch to Olmos's patriarch; as the series begins, they are in typically gender-related roles.

That is not to say, however, that traditional gender is a particular consideration in *BSG*. The third of the regulars on the show is Katee Sackhoff, who plays the role of Kara "Starbuck" Thrace. Starbuck also appeared in the original *BSG*, where *he* was a card-playing, cigar-smoking Viper pilot. This time around, Starbuck is a woman, but with many of the same attributes. Her status as a female soldier does not set her apart from her male colleagues; the women of the Colonial military serve in the same roles as the men, and they are just as tough. A punch-up between Starbuck and her commanding officer, Lee "Apollo" Adama, has no shades of sexism or woman beating.

Apollo, played by Jamie Bamber, is the estranged son of Commander Adama, and he is ordered to return to the ship to participate in the decommissioning ceremony. His appearance as part of a publicity stunt probably saves his life, and he takes up the role of CAG (Commander of the Air Group) after the *Galactica*'s CAG is killed in a skirmish with the Cylons.

The Cylons' success in attacking the Colonial fleet is largely thanks to Gaius Baltar (James Callis). A scientific genius entrusted with creating a new defense system for the military, Baltar is seduced by the Cylon agent Number Six (Tricia Helfer). Baltar unwittingly allows Six access to the defense system, into which she programs a critical weakness. Baltar's ego and libido are his undoing, and although he escapes the attack, he is haunted by visions of Six throughout the series.

The final regular on the show further represents the Cylon goal of subterfuge and infiltration. Sharon Valerii, as played by Grace Park, is a sleeper agent. A Raptor pilot on the *Galactica*, she initially has no knowledge of her true nature, which gradually comes to light when she finds herself carrying out acts of sabotage on the ship.

Like most quality TV programs, *Galactica* relies heavily on a large supporting cast; indeed, some of the most critical characters appear throughout the show as nonregulars, including the alcoholic executive officer of the *Galactica* Saul Tigh and Chief of the Deck Galen Tyrol. Such an expansive supporting cast helps maintain a sense of realism within the series; even minor roles, such as the journalists who attend Roslin's press conferences, are regularly played by the same actors to provide a sense of continuity.

Such a use of the cast is to be expected, considering Moore's pursuit of "naturalistic science fiction." *BSG* avoids many of the typical science fiction staples. For example, with the exception of the Cylons, there are no aliens in the universe of *BSG*. Indeed, Olmos once said in an interview that he would walk off the set the minute he saw an actor in a *Star Trek*–style latex mask. This is not the only stylistic disparity between *BSG* and other modern sci-fi shows. There are none of the familiar *Star Trek* view screens aboard the *Galactica*; instead, the Command Information Center, which serves as the bridge, is a multitiered, militaristic chamber filled with DRADIS screens and old-style telephones. The crew can't just grab a snack from a nearby food replicator; instead, supplies are rationed, and from the third season onward, the crew largely subsists on processed algae paste. And when the time comes for relaxation, no one just drops into the nearest holodeck; leisure time is sparse, and it often takes the form of a drunken fistfight.

The show is dark—and rightly so. After all, the human race has almost been wiped out, and the survivors live in cramped conditions, terrified that each moment may be their last. The writers are keen to explore the moral issues that arise from such extreme circumstances. *BSG*, since its inception, has never been one to shy away from addressing ethical concerns. The creative team behind the show has chosen to address a number of issues head-on, ranging from abortion rights to the freedom to vote, from religious persecution to personal responsibilities. Lesser shows might have sidestepped these moral quagmires with pat answers and deus ex machina solutions; *BSG* builds whole story arcs out of them.

A speech given by Adama in the miniseries is critical to the entire run of the show, which, by its conclusion in the fall of 2008, consisted of seventy-nine episodes, ten "webisodes," and a made-for-TV movie. During the decommissioning ceremony, Adama breaks from his prepared notes:

> The Cylon War is long over, yet we must not forget the reasons why so many sacrificed so much in the cause of freedom. The cost of wearing the uniform can be high, but. . . . Sometimes it's too high. You know, when we fought the Cylons, we did it to save ourselves from extinction. But we never answered the question: why? Why are we as a people worth saving? We still commit murder, because of greed, spite, jealousy, and we still visit all of our sins upon our children. We refuse to accept the responsibility for anything that we've done. Like we did with the Cylons. We decided to play god, create life. When that life

turned against us, we comforted ourselves in the knowledge that it really wasn't our fault, not really. You cannot play god, then wash your hands of the things that you've created. Sooner or later, the day comes when you can't hide from the things that you've done anymore.

Responsibility is a cornerstone of *Battlestar Galactica*; every action has a consequence.

One of the most significant plotlines of the show takes place at the halfway mark, from the last few episodes of season 2 through the first six of season 3. The second season of *Battlestar Galactica* concludes with the horrifying visage of Cylon centurions, polished and perfect, marching through the ragged and dirty New Caprica City while former soldiers and leaders look on, impotent and overwhelmed. Though echoing the miniseries in many ways — a surprise attack, with a certain Gaius Baltar partially responsible — the final few shots of "Lay Down Your Burdens" leave us with a huge sense of hopelessness for humanity. With Cylon forces marching into New Caprica City some three years after Coalition forces took Baghdad, Moore plunges headfirst into some of the most prominent concerns raised by the Iraq war and the wider "war on terror." From "Occupation" through "Exodus" and beyond, the show explores themes of occupational tactics, suicide bombing, collaboration with the enemy, and torture, both physical and psychological. Perhaps the most striking and controversial aspect of the occupation arc that opens the third season of *Galactica* is that, symbolically at least, our Colonial heroes are Iraqi citizens. Although some fans decried the lack of subtlety in what they dubbed the "New Iraqtica" story line, others embraced the show's bravery for daring to suggest that insurgents might be real people too.

If the creators of *BSG* have crafted a show that asks questions of the audience, the reverse is also true: many viewers are heavily invested in learning more about the religion, society, technology, and culture of both the Cylons and the Colonials. Although this curiosity has never quite reached the obsessive, feverish pitch of *Lost*'s most eagle-eyed viewers, keenly devouring each frame for the latest clue, one long-running mystery has gripped *BSG* viewers: the identity of the twelve Cylon models. The initial miniseries depicted four of the humanoid Cylons, but it would be the end of season 2 before another three were revealed. Season 3 answered a critical question that the audience had been asking: why have we seen only these (fan-dubbed) "Significant Seven"? Although most likely the result of practical concerns (such as the expense and narrative difficulty of servicing twelve actors), the writers of *BSG* capitalized on the enigmatic nature of these "Final Five" Cylons by making them a critical component of the last two seasons.

Suddenly, the audience had a new mystery to solve: who are the Final Five? Clues were drip-fed tantalizingly slowly during the third season, resulting in the revelation of four of the five at season's end. With only one remaining, speculation intensified concerning the identity of the final Cylon. Guesses ranged from Lieutenant Anastasia Dualla, whose first name derives from the Greek for "resurrection" (an important Cylon concept), to Roslin or Adama. Internet discussion forums were rife with opposing viewpoints. Some argued that the final Cylon would surely have to be a significant main character; anything else would be anticlimactic after the reveal of the other four Cylons. Others followed Moore's words when, interviewed about a promotional photograph for the fourth season depicting many of the central characters in a "Last Supper" scenario, he "let slip" that the final Cylon was not present in the tableau. More esoteric suggestions were also made: Is Earth itself the final Cylon? Is *Galactica*? Is the final Cylon the source of the incorporeal visions witnessed by several characters? Whoever or whatever the final Cylon turned out to be, there was a concerted effort to find out. The search term "final five cylons" elicits 13,400 results, a respectable amount for a television show that averaged between 2 million and 3 million viewers throughout its run.

Indeed, the strong online presence of *BSG* fans and their attendance at conventions featuring actors from the show are testaments to its cult success. The show has also leaped beyond the bounds of television; those fans who feel they need an additional or slightly more saucy fix of *BSG* can turn to fan fiction. One Web site currently hosts more than 3,000 fan-fic stories based on the show, ranging from alternative universe tales to crossovers with *Star Wars* and beyond. This Internet-based fandom was also in a prime position to enjoy the "webisodes," mini-episodes produced between the show's second and third seasons that depicted life on occupied Caprica. Twenty-five minutes long and broken into ten parts, the webisodes were broadcast online for U.S. viewers only; the international audience had to wait for their inclusion as DVD extras. The technique of using the Internet as both a marketing tool and a conveyor of additional (if ultimately unnecessary) narrative has also been used to great effect by *Lost*, another example of a cult television show tapping into the tech savvy of a modern audience.

Moore also regularly produced podcasts, much like DVD commentaries, to accompany episodes. Coproducer Eick frequently updated a humorous video blog on Sci-Fi's Web site—Lucy Lawless's appearance as a demanding, bitchy diva rooting through garbage cans is just one example. The eagerness of the show's cast and crew to interact with their audience reflected the amount of mutual respect in the relationship.

Many fans are already beginning to mourn for the show, although there seems to be a general acceptance that the story had run its course. *BSG*, by its very nature, was never going to match the extended run of its fellow Sci-Fi show *Stargate SG-1*. Fans do have something to cling to, however; rumors of additional made-for-TV movies are beginning to surface—one of them apparently to be written by Jane Espenson and directed by Edward James Olmos. Viewers can also look forward to seeing Colonial society before the attacks in the prequel movie *Caprica*, set at the time of the Cylon creation, which seems likely to serve as a pilot for a full-blown spin-off. *Galactica*'s journey may have come to an end, but the story may just be beginning.

Blake's 7

Steven Duckworth

Blake's 7 emerged during a difficult period for British television. In the late 1970s crippling industrial action and spiraling inflation saw programs canceled midshoot, budgets slashed (Howe, Stammers, and Walker 169), and, for three months in the autumn of 1979, the entire ITV network taken off the air. The National Viewers' and Listeners' Association was protesting loudly over TV violence, and in some cases these complaints were paid significant attention by television executives.[1] Elsewhere, *Star Wars* had both reawakened the notion that science fiction might be a marketable commodity and effectively redefined audience expectations of the genre. Given these obstacles and the BBC's famously apathetic attitude toward science fiction (Collinson), we might ask exactly how an effects-heavy space opera about the brutal exploits of a terrorist gang ever came to be made. Some commentators have argued that the 1970s constituted a "golden age" of innovation in British TV, and it was only in such an atmosphere that a show such as *Blake's 7* was possible (Bignell and O'Day 10–11). Whether this was the case or not, the presence of a "bankable" writer with a proven track record likely hastened the project's commission.

Terry Nation, described variously as a "craftsman" (Bignell and O'Day 9) and a "hack writer" (Stevens and Moore 11), cut his teeth writing comedy in the 1950s and 1960s and went on to write for *Doctor Who*, creating the Daleks—the Doctor's most famous enemy. Prolific and expeditious at his craft, Nation was reportedly able to knock out a *Doctor Who* script in "about eight hours" (Bignell and O'Day 18). More recently he had created the postapocalyptic drama *Survivors* (1975–1977) for the BBC, and his next venture would find him writing in a similarly dystopian and pessimistic vein. *Blake's 7* was initially discussed with the BBC's head of drama series, Ronnie Marsh, in September 1975 (Stevens and Moore 12), and Nation's high-concept pitch summed up the project as *"The Dirty Dozen* in space" (Sangster and Condon 117; Bignell and O'Day 32; Muir 8). Marsh accepted the pitch with the proviso that Nation script all thirteen episodes of the first season (Muir 8) to enable the BBC to promote the series on the back of the writer's established public profile (Stevens and Moore 18).

There was, perhaps, an air of inevitability about the production team assigned to *Blake's 7*. Both producer David Maloney and script editor Chris Boucher had worked on *Doctor Who* immediately before coming aboard—Maloney as a director, and Boucher as a scriptwriter. As the new project's "nearest living relative" at the BBC, *Doctor Who* seemed the ideal place from which to borrow available talent. Indeed, the two shows are largely indistinguishable on an aesthetic level, which is not surprising, considering they shared writers, directors, designers, effects technicians, and composer; recycled each other's props; and cast from the same pool of British character actors. And just as *Doctor Who* was well known for its shoestring budget, *Blake's 7* would find itself hampered by a similarly meager allocation of funds.[2] *Blake's 7* inherited both the time slot and the budget of *Softly, Softly: Taskforce*, a police procedural with an effects allocation of £50 per episode. Marsh attempted to secure funding to the tune of £70,000 per episode from independent production companies but was ultimately unsuccessful, and *Blake's 7* ended up with around half that amount for its first season (Bignell and O'Day 48). After overspending by £4,433 and using almost 2,000 man-hours on effects alone (Bignell and O'Day 49), the budget for seasons 2 and 3 was increased, but *Blake's 7* was never in a position to compete with big-budget U.S. genre shows in terms of production values. *Blake's 7* also stood apart from more expensive U.S. imports such as *Battlestar Galactica* and *Buck Rogers* in another key respect: Nation envisaged his protagonists as "villains," a group of convicted criminals who escape from a transport ship en route to a penal planet (Stevens and Moore 12). Although a number of ideas from his initial pitch were discarded at the behest of Boucher and Maloney, the idea of "villains as heroes" remained, and the resulting drama was shot through with moral ambiguities and uncertainties. As series star Paul Darrow commented, "Terry's characters were frightening heroes" (72).

Leading the corps of "frightening heroes" is political dissident Blake

(Gareth Thomas), falsely convicted of child molestation and sentenced to life imprisonment. He is accompanied by amoral embezzler Avon (Darrow), smuggler Jenna (Sally Knyvette), alcoholic kleptomaniac Vila (Michael Keating), murderer Gan (David Jackson), and alien guerrilla Cally (Jan Chappell). Citizens of a dystopian future where humanity is ruled by the totalitarian Terran Federation, the group escapes custody, commandeers an advanced spacecraft, and wages guerrilla warfare on the corrupt administration. The chief antagonists are Space Commander Travis (Stephen Greif, Brian Croucher), a man obsessed with killing Blake, and Supreme Commander (later President) Servalan (Jacqueline Pearce). The show ran for four seasons, and the first was scripted, as planned, entirely by Nation; then a team of writers headed by Boucher took over (although Nation contributed scripts until the end of season 3). Indeed, many consider Boucher to have been as instrumental in the series' development as Nation. Among them, Nation, Boucher, and producer Maloney forged a show characterized by twisting plotlines (often hinging on shock betrayals), sharp characterization, and ripe dialogue. At its best, *Blake's 7* had a peculiar intensity all its own and is perhaps best summed up by Darrow's observation that it was driven by "realism in an unrealistic situation" (quoted in Collinson).

Although the show essentially adopted a series format, with each individual episode offering a self-contained narrative (in much the same manner as the ITC and ABC series Nation had written for in the 1960s and early 1970s), it also made use of serial devices. Jonathan Bignell and Andrew O'Day identify *Blake's 7* as an early example of "flexi-narrative"—"episodic series that have new storylines each week as well as an ongoing storyline" (90). There are a number of story arcs operating at different points and at different levels over the course of *Blake's 7*'s four seasons. The overarching "rebels versus Federation" line runs through the series from beginning to end, but each of the four seasons also introduces an ongoing story to some degree, most notably season 2's "search for Star One" narrative. (In addition, certain characters are given continuing backstories, as examined later.) The program also makes use of cliffhangers at the climax of each season in an attempt to retain its audience during transmission breaks.

Both the cliffhanger and the story arc have been feted as influential on subsequent practitioners and programs (Muir 2–3, 171; Stevens and Moore 199–200; Collinson). Although the end-of-season cliffhanger is now common in all manner of genres, it is unclear to what extent *Blake's*

7 established the precedent (as has been suggested). Similarly, story arcs have become a primary component in science fiction television, with *Blake's 7* often cited as a key influence. Here, there are perhaps better grounds for accepting such an assessment, with both J. Michael Straczynski (*Babylon 5*) and Joss Whedon (*Buffy the Vampire Slayer, Firefly*) "self-confessed" fans of the BBC show (Stevens and Moore 199–200).

Blake's 7 is also notable for allowing significant character development over the course of its four seasons. Fans (Barrett, "The Way Back" 10) and critics (Collinson) alike have noted how the protagonists change over time due to their continuing involvement in the revolution. Perhaps more significantly, the show sometimes offers the villains a similar potential for character development. For example, both Travis and Servalan are explored psychologically over a sustained sequence of episodes. Season 4's "Sand" sees Servalan effectively served a "two-hander," trapped alone with Tarrant (Steven Pacey) and revealing details of her past that account for her current persona. However, not all the characters are allowed the same scope. In particular, the female protagonists are often reduced to secondary characters, with Jan Chappell's Cally notoriously degenerating from revolutionary fanatic to "ship's nurse and hand-holder" (McCormack 15).

Blake's 7's attitude toward gender representations and politics has drawn fire from a number of quarters (Bignell and O'Day; McCormack; Barrett, "The Way Back"), and it is difficult to disagree with the assessment that the female protagonists often "conformed to common stereotypes about women" (Bignell and O'Day 171). Although Servalan offers a potentially empowering female character through her transgression of established gender binaries, this nonconformity is closely bound up with her role as the show's primary villain. As Bignell and O'Day suggest, "positive characters conform to gender conventions, while negative characters distort them" (174).

Blake's 7 made its BBC1 debut at 6 P.M. on Monday, January 2, 1978, the same week *Star Wars* opened in the United Kingdom. This coincidence of dates has been afforded a degree of significance by those who view *Blake's 7* as little more than the BBC's attempt to cash in on the film's success (Newman, *Doctor Who* 94; Miller, "Servalan" 78). Whether this is the case remains open to debate, and it is certainly true that the BBC attempted to head off any unfavorable comparisons in its publicity material.[3] And although both *Blake's 7* and *Star Wars* chart the course of rebellion against an oppressive militaristic regime, the two are starkly different in terms of core philosophy. *Star Wars* is driven by a clearly (and rigidly) defined binary opposition, whereas *Blake's 7* is riddled with ambiguity. Despite setting up a relatively stable antagonism between Federation and rebellion, there is a lingering ambivalence about whether one is ultimately better than the other. The Federation espouses the pacification of its subjects (whether by chemical, psychological, or military means), colonialism, and organized crime and tolerates no political dissent whatsoever. Blake and his followers seek to overturn this status quo, but they do so by acts of terrorism and piracy in which civilian deaths are seen as little more than "collateral damage." Blake's ideological stance and plans for the post-Federation galaxy are barely articulated (indeed, it is questionable whether his campaign against the Terran administration amounts to much more than revenge for its attempts to brainwash and discredit him). Once the character disappears from the series and the unambiguously amoral Avon takes command, the revolution recedes into the distance, and the program edges closer to Nation's "*Dirty Dozen* in space."

On paper, the premise of *Blake's 7* reads like a fairly traditional "rebels versus tyrants" fable, a sci-fi variation on the Robin Hood myth of a closely bonded gang of roguish heroes fighting for a noble cause. In actuality, the protagonists are anything but a team, flung together by forces beyond their control and remaining together for selfish reasons and despite significant personal animosities. Avon quite clearly despises Blake but has designs on the *Liberator* and *Orac*, so he fights alongside him based on the agreement that Avon will inherit both once the Federation falls. Vila sticks around merely because the alternative (mental conditioning and prison) is a slightly less desirable option. Only Cally seems truly committed to Blake's cause, and once Blake is gone, the group drifts toward piracy and heists, tackling the Federation only when necessary or to satisfy personal grudges. The drama often hinges as much on conflict and even outright hostility between the rebels as it does on the battle of wits between Blake and Travis (later Avon and Servalan). The possibility that one of the crew might betray the rest for personal gain is a recurring theme: "They're not my gang. . . . We are together for mutual convenience. I imagine that if I double-crossed them, they would try and kill me" ("Gold," 4.10). Such possibilities occasionally yield genuinely shocking moments—none more so than in season 4's "Orbit" (4.11), written by Robert Holmes. Trapped on a shuttle that is doomed to crash unless enough excess weight is jettisoned, Avon realizes that Vila weighs the right amount to avert disaster and hunts him down. Although the crisis is eventually avoided by other means, the revelation of Avon's ruthlessness comes as a shock at this late stage in the series.

But then *Blake's 7* is relentlessly pessimistic in its worldview, in its opinion of human nature, and (perhaps surprisingly) in its attitude toward revolution. Despite a handful of minor victories early on, it becomes increasingly clear that Blake's campaign is futile, and we see Blake himself descend into dangerous obsession and madness over the course of his campaign. Alan Stevens and Fiona Moore offer an interesting perspective on the show's position, suggesting that as the post-Blake crew members move further toward a life of piracy and crime, they effectively become "supporters" of the system rather than attacking it: "The whole series has thus been predicated on the idea that revolution is a grim process, which is easily co-opted by greed and venality, and whose practitioners tend to meet violent ends" (196). Though not quite antirevolutionary, *Blake's 7* views "the cause" and those who follow it with a cynical eye. The show also offers a dystopian vision of the future, representing a "negative extrapolation from the television viewer's world" (Bignell and O'Day 119). The Federation starts off as an amalgamation of Nazi Germany and Stalinist Russia and degenerates into a tin-pot military dictatorship after the shambles of galactic war and Space Command's coup d'état ("Star One," 2.13). Technological progress is invariably bound up with the mechanics of terror; two of Nation's favorite obsessions—nuclear weapons and genetic engineering—feature prominently in the Federation's arsenal. *Blake's 7*'s pessimistic outlook also encompasses human evolution, with season 3's bleak finale ("Terminal," 3.13) revealing that the ultimate destiny of humanity is a reversion to the apelike savagery of our primal roots.

It is in the final episode ("Blake," 4.13) that the show's worldview reaches its nihilistic apotheosis. Just as it commences with the massacre of a rebel group, so *Blake's 7* ends in exactly the same manner. Here, however, it is the central characters who are systematically shot down—starting with Avon's paranoid murder of Blake. Critics and fans alike have described the events of the show's denouement as "apocalyptic" and "shocking" (Sangster and Condon 119). Apocalyptic it undoubtedly is, but given what has gone before, the final bloodbath seems like the only logical conclusion to the show's narrative arc. The production team decided that the final defeat of the Federation would be a "highly improbable" ending to the show (Muir 20). A precedent for shock exits had already been set in season 2's "Pressure Point" (2.5), with the death of Gan. Screened four days before Christmas in 1981, "Blake" ensured not only a lasting legacy for the show but also the circulation of an urban myth—that the episode triggered a spike in the U.K. suicide rate (Sangster and Condon 119).

For a show that has been off the air for more than a quarter of a century, *Blake's 7* retains an active fandom on both sides of the Atlantic. A number of organized fan communities exist, most notably the official *Blake's 7* fan club Horizon, and the program retains a strong cult presence on the Internet. However, the series was neither conceived nor broadcast as "cult." The BBC scheduled it in an early-evening time slot with the express intention of attracting a broad range of age groups, particularly parents and children (Bignell and O'Day 56–58; Stevens and Moore 12). Considered a ratings success, the show achieved viewing figures of over 10 million at its height (McAllister 118). Although *Blake's 7* enjoyed mainstream success in the United Kingdom, it remained an underground presence in the United States, where it was not seen until 1986, five years after its cancellation, and aired on public broadcasting stations. The formation of local *Blake's 7* fan groups led to a number of campaigns to persuade local PBS stations to purchase the rights to the show, and the *Blake's 7* cast and crew began appearing at U.S. sci-fi conventions in the late 1980s. To some, *Blake's 7* was "the hottest underground cult show in America" (Javna 115).

Why does *Blake's 7* remain such a firm cult favorite? Writing in the *Independent* on the show's twentieth anniversary, Robert Hanks argues that its continued popularity boils down to "the sheer crappiness of the series and the crappiness it attributes to the universe," suggesting that it is enjoyed both cynically (for its poor production values) and *for* its cynicism. Although the show undoubtedly holds an ironic or camp appeal for a number of its fans—for instance, Jacqueline Pearce and her Servalan character have a significant gay following ("The Steel Queen"; Linford)—other aficionados champion *Blake's 7* for its depth of characterization and visualization of a future society (Barrett 10). The show offers hyperdiegetic potential, with unexplored narrative space and character possibilities inspiring fan-writers to investigate the *Blake's 7* universe and its occupants more fully. In particular, a significant subgenre of *Blake's 7* fiction is the "post–Gauda Prime" story, exploring what might have happened after the massacre in the final episode (Bacon-Smith 162; Jenkins, *Textual Poachers* 164). Indeed, the final cliffhanger was designed to leave a question mark about the possibility of the show's return.[4] Matt Hills labels this an example of "Grand Non-narrative," a means by which cult shows can "ensure their immortality." Such a gambit might account for the durability of cult programs long after their cancellation, with the absence of officially sanctioned closure leaving the narrative "open to multiple fan productions, speculations and recreations" (Hills, *Fan Cultures* 137).

There have been numerous "re-creations" over the years, some circulated unofficially among fan groups, as well as a few officially sanctioned continuations. Two "new" *Blake's 7* episodes were recorded for BBC Radio in the late 1990s, reuniting most of the season 4 cast. The first of these met with a hostile reaction from both fans and the mainstream press (Stevens and Moore 207), and the second would be the last. A feature film, TV miniseries, and children's animation have been announced by *Blake's 7* Enterprises (which currently owns the rights), although none of these has surfaced yet.[5] However, in 2007 the company released a three-CD audio remake with a new cast and writing team, which was also made available on the Sci-Fi Channel's Web site. Given the current favorable disposition toward science fiction in the British television industry, a televisual revival of *Blake's 7* is by no means out of the question. However, as Stevens and Moore suggest, whether "a series about terrorism from the point of view of the terrorists would ever be considered in the present political climate" remains to be seen (200).

Notes

1. Following a complaint about a drowning sequence in the *Doctor Who* episode "The Deadly Assassin," the National Viewers' and Listeners' Association received a written apology from BBC director general Charles Curran (Howe, Stammers, and Walker 162). The offending sequence was later cut from a repeat broadcast, and *Doctor Who*'s incoming producer, Graham Williams, was asked in no uncertain terms to tone down the show's violent content (Chapman, *Inside the TARDIS* 119).

2. Muir (10) suggests that "in the final analysis, *Blake's 7* sported a lower budget than the pitifully low-budgeted *Doctor Who*."

3. "We've got something *Star Wars* doesn't have — time to develop our plots, characters and action. They've got two hours, we've got 12" (Maloney quoted in Evans, "Roaming" 116).

4. Chris Boucher suggests that he wrote it in such a way that if the show were once again reprieved at the eleventh hour, all the "dead" characters could return without destroying credulity.

5. BBC Entertainment news, July 3, 2000, http://news.bbc.co.uk/1/hi/entertainment/705922.stm.

Buffy the Vampire Slayer

Milly Williamson

When *Buffy the Vampire Slayer* aired on American network television, it entirely upended the tale of the vampire. In this television series, it is not vampires who dominate the screen, nor is the power to defeat them possessed by a patriarchal figure such as Dr. Van Helsing and his male-dominated Crew of Light. Instead, it is wielded by an American girl named Buffy Summers (played by Sarah Michelle Gellar), a teenage vampire slayer—the "chosen one"—who possesses supernatural strength and who regularly saves not only her classmates from vampires but also the world from annihilation at the hands of ancient evil. The series is set in Sunnydale, a typical Southern Californian town—except that it is also the Hellmouth, a magnet for the gathering of evil, which Buffy ceaselessly combats in its various incarnations.

The series has regularly been applauded for its feminist gender politics (Owen, "Vampires"; Daugherty; Playden). Indeed, series creator Joss Whedon declared *Buffy*'s feminist intentions from the outset: "The idea . . . came from seeing too many blondes walking into dark alleyways and being killed. I wanted, just once, for her to fight back when the monster attacked, and kick his ass" (quoted in Havens 21). Whedon's own commitment to feminist issues is well known—in 2006 the feminist organization Equality Now presented him with the award "On the Road to Equality: Honoring Men in the Front Lines," in recognition of his penchant for creating strong female characters. The theme of female empowerment marks the entire series—from Buffy's early refusal to accept without question the authority of her (adult male) "watcher," Giles, to the wonderful feminist and collectivist series denouement in which hundreds of young women—potential slayers—gather to fight together, a message that defies the suffocating individualism of our time and reminds us of collective power.

But to suggest that *Buffy the Vampire Slayer* deals simplistically or didactically with the issue of female empowerment would be to deny the complexity of the show and the manner in which it dramatizes the dilemmas it depicts, at both a narrative and a generic level. *Buffy* couples female empowerment to the theme of "outsiderdom" in a genre hybrid that successfully blends the codes of action-adventure with those of melodrama, teen drama, and supernatural horror to address the problems and powerlessness faced by young women (and adolescents in general) through a host of monstrous metaphors. From the first episode in which Buffy arrives in Sunnydale with her mother after being expelled from her school in Los Angeles, the series recognizes the impositions one must face, no matter how powerful one is. When Giles first tells Buffy that he is her watcher and that his role is to "prepare her," she retorts in what becomes her touchstone antiauthoritarian style, "Prepare me for what? For getting kicked out of school? For losing all my friends? For having to spend all of my time fighting for my life and never getting to tell anyone because I might endanger them? Go ahead—prepare me" ("Welcome to the Hellmouth," 1.1).

Buffy may be the "chosen one" and powerful, but she still has little control over her destiny. This supernatural dilemma mirrors the experience of many women in Anglo-American culture, which tells us that equality has been achieved while hiding the fetters of continued female subordination. Buffy's position as the slayer places her on the outside of her social milieu. She is drawn to the vacuous existence of high school queen bitch Cordelia (Charisma Carpenter) but chooses instead the friendship of outcast "geeks" Willow (Alyson Hannigan) and Xander (Nicholas Brendon). Giles (Anthony Stewart Head) is also depicted as an outsider, and this group of friends is eventually expanded to include Tara (Amber Benson), a lesbian Wiccan running from a domineering patriarchal family; Anya (Emma Caulfield), a fallen vengeance demon; Oz (Seth Green), a boy werewolf; Angel (David Boreanaz), a conscience-tortured vampire; and eventually the vampire Spike (James Marsters), who has fallen for Buffy and quips, in the quick-witted dialogue typical of the show, "I may be love's bitch, but at least I'm man enough to admit it." Even Cordelia gradually joins the outcasts after her own adolescent angst is revealed in "Out of Mind, Out of Sight" (1.11), in which a girl who is so unpopular that she literally disappears attempts to take revenge on Cordelia. The group is dubbed the "Scooby Gang," in a nod to the cartoon *Scooby Doo*, and its makeup is significant, for as Roz Kaveney has pointed out, the members are all "refugees from hierarchy of one sort or another" (7). Buffy's friendship circle thus both complicates the issue of monstrousness by including monsters and embraces socially marginal identities, speaking from and for the experience of outsiderdom.

The sympathetic approach to outsiderdom is reinforced by the use of melodrama to engage viewers' emotions. Whedon himself has remarked that emotions are at the heart of the series and that emotional investment with the characters forms the center of the program. It has long been acknowledged that melodrama addresses that which is culturally disavowed. It raises "what cannot be said" (Brooks 11). *Buffy* uses monsters and magic to address that which is usually not acknowledged as suffering at all, suffering that is therefore difficult to communicate — the limits of freedom and the lack of fulfillment that structure so many lives but are culturally unspoken. The melodrama of the series, however, is Gothic, not only in its use of the supernatural as a metaphor for the protagonists' problems but also because all the core characters, the humans and the demons, suffer the pathos of their predicament, linking the suffering of the "self" to the suffering of the "other." The Gothic has long given voice to the pathos of life because, as one critic comments, it "gives us glimpses of the skeletons of undead desires and makes them move again" (Punter 409).

Outsiderdom and otherness, then, are key themes in *Buffy* that are reinforced by the extratextual comments of the production team. For instance, co-executive producer David Greenwalt comments, "If Joss Whedon had had one good day in high school, we wouldn't be here" (Springer 13). Even Sarah Michelle Gellar (improbably) paints herself as a high school outcast when she comments, "Kids were hard on me. I was always excluded from everything because I was different" (Springer 13). The theme of the outcast is taken up again in the episode "Earshot" (3.18). Buffy has acquired the power to read minds and can hear someone in the school threatening to kill the students. She assumes that alienated outcast Jonathan Levinson (Danny Strong) is planning the shooting, but in fact, he is planning suicide. Buffy manages to dissuade him, and the Scooby Gang discovers that the voice Buffy hears belongs to the lunchroom lady. Buffy manages to subdue her, averting disaster. This is one of two episodes of *Buffy* that were postponed by the WB a month after the murders at Columbine High School in Littleton, Colorado. That it might be American society itself that produces such severe alienation in its youth is not generally acknowledged. Ironically, as Lisa Parks points out, programs like *Buffy* are held responsible "for violence in American high schools" (121), to avoid confronting the difficult issues of alienation that trigger such tragedies. Parks also comments that "the WB network became a temporary apologist for button-pushing content and then raced to capitalize upon it once Columbine faded from the news headlines" (122).

In the United States, *Buffy the Vampire Slayer* repeatedly upset the sensibilities of members of the Religious Right, and many episodes comment directly on their authoritarianism and hypocrisy. For example, in "Gingerbread" (3.11), adult authority is shown to be part of the problem rather than part of the solution. Joyce Summers, Buffy's mother, wants to learn about Buffy's life as the slayer but becomes very upset at the death of two children (who are actually a single demon in disguise) and decides that Buffy and her friends are ineffectual. She sets up MOO (Mothers Opposed to the Occult), but the group's activities spiral out of control when Willow and Buffy are denounced as witches and are set to be burned at the stake by MOO members—their own parents. Buffy and Willow are eventually saved by the Scooby Gang, but not before library books are confiscated at the behest of Joyce and her organization to "weed out offensive material." Buffy digs at this presumed adult authority with the jibe, "Maybe the next time that the world is getting sucked into Hell, I won't be able to stop it because the anti-Hell-sucking book isn't on the Approved Reading List." Buffy's surface wit reveals the show's deeper critique of conservatism, moral panic, and authoritarianism.

But the Religious Right in America was actually more offended by the show's polymorphous sexuality than its antiauthoritarianism. Moral ambiguity and sexual libertarianism become key themes in later seasons as the characters grow up, putting the show deeply at odds with the morally conservative climate of Anglo-American culture in the late twentieth and early twenty-first centuries. As members of the Scooby Gang begin to pair up, Willow and Tara, both Wiccans, become a lesbian couple, and Whedon insists to the WB that the kiss between them in "The Body" (5.16) is "not negotiable." Moral ambiguity begins in the first season, however, when Buffy, who is supposed to kill vampires, finds herself attracted to Angel. But the polymorphous perversity inherent in the figure of the vampire is most fully explored in the relationship between Buffy and Spike. As Dee Amy-Chinn argues, this is not a straightforward heterosexual pairing, because of the gender mobility of the two characters involved. For instance, Buffy assumes the dominant role, while Spike adopts the traditionally feminized role of being "in love" with Buffy. In season 6 Buffy uses Spike as her sexual toy. She regularly abuses him—physically, mentally, and sexually. She beats him, calls him an "evil, disgusting thing," and insists on sex even when he says no. In "Smashed" (6.9), the pair's first sexual encounter occurs when Buffy throws Spike against a wall, unzips his trousers, and has sex with him. In "Gone" (6.11), she breaks into his room, throws him against the wall, and initiates sex. The act of sex (which, for these two, is violent and out of control) is the only possible comfort for "a pair of lovers whose own problems are too vast for them to find anything but transitory comfort" (Saxey 202). Even this is fleeting and physical, leaving psychological and emotional suffering neglected. When, in "Seeing Red" (6.19), Spike tries (unsuccessfully) to rape Buffy (she beats him off), this act leads to his further feminization; it is the catalyst for his decision to get his soul back—because of his love for Buffy. Once his soul is returned, for which he must suffer torture, he can admit his love:

> BUFFY: How did you do it? How did you get your soul back?
> SPIKE: Saw a man about a girl. I went to seek a legend out. Travelled to the other side of the world. Made a deal with a demon. . . .
> BUFFY: Just like that?
> SPIKE: No, not like that. There was a price. There were trials, torture, pain and suffering . . . of sorts. . . .
> BUFFY: Meaning?
> SPIKE: Meaning I have come to redefine the words *pain* and *suffering* since I fell in love with you. . . . You hated yourself and you took it out on me. . . . The soul's not moonbeams and whistles, luv. It's about self loathing. I get it. I had to travel round the world, but I get it now. I understand you now. I understand the violence inside you.
> BUFFY: William the Bloody now has insight into violence?
> SPIKE: Not the same. As bad as I was, as evil and wretched as I was, I never truly hated myself back then. Not like I do now. ("Never Leave Me," 7.9)

Spike's story arc puts him in a long tradition of sympathetic bad-boy vampires stemming back to Byron (it's no accident that Spike was a poet in his human life, although not a very good one), which has contributed to the show's cult fan following. The complexity with which issues of sexuality are handled on *Buffy*, the intertextual references to other fiction, and the moral ambiguity surrounding the relationship between Buffy and Spike led to an enormous amount of online erotic fan fiction (known as slash fiction), with pairings between most of the characters, although Spike and Buffy remained a favorite. *Buffy*, like other cult TV shows, invited the audience to read its subtext, particularly around the character of Spike.

Cult texts, according to Jancovich and coauthors, are "not defined by any feature shared by shows themselves, but rather by the way they are appropriated by specific groups" of cult fans (*Defining Cult Movies* 27). *Buffy*, however, is deliberately constructed to be consumed by fan groups in a fannish or cult manner—in other words, fans are invited to immerse themselves in the text and produce subtextual readings from the many textual clues. Whedon posted a message on the *Buffy the Vampire Slayer* fan discussion board, the Bronze, suggesting that the attraction of the "Buffyverse" is that "it lends itself to polymorphous perverse subtext. It encourages it. I personally find romance in every relationship [with exceptions], I love all the characters, so I say B.Y.O. Subtext!" (www.cise.ufl.edu/~hsiao/media/tv/buffy/bronze). *Buffy*'s extended plotlines, intertextual and metatextual references, serial nature, and lack of closure are deliberately intended to produce active fan involvement, as Whedon's comments indicate.

Yet *Buffy* always treated its audience intelligently. The combination of fantasy story lines, superb dialogue, emotional realism, and moral complexity demonstrated the commitment of the show's producers to the astuteness of its viewers. It also meant that *Buffy* was not only a cult TV show; despite its small audience,[1] the show made an impact on mainstream television culture, winning awards and critical acclaim. The episode entitled "Hush" (4.10) was nominated for an Emmy award; in that episode, monsters called the "Gentlemen" steal the voices of everyone in town, so for more than half an hour, there is complete silence. In 2001 *Buffy* won a Saturn Award for Best Genre Network Series. *Buffy* was ranked among the top ten shows by *USA Today*, it was ranked number five by the American *TV Guide*, and *Entertainment Weekly* called it "one of TV's all-time great dramas" (Susman).

So how did a show like *Buffy*, with its challenging themes and relatively small audience, not only survive a neoconservative social climate and American network television but become feted by its critics? The key to *Buffy*'s fortunes was its placement on newly fledged television networks. In the United States, *Buffy* aired initially on the WB network as a midseason replacement in March 1997, until it was poached by UPN in 2001. Both networks were set up in 1995 by "studio-based conglomerates in the throes of deregulation" (Holt 12). The combined force of the 1995 repeal of the financial and syndication rules in the United States (which had prevented networks from having an ownership stake in their prime-time programming) and the Telecommunications Act of 1996 (which abolished network ownership caps on stations and increased the audience limitation for networks from 25 to 35 percent) led to a "phase of frenzied merger and acquisitions activity" (Holt 12), out of which the new networks that aired *Buffy* were born. The WB was owned by AOL Time Warner, a result of the largest merger in media history and the second largest media conglomerate in the United States.[2] UPN was owned by another big player, Viacom-CBS.[3] However, despite the scale of conglomeration, American network television was going through a demographic crisis that deregulation could not solve. These new networks emerged at a time when network television audiences overall were declining as a result of competition with cable and satellite channels. Network television's 90 percent share of the audience in the 1970s had shrunk to 57 percent by the 1990s (Holt 16). Less concerned with attracting mass audiences, the new networks focused on reaching "the most valuable audiences: affluent viewers that advertisers were prepared to pay the highest rates to address" (Jancovich and Lyons 3). *Buffy* had a high concentration of the WB's target audience: eighteen- to thirty-four-year-old, educated, white, affluent viewers—a demographic that advertisers are keen to reach. UPN was reportedly prepared to offer $2.3 million per episode, as opposed to the WB's $1 million, indicating that the program was reaching the young, white, educated audience both networks were courting. UPN had struggled to get a solid hold in prime-time television, and *Buffy* guaranteed a substantial increase in viewers who made up the station's key demographic target.

Ironically, the "press of forces" (Wilcox and Lavery xvii) that all television programs grow within unwittingly provided the conditions that contributed to the success of a television show that critiqued those very forces. In the process, viewers were treated to one of the most intelligent and thought-provoking shows to emerge from American network television—a show that challenged us, at the turn of the millennium, to question what it means to be human.

Notes

1. According to *USA Today*, *Buffy* had about 4.5 million viewers per episode at its highest point.

2. In 2006 Time Warner had a revenue of $44.2 billion. See *Columbia University Journalism Review*, http://www.freepress.net/ownershipchart.php?hart=main.

3. The WB and UPN have since merged into the CW television network, jointly owned by Time Warner and CBS. The Viacom-CBS merger was approved by the Federal Communications Commission despite the fact that the new conglomerate exceeded the 35 percent audience share regulation. Viacom-CBS has a 41 percent audience reach (Holt 22; http:mediasharx.com/index.php.news/119).

The Comeback

Joanne Morreale

In 2005 Michael Patrick King, writer for *Sex in the City*, and Lisa Kudrow, star of the sitcom *Friends*, created *The Comeback* for HBO, a comedy about aging ex–sitcom star Valerie Cherish, played by Kudrow. Kudrow was not, however, enacting a version of herself or her character from *Friends*. She was virtually unrecognizable in an outdated, titian-red wig and a slight southern accent. The show's conceit was that Valerie had been the star of an early 1990s sitcom called *I'm It!* but since then had not had a successful series. Valerie has landed a role in a new sitcom, *Room and Bored*, under the condition that she allow herself to be filmed for a reality show that documents her "comeback," thus allowing the network to combine two shows in one.

Like many HBO comedies, *The Comeback* exemplifies what Brett Mills refers to as "comedy verité" by using the aesthetics and conventions of reality television for comedic purposes ("Comedy Verité" 63). It provides a reflexive behind-the-scenes look at the entertainment industry, which has been a sitcom convention since *The George Burns and Gracie Allen Show* and *I Love Lucy* in the early years of television. Unlike conventional sitcoms, however, *The Comeback* is shot in documentary style, with both reality cameras and cameras recording the reality cameras; further, it combines interior and exterior locations and, like other HBO comedies, has no laugh track to emphasize its "liveness." It fits into the genre most often referred to as cringe comedy; its dark, satirical humor is based less on set jokes and repartee than on discomfort and humiliation.

The show-within-a-show, filmed as if it were a reality show in the making, depicts the struggle between situation comedy and reality television as primary modes of entertainment, even as it blurs their boundaries. In so doing, it lays bare the processes by which all television is constructed and the way that both cringe comedy and reality television rely on humiliation and embarrassment. It is also a Goffman-like rumination on the presentation of self, with Valerie attempting to control her image, the reality show producers attempting to shape their version, and *The Comeback* presenting a (fictional) glimpse of the "real" Valerie Cherish that occasionally emerges through the facade.

Erving Goffman's concept of *face* explains much of *The Comeback*: "A person may be said to *have, to be in,* or to *maintain* face when the line he effectively takes presents an image of him that is internally consistent, that is supported by judgments and evidence conveyed by other participants, and that is confirmed by evidence conveyed through interpersonal agencies in the situation" (6–7). Throughout *The Comeback*, the face presented by Valerie Cherish contrasts with the perceptions of those around her, and both tension and humor come from the fact that she seems unaware of the discrepancy between her elevated self-image and her marginal status. She is the consummate performer who does her "facework": she says and does only what conforms to how she wants to be seen, yet the relentless reality cameras occasionally offer glimpses of her pain. *The Comeback* presents Valerie as simultaneously authentic and inauthentic, sincere and insincere. It remains unclear to what extent she is aware of her self-contradictions or her humiliation, making her a remarkable characterization of the way people try to present a consistent face to the world but are blind to their own failings and inconsistencies.

Although Kudrow was nominated for an Emmy for Best Actress in a Comedy and King for Best Writer, *The Comeback* was canceled after one season. Perhaps, as Valerie Cherish notes in one episode, "Edgy is good. Too edgy is cancellation." Critic Alessandra Stanley referred to it as "the saddest comedy on television," and many viewers found Valerie's embarrassments and humiliations too difficult to watch. Yet *Boston Globe* critic Matthew Gilbert wrote, "I believe that, beginning with its release on DVD, *The Comeback* will find its destiny as a cult TV classic." He added, "What still awes me about *The Comeback* is probably what kept it from developing a big audience: its entire willingness to risk its own likeability to sling its ugly truths."

The Comeback was a complex and innovative form of television comedy. According to King, it was "a satiric look at ego and vulnerability laced through the landscape of television and popular culture." In the process, *The Comeback* critiqued the relationship between reality television and the sitcom, stars and writers, filmmakers and subjects, and women as subjects and objects of comedy. As in the more successful satire *The Office*, the main character is an outsider who desperately wants to become an insider. But her inflated view of her own importance is as much a comment on the marginalized status of older women in Hollywood as it is on ego and identity. For example, in "Valerie Triumphs at the Upfronts" (1.2), she repeatedly tells everyone that the network executives will expect her to make a speech about her comeback on *Room and Bored*. Instead, they almost forget to announce her as a cast member.

Throughout the series, Valerie attempts to control her performance in both the sitcom and the reality program that documents her every move. For thirteen episodes, she tries to project herself as dignified in the face of a constant barrage of indignities. In the pilot, actresses Marilu Henner from *Taxi* and Kim Fields from *The Facts of Life* audition along with Valerie, but they balk at doing a reality show. But the fictional Valerie, who is desperate for fame and recognition, welcomes the idea of having cameras document her life. She is, however, aware of the low status of reality programs and is determined to produce "a reality show with dignity." Always performing for the cameras, she appears oblivious to slights and disappointments, although close-ups that linger a little too long allow Kudrow to display signs of embarrassment and humiliation: a frozen smile, a downward glance, or nervous laughter. Valerie is humiliated on multiple levels: by the reality show producers, by the sitcom writers within the reality show, and, ultimately, by Kudrow and King.

The Comeback is shot as if it were a reality show in process. Each episode begins with a color bar that reads "raw footage" rather than opening credits. It is what Roscoe and Hight refer to as a "degree 3" mock-documentary, in which "the filmmakers are attempting to engage directly with factual discourse, and effectively to encourage viewers to develop a critical awareness of the partial, constructed nature of documentary" (16). Both the reality program producer, Jane, and her crew appear on camera, and particularly at the beginning of the series, camera movements are shaky and awkward, as if the filmmakers are unsure of what to follow. They deliberately include mundane moments; in a visual joke, Valerie and her husband Mark watch paint dry on a wall.

In "Valerie Relaxes in Palm Springs" (1.8), the requisite product placement—a crucial part of reality programs, though not meant to be noticed—plays a central role. Valerie and Mark are given a Ford Navigator to drive to Palm Springs for a weekend break. The press representative sits in the back and feeds them lines about the car to repeat for the reality show, and Jane makes sure the Navigator name is prominently displayed on camera. During their stay, Valerie's friend, a cancer survivor, tells her that bottling up her emotions will make her ill, and she points out that Valerie is always looking to the reality cameras for validation. In the midst of dinner, the young star of *Room and Bored*, Juna, calls Valerie to ask why she isn't at head writer Paulie G's party, and Valerie learns that she is the only cast member who has not been invited. At the end of the episode, Valerie calls Paulie G. and tells him that he has hurt her feelings. As they drive home, she tells the Navigator's press representative to shut up or she will throw him out of the car, and she plays music despite Jane's protests that it's too expensive to air on the show. Although this was the eighth episode of the series, it was one of the first in which Valerie expresses her vulnerability and asserts herself, thus emerging as a sympathetic character with whom viewers can empathize.

In her illusion of control, Valerie tells Jane to cut or rewind the tape when a scene or incident is not to her liking. For example, in her first video diary, she pompously describes *The Comeback* as the story of a woman's "journey back to herself." In the background, viewers can hear Mark defecating in the bathroom. Of course, these moments delight the filmmakers, and Valerie does not realize until the penultimate episode (when the pilot for *The Comeback* airs) that Jane has never stopped filming at her request. In "Valerie Demands Dignity" (1.5), Jane sets up a scene in which Valerie's housekeeper finds a pornographic videotape. When Valerie first enters the room, she orders Jane to stop the cameras because she doesn't have her "face" on. When Valerie reenters the room, she notices the pornographic tape. She initially laughs it off, then suddenly tells Jane to stop shooting because "this is a reality show about dignity and a woman's journey," not about sex. But later in the episode, Valerie sees an *Entertainment Weekly* headline that reads, "Reality Show Ratings Are Slipping; Sex and Stunts Provide a Much Needed IV." Jane then tells Valerie that the network has decided to cross-promote *The Comeback* with another new reality show, *The Celebrity Apprentice*, starring a midget who assists celebrities. Although Valerie protests that this is not dignified, she eventually acquiesces. When the otherwise able apprentice runs out of gas on the freeway, Valerie is forced to walk to a meeting, at one point falling and cutting her knee. When she loses her temper, the apprentice tells her it was a stunt set up to make the show more interesting. Instead of getting angry, at the end of the episode Valerie "forgets" to turn off the mike when she and her husband have sex in the bathroom (as in all reality shows, the only room where they have privacy). Through the reality show, the comedic point is made that Valerie's narrative about dignity is just a performance.

Valerie is humiliated by the reality show, and also by her role in the sitcom. Throughout the series she seeks but never attains the approval of her nemesis, Paulie G. Initially, she is supposed to play an architect in her forties who shares an apartment with three thirty-something roommates. But the network decides it needs to attract a younger demographic, so the writers change her role to Aunt Sassy, an older woman who owns the apartment and lives upstairs, and the roommates become two men and two women in their twenties. Valerie, who initially sees herself as the star, is relegated to a minor role as comic relief. Her dressing room is upstairs, away from the rest of the cast, and even the publicity photo has her standing behind the four attractive young stars, nodding disapprovingly as they huddle together. The writers, who resent the network's interference with their sitcom, give Aunt Sassy humiliating lines (and as few as possible) and dress her in a pastel pink running suit that contrasts with the bikinis and swimming trunks worn by her tenants.

Despite her treatment on the set, Valerie still tries to exert control. In "Valerie Stands Up for Aunt Sassy" (1.4), she contests a line written for her character: upon seeing that her tenants have taken in a litter of puppies, Aunt Sassy complains, "You see a box of puppies. I see Korean barbeque." Valerie protests that such a crass remark will make her character unlikable. She attempts to convince the one female writer to change the line, claiming that she loves puppies, and the owner of the puppies insists that she adopt one. Valerie agrees, although she really has no interest in dogs and the puppy is a constant annoyance—refusing to sleep in a crate or walk on a leash and pooping in her hair. At the end of the episode, Valerie pretends she doesn't know the puppy is behind her car and almost runs it over. She stops the car, gets the dog, and gives it to Jane. "You'd better keep it," she says. "If I take this dog home it *will* be Korean barbeque." She thus makes the same statement in "real" life that she contests in the sitcom. This episode demonstrates the tension between sincerity and insincerity that makes up Valerie's character, and her inability to control her image. The ending is humorous, yet it is also uncomfortable because it makes the contradictory and performative nature of Valerie—and perhaps all of us—apparent.

At the same time that it turns a comedy into a faux reality show, *The Comeback* interjects elements of the traditional sitcom into the reality program, thus blending the two competing forms. Stereotypical comedic characters are found in the reality show. In addition to villain Paulie G., Valerie's devoted gay assistant and precocious preteen stepdaughter provide traditional sitcom humor. Sexy young star Juna effortlessly gets the attention Valerie craves. Valerie's husband Mark plays the straight man, while Valerie herself is a "clown." Even in the so-called reality show, she performs physical comedy; for example, she falls while running on the freeway, crawls down the aisle of a plane, and bumps into her dressing room door. She also speaks in sitcom clichés, often repeating the one line that sums up her character— "I just want to be heard"—or her catchphrases from the sitcom—"Note to self" and "I don't need to see that!"

Room and Bored, the sitcom within the reality show, is also written and produced like a real sitcom on the order of *Three's Company*. James Burrows, who directed episodes of *The Mary Tyler Moore Show* and *Taxi* and cocreated *Cheers*, plays the director. The dialogue is laden with sexual innuendo, the well-toned characters (except Aunt Sassy) are scantily clad, and there is the requisite three-camera setup and studio audience at each taping. There are subtle scenes in which characters prepare to do a read-through of their lines, and while Juna underlines frantically, Valerie searches through the script. In one particularly harrowing scene, Valerie bakes cookies for the writers, who are working overtime after the show's premiere gets mediocre ratings. When she delivers them, she finds Paulie G. pretending to perform a sexual act with another writer dressed as Aunt Sassy—the writer's ultimate act of hostility to the character. Valerie, always performing for the cameras, cheerfully shrugs it off as part of the creative process.

In another scene, dubbed by *Entertainment Weekly* as one of the most humiliating moments in television history, Valerie complains that she is not being given enough lines, and Jane intervenes on behalf of the reality show. In response, Paulie G. develops a dream sequence in which Valerie, dressed as a giant cupcake, performs a pratfall. The episode is poignant because viewers learn that she has a metal rod in her back and went through high school in a full body cast because she had scoliosis. She tells Jane (while looking into a mirror rather than at the reality cameras) that she had been on the lacrosse team and attended every game and practice despite her cast. "But," she adds, "they still wouldn't allow me in the team picture." There is a pause. Jane wipes away a tear, and the camera tightens on Valerie's face so that viewers see, briefly, her pain.

Valerie, however, wearing her cupcake suit, insists on doing take after take to get it right in order to please Paulie G., who eats pizza and ignores her. Finally, she decides to fall backward because it is funnier, even though it causes her extreme pain. Paulie responds by telling her that he thought the first take was better and then makes an insulting comment about her having a metal rod up her ass. Finally, she strikes out and punches him in the stomach. He vomits, and she vomits in return. The reality show cameras are on, and Valerie orders Jane to turn them off (to no avail).

In the penultimate episode of the series, the reality show pilot of *The Comeback* airs. Valerie hosts a party, despite being disconcerted when the publicity poster for the show portrays her in a comedic fashion rather than as a dignified actress. Jane does not attend the party, and Valerie finally learns that they have been at cross-purposes throughout. The show is edited to depict all the most humiliating and embarrassing moments of the previous eleven episodes, culminating with Valerie punching Paulie G. in the stomach. Valerie protests that the shots are taken out of context and everything is manipulated, but she is crushed and retreats to the bathroom, supposedly the only room that is off-limits to the cameras. As she and Mark smoke cigarettes (which she has banned throughout the series), the cameras peek in from outside and capture their conversation. Enraged, she announces that she is quitting the show. She drives to Jane's house (followed by the cameras), knocks on the door, and asks Jane how it feels to be intruded upon. As she leaves, a crew member queries, "Didn't she sign up for this?"

It seems here that Valerie, by expressing her anger, is achieving a measure of dignity in lieu of her need for the spotlight. However, in the final episode she appears on *The Tonight Show* to discuss the pilot. She initially plans to announce that she has quit *The Comeback*, but Jay Leno tells her, "Everyone is talking about the cupcake scene." The studio audience laughs uproariously when he shows the clip. Leno then asks her to spar with him, and when she playfully punches him in the stomach, he pretends to vomit. The audience cheers, and Valerie accepts their kudos. Later, in the dressing room, a network executive calls to say that *The Comeback* is such a hit it has already been renewed for a second season. The series ends as Valerie walks through a crowd of adoring fans from *The Tonight Show* and signs special "vomit bags" they had received as gifts. The classic 1960s song "Cherish" plays, ironically indicating that she has "made it." Valerie accepts her role as comic butt and sells her soul for fame.

The plight of *The Comeback* speaks to the dilemma of the female comic in one of the few domains still considered male. Classic theories of comedy, from Freud's view of tendentious humor to Bergson's superiority theory, privilege the male as the subject of humor, while the female is the victim of the joke. A controversial *Vanity Fair* article written by Christopher Hitchens was titled "Why Women Aren't Funny." A *Christian Science Monitor* review of *The Sarah Silverman Show* was titled, "Are Women Allowed to Be Funny?" In the article, Drew Carey explains that prejudices against female comedians are real: "Comedy is about aggression and confrontation and power. . . . As a culture we just don't allow women to do all that stuff" (Goodale). Female comics who play into male stereotypes, such as the ditzy Phoebe on *Friends* or the childlike Sarah Silverman, are not threatening, but women who are mature, attractive, and assertive are rare in comedy. As producer and star, Kudrow was in control of the typically male domain of comedy. She was a "woman on top," yet the show's humor was based on the constant put-down of her fictional character, who was made to look unattractive and powerless as she attempted to exert control. The end of the series is the character's final humiliation, this time at the hands of the show's creators. She has indeed traded dignity for fame, and the female comic retains her traditional role as target of humor.

While sitcoms such as *Curb Your Enthusiasm*, *The Office*, or *Extras* appropriate the conventions of reality television in the service of their fictional narratives, *The Comeback* appropriated the conventions of both reality television and the sitcom in order to attack them. It provided incisive social criticism of the entertainment industry, reality television, sitcoms, and the egotistical need to brand the self. It was a discomforting program that illustrated the way the self is constituted and performed in contradiction. It highlighted rather than resolved tensions and subverted television's ideological function to provide reassurance by smoothing over contradictions. Although this is a characteristic of many cringe comedies that rely on humiliation and embarrassment, *The Comeback* may have failed because it reproduced the cultural discomfort with a female comic who attempted to exert control—whether through the character of Valerie Cherish or through producer and star Lisa Kudrow—and succeeded only in putting down her character and making her, like many women before her, the butt of humor. *The Comeback* may have attempted to use self-abjection—whether Aunt Sassy as comedic clown or Valerie Cherish as parody of an actress living in the past—as a critique of gender, but in the end, its message was ambiguous. *The Comeback* may have offered not enough pleasure and too much pain, but is still worth watching for its insights into contemporary culture, and it may indeed become a cult classic.

The Daily Show and *The Colbert Report*

Sam Ford

News parody is hardly new. Lampooning politicians has long been the job of political cartoonists. Publications such as the *Onion* have been making a reputation for quality satire for decades now,[1] and parody news has been a staple on NBC's cultural icon *Saturday Night Live* since its first broadcast in 1975.[2] Those with a historical eye would point even further back, to the central role the court jester played in criticizing the decisions of monarchs in the Middle Ages.

That Comedy Central's *The Daily Show with Jon Stewart* and its spin-off *The Colbert Report* fit firmly within a rich history of political commentary through comedy does not make the accomplishments of these shows any less significant, however.[3] Rather, this tradition demonstrates the powerful cultural history these shows have tapped into in becoming must-see television for a cross section of U.S. citizens and international viewers. These viewers have increasingly used the onscreen parody of hosts Jon Stewart and Stephen Colbert to express their own frustration with politics and to give voice to a cynicism that many scholars have become interested in over the past several years.[4] This expression includes the circulation of clips online and both figures' permeation throughout U.S. popular culture.

The Daily Show

The Daily Show debuted on Comedy Central on July 11, 1996, originally hosted by Craig Kilborn. When Kilborn left the show to become a late-night host on *The Late Late Show* in 1998, Jon Stewart took over, with his first episode airing in January 1999. Stewart, who had developed a following as the host of MTV's talk show *The Jon Stewart Show* (1993–1995), rapidly rose to greater prominence. In the decade since Stewart's debut, *The Daily Show* has risen to critical acclaim, with ten Emmy Awards and nine additional Emmy nominations. With the popularity of *The Daily Show* and its now established place in popular culture, many current fans know little about the show's origins during Kilborn's tenure. In particular, Stewart's involvement as a writer and co–executive producer has helped create a stronger political focus, and the show's political coverage of the 2000 election helped increase its visibility.

Subsequently, *The Daily Show* developed a dual status, not only providing savvy political satire but also presenting major political figures as serious guests, including Madeleine Albright, John Ashcroft, John Bolton, Jimmy Carter, Bill Clinton, Hillary Clinton, Bob Dole, John Edwards, Vicente Fox, Al Gore, Alan Greenspan, John Kerry, Henry Kissinger, John McCain, Evo Morales, Pervez Musharraf, and Colin Powell. The show also regularly features entertainment stars, scholars, and journalists. By October 2007, before the writers' strike that took the show off the air for several weeks, *The Daily Show* was drawing about 1.6 million viewers per episode.

Airing four nights per week throughout the year (allowing for several weeks' vacation for the cast and crew), *The Daily Show* typically draws from a team of four or five regular comedians who act as "news correspondents." The show includes a rundown of major news stories for the day in the opening segment, followed by a second segment that features either a continuation of news commentary or a prepackaged correspondent's report. The third segment is always an interview with the evening's guest, followed by a commercial break and a final short segment called "Your Moment of Zen," which typically features some sort of ironic commentary related to a topic from earlier in the show or to a stand-alone video, often lampooning the coverage of network news broadcasts. After the launch of *The Colbert Report* in 2005, the final segment often includes a witty exchange between Stewart and Colbert, through the guise of offering a preview of what is coming up on Colbert's show, which immediately follows *The Daily Show*.

The Colbert Report

With the rising cultural status and popularity of *The Daily Show*, Comedy Central launched a spin-off series to air immediately after it in the 11:30 P.M. time slot. *The Colbert Report*, starring longtime *Daily Show* personality Stephen Colbert, debuted on October 17, 2005, and has developed a strong following tied to but also distinct from its relationship with *The Daily Show*. Colbert's history with *The Daily Show* predates Stewart's as an on-air talent, and Colbert served as a cowriter for *The Daily Show* during his tenure there. The spin-off was built around the extreme conservative stereotype Colbert had developed for his on-air character, serving as a parody of personality-driven news commentary shows such as Fox News's *O'Reilly Report* rather than newscasts.

While Jon Stewart performs as himself, Colbert is always explicitly playing an on-air persona and is rarely out of character, even if he often winks at the camera (sometimes literally). Colbert received even more attention after his 2006 appearance as the featured entertainer at the White House Correspondents' Association dinner, where he excoriated President George W. Bush and U.S. journalists alike through his satirical monologue. By October 2007, before the writers' strike, *The Colbert Report* was averaging 1.2 million viewers per episode, and the show earned a combined eight Emmy nominations in 2006 and 2007.

Colbert's show generally begins with a rundown of the night's top stories before the hyper-American opening titles, followed by Colbert's opinion on the featured news stories of the day. This part of the show concludes with "The Word," in which Colbert's spoken commentary is supplemented by an ironic written subtext running on the other side of the screen, often directly contradicting what he says. The second segment may focus on other current events or introduce a prepackaged segment, an unadvertised interview, or one of Colbert's recurring segments. These include "Tip of the Hat, Wag of the Finger," in which Colbert praises or criticizes those involved in recent news events; "Better Know a District," in which Colbert interviews members of Congress and rather famously creates humorous postproduction edits of political figures' comments (see Baym, "Representation"); "Threatdown," in which Colbert lists what he considers to be the major threats to U.S. citizens; and less political segments such as his animated series "Tek Janson" and "The Sport Report." The final segment features an interview, which

Colbert also does in character. In an inversion of the traditional television interview format, Colbert makes an entrance onto the interview set, complete with applause and with all the cameras focused on him, while the guest is already seated, waiting for Colbert to arrive and start asking questions. Although *The Colbert Report* does not feature a regular cast of contributors, recurring characters occasionally show up, but they play a less prominent role than Stewart's correspondents.

Politics and Media Culture in the United States

Most scholarship on *The Daily Show* has looked at the show's effects on democracy, citizenship, and journalism. For instance, in his 2005 essay in *Political Communication*, Geoffrey Baym argues that "the show uses techniques drawn from genres of news, comedy, and television talk to revive a journalism of critical inquiry and advance a model of deliberative democracy." Conversely, other scholars—along with many journalists—argue that these parody shows only encourage further cynicism and apathy (see Baumgartner and Morris). Other studies have focused on a comparison between *The Daily Show* and news broadcasts (see McKain; Fox, Koloen, and Sahin).

Targeted to a young audience with a leftward political slant, *The Daily Show* and *The Colbert Report* rely on at least some degree of implied common "agreement" with their viewers. For instance, the punch lines of many routines appeal to the supposed shared sensibility among viewers. Thus, news content can often be shown with only minimal commentary, and new meaning is created just from the appearance of these events on *The Daily Show*. In contrast, *The Colbert Report* can present its host's often ludicrously extreme conservative viewpoints because it relies on the core audience's knowledge that he is always in character. As Henry Jenkins said of *The Daily Show*, the program "challenges viewers to look for signs of fabrication. . . . In such spaces, news is something to be discovered through active hashing through of competing accounts rather than something to be digested from authoritative sources" (*Convergence Culture* 227).

One could argue, then, that these shows have actively encouraged a political media literacy that can be tied to the rise of political parody videos through Web sites such as YouTube.[5] Certainly, one of the greatest contributions of *The Colbert Report* is its instigation of online campaigns, such as encouraging fans to submit user-generated videos using images of Colbert in a contest called "The Green Screen Challenge"; driving fans to enter Colbert's name in a Hungarian government initiative seeking public advice for the naming of a bridge over the Danube, and subsequently winning the contest; and encouraging viewers to participate in a campaign to change the truth about elephant populations by editing the Wikipedia entry to say that the African elephant population had tripled in a six-month period. These initiatives demonstrate a type of activism similar to grassroots political campaigns, but operating through the elements and aesthetics of online fandom. In fact, many of these initiatives stem from Colbert's active attempt to foster a relationship with his online fans through the "Colbert Nation," including a Web site that Colbert regularly refers to on his show. He often parodies political activism in the way he calls on "his nation," but the show's ability to foster and maintain a vibrant online fandom has helped make it one of Comedy Central's top programs, along with *The Daily Show*. Their immense online popularity also explains why *The Daily Show* and *The Colbert Report* are at the center of copyright debates surrounding video-sharing sites such as YouTube.[6]

The Daily Show and *The Colbert Report* as Cult Television

What in particular makes these two programs part of this collection on cult TV, though? If one accepts their impact on the political process, on journalism, and on parody, that still does not qualify them as cult media. This volume doesn't include chapters on *Meet the Press* or late-night talk shows, despite their influence on citizenship and politics in the United States.

What does cult media refer to, then? Popularly, the term *cult media* seems to refer to content outside the mainstream, so a cult television program might be one that isn't widely popular but is particularly beloved by those who watch it. One might question, however, whether a show watched by millions in its regular airings on Comedy Central and through various online methods—legal and illegal—can really be considered cult. My concept of *cult* relates less to quantitative measures and more to a position outside the cultural mainstream. Programs like *The Daily Show* and *The Colbert Report* present themselves as embodying a particular lifestyle or mind-set. Thus, viewers of these shows might position themselves as a particular kind of television viewer, fan, *and* citizen. That identification is central to the cultural resonance of both these programs.

Further, both *The Daily Show* and *The Colbert Report* engender a certain dedication among viewers, leading to a greater depth or quality of viewership that exceeds the quantitative numbers these shows register. A large segment of the viewership doesn't just watch these shows; viewers identify with these programs in a deeper way, whether that means subscribing to Stewart's skepticism or being a professed member of the Colbert Nation.

In addition to actively participating in the building of their fan followings, these shows define themselves as cult by operating outside the cultural mainstream through two methods. First, they create a common identification for their viewers by defining themselves against particular figures through regular political parody. Fans of *The Daily Show* and *The Colbert Report* can define who they are through the shows' lampooning of who they are not. Second, these shows foster the feeling of an "in crowd" among regular viewers through the repetition of particular jokes. Both hosts rely on information or cultural references that might resonate with a younger audience, such as those who consider themselves digitally savvy or those who prioritize civil liberties over security issues, for instance. In short, these shows build a dedicated viewership through their constant reference to "externally located content" that dedicated viewers are assumed to already know (see Ford, "Externally Located Content"), just as members of a religious congregation might be expected to know a parable or a reference to scripture without the need for explanation (to return to the religious connotations at the core of the term *cult*).

Certain entertainment products develop into "immersive story worlds," properties that have a serial storytelling structure, multiple creative forces that author various parts of that story, a sense of long-term continuity, a deep character backlog, contemporary ties to the media property's complex history, and a sense of permanence (Ford, "As the World Turns"). U.S.-style soap operas, comic books, and professional wrestling are the fullest manifestation of this phenomenon, and all could be considered among the most robust forms of cult media. They are all perceived to exist outside the cultural mainstream, and all foster a deeper sort of fan involvement, in part because of the many ways they require fans to actively make sense of their history.[7] Looking at *The Daily Show* and *The Colbert Report* as fictional entertainment programming, these shows similarly have a large volume of content, with four new episodes per week and no off-season. They likewise feature a cast of common characters, multiple creative forces, and a type of continuity that often requires knowledge of the show's history to understand the relevance of recurring jokes.

There is little doubt that the degree of fan identification with these two programs has led to intense interest among cultural critics and scholars. Although a centralized meaning of the term *cult media* will likely remain a debated topic, these shows' development of an immersive story world of sorts—coupled with their existence at the intersection of journalism, parody, and fictional storytelling—positions them at the center of the debate about what *cult media* means. Whether one considers the fan activity and intense engagement with these shows as cultish depends on that definition. However, with no end date in sight, *The Daily Show* and *The Colbert Report* might be seen as among the strongest cult media texts included in this volume.

Notes

1. The *Onion*, which began in 1988, was originally published by two students at the University of Wisconsin–Madison. It was derived from a college spread published by students in the university's Tripp Hall dormitory starting in 1986.

2. The "Weekend Update," originally anchored by Chevy Chase, is the only comedy segment to survive throughout the duration of *Saturday Night Live*. For a variety of other news parody television series, see the BBC's *Not the Nine O'clock News* (1979–1982), HBO's *Not Necessarily the News* (1983–1990), ITV's *Spitting Image* (1984–1996), TQS's *100 Limite* (1988–1992), CBC's *This Hour Has 22 Minutes* (1993–present), BBC2's *The Day Today* (1994), and Channel 4's *The 11 O'clock Show* in Britain (1998–2000).

3. I feel obliged to disclose that the MIT Convergence Culture Consortium, a project I am affiliated with, partners with MTV Networks, the parent company of Comedy Central. However, I had no interaction with anyone at the company regarding these two shows during the writing of this chapter.

4. See, for instance, Rahn and Transue; Henn, Weinstein, and Forrest. This idea of a skeptical or cynical youth has become an accepted fact in the popular press of many countries.

5. For more on political parody and online videos, see Henry Jenkins's essay entitled "Why Mitt Romney Won't Debate a Snowman," which appears in the paperback version of *Convergence Culture*, released in 2008.

6. When Viacom pulled many of its clips off this Google-owned video-sharing site in 2006, most media attention focused on these two shows.

7. Unfortunately, none of these texts is included in this volume (with the exception of the Gothic-style soap opera *Dark Shadows*). For comic books, the reason is obvious: they are not television programs. And despite being mainstays since the origins of television, perhaps professional wrestling and soap operas are considered too culturally marginal to be "essential" cult TV texts.

Dark Shadows

Jonathan Malcolm Lampley

Of the many television programs that define the baby boom generation, few have inspired the sort of cult following that *Dark Shadows* enjoys today. Indeed, among 1960s TV staples, only *Star Trek* is more popular in terms of the size and devotion of its fan base, a situation partially accounted for by its greater promulgation and reinvigoration through the success of later movie and TV incarnations. *Dark Shadows* is also unique because it was developed as a daytime drama, becoming the first soap opera to incorporate genuinely supernatural elements into its story line. Furthermore, *Dark Shadows* enjoys more fanatical devotion than any other soap, even though its relatively brief five-year run is insignificant compared with the decades-long legacies of such afternoon serials as *Days of Our Lives* and *All My Children*.

Dark Shadows was a Gothic-themed series, and like many of the classic Gothic novels it borrowed from, it was inspired by a dream. The show was the brainchild of veteran TV producer Dan Curtis (1927–2006), who is probably best known for two colossal miniseries of the 1980s: *The Winds of War* and *War and Remembrance*. In the summer of 1965, Curtis dreamed about "a girl with long dark hair. She was about nineteen, and she was reading a letter aboard a train and occasionally staring out the window.... The girl got off the train and started walking. Finally, she came to a huge, forbidding house. At the door, she lifted a huge brass knocker and gently tapped it three times. I heard a dog howl, and then—just as the door creaked open—I woke up!" (Thompson, *Television Horrors* 79).

Encouraged by his wife Norma, Curtis developed his odd dream into a proposal for a TV show. Much of the dream was re-created for the first episode of what became *Dark Shadows*, which was broadcast on June 27, 1966, on ABC. Although Curtis himself only rarely wrote or directed episodes, he "was the idea man behind the show. . . . Whatever concept or character captivated Curtis was incorporated into the show. Whenever Curtis became bored with a certain story, the storyline changed" (Thompson, *Television Horrors* 80). The mysterious house of Curtis's dream became Collinwood, ancestral home of the Collins family of the ancient shipping town of Collinsport, Maine. The young girl became Victoria Winters, played by Alexandra Moltke (who years later gained notoriety as the mistress of accused murderer Claus von Bulow). Victoria was hired as a governess for the troubled David Collins (David Henesy), youngest of the dysfunctional family overseen by matriarch Elizabeth Collins Stoddard (Joan Bennett).

For nearly a year, *Dark Shadows* was presented as a slightly more mysterious variation on the soap opera formula, spooky but no more rooted in the supernatural than such classic Gothic movies as Alfred Hitchcock's *Rebecca* (1940) or Joseph L. Mankiewicz's *Dragonwyck* (1946), based on popular novels by Daphne du Maurier and Anna Seyton, respectively. The ratings were not impressive, and because Curtis feared the show would be canceled, he decided to make it overtly supernatural—at the suggestion of his children (Thompson, *Television Horrors* 81). Story lines involving ghosts and a phoenix boosted the ratings, so in April 1967 Curtis decided to add a vampire to the proceedings. Thus was born an unlikely pop superstar: tortured bloodsucker Barnabas Collins (Jonathan Frid).

The impact of Barnabas's introduction to the show cannot be overstated. Ratings eventually doubled, reaching a peak of roughly 20 million viewers by the end of the decade (Melton 155). Fans of all ages were fascinated by Barnabas, a reluctant vampire doomed to eternal life and a fruitless search for a cure for his affliction, and the middle-aged, hitherto unknown Canadian actor Frid became something of a sex symbol. Yet it was younger viewers who made up the primary audience; to this day, aging baby boomers wax nostalgic at the mere mention of the show, inevitably noting that they used to rush home from school to watch *Dark Shadows* (a sentiment famously captured on a popular bumper sticker of the late 1980s).

Initially introduced as a purely villainous character, Barnabas soon became the main attraction of *Dark Shadows* and developed into a more sympathetic protagonist—an antihero of sorts. Other supernatural characters were introduced, most notably a Frankenstein's monster homage called Adam (Robert Rodan), a spiteful witch named Angelique (Lara Parker), and a handsome werewolf, Quentin Collins (David Selby), who became the program's second most popular character. As the series progressed, Curtis and his writers borrowed liberally from such recognized horror classics as Henry James's *The Turn of the Screw*, Edgar Allan Poe's "The Cask of Amontillado," and the writings of H. P. Lovecraft, whose extradimensional Great Old Ones inspired Curtis's alien monstrosities the Leviathans.

The popularity of *Dark Shadows* led to a merchandising campaign that rivaled the promotions associated with such contemporary fantasy-related shows as *Batman* and *Star Trek*. By the time the show was canceled, eager fans had snapped up millions of *Dark Shadows* board games, Halloween costumes, sound track records, and gum cards. Thirty-three paperback tie-in novels, all of which were authored by romance novelist Dan Ross (under his wife's name, Marilyn), appeared between 1966 and 1972. In 1968, Gold Key began publishing a series of *Dark Shadows* comic books in which Barnabas Collins was prominently featured—even though the depiction of vampires had been expressly forbidden by the Comics Code Authority years before (Melton 156).

One of the hallmarks of *Dark Shadows* was its incorporation of time travel and what Curtis called "Parallel Time," a method of transporting Barnabas and company back and forth between different realities and epochs in history. Through the use of Parallel Time, different aspects of the complicated Collins family history could be explored, and characters could be introduced and killed off with impunity. Actors need not worry about their characters' demise and the loss of future paychecks, for they could always be brought back as ghosts or recast as other members of the Collins family. Thus, Louis Edmonds, who initially played Elizabeth's hard-drinking brother and David's neglectful father Roger Collins, also portrayed Barnabas's father Joshua Collins; Kathryn Leigh Scott, who debuted as waitress Maggie Evans, turned up as Josette DuPres, Barnabas's long-lost true love; and Grayson Hall, whose Dr. Julia Hoffman suffered an unrequited love for Barnabas, also played Josette's aunt, Natalie DuPres, and an over-the-top gypsy named Magda.

The show was so popular that Curtis was able to secure funding for two feature films, *House of Dark Shadows* (1970) and *Night of Dark Shadows* (1971), only the first of which involved vampires. By the spring of 1971, ratings for the show had declined to their pre-Barnabas levels.

Jonathan Frid, no doubt mindful of the typecasting that had haunted earlier vampire players Bela Lugosi and Christopher Lee, no longer wished to continue in the Barnabas role. The final story line, inspired by Emily Brontë's *Wuthering Heights*, was more akin to the nonsupernatural themes of the program's earliest episodes. Thus on April 2, 1971, *Dark Shadows* ended its brief but enormously influential run with an epilogue by Thayer David, who played Professor Stokes, the Van Helsing of the show. David assured viewers that "the dark shadows at Collinwood were but a memory of the distant past."

Dark Shadows was gone, but it was far from forgotten. Devoted fan Kathleen Resch began publishing a fanzine, *The World of Dark Shadows*, in 1975; two years later, fans at a San Diego science fiction convention initiated Shadowcon, which by the end of the decade was a separate entity dedicated entirely to the fondly remembered serial. In 1983 a new convention, the Dark Shadows Festival, superseded Shadowcon and remains the leading gathering of *Dark Shadows* fans today (Melton 553). Although Curtis never attended a fan convention, most of the other notables associated with the show, including Jonathan Frid, have appeared at the festival, where they "regularly endure writer's cramp signing autographs" (Skal 70).

For many years Curtis remained associated with TV horror — he produced the classic TV movie *The Night Stalker* in 1972 (a major ancestor text of *The X-Files*) and oversaw televised adaptations of *The Strange Case of Dr. Jekyll and Mr. Hyde* (1968), *Dracula* (1973), and *The Turn of the Screw* (1974). By the 1980s mainstream dramas such as *The Winds of War* had replaced Gothic horror as his idiom of choice. Yet fans of Curtis's scary soap opera never gave up hope of revisiting Collinwood, and a new generation of fans discovered Barnabas and his ilk thanks to the miracles of syndication and cable television. In January 1991 *Dark Shadows* rose again, this time as a nighttime drama on NBC. Unfortunately, the program debuted just as the first Iraq war broke out, and the new show never caught on; it was canceled after just twelve episodes were broadcast. One of Curtis's last projects was a second revival in 2004 on the WB network, but this time, *Dark Shadows* never made it past the pilot stage.

Nevertheless, *Dark Shadows* lives on. The entire series has been released on VHS and DVD by MPI Home Video, which has also put many of Curtis's other TV thrillers back in circulation, most notably *Trilogy of Terror* (1975), an anthology adapted from the stories of Richard

Matheson (*I Am Legend*). Fans still flock to the Dark Shadows Festival, which alternates between Los Angeles and New York (where the series was originally taped). A random search of eBay revealed 354 items up for bid, indicating that *Dark Shadows* memorabilia is still highly sought after by collectors.

What is it that keeps the undead soap opera from dying? The cult of personality that developed around the Barnabas Collins character is a significant factor. Barnabas was introduced as an outright villain, but when the character caught on with viewers, his more complicated nature was explored. Although a few minor films had suggested sympathy for the undead years earlier (including the Universal horror classics *Dracula's Daughter* [1936] and *House of Dracula* [1945], in which vampires vainly seek cures for their affliction), *Dark Shadows* was the first major text to emphasize the suffering of vampires. "As a reluctant, angst-ridden bloodsucker," David Skal notes, "Barnabas Collins is an important transitional figure in the history of vampirism, providing a popular link between the predatory evil of Dracula and the introspective, conflicted vampires of novelist Anne Rice" (70). Indeed, only Count Dracula and Rice's Lestat de Lioncourt are more famous vampires than Barnabas Collins, although some of the supernatural supporting characters on *Buffy the Vampire Slayer* and *Angel* come close.

The quality of the show is debatable. Though imaginative and often well acted (Kate Jackson, Conrad Bain, and Marsha Mason all made early appearances, and a very young Harvey Keitel can plainly be seen dancing in the background of episode 2), *Dark Shadows* was produced on a very low budget at a time when expensive retakes were a luxury the producers could ill afford. Thus the series is riddled with flubbed lines (particularly in the early days from a visibly nervous Frid), stray insects, and wobbly sets; in some scenes unwary technicians wander into the background only to hastily scurry away at some behind-the-camera prompting. The end credits were recorded "live," and on one occasion a hapless Frid wanders back onstage with his Barnabas costume draped over his arm! Yet it is precisely this unpolished quality that endears the show to many fans, particularly those who enjoy its camp.

As a daytime serial broadcast five days a week, *Dark Shadows* follows the conventions of the form and unfolds its plots gradually. This is an acceptable format for soap opera fans, but to the uninitiated, particularly those watching the show on video today, the long expository scenes can be irksome. That being said, some genuinely creepy moments remain effective, such as a scene in which the evil Reverend Trask (Jerry Lacy) is walled up alive by Barnabas. The higher budget and more leisurely production pace of the two feature films and the 1991 revival result in more technically proficient offerings, yet none of these projects seems to resonate with fans in quite the same way as the original show.

One of the show's strongest elements is the music of composer Robert Cobert. The spooky theme was recorded several times during the show's heyday, and Cobert's "Quentin's Theme" was an even bigger hit as a single. Cobert's moody, atmospheric cues make brilliant use of flute, percussion, strings, and early synthesizers. Curtis was so pleased with Cobert's music that he hired the composer over and over again for various projects, including the feature films and the 1991 series. Indeed, Cobert's music is an essential ingredient in what might be called the "Curtis universe." An examination of Curtis's TV terror offerings reveals a consistent fictional construct in which the same actors (especially John Karlen, Barnabas's Renfieldesque servant on *Dark Shadows*), thematic concerns (such as sympathy for the monster), and (thanks to Cobert) sounds continually reappear, often reconfigured but ultimately suggestive of an organic alternative reality that is as distinct and defined as the fantasy worlds presented in the classic horror films produced by Universal Studios in America and Hammer Films in England.

Perhaps the most important reason for the cult status of *Dark Shadows* is the simplest: the program is purely escapist in nature. It is significant that *Dark Shadows* was produced and enjoyed its greatest popularity during a period of enormous social and political upheaval, yet there is almost no acknowledgment of these momentous changes in any of the 1,225 original episodes. There is no mention of the Kennedy or King assassinations, no reference to any characters serving in Vietnam, no allusion to the civil rights movement (in fact, not one significant minority character appeared in the show's five-year run). In spite of its many grim plot twists, *Dark Shadows* seems wholly devoid of any connection to real-life problems; its horrors are mild compared with those that plague the real world, no matter how many characters are killed off (and they usually come back in spectral form anyway, suggesting that death itself is more a vexation than an actual threat). Whether fans flock to *Dark Shadows* out of a sense of nostalgia or a love of camp, they keep coming back in large measure because they recognize the timeless and otherworldly qualities that only a vampire-haunted old mansion can offer.

Dexter

Michele Byers

In 2004 little-known American crime novelist Jeffrey P. Freundlich—under the pen name Jeff Lindsay—published *Darkly Dreaming Dexter*, the first of what would become a series of popular novels about a serial killer named Dexter Morgan.[1] The novel was adapted and developed for television by James Manos Jr., an Emmy-winning writer-producer on *The Shield* and *The Sopranos*. The series first aired in early October 2006 on the Showtime network. Although Showtime has been airing original programming for more than two decades, its profile as a purveyor of high-quality series has risen exponentially since 2000 in the increasingly fragmented world of television. Like HBO, Showtime produces edgy work that would never make it past the network censors.[2] In recent years especially, the premium cable network has distinguished itself by pushing the limits of what can be shown on television with series such as *Californication*, *Dead Like Me*, *Huff*, *The L Word*, *Queer as Folk*, and *Weeds*. This would be a perfect home for a show like *Dexter*.

Its appearance on Showtime may account in part for *Dexter*'s rapid achievement of cult status. Given the shows it has brought to the air in recent years—shows about the quirky side of sex, drugs, and death—Showtime seems to be trying to make itself the home of cult TV. For *Dexter*, cult status may be a question of location, location, location. But there's something else about *Dexter* that makes it a natural cult hit: it's on the pulse; it's part of the cultural zeitgeist. As I outline here, *Dexter*'s cult status comes largely from the novel ways it lets us explore relationships among social identity, violent crime, and the state. It's a cult show because it draws us in, in a way that feels so good, even while it makes us extremely uncomfortable. This is the hallmark of cult TV: it keeps us on our toes.

The quirk at the center of the *Dexter* cult is Dexter himself, a serial killer whose day job is working for the Miami police department as a blood spatter expert. Here is a little of the backstory: A Miami police officer and his wife adopted Dexter when he was just a child. As the series opens, Dexter knows and remembers nothing about his life prior to his adoption into the Morgan family. What he does know, and what quickly became apparent to his adopted father Harry (James Remar), is that Dexter has a proclivity for killing. Harry both mitigates and encourages this inclination, creating a code of ethics through which he hones his adopted son's talent as an enforcer of vigilante justice. Dexter grows up, outlives his adoptive parents, and, like his adoptive sister Deb (Jennifer Carpenter), follows in the family business (or at least one of them) of policing (I'll get to the other one later).

On the flowtv.org Web site (an online forum for television scholars), there has been some discussion of *Dexter*. A few people have noted that the series and its title character are simply one more in a long line of vigilante antiheroes we love to love. I do not dispute this. We *do* love the idea that there are powers out there that can rectify the failings of the system, and we are safe in our belief that these same powers will pass us over because we are "good." There is a sense of moral ambiguity here that isn't really morally ambiguous at all. What is different about *Dexter* is how the text is read in relation to the particular cultural moment when it emerged, was produced, and was critically acclaimed—a time, in the American context especially, increasingly circumscribed by neoliberal beliefs about personal responsibility and neoconservative moral demands. The line Dexter Morgan feeds us is clear: he kills only "bad" people, and he does this to make the world "better." What's not to like about that? The question is, what makes this line and this story so compelling right now?

I would say it's Dexter himself. Much of the show hangs on the shoulders of the series' title character. This burden is well placed on Michael C. Hall, who rose to stardom in the role of repressed mortician David Fisher on the HBO drama *Six Feet Under*. The two characters are decidedly different, but especially in the first season, there seemed to be something just under the surface that linked them together and drew *Six Feet Under* fans into the captivating circle of Hall's new show and character. Both characters are tightly coiled to the point of springing apart.

Both are insiders in worlds where they also stand outside, watchful, vigilant, critical. David's queerness and troubled relationship with Keith on *Six Feet Under* is even mirrored in Dexter's relationship with Rita (Julie Benz), the troubled young woman whose psyche is as damaged as Dexter's. Her fear of sex, having been raped by her junkie husband Paul (Mark Pellegrino), allows Dexter to play house without having to get close enough to Rita to expose his lack of true emotion—or so we would believe as the show opens.

Stylistically, *Dexter* is pretty slick. Its visuals reflect the ironic quality that is so central to the narrative. This is best evidenced in the opening credit sequence, which shows Dexter getting ready for work. In a series of cutaways shot very close up (to disrupt our certainty about what we are seeing), we witness a straight razor against a neck followed by a couple of drops of blood; something that looks like a tongue (it's a piece of ham) being sliced and thrown into a hot pan; white string being wound around fingers and cords being wrapped around hands, which moments later are revealed to be preparations for tooth-flossing and shoe-tying rather than murder; a face pressed against a white cloth that is simply making its way into a T-shirt, not being smothered. On *Dexter* we quickly learn to accept the extraordinary as mundane and to perceive the ironic juxtaposition of the extraordinary and the mundane—as evidenced by the jaunty music that accompanies this title sequence.[3] Not unlike on *CSI: Miami*, we learn that darkness doesn't have to happen in the dark; death can happen on the brightest of sunny days.

The second major stylistic device the series employs routinely is the voice-over. Specifically, we spend a lot of time in Dexter's head, and this helps position us in his particular moral framework where vigilante justice makes perfect sense. Through this device (which is indebted to the novels, written in the first person), *Dexter* keeps us very close to the title character; we feel as though we are with him in all his choices and in each new phase of his self-discovery.

Like any good serial worth its salt these days, explaining the intricacies of the *Dexter* narrative is no easy task. But let me try. The first season begins with the introduction of the "Ice Truck Killer" (ITK), a serial murderer who leaves his victims as disassembled and bloodless as high-end cuts of beef. The ITK enters into a vaguely erotic game of cat-and-mouse with Dexter, whose own blood-related proclivities the ITK clearly knows about. As Dexter and his coworkers pursue this serial killer, with slightly different intentions in mind, two things happen: Ser-

From left: Sergeant Doakes (Erik King), our favorite serial killer Dexter Morgan (Michael C. Hall), and his sister Debra (Jennifer Carpenter).

geant Doakes (Erik King) becomes increasingly suspicious of Dexter, and Dexter begins to remember more and more about his past. What he remembers (it is eventually revealed) is that his mother was involved in the drug trade and was killed with a chain saw while Dexter watched. He then waited for hours in a warehouse filled with her blood until the police came. But he didn't wait alone. Waiting with him was his brother Rudy Cooper (Christian Camargo), whom we eventually discover is the ITK. Dexter is thrilled to finally find someone who understands him, but his oath to his adoptive father Harry proves stronger than any potential blood ties: he dispatches the ITK.

It is through Dexter's relationships with women—particularly Rita and Debra in season 1—that the nuances of his emotional life are played out. But through his relationships with men—notably, Harry, Doakes, and Rudy—the politics of the series are made most visible.[4] The men on this series are all broken, at least in part by the system's failure to help them be men in a traditional sense. Their violence, enacted in different ways by each character, stems from this inability to reconcile the men they would like to be or have been with the men they *can* be in the world they have been forced to fit into. In this way, the series is deeply neoliberal and neoconservative, even though it also offers a critique of these sociopolitical and moral positions. It begins with an assumption that the state is a failure and refuses any view of crime and criminality outside a discourse of individual choice. The only time we slip out of this view for a second is when we find out about Dexter's past and recognize that his urge to kill is not biological but the result of severe trauma. This is not really disruptive, though, because once we have Rudy, we see that Dexter, unlike his brother, has made a moral choice to use his brokenness for the greater good.[5] Good and evil remain intact terms; individuals must care for and account for themselves: this is what Harry ultimately teaches Dexter.

Doakes comes into play in a somewhat more complicated manner. An African American police officer and former Special Forces operative, he is the only character who suspects that Dexter is not what he seems. The *Dexter* cast is multiracial and multicultural, so the juxtaposition of Doakes and Dexter (who is more "white" than any of the other key characters, aside from his sister and lover) creates a great deal of tension. Doakes critically and continually draws our attention to the relative impossibility of reading middle-class, white, educated masculinity as deviant. The neoconservative moral reasoning behind this—and the neoliberal understanding of who can care for and name him- or herself in ways that those in positions of authority will accept—becomes even more explosive in the second season, when the Miami police force is hunting a new serial killer. They call him the "Bay Harbor Butcher" (BHB), and we already know his identity: Dexter, who has been dumping bodies off the side of his boat into the ocean for years. Doakes is increasingly suspicious of Dexter, but this merely makes *him* the object of suspicion by his peers and superiors. The more Doakes tries to show people what they don't want to see, the more they see it reflected back on him.

In season 2, Dexter meets Lila (Jaime Murray), a British artist he becomes involved with when she offers to be his Narcotics Anonymous sponsor (Dexter has joined NA to throw Doakes off his trail). Lila is revealed to be a sociopath, but unlike our hero, she has no moral scruples, going after Dexter's friends and family when she doesn't get what she wants. But Lila's real use to the narrative lies elsewhere: she helps liberate Dexter in a variety of previously impossible ways. One of these is sexual, but the other is much more interesting: Lila helps liberate Dexter from the law of the father, from Harry's moral code. When Doakes finally discovers the truth, Dexter locks him in a cabin in the Everglades, but since Doakes is an innocent man, Dexter cannot bring himself to kill him. Enter Lila, who does it for him (unasked). Where does this leave us at the end of season 2? Doakes is dead, blown to pieces and burned alive, and everyone thinks that he was the BHB. Lila flees to Europe, only to be tracked down by Dexter and killed. Dexter is liberated from Harry. He has his job, and accolades for helping to solve the BHB case. He has Rita and the kids back. He has his name. Vigilante justice results in the moral victory of white masculinity. White femininity can play at equality but must ultimately be put back in its place. Black masculinity carries the penalty for crimes enacted by those in power; the "truth" Doakes wanted us to see is one we cannot and will not look at, even those of us who know the whole story. There's no need to feel bad about this, though—after all, Lila, not Dexter, killed Doakes. And isn't it better that we have Dexter around, when there are so many other killers out there just waiting to slip through the cracks in the system?

So *Dexter* (and Dexter) is a new version of an old story, but that doesn't make it any less fascinating. In fact, it is a real variation on a theme that offers us a great deal of insight into the world we live in and how it has changed since an earlier version of the same story was told. *Dexter* is so compelling, in my view, because it is ironic and thus deeply ambivalent about the way it wants us to see the world. It's dark but light. It's violent but relatively gore free—something worked into the story at a narrative level—compared with network fare such as *CSI* and *Criminal Minds*.

One more thing about *Dexter* makes it a trendsetter: it's the first premium cable show to get a full-season shot at a network run. Under the duress of the 2007–2008 Hollywood writers' strike, CBS decided to broadcast the first season of *Dexter* in its entirety on prime time. The show did remarkably well, earning CBS its highest ratings in the 10 P.M. time slot since the end of 2007 (Kissell). According to the *New York Times*, *Dexter* brought 8.1 million viewers to CBS, or about 7 million more than tuned in to the series on Showtime during its first season (Stelter). The move was not without some discomfort for all involved, but even that is telling in what it suggests about the show, the viewing public, and the televisual world. The series had to be edited to meet various network moral regulations, but perhaps not as one might anticipate. For instance, as reported in the *Los Angeles Times*, "the severed head still bounced on the freeway and the mutilated corpse was still neatly laid out by the motel. But profanities, sexual foreplay, genitals secured with plastic wrap? Cut, cut, and blurred" (Smith, "Slicing"). More complicated was the editing of the wonderful but lengthy opening credits—seen as something a CBS audience would refuse to sit through—and the need to cut the episode to allow space for commercial breaks—perhaps something a premium cable audience would not sit through.

The most outspoken critics of the move were groups such as the Parents Television Council, who argued that editing couldn't eliminate the core message of the series: serial killer as hero. Bob Greenblatt, the president of entertainment at Showtime, offered the following argument: "Dexter kills people who deserve to be killed after he's proven they've done the crime. . . . There's a fine line between vigilantism and murder" (Smith, "Slicing"). But this goes back to my earlier point: Is there a line? Who decides? Aren't we asked to consider the case of murderers of various kinds every day in the news? *Dexter*, like any great TV series, swings that hyperbolic boom right back at us, putting it in a language that makes it much harder to walk away from completely unscathed.

Notes

1. Two interesting bits of trivia about Freundlich/Lindsay: his wife is the niece of Ernest Hemingway, and in 1997 he cowrote a novel (*Time Blender*) with actor Michael Dorn (Worf) of *Star Trek: The Next Generation* fame.
2. Just to drive home this point, in 2007 Showtime promoted its new slogan: "The best shit on television." As the *New York Times* pointed out, much like its programming, this slogan was "inappropriate for the networks" (Newman, "Showtime's New Slogan").
3. As I noted on flowtv.org, this always makes me think of the scene in *Reservoir Dogs* where Michael Madsen cuts off the security guard's ear while listening to "Stuck in the Middle with You" by Stealers Wheel.
4. This gendering is itself a clue to the deeply neoconservative (yet ambivalently so) themes that run through this series.
5. The dual serial killer motif is not new. It's most dramatic use, in my mind, is in the film *The Silence of the Lambs* (1991). In that film, one of the techniques that allows us to identify positively with Hannibal Lecter (Anthony Hopkins) is his juxtaposition with both the failed representatives of the state (his psychiatrist, the police, the FBI) and a host of morally bankrupt serial killers, particularly Buffalo Bill. Offering clear binary structures in which Lecter (like Dexter) is both correct and superior helps tie the viewer to the character and to the moral-political position he offers.

Doctor Who

Matt Hills

Doctor Who might seem to be a textbook example of a cult TV series: it falls into the genre of "telefantasy"; it has a well-established and vocal international fan base (the *Doctor Who* Appreciation Society was formed in 1976); it has run, with lengthy interruptions, since 1963; and, as such, it arguably occupies a place in British TV history as a cultural institution in its own right (Hills, "*Doctor Who*"). The show concerns the adventures, across space and time, of a time lord known only as "the Doctor," an alien with two hearts who can "regenerate" or change his bodily form. Often accompanied on his travels by human companions, the Doctor has transformed many times and at the time of this writing is played by David Tennant.

However, *Doctor Who*'s cult status may not be quite so clear-cut. Recently, Tom Spilsbury, editor of the official *Doctor Who Magazine*, argued that the 2005 version of the program, made by BBC Wales, should not be described as a cult show: "There's something about the word [*cult*] that somehow implies it's a *minority* interest. You wouldn't call football 'a cult sport,' would you? Or The Beatles 'a cult band'? . . . So does 'being a bit spacey' automatically qualify a TV series as 'cult'? . . . Last Christmas Day, *Doctor Who* was watched by over 13 million viewers. . . . That's more people than watched anything else on TV [in the United Kingdom] last year, bar the immediately following episode of *EastEnders*. . . . So if you ask me, it's high time we dropped the whole 'cult' thing" (Spilsbury 3). The suggestion here is that *Doctor Who*'s recent ratings success and newfound status as a flagship BBC program make it a "mainstream" TV program rather than cult TV, which Spilsbury links to a "niche audience" or so-called minority tastes.

If the equation of cult with a non- or anti-mainstream identity is accepted, then Spilsbury's contention carries some force. Indeed, it could be asserted that for much of its cultural life *Doctor Who* has actually occupied the mainstream of British television programming: "Unlike . . . Trekkers. . . *Doctor Who* fans in the UK didn't think of the series as in any way 'Cult.' It was as mainstream as it got until 1980, and the foundation of fandom came at the time when activities associated with Punk . . . seemed more useful to us. . . . It was a very blokey world, characterised by piss-taking, quite unlike the . . . American [cult TV fan] scene" (Wood 171). Fan critic Tat Wood views *Doctor Who* as a TV series that wasn't born into cult status but rather had cult identity thrust upon it at a certain point in its history. As the show began to lose ratings and apparent popularity during the 1980s, Wood suggests that it was recontextualized and viewed as cult, whereas previously it had been thoroughly part of the cultural mainstream.

In his cultural history of the program, *Inside the TARDIS*, James Chapman similarly notes: "The trend in the 1980s . . . was towards an increasingly segmented and compartmentalised view of audiences . . . the family audience was dissipating. . . . Thus it was that in its final years, *Doctor Who* became a marginal series made for a 'cult' rather than a mainstream audience" (162; see also Johnson, *Telefantasy* 13; Hills, *Fan Cultures*). Rather than this shift from mainstream to cult being a matter of changing audience tastes or loyalties or some reflection of the program's alleged loss of quality, Chapman attributes *Doctor Who*'s shifting fortunes to a changed TV industry. Discourses of cult fandom as constituting a niche, or specialist, audience emerged in the United Kingdom in the 1980s, repositioning *Doctor Who* within the concept of mass audience "fragmentation" and displacing those discourses of a "family," demographic-crossover show that had previously given rise to, and made sense of, the program's format in the U.K. context (Tulloch and Alvarado).

Following the likes of Chapman, Spilsbury, and Wood, it seems that rather than always being a cult TV program, *Doctor Who* may well have veered into and out of this realm. Apparently, it became cult from the 1980s to its reimagining in 2005, at which point it reverted to its 1960–1970s status as mainstream and widely popular (Hills, "'Gothic' Body Parts"). Nevertheless, this argument neglects to consider differences in the program's transnational career. As Wood notes, the activities and cultures of U.K. fans may well have strongly differed, historically, from

U.S.-based fan cultures surrounding TV science fiction, the assumed heartland of cult television (Wood 213). Francesca Coppa's useful history of American media fandom points out that "it was only in 1978 that the Tom Baker seasons were sold to PBS, where they attained a growing and fervent cult status through the 1980s.... Media fandom's affinity for the Doctor was only the most recent example of its growing BBC obsession ... and 'British Media' became a catchall phrase indicating a love of a number of otherwise disparate British shows" (51).

Therefore, we may need to consider not just the changing *times* of *Doctor Who*'s cult status in the United Kingdom but also the different national *spaces* of its cultishness. As part of the British media not widely watched or recognized in the States, and appealing to specialist fan tastes there, *Doctor Who*'s status as cult TV may have been more consistent in America, connoting a foreign exoticism or cultish "otherness" that it lacked in its British home. Scholars such as Catherine Johnson (2–3) have stressed the importance of analyzing cult TV as a matter of audience interpretations and activities rather than seeking to root it in genre-like categories such as telefantasy. However, this binary of text and audience tends to downplay how the textual qualities and attributes of *Doctor Who* may have incited, invited, or variously led to audience responses and classifications as cult.

Chief among these textual attributes is the program's highly unusual conflation of ordinary, everyday elements and extraordinary, fantastical aspects. In the book-length academic study *Doctor Who: The Unfolding Text*, John Tulloch and Manuel Alvarado emphasize that the series' 1963 inception insistently constructed its own "television discourse" as one of the "normal and uncanny" (16). The show is marked by recurrent "strangeness," depicting ordinary cultural objects, such as the then-common police box (a construction used by police to temporarily confine suspects), as unearthly and weird: "From the beginning the TARDIS [police box] was conceived as something concrete and familiar, fitting in naturally with its environment, and yet narratively defined as 'odd' and 'incongruous'" (Tulloch and Alvarado 27). Far from beginning as out-and-out science fiction, *Doctor Who*'s format was initiated via this narrative-visual collision of present-day settings and fantastical content, amounting to a wholesale making-strange of the familiar.

In *Time and Relative Dissertations in Space*, David Butler contrasts the opening 1963 episode with the 1996 TV movie starring Paul McGann, arguing that the balance of strangeness and familiarity, surrealism and realism, is entirely different in the latter: "Whereas the 1963 episode takes familiar genres and icons and makes them strange . . . the 1996 TV Movie goes out of its way to explain *Doctor Who*'s strangeness through familiar models (incorporating elements . . . and terms from *The X-Files* . . . , *Terminator 2*, *ER* . . . , *Star Trek*, and so on) right down to the music as the uncanny electronic theme tune is transformed into a generic piece of orchestral bombast" (Butler, "How to Pilot" 28). The spirit of *Who* as cultish invoked here is one of defamiliarization; by contrast, the TV movie is interpreted as textually conventional and conservative due to its attempts to contain strangeness. In the early series, audience-identificatory characters are shocked by the TARDIS and by the fact that it is "bigger on the inside." In the later movie, these moments of character hesitation—can such a thing as the TARDIS possibly exist, or is its console room some sort of illusion?—are displaced by far more blasé narrative responses: "What is crucially missing [in the 1996 TV movie] is the [natural-supernatural] hesitancy that Todorov argues is an essential feature of the . . .'fantastic' . . . glib reaction to the TARDIS' mindboggling nature removes the sense of wonder but also deprives the audience of a character through which their own hesitancy at *Doctor Who*'s narrative can be expressed" (Butler, "How to Pilot" 29).

However, the balance of uncanniness and normality is pushed firmly back toward defamiliarization and natural-supernatural hesitation in the opening episode of the show's 2005 reimagining. It introduces the ninth Doctor (Christopher Eccleston) battling against animated shop-window dummies, all viewed through the eyes of department store assistant Rose Tyler (Billie Piper). Rose refuses to accept the existence of alien entities, speculating instead that the spookily sentient mannequins are the result of some sort of student prank. This story is "strong as both a pilot [for new audiences] and a restoration [for the show's established fan audiences], told completely from the angle of a supporting character" (Lyon, *Back to the Vortex* 225).

Doctor Who seems to have inspired and earned cult status, then, in large part due to its "genuinely disturbing, radical and unusual" conflations of fantasy and contemporary reality, as well as the fact that the main character's ability to change his appearance and regenerate prevents audiences from settling into a sense of cozy familiarity (Newman, *Doctor Who* 63). But it can also be argued that the program's iconic sound and design have contributed greatly to its cult status, especially given that the soundscape has remained virtually unchanged from 1963 to

2008, as has the appearance of many visual designs, such as the TARDIS interior. In each case, sound and visual imagery have been tweaked over the years, but identifiable fundamentals have remained in place, perhaps as a testament to their very alienness: "The series used sound in an iconic way. . . . One could argue that sound 'starred' rather than simply being there to convince audiences of the veracity of screen representations. The relaunched 2005 series . . . has demonstrated great awareness and respect for these 'sonic stars,' with returning effects including the TARDIS materialisation/dematerialisation, the Autons' handgun, and the . . . Dalek control room" (Donnelly 197).

Fans have always paid very close attention to the sounds and designs of *Doctor Who*, but most scholarship has focused on the show's narratives, genres, and ideologies. Along with Kevin Donnelly's work, another rare exception to this rule is the outstanding study of visual design by Piers Britton and Simon Barker. These writers argue that it would be "no exaggeration to say that the long-term success of the show was based on two virtuosically stylised designs. Both almost verged on abstraction. . . . First came the interior of the Doctor's ship, the TARDIS. . . . Even more popular were the inhabitants of . . . the planet Skaro . . . the Daleks. . . . [Both] established the benchmark for spectacle in the series" (134; see also Schuster and Powers 27). In each case, these visual spectacles—pop-modernist images of the alien—were frequently represented in conjunction with cultural ordinariness; the TARDIS console room was diegetically inside a police box disguise, and the Daleks invaded Earth as early as their second appearance on the program in 1964 and were still trying in 2008. Just as the BBC Wales's incarnation of *Doctor Who* has respected "sonic stars," so too has it respected "visual icons," modifying the TARDIS interior but in such a way as to echo the hexagonal and circular motifs of the original Peter Brachacki realization (Britton and Barker 185). And even though the Dalek casing design has been updated to make it seem more metallic, tanklike, and solid, it is still very much iconically recognizable. If *Doctor Who*'s textual address can be described as cultish due to its uncanniness, with the familiar becoming strange, then it can also be described as cultish thanks to its specific aural and visual icons of otherworldly otherness sustained across some forty-five years.

These arguments all suggest that *Doctor Who*'s cult status might be both text based and audience based rather than a binary either-or. That other binary—cult versus mainstream—also has a major conceptual difficulty: it implies that TV shows can be objectively and univocally fixed in one or the other category at any given moment in time in any given broadcasting environment, rather than approaching cult status as potentially multivocal and linked to a range of different interpretive communities. To put it another way, a text can be ostensibly mainstream, perhaps in the manner of the BBC Wales *Doctor Who*, yet still have cult fan audiences reading it in the light of detailed fan knowledge of the show's longer history. Similarly, if one accepts that *Doctor Who* was mainstream and not cult in the United Kingdom prior to the 1980s, then the 1976 formation of the *Doctor Who* Appreciation Society—bringing together generations of fans who had watched the show since the 1960s and built up years of textual expertise—seems to run counter to the idea that the program was definitively and univocally mainstream at that point in time, lacking any cult following or identity whatsoever. By contrast, it may be entirely possible for a TV show to be both cult and mainstream at the same time. Once a show has been dubbed cult and attracted a fan culture, even if it subsequently gains (or regains) widespread cultural recognition and mainstream ratings, its cult following will surely continue to operate, distinctively reading and speculating over the particular program.

Specific attempts to fix *Doctor Who* as either cult or mainstream have also marginalized another unusual change in the program's status, something that has occurred partly as a result of the program's long history. When the show's return was announced in 2004—it had been off the air as an ongoing series since 1989—an article in the British broadsheet the *Guardian* reported the following: "The Time Lord's new lease of life could be put down to simple nostalgia, but according to Clayton Hickman, [then] editor of *Doctor Who* magazine, more sinister forces are at work. 'The Doctor Who mafia,' he says. 'That's why the show's coming back. If it wasn't for all the fans in high places, it would have just faded away.' Russell T. Davies, the writer overseeing the show's revival, is a case in point" (Bodle 4). Davies, a longtime fan of *Doctor Who*, had previously written a spin-off novel, *Damaged Goods* (1996), targeted squarely at the program's cult fandom. In this case, then, fandom is not just an audience identity: *Doctor Who*'s fans have officially taken over the running of the show.

Davies is not alone. Many writers on the BBC Wales version, along with its producer Phil Collinson, are self-identified fans. Many have participated in socially organized fandom and have published niche, fan-targeted fiction, including Paul Cornell, Mark Gatiss, Steven Moffat, Gareth Roberts, and Robert Shearman. The actor playing the tenth Doctor, David Tennant, has also been a fan of the program since childhood. This version of the show, whether or not the current editor of *Doctor Who Magazine* believes it should be described as cult, is made by and stars media professionals who are also part of *Who*'s cult fan audience. Rather than directly contrasting fan audiences' interpretation of the text with producers' control over it (see Tulloch and Jenkins 145), these highly privileged producer-fans can seemingly have it all.

Such fan-pro crossing over has also given rise to instances of metacult television, or cult TV about cult TV. For example, the episode "Love & Monsters" concerns one of the Doctor's fan groups: "I don't recall ever seeing a more controversial episode. . . . [This] shows us who we are, rather than who the Doctor is . . . [representing] *Doctor Who* fans and their experiences" (Lyon, *Back to the Vortex—Second Flight* 297). This metacult strand even extends to the Doctor appearing as a kind of uncanny DVD extra in "Blink" (Walker, *Third Dimension* 218–19) and to Tennant's own fandom being connoted by dialogue between the tenth and fifth Doctors in "Time Crash": "You were *my* Doctor." If anything, it is perhaps unsurprising that it has taken *Doctor Who* more than forty years of time travel to edge from cult status toward sustained metacult. The program has been loved by generations of fans, and right now it is being created in Cardiff by a lucky few of those self-same fans.

Farscape

Jes Battis

Farscape remains one of those impossible shows: too strange and vast to conceive of, too weird and idiosyncratic to make, and too outrageously wonderful to be canceled. An idea for the show—which was almost called *Space Chase*—flowered secretly in the minds of creator Rockne O'Bannon and producer Brian Henson throughout the early 1990s until it became a viable product in 1999. The blueprint for *Farscape* destined it for either instant cult status or total oblivion: a living "biomechanoid" starship (Moya), designed through a mixture of costly computer-generated images and intricate set building, populated by aliens who really looked alien. The entire cast hailed from Australia, New Zealand, and Britain except for the lead—Ben Browder—whose sexy Memphis drawl immediately marked him as American. He was a kind of U.S. astronaut launched into Australia, an "alien" out of his element and surrounded by accomplished "native" actors. Since programs that air in the United States are made or broken by the recognizability (and sex appeal) of their cast, *Farscape* was banking almost solely on Browder's ability to carry the show for American audiences. The crux of the show, then, would have to be the romance between John Crichton (Browder) and his original antagonist, the Sebacean pilot Aeryn Sun (Claudia Black), whose relationship emerged slowly and far too cryptically and organically for American audiences, who were used to watching instant freeze-dried romances between modelesque twenty-somethings on network TV.

O'Bannon and Henson had nearly everything working against them. *Farscape* was much too expensive to produce, at $1.2 million per episode (Battis, *Investigating* 1); none of the actors had immediate popular appeal with American viewers; the story arc was epic and literally stretched across galaxies, with a deeply critical undercurrent of discussion around issues of racism, xenophobia, miscegenation, and sexual freedom; and the pivotal romance was subtle rather than instantaneous. The pilot episode builds slowly, beginning with astronaut John Crichton's launch into space and his disorientation as he is sucked into a wormhole and deposited in the "uncharted territories."[1] Brought aboard Moya by sheer accident, Crichton is at first unable to communicate at all with the ship's crew—they actually speak in alien languages, without subtitles, placing them in sharp contradistinction to the English-friendly aliens of *Star Trek*. This "crew" has, in fact, hijacked Moya (Moya is essentially a slave to the Sebacean "Peacekeepers," who are a mixture of postmodern Nazis and *Trek* Federation bureaucrats), so when we meet them for the first time, they are in the midst of a galactic felony. Nobody is wearing a starched uniform.

Crichton's new friends are all criminals, and their psychological scars and dark histories are brought to the surface as the show progresses. D'Argo, a Luxan general (Luxans are like Klingons, only with prehensile tongues and "mivonks"), is actually not a general at all; he has been incarcerated for allegedly murdering his Sebacean wife, Lo'Laan, and we don't learn whether he is guilty of this crime until the final season ("Mental as Anything," 4.15). Zhaan, a Delvian priest (Delvians are actually evolved plant life), admits to being her world's leading anarchist and freely acknowledges having killed in the past for political reasons. Rygel, a Hynerian Dominar, is a three-foot-tall slug on a floating throne and is undoubtedly the least ethical member of the crew (he sells everyone out to the Peacekeepers in "Family Ties," 1.22). Pilot, a six-armed giant alien who exists in a symbiotic relationship with Moya, actually colludes with the Peacekeepers (resulting in the death of Moya's original pilot) to fulfill his dream of exploring the stars. Chiana, a Nebari prisoner, is linked to political dissidents; she also maintains a proud identity as a sexual nonconformist.[2] And Aeryn Sun, a prowler pilot, betrays her former lover, Velorek, to gain military advancement.[3] Crichton thus becomes the ethical locus of *Farscape*, even as he is revealed, with each episode, to be physically and intellectually inferior to the rest of the crew.

Part of what makes *Farscape* such a surprising cult classic is its commitment to invest in *all* its characters, including the antagonists. There are no throwaway enemies or disposable ensigns on the show. Crichton's primary foe in seasons 1 and 2, Bialar Crais, is a Peacekeeper commander who becomes irrationally convinced that Crichton murdered his brother. He also deems Aeryn to be "irreversibly contaminated" due to her contact with a genetically inferior species (i.e., Crichton), forcing her to abandon the Peacekeepers and become a fugitive. But Crais becomes a curious ally in season 3 and ultimately sacrifices himself to save Moya and her crew. Scorpius, meanwhile, is an antagonist of epic, even operatic, proportions. An illegal hybrid of Sebacean and Scarran bloodlines (Scarrans are fascist reptiles who compete with the Sebaceans for galactic dominance), Scorpius is actually disabled because he requires a special cooling rod to regulate his unstable body temperature, as well as a body suit for the same purpose. He is despised by both Sebaceans and Scarrans, even as they value his brilliance and tenacity, and over the course of four seasons he develops an intimate relationship with Crichton. John even promises to give up the object of Scorpius's neurotic obsession—his knowledge of wormholes—if Scorpius will help him rescue Aeryn after she is taken captive by the Scarrans ("Prayer," 4.18). The two exchange a very sexy blood vow, and Crichton slyly calls him "lover." There are times, in fact, when Scorpius is John's only "friend," even as his interests remain clandestine and selfish.

Farscape also gives an intense and consistent narrative focus to its female characters, allowing them to explore side arcs and personal conflicts that have nothing to do with Moya or the Peacekeepers. In the episode "Taking the Stone" (2.3), Chiana journeys to a "royal cemetery planet" to grieve the death of her brother. Neither Crichton nor Aeryn can dissuade her from participating in a native ritual that will most likely be fatal, and she dismissively tells Crichton, "It's not about you. . . . I'm not your kid, I'm not your sister, and I'm only your *tralk* in your dreams."[4] In the beautifully shot episode "The Choice" (3.17), Aeryn leaves Moya to deal with her own private grief on a remote planet. Agreeing to speak with a deformed, fetus-like "psychic" named Cresus, who promises that he can contact her dead lover, Aeryn strokes his repulsive flesh and admits softly: "He loved me. He was very—he made me better." As I state in *Investigating* Farscape, "[her] memory is phallic . . . [and] Cresus acts as a speculum" (Battis 132–33). Zhaan is also forced to confront her violent past in the episode "Rhapsody in Blue" (1.13), wherein we learn that she too killed her lover (a refrain in *Farscape*) to maintain her mission of political resistance. And Moya herself, perhaps the most crucial female character on the show, becomes pregnant, gives birth, and then agonizingly chooses to sacrifice her own child ("Wolf in Sheep's Clothing," 3.21) to keep him from being captured. Much of the show's final season, in fact, revolves around female reproductive rights, as Aeryn's unborn child becomes the target of Scarran military curiosity.

As I have previously argued, *Farscape*'s covert queer-feminist potential lies in its exploration of the links between sexuality and kinship, as well as its attempts to expose John Crichton as a vulnerable and emotional human being. Crichton's relationship with Chiana, for instance, is a sisterly one, but edged with sexual flirtation (Chiana initiates this; she is always in control). Scorpius becomes a kind of surrogate father figure to John, invading his dreams and offering him unsolicited advice. Aeryn is physically stronger than Crichton, overpowering him on more than one occasion, but the show never reduces this to a bland sadomasochistic relationship (and Crichton never appears to be threatened by Aeryn's military training). He cries openly, playfully telling his newborn son, "Crichtons don't cry . . . often," at the end of *The Peacekeeper Wars* (a two-part miniseries that aired after the series was canceled). Rygel becomes a kind of student, taking ethical instruction from John, who even dares to kiss the Dominar gently on the head ("Family Ties," 1.22). Moya's crew enjoys complex and durable ties with one another, limned with sexuality but not necessarily limited to carnal expression. They do have a lot of sex, though. Crichton sleeps with Aeryn; D'Argo sleeps with Chiana; Zhaan has an interesting form of mind sex with both Crichton and Aeryn; even Rygel finds a sexual partner, and we get to see two Hynerians in a postcoital embrace, which is no mean feat of puppetry.

In "The Hidden Memory" (1.20), Crichton is taken captive by Scorpius and placed in the Aurora Chair, a kind of psychic torture device. After he can endure no more, he is thrown into a cell with another prisoner, Stark, a Stykera mystic who will eventually become a significant character on the show. The audience expects a colorful interaction between Stark, who has been driven insane by his captivity, and Crichton, the long-suffering American prisoner of war. But viewers are given something very different. Stark grabs Crichton and sort of cradles him; Crichton puts his head in Stark's lap, exhausted. Can we imagine Picard or Janeway appearing so vulnerable in a same-sex situation? A tear courses down Crichton's cheek as Stark reveals his own "hidden memory." As I discuss in *Investigating* Farscape, "Crichton lies here in Stark's embrace—in the hands of Stark, of insanity, being comforted by madness itself—and rather than squirming away, he submits to the touch" (Battis 72). I can think of no other science fiction program that offers a comparable scene of its protagonist, a heterosexual male, lying with his head in the lap of a male alien and letting that man stroke his hair and whisper to him. Yet Crichton coheres as a heterosexual male; his masculinity is made durable precisely *as a result* of its flexibility, its assailability. *Farscape* tell us that if Crichton didn't cry, if he didn't participate in same-sex affection, he wouldn't be a man.

Similarly, the women aboard Moya have intense, affiliative connections with one another. Zhaan, as a priest, becomes a confessional figure for both Aeryn and Chiana. She also officially "names" each character in the episode "Wait for the Wheel" (3.4), calling Crichton "innocent," Chiana "exuberant," D'Argo "sensitive," Rygel "wise," and Aeryn "selfless."[5] Earlier in season 2, Zhaan shares an intimate mind connection with Aeryn, telling her, "I love you." All three women are imbricated in a kind of pedagogical relationship with one another: Chiana offers lessons in erotic freedom, Aeryn tries to instill military precision and pragmatism, and Zhaan imparts spiritual wisdom (also grounded in bodily acceptance and love). Finally, Moya, the crew's unofficial mother figure, constantly teaches them the value of positive symbiosis and what Donna Haraway calls the "companion species" relation: "co-constitutive relationships in which none of the partners pre-exist the relating, and the relating is never done once and for all" (Haraway 300). In "I Do, I Think" (2.12), when Moya finally speaks, her address is enigmatic: "Moya . . . willing. Fulfilled. Yes." Her crew understands that rather than existing in a utilitarian relationship with a vessel, they are actually sharing a biological space with a living entity—a symbiosis that fulfills everyone.

So what gives *Farscape* cult status? What makes it a unique text? To state it simply, there has never been another show like it. Borrowing ideas from science fiction writers such as Anne McCaffrey, *Farscape* was the first SF program to showcase a living vessel (arguably the main character) rather than a mechanical starship that was primarily utilitarian. Whereas the USS *Enterprise,* in all its various incarnations, attains cultural capital and sex appeal because of its sleek appearance, weapons technology, and endless mechanical minutiae, Moya is a *female* starship inscribed with ideas of maternity and reproduction. We don't have to worry about the *Millennium Falcon* giving birth anytime soon, but for Moya, parturition and its attendant consequences become a very real part of *Farscape*'s unfolding story. Unlike other starships, Moya has no real weapons and an inadequate defense system (consisting of a "defense screen" the crew stole from another vessel—they're criminals, remember?). Pilot, who guides (but doesn't control) Moya, is a pacifist living with violent and sometimes unstable crew members. Like the renegade crew of Joss Whedon's *Firefly*, Moya's crew is composed of people who don't necessarily trust or even like one another. Rygel, in "Could'a, Would'a, Should'a" (3.3), admits freely that "we were thrown together against our will, and we're all just trying to make the best of it until we get the chance to screw the others"—and this after *three years* of living together.

What else does *Farscape* do differently? It kills central characters (at least four by the end of *The Peacekeeper Wars*). In one episode, Chiana and Rygel get stoned from interdimensional energy and compose a song to each other ("Through the Looking Glass," 1.17). Another episode revolves almost entirely around explosive diarrhea and ends in mass purgation ("Lava's a Many Splendored Thing," 4.4). Noranti, an older alien, does a striptease in the same episode. Noranti also becomes a pusher for Crichton's drug habit, offering him a narcotic to help him deal with depression throughout season 4. Crichton is cloned in "Eat Me" (3.6), and the clone isn't eradicated but actually becomes a secondary character; so there are two Crichtons running around. Aeryn kills her own mother—twice. Rygel eats Crichton and Aeryn. In "Out of Their Minds" (2.9), the crew switches bodies, and Crichton-as-Aeryn spends some time playing with his new breasts. In "Crackers Don't Matter" (2.4), everyone goes crazy, and D'Argo assaults Rygel by shoving food down his throat (he later apologizes). In fact, much earlier than this, the crew colludes to gain valuable information about their home worlds. The only catch is that they have to cut off one of Pilot's arms—so they do. Luckily, it grows back, and then D'Argo feels bad and plays Pilot a beautiful song on the *shilquen*, a Luxan guitar.

Farscape doesn't do anything in a predictable way. Two of its main characters—Pilot and Rygel—are puppets, but they are so vividly real (far more real than any computer-generated rendering could be) that we quickly forget about their mechanical origins. When we see Rygel's dissected body in "A Human Reaction" (1.16), the sight is horrifying, unendurable, despite the fact that we know Rygel is a puppet. In "The Way We Weren't" (2.5), when the Peacekeepers digitally record the killing of Moya's original pilot, the result is an alien snuff film. The pilot screams as she is torn apart by laser blasts, and it ceases to matter that she is a complex animatronic puppet. *Farscape* attempts not only to infuse its mechanical and "nonliving" characters with human life but also to reveal that everyone—human and alien alike—is animatronic in some way. Thus, the show participates in deconstructing what Judith Butler calls the category of the "grievable life," which dictates that "certain lives will be highly protected, and the abrogation of their claims to sanctity will be sufficient to mobilize the forces of war" (*Precarious Life* 32). In this episode, *Farscape* effectively convinces us to mourn and grieve for something that never existed—a puppet, a special effect; yet she is real.

Although it was canceled after just four seasons, fan engagement with the show continued. Noah Porter notes that only a day after its cancellation was announced on September 6, 2002, the "Save *Farscape*" campaign had already been launched by fans. In 2004, largely due to fan pressure, the Sci-Fi Channel aired the miniseries *The Peacekeeper Wars*, whose reception was largely positive. As with many canceled programs, there has been talk of a feature film, but it's more than likely that we have seen the last installment in *Farscape*'s epic story line. Luckily, both Claudia Black and Ben Browder have participated in conventions and other fan events with great enthusiasm, and *Farscape* fan fiction still circulates online. In 2007 I published the first academic book to analyze the show's various engagements with feminism, critical race studies, queer theory, and science fiction cultures. Hopefully, there will be more discussions to come.

Notes

1. For legal reasons, the NASA logo on Crichton's suit had to be changed to "IASA."

2. It's interesting to note that the Nebari, with their bleached gray skin and conservative sexual mores, are both visually and ethically the *whitest* aliens. When Chiana first comes aboard Moya (escorted in chains by a Nebari handler), she tells Crichton: "They won't tell you what I've done because they're embarrassed. You wouldn't consider it a crime" ("Durka Returns," 1.15).

3. In "The Way We Weren't" (2.5), we learn that Aeryn was one of the Peacekeeper soldiers who murdered the original pilot. This episode remains one of the most disturbing and brilliant in the show's run, and I discuss it in detail in *Investigating* Farscape.

4. *Tralk* is a kind of pidgin slang that translates as "whore." Chiana spends much of the show's run attempting to challenge and deconstruct this term.

5. When Zhaan also refers to the crew as a family, D'Argo tells her, "You birthed it."

Firefly

J. P. Telotte

Every cult text is an "accident," a disruption in our normal experience, a work that, for various reasons, should not have retained its following. But as Paul Virilio observes, such disruptions of the norm and of our expectations can offer something important, a glimpse of "symmetry," a possible payback for other, less resonant texts: "The beginning of wisdom would above all mean recognizing the symmetry between substance and accident, instead of constantly trying to hide it. Acquiring a tool, any new piece of equipment, industrial or otherwise, means also acquiring a particular danger; it means opening your door and exposing your private world to minor or major hazards" (55). Through the juxtaposition it foregrounds, the accident—or accidental text—affords a new and even necessary perspective; it reveals "something important that we would not otherwise be able to perceive" (Virilio and Lotringer 63). That "something" might be little more than a glimpse of the romance and purpose that seem drained from much of modern life, as the classic cult film *Casablanca* suggests. Alternatively, it might open onto a wholly different and subversive view of the real, or even of human nature, as we find in the series *Twin Peaks*. In either case, the cult text is not something that can be easily forgotten, dismissed, or apologized for (as when we say, in other contexts, "Accidents happen!"). Rather, it serves as a kind of unpredictable revelation, an "opening ... door." This perspective, I suggest, can be useful when thinking about a series like *Firefly*, which, despite having an initial run of only eleven broadcast episodes, developed an intensely loyal fan base, gave birth to the highly praised feature film *Serenity* (2005), and even inspired its own fan conventions. That sort of response suggests that "something important" is indeed afoot and that the series has valuably "accidented" contemporary media culture.

That *Firefly* would have such resonance is surely a surprising achievement in light of two factors. The first is its treatment by FOX, which promoted *Firefly* essentially as an adventure-comedy; gave it a difficult time slot—Friday night at eight, described by Ginjer Buchanan as the programming "death slot" (52); and then ran the episodes out of order. FOX executives insisted that the series premiere not with the two-hour introduction (entitled "Serenity") shot by series creator Joss Whedon but with a hastily created action-oriented episode, "The Train Job." That move not only created problems of narrative continuity but also made it more difficult to establish the show's characters and situation, arguably its key and most attractive elements. Under such conditions, the entire creative team as well as the cast were all aware that another sort of accident was looming. That is, they were "under constant threat of cancellation" ("Still Flying" 8) as audiences were having a difficult time finding—and finding their way into—the series.

The second factor is the series' curious character as a genre pastiche—a science fiction Western that draws much of its atmosphere and its most compelling situations from its parallels to the post–Civil War American West. Whedon readily admits that his primary narrative inspiration was the classic Western *Stagecoach* (1939).[1] In the most ambitious analysis of *Firefly* to date, Fred Erisman examines both the structural and thematic similarities between *Stagecoach* and the series—a link that supports some of the latter's central concerns, including its skepticism about the nature of "civilization" and its emphasis on individual freedom. Many other commentators have pointed precisely to this genre hybridity as the series' greatest drawback. Buchanan, for example, blames Whedon for not recognizing "that the western was . . . totally moribund" (53). John C. Wright suggests that many elements of the Western are simply "incompatible" with science fiction and that using those conventions worked to "alienate a large segment" of the audience (166). In short, many critics—and even viewers who claim a great fondness for the series—believe that *Firefly* was too much a Western at a time when that genre no longer struck a responsive chord with audiences.

Yet the series did find a devoted—if initially small—audience. In fact, in response to rumors of its impending cancellation, those fans raised enough money for a full-page ad in the show business publication *Variety*, urging that *Firefly* be kept on the air. The series has subsequently maintained an interesting afterlife, with organized campaigns to get the series released on DVD and then to promote its sales, the marketing of a wide range of series-related products, conventions and convention appearances by its creators and stars, and even special discussion sessions at academic conferences. This afterlife might be partly explained by *Firefly*'s resemblance to a number of other popular texts that have inspired similar responses: *Star Wars* and its various offspring; the entire *Star Trek* family of shows (in fact, *Firefly* screenwriter Jane Espenson says that working on the series felt like "being on the set for the first few episodes of the original *Star Trek* and getting a tingly sense of what it would become" ["Introduction" 2]); and even some recent anime, most obviously a series with a similarly hybrid feel, *Cowboy Bebop*.

However, resemblance to other shows ultimately seems like a weak explanation, and in light of the series' many difficulties, it makes at least as much sense to suggest that *Firefly*, in the best cult tradition, resonates with its special audience quite by "accident." To be more precise, I suggest that the series works for those viewers because it consistently foregrounds or *evokes* the accident; it looks at the consequences of accidents both large and small, of the dangers and benefits of (as Virilio says) "exposing your private world," much as cult audiences have always exposed something of themselves in admitting or embracing their various fascinations. *Firefly*'s postwar setting already suggests that its central characters are living in the aftermath of what was, for many of them, a life-altering accident. During the Alliance versus Independents civil war, friends and comrades were killed, much freedom was lost, and deeply held values, including Malcolm Reynolds's original religious convictions (suggested by the cross he wears and several comments made in the "Serenity" episode), were drained away. In this aftermath, Mal and his crew spend much of their time simply trying to avoid encounters with Alliance forces, involvements, and other sorts of accidents. And yet those accidents are, as episode after episode demonstrates, simply unavoidable, and the folks of the spaceship *Serenity* are constantly "exposed," their characters tested and revealed by chance experiences.

In fact, accidents seem to be a normal occurrence. Even in the vast emptiness of deep space, as we see in the episode "Bushwhacked," one can suddenly hit a floating body, come upon a transport that had accidentally run into a Reaver raiding party, and then happen upon an Alliance cruiser—one incident right after the other. Amid the good cheer and fellowship that begin "Out of Gas," *Serenity* can suffer a catastrophic

From left: warrior woman Zoe Washburne (Gina Torres), Captain Mal Reynolds (Nathan Fillion), and hired gun Jayne Cobb (Adam Baldwin) in *Firefly*.

accident when its engine catalyzer produces a blast that nearly kills Mal's second in command, Zoe, and leaves the crew without life support and only enough oxygen to sustain them for a few hours. And in this universe of improbabilities, a thug and mercenary like Jayne Cobb can, by chance, become a hero and even have a statue erected in his honor in "Jaynestown," all because he accidentally drops his loot from a robbery over a town of needy and downtrodden "mudders" and is thereby mistakenly perceived as a futuristic Robin Hood. Of course, these and similar incidents finally represent something more than bits of chance, and Mal's fascinated pronouncement upon seeing Jayne's statue—"Here's a spectacle that might warrant a moment's consideration"—might well be our guide in this matter as well.

As the episode's title suggests, "Bushwhacked" starts with the premise of an unexpected encounter. *Serenity*'s proximity alert alarm suddenly interrupts a game among the crew that, as the thoroughly rational Simon observes, they do not seem to be "playing by any civilized rules I know." But more than just approaching another ship, *Serenity* has run over a body floating in the depths of space—an odds-on impossible, unpredictable, even absurd occurrence with conflicting consequences.

On the one hand, it confronts Mal and his crew with a disturbing situation, a kind of affront to their humanity, as they find a ship containing the bodies of settlers slaughtered by the cannibalistic Reavers and hung up like horrific decorations. And on the other hand, it presents an irresistible self-serving opportunity to salvage supplies and materials, gaining "about a fortune," as Mal calculates. Yet no sooner do they work out a compromise—Shepherd Book is allowed to "say words" over the butchered settlers while Jayne loads the salvaged booty—than another proximity alert sounds, indicating another improbable encounter in deep space. This time, the encounter is with an Alliance cruiser that quickly captures the *Serenity* and reverses the situation, seizing the booty and accusing the crew of murdering the settlers. However, when the Alliance commander questions Mal and the others, Book cautions him about reading the situation too logically, noting that "rules can be a mite fuzzy" on the frontiers of space.

His comment obviously echoes the narrative's opening, when Simon offers a similar observation about "rules," suggesting not only a pattern of doubling but also a key implication of these accidental encounters. What we repeatedly see is evidence of just how unpredictable, irrational, accidental—literally un-rule-y—this universe is and, given that situation, how contingent, even precarious, humanity's own situation is. Certainly, the accidental encounter between the settlers' ship and the Reavers in the midst of what Kaylee describes as "the vasty nothingness of space" dramatically illustrates that contingency. This point is also foreshadowed when Simon watches Mal and Zoe don space suits to explore the derelict ship and is suddenly struck by "the thought of a little Mylar and glass being the only thing separating a person from *nothing*." It is a shock of recognition that also comes to the very rational, rule-bound Alliance commander, who is new to patrolling deep space, when the one survivor among the settlers—an individual the commander believes he has rescued from the "pirates" of *Serenity*—again reverses things. In Reaver fashion, he mutilates himself, kills a number of Alliance medical personnel and soldiers, and is about to dispatch the commander when a handcuffed Mal intercedes. This unexpected encounter with something—a Reaver—whose very existence the commander had doubted upsets his view of things and leads to the sort of new understanding that accidents, like cult texts, always carry with them. Despite the "rules," the commander lets Mal and the others go and even destroys the derelict ship, just as Mal suggests. He does keep all the salvage, however, perhaps as a show of his lingering if superficial commitment to the worldview the Alliance espouses—one of reason, control, utopian possibilities; one where *things* still stand solidly against the *nothing*ness that has apparently made Reavers out of men.[2]

The most intricately structured episode of *Firefly*, "Out of Gas," works backward from its opening imagery to point out that some sort of serious accident has already occurred. A wounded Mal falls directly into the foreground, and we see his blood dripping through the floor grate. The succeeding flashbacks follow no logical pattern but seemingly flow from Mal's ebbing consciousness. These scenes consist of a series of contingencies or accidents that randomly flesh out not only how Mal came to this point but also how, through a series of unlikely events, he acquired many of his crew and "boat": Kaylee when he almost stumbles over her while she makes love to his former mechanic in the engine room; Jayne when he is helping to hold up Mal and Zoe but is dissuaded by a better offer; Inara when she suddenly appears and insists that he rent the shuttle to her, even though he already has a surveyor interested at a higher price; and even the *Serenity* itself—which Zoe describes as an accident waiting to happen, "a deathtrap"—when it catches his eye just as he is about to close a deal on a newer ship. Drawing these different stories together, we gather, Mal finds a kind of solace as he seems to be dying. Perhaps he even draws "something important" out of these random memories that flood into and out of his consciousness—in this case, the inspiration to keep going and ultimately save his ship.

Although this episode seems to be about accidental events and their sometimes terrible consequences, it also demonstrates how we might draw strength from such events and even rise above them. Pressed to find a way to fix the ship, even without a spare catalyzer, Kaylee recalls that sense of contingency and the importance of "things," yet she insists on the power of the accident when she observes, "Sometimes a thing gets broke and can't be fixed." But even as everyone resigns themselves to the consequences of this accident, as Mal sends everyone off in the shuttles and he prepares to die with his ship, Wash sounds an alternative, even illogical note, instructing Mal how, "when your miracle gets here," he might recall the shuttles. And indeed, another accident—or miracle—happens when salvagers stumble upon the *Serenity*, Mal survives a gunshot to chase them off (after getting the necessary spare part), and he finds the strength to endure long enough to get the ship running. With the *Serenity* and Mal both returned to life, "Out of Gas" reminds us that while an accident might entail "exposing" oneself to "major hazards" (as Virilio puts it), it can also open onto a horizon of possibility. In this case, the result is an almost familial feeling as the others, determined in spite of all reason to cast their lot with Mal, return in time to save him from his wound. What began as a voyage carefully plotted to avoid accidentally encountering the Alliance eventuates in a series of accidents. Yet from them comes not only survival but also an affirmation of the group, of their feelings for one another, and even of the possibility of miracles.

Though hardly as complex an effort as "Out of Gas," the "Jaynestown" episode amplifies this sort of payback that our accidents harbor. In fact, through its rather straightforward comic irony, it suggests the accident's broader social implications. This is illustrated in the story of Jayne's effort to steal a payroll from Magistrate Higgins on Higgins's Moon, populated by the downtrodden workers known as mudders. When his aircraft is hit by ground fire, putting his getaway in doubt, Jayne is forced to dump his box of stolen money in the middle of the mudder town of Canton. Misreading this move as evidence that Jayne heard "the mudders' lament" (as a ballad in his honor suggests) and tried to help them, Jayne accidentally becomes the town hero, and a statue—suitably of mud—is erected. Hailed as a revolutionary leader, someone who "stood up to the man," Jayne, against all logic, becomes a symbol of defiance, of heroic action, and of social justice (as Simon offers, "This must be what going mad feels like").

Even when Jayne admits the truth in the town square and tries to convince the people that no one would just "drop money on you," the effect remains. Though he denies that there are selfless, heroic types ("just people like me"), one of the mudders throws himself in front of Jayne to save him from a bullet—at the cost of his own life. That action leaves the "hero of Canton" both stunned and puzzled, as his final remark underscores: "It don't make no sense." And indeed, to someone like Jayne, self-sacrifice seems illogical and incomprehensible, but the point is clear enough to the others: Jayne's quite inadvertent and misinterpreted act of "social justice" inspired the mudder and others like him, generating a spirit of defiance and selflessness among Canton's poor and repressed. As one of them observes, "If the mudders are together on a thing, there's too many of us to be put down." The "box-dropping, man-ape-gone-wrong," as Simon describes Jayne, has accidentally produced the potential for his opposite—a true hero. The episode then underscores this pattern when the magistrate's son demonstrates that same rebellious spirit, defying his father and helping the *Serenity* to escape. Seeds accidentally planted in the mud of the mudders' moon have already begun to produce fruit.

If that social development initially seems inexplicable to the "man-ape-gone-wrong," it may yet make sense, or at least its illogic may fall into place. The positive impact of any accident lies in the fact that it "is going to provoke, [or] has already provoked a reversal of tendencies and values"; it might well prove to be a "revelation" (Virilio and Lotringer 64–65, 107). And subsequent episodes—no less than the feature film *Serenity*—emphasize that element of growth in Jayne and, more importantly, an increasing sense of family or connectedness among all the crew and even in terms of the larger human situation on this new frontier. It is an impulse central to the episode "Heart of Gold," when the *Serenity*'s crew comes to the aid of Inara's friend Nandi, saving her fellow prostitutes from Ranse Burgess—essentially another version of Magistrate Higgins and yet another of those recurring Alliance figures who insist on a thoroughly logical, predictable, and rigidly controlled world.

Of course, the cult text has always suggested the possibility of other values. As Bruce Kawin notes, it typically "represents a disruptive rather than a conservative force," functioning as "a site of audience power" (19, 21). In fact, its rather "accidental" embrace, its acceptance by the small cult audience that manages to find the text, provides the surest sign of its own vision of otherness and of the need for those other, compensatory values it represents. In the case of *Firefly*, its dedicated audience has fittingly adopted the nickname of the rebel "Browncoats," the term used to describe the soldiers (like Mal and Zoe) who fought for the Independent faction against the Alliance and its repressive order. That link underscores how the series' rebellious spirit, its emphasis on the importance of individualism, its questioning of what the mainstream would deem civilization, and its persistent reminders of the "fuzzy," often illogical and unpredictable nature of things have managed to resonate with this audience, offering them, in the best cult tradition, a vision of "something important," even if seemingly by accident. It is a vision, of course, that is too rare in the world of series television—an accident to which we have profitably been exposed.

Notes

1. In the interview "Into the Black," Whedon describes how he planned the series to be "a *Stagecoach* kind of drama with a lot of people trying to figure out their lives in a bleak and pioneer environment" (6).

2. Although the film version offers another and far less mysterious rationale, here Mal articulates an explanation for the Reavers that is more in keeping with the thrust of this episode. He explains: "They got out to the edge of the galaxy, that place of nothing, and that's what they became."

Freaks and Geeks

Jonathan Gray

Writing of his doomed show in its DVD liner notes, *Freaks and Geeks'* creator and co–executive producer Paul Feig observes:

> Everything about this show from the very beginning has been like the characters who populate it. Because *Freaks and Geeks* is about outsiders. It's about people who don't tend to get the respect of the "normal" world, who are individuals no matter how hard they try to fit in. And, from the start, this show has been like a freak or a geek who has moved to a new school district. It showed up, hoping to be accepted, was introduced to the class, got ignored for a while, but then found other people who had similar tastes and hopes and dreams and suddenly it had a home, a support group. It felt wanted. It felt appreciated.
> Then, unfortunately, it got cancelled. I think the metaphor kind of falls apart there.

Created by Feig and produced by Judd Apatow, *Freaks and Geeks* is an eighteen-episode high school dramedy set in the 1980–1981 school year at William McKinley High School in Michigan. Banished to a Saturday evening time slot, an American television graveyard, the show had an ill-fated and short life on NBC in the 1999–2000 season. Despite a fast-developing cult following and widespread critical acclaim, it was canceled midseason, after only twelve episodes. An additional three episodes would air in the summer of 2000, following a concerted campaign by fans, and the final three episodes aired later in 2000 when FOX Family Channel picked the show up in syndication. Another fan campaign, including an online petition, later resulted in the series' availability on DVD, where it became a considerable hit.

Though *Freaks and Geeks* struggled to obtain network-sized audiences, much like its fellow doomed high school cult favorite *My So-Called Life*, the show ranks highly on many lists of quality American television programming. It is also notable for launching the more successful careers of several of its cast and crew, in particular, Apatow (writer-director of hit cult-mainstream crossover films *The 40-Year-Old Virgin* and *Knocked Up* and producer of numerous other comedies, including *Superbad*, *Anchorman*, and *Walk Hard*) and actors Linda Cardellini (a regular on *ER* since 2003), Seth Rogen (Apatow regular and star of *Knocked Up*), James Franco (most prominently known as the Green Goblin's son in the *Spider-Man* franchise), and Jason Segel (another Apatow regular and star of the sitcom *How I Met Your Mother*).

Under the Bleachers: A Different Sort of High School Life

Fans welcomed *Freaks and Geeks* as a breath of fresh air in its portrayal of high school life. American film and television too often bow to the hegemonic portrayal of high schoolers as either wholly sex obsessed (*American Pie*), mindless shopper-gossipers (*Laguna Beach*), saccharine, squeaky-clean Disney creations (*Saved by the Bell*), or edgy teens moving from one controversy and drug addiction to the next (*Beverly Hills 90210*). Teen depictions often reflect out-of-touch projections by adults, producing an image of either desired youth or feared youth. Moreover, following the advertiser-driven needs of network television, many high school shows are populated with beautiful people—young men with chiseled physiques and square jaws and endless young girls with plastic bodies, flat stomachs, and plenty of outfits to display them.

Amid this intertextual backdrop, then, came *Freaks and Geeks*, a show that focused on, as the title suggests, a group of high school outsiders—the socially awkward and normatively unattractive "geeks" and the disaffected outcast "freaks." Shifting the camera away from the cheerleaders, football team, and Most Likely to Succeed nominees, *Freaks and Geeks* offered a wonderfully humorous, and often painfully accurate, depiction of the awkwardness of the teen years.

This shift of attention is rendered explicit in the opening scene of the pilot episode. We see a football player and a cheerleader chatting, hand in hand, at the top of the bleachers while the rest of the team trains:

ASHLEY: You seem so distant these days, Brent. Is there something I did? 'Cause, if there is, I want you to tell me.
BRENT: Ashley, it's just that . . .
ASHLEY: We need to work through whatever it is that we need to work through. But we need to communicate. I need you to talk to me.
BRENT: Ashley, it's just that I, I love you so much, it scares me.

As Ashley and Brent lean in to kiss each other, the camera grows bored and pans down, under the bleachers, where we meet the freaks, and the background music changes abruptly to hard rock. The freaks discuss getting kicked out of church because of wearing inappropriate clothing, until Nick Andropolis (Segel) proclaims with religious zeal, "Hey, I believe in God, man. I've seen him, I've felt his power! He plays drums for Led Zeppelin and his name is John Bonham, baby!" With this, the camera then pans out to the geeks, Sam Weir (John Francis Daley), Neal Schweiber (Samm Levine), and Bill Haverchuck (Martin Starr), acting out a scene from *Caddyshack*. In clear fashion, the show's opening minute thus announces its lack of interest in the sort of saccharine dialogue and clichéd high school stereotypes of the Brents and Ashleys and its greater interest in those under the bleachers. Rounding out the scene, a group of bullies accosts Sam and his friends, who are then defended by Sam's older sister Lindsay (Cardellini), who quickly dispatches the bullies verbally. When Sam is less than thankful to his sister for getting involved, Lindsay shrugs, exasperated, and grunts, "Man, I hate high school." And with this incantation, we cut to the opening credits.

Characters, Not Caricatures

The plot centers on Lindsay and Sam. Lindsay is struggling not so much to fit in but to "fit out." She is academically gifted, a whiz at mathematics, well liked by her teachers, and socially sure on her feet. But she finds herself dissatisfied with the school's norms and wondering what point there is in conformity. At the end of the pilot episode, she recounts to her brother the experience of being with their grandmother when she passed away. She asked her grandmother whether she saw something—a light at the end of the tunnel, anything—only to be told that there was nothing there. Gravitating away from her mathlete ways and her God-fearing friend Millie (Sarah Hagan), Lindsay becomes attracted to the freaks, who distance themselves from the high school's norms and resist them. At the same time, part of her discomfort with the freaks lies in the way they so gleefully separate themselves from others, accepting the binary that has been posited between them and the rest of the school, yet flipping its evaluative terms so that they become the smart ones and all the others are losers. Lindsay is not so keen to give up on her old friends; nor is she comfortable deriding them as a bunch of losers and stiffs. Through Lindsay's internal conflict, then, *Freaks and Geeks* offers a complex and thoughtful treatment of belonging, behavioral norms, and what counts as "normal" and "freak" or "outsider."

Lindsay's younger brother Sam is definitively one of the geeks. He and his best friends Neal and Bill are conventionally unattractive, wear uncool clothes, and are socially awkward. Sam has a passion for all things Steve Martin, especially *The Jerk*; they are the frequent butt of jokes from many of their fellow students; and as Neal says to Sam when the latter dreams of taking Cindy, a cheerleader, to the homecoming dance: "She's a cheerleader, you've seen *Star Wars* twenty-seven times. You do the math." Yet in many ways Sam proved to be one of American network television's first instances of "geek chic"—something of a social pariah yet a likable, funny, deeply identifiable one whose geek knowledge and fandoms provide the basis for many a cool and knowing reference or joke. In other words, rarely does *Freaks and Geeks* ask us to laugh *at* Sam; more often we laugh *with* him.

In Sam's wake, Josh Schwartz would champion geek chic with Seth Cohen on *The OC*, then Chuck Bartowski on *Chuck*; others, too, would follow in Sam's footsteps. Crude caricatures of media fans and geeks still populate television. However, in recent years, as channel proliferation, strategies of narrowcasting, and increased competition for viewers' leisure time have forced Hollywood to shift to a model of "affective economics" (see Jenkins, *Convergence Culture*) that values fans rather than chastises them, we have seen more complex, interesting, and heroic depictions of geeks. Sam Weir was an early path setter in this regard. Sam eventually gets the girl but soon realizes, as he tells his friends, "She's kind of boring. It's weird hanging out with her friends. And, I mean, all she wants to do is make out and stuff."

Beyond Lindsay and Sam lie their similarly well-fleshed-out friends. On *Freaks and Geeks*, cliques and in-groups operate more organically than do countless televisual and filmic counterparts. When Sam breaks up with Cindy, she angrily exhorts a jock to beat him up, but the shocked jock protests that he likes Sam too much to fight him. In moments such as this, the barriers between in- and out-groups are obvious, but the writers and actors give a significantly more nuanced and layered picture of exactly how these groups interact. Importantly, too, in spite of the show's title, they ultimately show less interest in the *groups* that populate high school life and more care and attention to charting *individuals*. As such, characters are characters, not caricatures, and plots are thus rendered more interesting because actions and reactions are less predictable. Even Sam and Lindsay's parents and the teachers buck stereotypes, sounding like actual parents and teachers with real-life, relatable concerns, hopes, and issues, even though their roles are otherwise often familiar and archetypal.

Nostalgia: A Conflicted Glance Backward

Freaks and Geeks was able to play a clever game with time and generations. Though focusing ostensibly on preteen and teen characters, by setting its action in the 1980s, it could also address a late twenty- or thirty-something audience that would have been that age in the 1980s. Such a move was hardly new to television, with shows such as *Happy Days, The Wonder Years, American Dreams,* and *That 70s Show* prominently setting their action in the past. However, many of television's experiments with time shifting have been characterized by a rich and enveloping sense of saccharine nostalgia, seeming to offer a "better, simpler age" when moral issues could be wrapped up in twenty-two or forty-five minutes. By contrast, *Freaks and Geeks'* nostalgia is more complex. *Happy Days,* for instance, offers the 1950s as a time when small social rebellions are occurring (the Fonz wears a leather jacket, after all!) but the world is safe, warm, and knowable. No real risk exists, parents and teachers always have the best intentions, kids ultimately listen to their parents, and society is small—everyone knows everyone else. *Happy Days* thus creates a golden age, a Garden of Eden that existed before the supposed fall of the 1960s and progressive politics, and it is conservative and closed-minded in its construction of utopia. The Fonz is one of television's most watered-down rebels (though the clear model for *Full House*'s Uncle Jesse), as *Happy Days* polices a firm notion of normative behavior and socialization—a world where the boys wear letters on their jackets and everyone at school thinks they're just swell, and where the girls all shop for their skirts and red lipstick at the same store and dream of hanging off boys' arms while chatting at the soda shop.

Freaks and Geeks also peddles nostalgia, but of a very different nature. Its heroes are those who don't fit in—like Lindsay, who wears an army jacket, not a patent skirt, or like Sam, who wears a secondhand tracksuit top that doesn't match his slacks, not a letter jacket. Whereas *Happy Days* asks viewers to look back to a golden age and identify with the normative teens, *Freaks and Geeks* refuses to sprinkle the 1980s with fairy dust and asks viewers to identify with its titular characters, those who never fit in and who either feel excluded or who actively exclude themselves. Hence, the nostalgia speaks to, of, and for nonconformists and for difference and variety, rather than policing a firm sense of what teens, families, boys, and girls *should* look, act, and talk like. In this regard, its power as a cult television show lies in inviting older viewers who may not have fit in to look back with pride and teen viewers who have more in common with Sam, Neal, Lindsay, and Nick to be comfortable in their skin. Certainly, the feeling of not belonging is rife in teen television, but more often viewers are asked to experience these emotions through beautiful, popular people. In contrast, *Freaks and Geeks* gives us a host of regular-looking characters that we might expect to be our freak or geek friends, not the captain of the football team or the homecoming queen.

Beyond its challenging of the norms of nostalgic television, *Freaks and Geeks* manages a careful balancing act between cynicism and heart. Somewhat like *The Simpsons* and *Buffy the Vampire Slayer*—pros at this balancing act—*Freaks and Geeks* can seethe with snark at one moment yet pull on viewers' heartstrings at the next. Freaks Ken Miller (Rogen) and Kim Kelly (Busy Philipps), in particular, often fire off cynical quip after quip, giving voice to a disgruntled attack on high school life. This caustic sniping is repeated throughout the script, as evident in its treatment of the largely ineffective teachers and the guidance counselor who wants to "rap" with the kids on a first-name basis, or when we see a classroom of bored-stiff students forced to watch an instructional video entitled "Is a Career in the Professions for You?" When Sam's mother asks whether he's going to the homecoming dance, he scornfully asks, "Why would I do that?" Yet the crisp scripts and superb acting from a gifted cast often pull us forward with emotional hooks. For example, Ken falls in love with the "tuba girl" from the band, only to find out later that she was born androgynous. This plot, reminiscent of the Farrelly brothers, gives rise to Ken's rather touching evaluation of what really matters, not, as might be expected, countless sophomoric jokes. Similarly, Sam does attend the homecoming dance, and we are invited to enjoy his dance with Cindy and a rare unabashed smile from him in public. Meanwhile, amid her own equally isolating and confusing life, Lindsay (like Buffy) finds moments to be a good friend and to connect with her family, friends, and others in an endearing manner. It is through this oscillation between and mixing of cynicism and heart that *Freaks and Geeks* deals with nostalgia most effectively, exhibiting passion for high school life and for life in the 1980s, yet refusing to be overtaken by that passion to the point of forgetting the colder, less picturesque aspects of high school life.

A Survivor's Tale

Freaks and Geeks' pilot episode is notable for its many references to death: Lindsay discusses the death of her grandmother; her father's moral lectures take the form of telling his children that those who cut class, smoke, and the like end up dying; the dodgeball game the geeks play is replete with the fear of being "killed"; Alan the bully tells the three geeks that they're dead; and a senior geek counsels Sam, Neal, and Bill on the many ways they might die while fighting Alan. Through its multiple references to death, though, the episode exhibits what would become one of the show's key interests: survival. *Freaks and Geeks* is a deeply funny story for survivors of high school—for those who remember the slings and arrows of high school or those who are currently suffering them. It is also a testament to survival in terms of its own survival in the face of network cancellation. *Freaks and Geeks* would never have worked as a story for Ashley the cheerleader or Brent the football player, but its cult popularity is all the stronger for it.

Heroes

Nikki Stafford

"Save the cheerleader; save the world." It sounds ridiculous, like a tagline made up by *Saturday Night Live*, but when it became the mantra of NBC's newest sci-fi series, *Heroes*, it became a pop culture phenomenon.

Heroes debuted on September 25, 2006, riding a new wave of sci-fi programs that had become mainstream, with *Lost* leading the way. The surprise success of *Lost* led to many copycat shows, and the fall 2006 season was full of pilots that owed a debt to it. These included *The Nine* and *Six Degrees* (stories told through flashbacks that show how the characters are all connected), *Dexter* (a sociopath who believes the system is letting everyone down takes the law into his own hands, blurring the moral line between good and bad), and *Jericho* (an apocalypse throws people together).

Lost wasn't the only show creating a television zeitgeist. *Battlestar Galactica*, despite being relegated to the smaller Sci-Fi Channel, had erased the earlier, sillier incarnation of the series from most people's minds. *Time* named it the best television series of 2005, describing it as "a ripping sci-fi allegory of the war on terror, complete with religious fundamentalists (here, genocidal robots called Cylons), sleeper cells, civil-liberties crackdowns and even a prisoner-torture scandal" (Poniewozick).

The best science fiction has always offered a commentary on current events, and *Lost* and *Battlestar Galactica* were no exception. By the time *Heroes* debuted, there was a *lot* to comment on: September 2006 was the fifth anniversary of 9/11; Bush's second term had begun in 2005, and he had managed to make the entire country distrustful of his administration; Vice President Dick Cheney had accidentally shot a friend in the face while hunting (causing endless hilarity on *The Daily Show*); the so-called war on terror and Operation Iraqi Freedom had devastated a nation and escalated world violence; images from Abu Ghraib turned heroic soldiers into villains; suicide bombers were in the news daily; and the Israeli-Palestinian conflict had intensified.

Heroes conveys a simple yet poignant theme: in a world where heroes are hard to find, ordinary people will evolve to become the very heroes we all need. Creator Tim Kring's saviors include a lovable Japanese office drone, a wannabe congressman with the ability to fly, a woman with a split personality, a man who hears voices, and one hell of an invincible cheerleader. Boasting a large ensemble cast, an overriding mystery, time travel, astounding cliffhangers, characters who cross paths without knowing it, and an extended social commentary, *Heroes* is the perfect combination of all the TV elements people crave.

The premise of the show is this: Ordinary people suddenly begin to develop extraordinary powers. Individually, they have no idea why they've evolved; some see it as a curse, others as a gift. As they slowly learn how to use (or harness) their abilities, their paths start to cross, and it soon becomes clear that others are aware of their existence. A mysterious entity named Sylar is hunting down and killing them one by one, and an even more mysterious group called the Company is either protecting them or giving them up to Sylar. The new heroes begin to fear for their lives. But as the story progresses, they realize that if they join forces, they can stop whatever evil comes their way.

The immediate fan favorite of the show (creating a breakout star in actor Masi Oka) is Hiro Nakamura, a Tokyo office worker and comic book lover who discovers that he can alter the space-time continuum. Claire Bennet (Hayden Panettierre) is a cheerleader who can heal herself from any injury. Nathan Petrelli (Adrian Pasdar), an ambitious New York district attorney who is running for Congress, can fly. His brother Peter (Milo Ventimiglia) can absorb the abilities of any other hero with whom he comes into contact. Niki Sanders (Ali Larter) has an alternate personality named Jessica with homicidal superstrength, and there is a constant internal struggle between the two. Matt Parkman (Greg Grunberg) is a Los Angeles cop who can read minds. Isaac Mendez (Santiago Cabrera) is a New York artist and heroin addict who can paint the future when he's high.

Surrounding these people are other characters who want to study them, save them, or stop them. Bennet (aka Horn-Rimmed Glasses) works for the Company as a way to hide his more humane objectives (like being Claire's father). A genetics professor from India, Mohinder Suresh, is trying to locate all the heroes to protect them from the dangerous Sylar (played with wicked fun by the excellent Zachary Quinto). Another group of people, led by the omnipresent Mr. Linderman (Malcolm McDowell), also wants to get the heroes together, but for nefarious reasons: to make them destroy New York City.

The fun and fascination of the first season were the revelations of the characters and their abilities, their connections to other characters, and their purpose in the story. Horn-Rimmed Glasses went from bad to good to bad again, sometimes in the same scene. Peter Petrelli's powers were similarly unclear — was his ability flying, time travel, invisibility? — until it became obvious that he was exhibiting the power of the other hero nearby.

Like *Battlestar Galactica*, *Heroes* is a commentary on the current state of the world, and in many ways, it is a more realistic depiction of the world than the one created by the Bush administration. The good guys are flawed — Ted Sprague, a man with radioactive powers, accidentally kills his wife, and Peter almost obliterates New York when he takes on Sprague's powers. The bad guys are sympathetic — for one brief moment near the end of the first season, we see that Sylar used to be Gabriel Gray, and he's tortured by the man he has become (his apprehensions pass quickly, however). *Salon.com* referred to *Heroes* as "a thoughtful critique of Vice President Dick Cheney's doctrine on counterterrorism" (Cole), pointing out its more leftist tendencies in comparison to a right-wing show like *24* (the baddies aren't all from the Middle East, for example).

Season 1 was full of awe-inspiring cliffhangers, twists, and, most importantly, revelations. In an article in *Entertainment Weekly* (aptly plugged on the front cover as "Save the Cheerleader, Save the TV Season!"), Kring (until then, best known as the creator of *Crossing Jordan*) said his show was not going to force fans to endure the frustrating mysteries of a show like *Lost*, which offered many questions but few answers. "We tried to learn from the pitfalls that other shows had fallen into," he said. "We sort of made a pact internally that we weren't going to be the show that made you wait for stuff" (Jensen, "Powers That Be"). As promised, the first season moved at a fast pace because the show kept reinventing itself. The cheerleader was saved a third of the way through the season ("Homecoming"), and the rest of the season concerned itself with Peter's prophetic vision that he was going to annihilate New York.

When *Heroes* debuted, the critics loved it. The *Hollywood Reporter* raved, "Part sci-fi, part mystery and wholly unique, *Heroes* is one of TV's most imaginative creations and might, with luck, become this year's *Lost*. Its mix of danger, humor, drama, romance and science creates a unique and surprising flavor of programming" (Garron). Rob Owen of the *Pittsburgh Post-Gazette* gushed, "NBC's *Heroes* is the best pilot of fall 2006."

The show premiered to over 14 million viewers, and NBC knew it had a hit on its hands. Suddenly *Heroes* was the hottest thing on television. Countless parodies surfaced, borrowing *Heroes*' famed (and easily satirized) tagline — from *Ugly Betty*'s "Love the Ugly, Love the World" to *The Family Guy*'s "Save the Baby, Save the Planet" (Schneider, "Rival Blurbsters"). In its first season, *Heroes* created some of the most memorable TV moments in recent memory: Hiro standing in Times Square with his arms raised, shouting, "*Yatta!*"; Claire waking up on an autopsy table to find her rib cage peeled open; Sylar and Peter battling it out, with Peter becoming invisible and Sylar shooting shards of glass around the room to find him; Ted Sprague losing control and going radioactive in Claire's home.

Despite its millions of viewers, *Heroes*, like *Lost*, is a show that can be watched casually, or it can be dissected and analyzed endlessly by viewers. The latter group is what makes a show cult TV. *Heroes* immediately became a cult hit, discussed the night of its initial broadcast into the wee hours of the morning on countless message boards and Internet forums. The show boasts sci-fi elements and several Easter egg–like recurring motifs: a helix, a solar eclipse, a cockroach. Taking another page from *Lost*'s various interactive marketing techniques, NBC started an online graphic novel that offers extra insight into the characters, including details that can't fit into the hour-long episodes. For example, Hana Gitelman, a character only briefly seen in a couple of broadcast episodes, is a major character in the graphic novel series. When the character made her first appearance in the television episode "Unexpected," it was a nod to the fans who had been loyally following the story line in the comics.

Spinning *Heroes* off into a Web comic made sense — the action is very comic book–like; the characters' abilities have been "influenced" (the most charitable choice of words) by some of the greatest comic book heroes; and, most important, Hiro carries a copy of the prophetic comic book *9th Wonders*, written and illustrated by Isaac Mendez—or, as the fans call him, "Mystery Sock," based on Hiro's pronunciation of "Mr. Isaac" (Erin). Ironically, Kring was a complete novice when it came to comic books and their mythology, as he readily admits. So he waded into this unknown territory armed with consultants who were experts in comics, counting on them to let him know if he was doing something that had already been done.

One of those consultants—and the co-executive producer of the show—is Jeph Loeb, a past supervising producer of *Lost* and *Smallville* who has worked on such legendary comic book heroes as Superman, Spider-Man, Batman, the Hulk, and Daredevil, usually in collaboration with artist Tim Sale. Loeb introduced Kring to Sale, who then painted all of Isaac's work for the show (Porter, Lavery, and Robson 78). Loeb realized how important his job would be when he first began talking with Kring about show ideas. "At one point," Loeb explained to *Entertainment Weekly*, "[Tim] said, 'I think there should be a character who with a sweep of his hand lifts up a car and magnetically throws it across the street.' I said, 'Tim, that's [*X-Men's*] Magneto'" (Jensen, "Powers That Be"). But at the same time, it is Kring's naïveté that lends such freshness to the series. Rather than trying to come up with new ideas, as someone familiar with the comic book canon might do, Kring takes ideas that he doesn't know are already out there and treats them as if they are new and exciting. Television fans who aren't familiar with comic books can enjoy the characters the same way Kring does, and the comic book fandom can dissect which characters and series and story lines Kring has borrowed heavily from.

Kring's method of storytelling served him well, until the end of the first season. In the comic book tradition, one would expect several threads to build up to an explosive battle at the end of the volume, but in the season 1 finale, many fans were disappointed when the long-awaited showdown between Sylar and the heroes elicited barely more than a five-minute shoving match.[1] Kring had teased the finale in advance, suggesting that it would take on epic proportions: "The fifth act is *ridiculous*," he said. "It's like a $90 million movie. It's just . . . big" (Jensen, "Bomb Squad"). The reality was anything but, due to budget restrictions and edits to keep the show under forty-five minutes.

The cast defended the finale, with Jack Coleman (Mr. Bennet) arguing that "a TV show can't do what *Spider-Man 3* can do," causing some fans to reiterate Kring's "$90 million movie" promise. Masi Oka explained that a lot of the bigger battle scenes ended up on the cutting-room floor but added, "in terms of the story, it served its purpose" (Jensen, "*Heroes* Comes Out Swinging"). Kring admonished fans for being sticklers and argued that the finale required "the proverbial suspension of disbelief" (Mitovich, Webb, and Logan).

Heading into season 2, Kring decided to divide the story into several smaller parts rather than the twenty-three-episode arc of the first season. The concern wasn't just the critical backlash over the finale but also the fact that the ratings had dropped during the show's hiatuses throughout the year. To help solve the problem, NBC announced a spin-off show called *Heroes: Origins*. This six-episode series would introduce a new character in each segment; fans would then vote for their favorite character, who would become a regular on the show. NBC Entertainment president Kevin O'Reilly told reporters that with this show plus the twenty-four installments of *Heroes* ordered, the show would be able to run without a hiatus for the full season. "We'll keep the pedal to the metal next year on 'Heroes,'" he said (Schneider, "NBC").

Sadly, it seemed as if Linderman had a hand in the fate of television's 2006–2007 season, because nothing went as planned. First, season 2 of *Heroes* was full of problems. The primary story line concerned the Shanti virus (named after Mohinder's deceased sister), which Peter discovers will wipe out 93 percent of the world's population, and the Company's role in preserving it. The second season also explored the previous generation of people with special abilities, who are mysteriously being killed one by one. The new direction had a lot of promise, but the criticisms began after the season 2 premiere. The new heroes annoyed fans (Maya and Alejandro Herrera), boasted abilities that were boring at best (Monica Dawson, who can double-Dutch her way out of a conundrum or fashion roses out of tomatoes—perhaps to throw at people?), or had all the charisma of a slug (Claire's dull boyfriend West Rosen, who can fly like Nathan, prompting questions of whether Kring had already run out of ideas). Hiro was turned from comic relief into a fawning man in love as he travels back in time to feudal Japan to meet his hero, Takezo Kensei, and then woos Kensei's woman. The action from season 1 was gone, replaced by a slow-paced story line that spent far too long building things up.

After the first nine episodes, Kring released a mea culpa through an interview with *Entertainment Weekly*—something almost entirely unheard of in Hollywood, where the blame is always put on someone else. He agreed that Hiro had been out of commission too long, that the pacing was too slow, that the new characters hadn't been introduced properly, and that the little romances didn't click (Jensen, "'Heroes' Creator").

But just as the next two episodes seemed to remedy some of the problems—offering a fast-moving plot, amazing cliffhangers, and everything that made us love the show in season 1—the Writers' Guild of America went on strike on November 5, 2007, putting all of Hollywood on hiatus for three months and shutting down television shows. NBC canceled *Heroes: Origins*, saying that dealing with the scripts for the main production would be difficult enough, and it didn't have the resources to worry about the spin-off (Battaglio). When the writers went back to work on February 10, 2008, NBC decided that due to the loss of momentum, it would be better for *Heroes* to start fresh in the fall of 2008. The giant season of thirty episodes had been reduced to a mere eleven.

All was not lost, however. Because the final two episodes of season 2 had returned the show to its former glory, fans were excitedly anticipating its return. Kring's apology to the fans was a huge step forward in renewing their faith in the show. *Heroes*' cult status was secure, and its future appeared to be safe. Then season 3 continued the show's rollercoaster run by alternating between strong episodes with intriguing characters and dreadful installments that caused the loyalty of even diehard fans to waver.

Heroes is that rare hour of television that informs as well as entertains. It can't be easily written off as a one-trick pony, and even the fans who were upset with the third season didn't stop watching. One of the cornerstones of cultdom is the emotional connection between fans and the series, meaning that they will stick with a show through thick and thin. *Heroes* has undoubtedly created that connection with its viewers. We were shocked by Nathan's fate in the season 2 finale. We breathed a sigh of relief when Bennet wasn't dead. We want to see Claire happy. We secretly adore Sylar. And as for the lovable Hiro? He had us at "*Yatta!*"

Note

1. See the chapter "Finale Face-off" in Porter, Lavery, and Robson (165–79) for my complete take on how disappointing "How to Stop an Exploding Man" was, with a counterargument written by David Lavery.

The League of Gentlemen

Leon Hunt

Part sketch show, part sitcom, part "northern grit," part Gothic horror, *The League of Gentlemen* is one of British television's most innovative and unusual comedy series. Critically acclaimed and much awarded, it is one of the benchmarks of a period from the early 1990s to the early 2000s that has been celebrated as a "golden age" of British TV comedy (Thompson, *Sunshine*). But it also belongs to a longer tradition of "alternative" TV comedies that includes *Monty Python's Flying Circus*, with which it shares a penchant for cross-dressing and the grotesque, and the work of Vic Reeves, whose surreal reinvention of "light entertainment" paved the way for the post–alternative comedy of the 1990s. The program's cult credentials rest even more on two other qualities. First, it meets one of the prerequisites for cultdom established by Umberto Eco, providing a "fully furnished world so that its fans can quote characters and episodes as if they were aspects of the fan's private sectarian world" (198).[1] The fictional northern English town of Royston Vasey is so richly detailed and immersive that one is tempted to speak of a "Vasey-verse," even though we are talking about a location no bigger than that of a soap opera. The "Vasey-verse" would be expanded both in the narrative "bubble" of the 2000 Christmas special and in the competing fictional worlds of the feature film *The League of Gentlemen's Apocalypse* (2005). Second, like Joss Whedon and Quentin Tarantino, the *League*'s creators' status as fans is part of their allure. Although their influences were diverse, it was their channeling of horror that particularly attracted cult devotion—the series is remembered as one that genuinely chilled and disturbed its viewers as well as making them laugh.

Two words, in particular, are inextricably linked to *The League of*

Gentlemen. The first is *local*, the totemic adjective wielded defensively by misshapen rural shopkeepers and serial killers Tubbs and Edward—"This is a local shop for local people. There's nothing for you here!" they warn visitors ("strangers"), usually as a prelude to terminating them. *Local* captures the insularity of hostile communities (the shopkeepers are both siblings and spouses) as well as the metropolitan fear of the rural often found in horror films. The second word is *dark*, encompassing not only the series' macabre aspects (murder, incest, blood-soaked epidemics) but also its cruelty, tragedy, and willful "bad taste." Mark Gatiss's performance as a cave tour guide implicated in the accidental death of a young boy is a tragicomic tour de force to rival Alan Bennett's *Talking Heads* monologues (1.5). "Dark comedy" took on a particular currency at the turn of the millennium, and the comedy team responsible for *The League of Gentlemen* was often identified as its prime exponents. The early development of the show on stage roughly coincided with the arrest and horrific revelations of English serial killers Fred and Rosemary West. Once the atrocity had sunk in, it was not uncommon for the Wests to appear in the sort of "sick" jokes that often circulate after high-profile murder cases. Provincial grotesques, the Wests seemed too "local" and unsophisticated to be capable of their crimes, an incongruity inherent in some of the humor surrounding Royston Vasey's shopkeepers—"We didn't burn him!" blurts out Tubbs, unprompted, just as a policeman investigating a hitchhiker's disappearance is about to leave (1.1).[2]

Like Monty Python, *The League of Gentlemen* is the name of both a TV series and a comedy team. Mark Gatiss, Steve Pemberton, and Reece Shearsmith studied theater arts at Bretton Hall, an arts college affiliated with Leeds University. Jeremy Dyson, the team's nonperformer, studied philosophy at Leeds and met Gatiss through a mutual friend. After working in various combinations on diverse projects, the four began to stage shows at the end of 1994. They largely wrote in pairs—Dyson with Gatiss, Pemberton with Shearsmith. Early shows were performed in tuxedoes and Brylcreem; signature characters were created without the distinctive makeup designs that would become a hallmark of the TV series. A turning point came with two residencies at the Canal Café in London in 1996. The League began to inject an element of seriality into what was effectively a sketch show, a move motivated partly by expediency—"Never the same show twice!" claimed the posters in a bid to persuade audiences to return. Key characters began to accumulate something resembling story lines through follow-up sketches. In 1997 the show won the prestigious Perrier Award at the Edinburgh Festival and made the transition to radio, where *On the Town with the League of Gentlemen* further synthesized the sketch material into something more unified. Producer and script editor Sarah Smith played a key role in honing the series into something unique. According to Dyson, she "had a kind of clear grasp of what the thing was at the heart of what we did that was different from what other people did." He described the process as "a gradual weeding out of the kind of stuff that other people might have done."[3] The town setting, something Smith was especially keen on, played a key role in this "weeding out" process, retaining those characters who could plausibly coexist in the same locale. On radio, the town was named Spent, an apparent nod to the faded northern industrial towns often found in "kitchen sink" and "Brit-grit" movies. On television, it would become Royston Vasey, the real name of foul-mouthed English comic Roy "Chubby" Brown. Brown later appeared in the series as Mayor Larry Vaughan, who manages not to swear during a TV interview until he is thanked at the end. "It's a fucking pleasure," he replies (2.4). The TV series would become a flagship comedy on BBC2, considered by many the "home" of innovative British TV comedy before the emergence of digital channel BBC3 in 2003. *Radio Times* promised "characters who would not look out of place in *Twin Peaks* or *The Fast Show*" (Graham, "Pick" 90).[4] Although its ratings were modest but respectable, it was an instant cult, prompting many fans to visit Hatfield in Derbyshire where the series was filmed, often dressed as their favorite characters.

Tubbs and Edward had been omitted from the radio series, but they quickly became the most popular characters on the TV show. Controversially, they were seemingly killed off at the end of season 2 and then more conclusively at the start of season 3, shortly after their fleeting resurrection (although they returned again in the feature film). In the first season their ongoing story line finds them resisting a new road that will bring strangers to the shop, while in season 2 they seek a "no-tail" (a woman) for their monstrous attic-bound son. "Welcome to Royston Vasey. You'll never leave," proclaims the town's sign, and the shopkeepers embody the implicit threat in that tourist slogan (a slogan allegedly considered by Gloucester Council, the town where the murderous Wests lived). Harvey and Val Denton, equally freakish but less murderous in intent, are similarly difficult to escape. Seasons 1 and 2 follow the trials of their nephew Benjamin, an ostensibly short-term guest who endures a suffocating domestic regimen obsessed with hygiene and labyrinthine classifying systems (keys, towels, which toilet to pass "solids" into). He is constantly policed for signs of masturbation (or "cavorting with Madame Palm and her five lovely daughters," as one of Harvey's prodigious euphemisms puts it). By season 2, the toad-obsessed Dentons have murkier designs on Benjamin, who has recently escaped from untold torments at the Local Shop. Benjamin is the unifying figure of the first two seasons, a normative audience avatar who passes between Vasey's two monstrous families. Meanwhile, at the unemployment office, Restart Officer Pauline bullies the "dole scum" she is supposed to be helping, particularly the lovable idiot Mickey and the educated Ross, who soon becomes her nemesis. Based on Shearsmith's experiences collecting unemployment benefits, Pauline captures the ambivalence of the League's female grotesques. She is a middle-aged, sexually frustrated (and sexually ambiguous) tyrant who seems to embody a streak of misogyny in the series. But Pemberton gave her character a warmth and energy that increasingly made audiences side with her against the initially more sympathetic Ross, who progressed to outright villainy in season 3.

Two other characters in the pantheon of popularity represent the dark heart of *The League of Gentlemen*. Hilary Briss, a sinister butcher with muttonchop whiskers on ruddy cheeks and a lisping, James Mason–toned voice, sells his "special stuff" to an elite clientele. Teasingly macabre, filled with unresolved innuendo about what it might be—nothing so prosaic as human flesh, with hints of addictive narcotics or the most unconscionable pornography—the "special stuff" was enough of a hook in season 1 to be promoted to a loose story arc in season 2, linked to a graphic nosebleed epidemic. The first episode of season 2 also introduced a character whose onscreen presence would be judiciously rationed, returning in only two additional episodes but almost rivaling Tubbs and Edward in iconic resonance. Papa Lazarou is a demonic circus ringmaster in a long leather coat, bandana, and minstrel blackface who sets up his Pandemonium Carnival in Royston Vasey. In his signature sketch, he forces his way into the spotless suburban home of a housewife and initiates her into a dark and unfathomable world in which she becomes one of his many "wives." Pitched somewhere between *Chitty Chitty Bang Bang*'s Childcatcher, Freddie Krueger at an Al Jolson convention, and a more mythic trickster archetype, Lazarou is simultaneously absurd, primal, and nightmarish. He subverts the familiarity of the comedy catchphrase by injecting an extraordinary menace into the greeting "Hello, Dave" (the name applied indiscriminately to every woman he meets) and concluding most of these encounters with the rasping declaration, "You're *my* wife now!" When he returns for the Christmas special, the League seems to have given up any pretense of Papa being a comic character. He emerges from a childhood nightmare clad in Santa Claus outfit like a character from an EC Comics horror tale.[5] In season 3 he adopts the alter ego of effete Keith Drop, applying Caucasian flesh tones to his "natural" skin, like Jack Nicholson's unnaturally white Joker. The ultimate fate of his wives produces one of the series' most grotesque images: they are placed inside living circus animals (3.6). "You're going to be an elephant" feels like a bid to outdo "You're my wife now" as comedy's creepiest catchphrase, but don't hold your breath for it to appear on a T-shirt.

Along with hapless vet Mr. Chinnery, the unwitting exterminator of domestic pets and livestock, these characters became the series' most popular. But the League created equally memorable if less celebrated characters, such as failed rock star Les McQueen and the terrifying immigrant patriarch Pop. Special mention should go to Geoff Tipps, underachieving worker at the local plastics factory and an aspiring comedian who cannot comprehend the mechanics of comedy. His signature sketch finds him struggling with the rituals of social joke-telling, especially problematic when the joke in question has been only partially memorized (1.1). But arguably his finest moment comes when delivering the best-man speech at his best friend's wedding. Clad in a jester's outfit, his reminiscences degenerate into a catalog of perceived defeats, injustices, and other grudges until he arrives at one moment of petty triumph. When both their mothers became seriously ill, only Geoff's survived. "I won that!" he crows with extraordinary venom. "At least I won the Mums!" (1.5). Season 3 finds him pursuing his ill-advised comedy ambitions in London, the first Vasey character to hit the "Big Smoke." In a bravura piece of "cringe comedy," he dries when his all-too-local jokes fail to impress the "clever London people" and dissolves into an undignified rage until the lights are turned off (3.3). Shearsmith plays the rage and disappointment to comic perfection but never loses sight of Geoff's humanity, so the character remains sympathetic in spite of having no conspicuous redeeming features.

Regardless of its previous lives onstage and on radio, *The League of Gentlemen* arrived on BBC2 fully formed as a televisual experience—

densely packed with visual jokes (particularly during the title sequences) and displaying the flair that often earns visually striking television the label "cinematic." In addition to the four gents, it benefited from an ongoing production team that included director Steve Bendelack, production designer Grenville Horner, costume designer Yves Barre, and composer Joby Talbot. What it inherited from its stage origins was not only tried-and-tested characters but also the extraordinary versatility of Gatiss, Pemberton, and Shearsmith—an edition of *Radio Times* provided a chart to help viewers recognize who played who (Graham, "Are You Local?"). If narrative initially felt like icing on a cake that would have tasted pretty good without it, it would grow in importance. For season 3, each episode offered a more sustained story focusing on particular characters—Pauline, Ross, and Mickey (3.1), one-armed joke shop owner Lance (3.2), Geoff (3.3), hotelier Alvin and his swinger wife Sunny (3.4), warring couple Charlie and Stella (3.5), charity shop workers Vinnie and Reenie, and the return of Papa Lazarou (3.6). Each episode was filled out with new subsidiary characters, of whom tyrannical Dr. Carlton ("Go out, would you") and childlike debt collector Barry Baggs were especially memorable. The episodes were interlinked by an event that provided the climax each week—an accident involving a white van and a red carrier bag—with more information gradually revealed about the fate of the characters involved. This show felt very different from the first two seasons, with a new arrangement of the theme music and (like the Christmas special) no studio audience to ease viewers through the darker scenes. Not everyone appreciated this new format. For some viewers, the show jumped the shark at precisely the moment a train hit Tubbs and Edward in the first episode. Says Gatiss, "We didn't jump the shark, but we certainly got one foot on the water ski in terms of what the public were expecting versus what we wanted to do."[6] The third season divided the show's cult following, but its reputation has improved considerably since its original low-key reception, critically overshadowed by the second season of *The Office*.

The Christmas special, by contrast, represents a more acclaimed break from the restrictions of the sketch format, as well as the culmination of the League's love affair with the horror genre. Arguably their finest work on television, the Christmas special derives its narrative structure from the portmanteau horror film, particularly those associated with Amicus Studios (*From Beyond the Grave* was a particular favorite of the gents). On Christmas Eve, three visitors tell their stories to Vasey's vitriolic Reverend Bernice Woodall. The first tale ("Solutions") throws Charlie and Stella into a volatile cocktail of marital discord, voodoo, and line dancing. The second ("The Vampire of Duisberg") is a vampire story set in the 1970s that stars Herr Lipp, the innuendo-dispensing German pedophile from season 2, seen here spying on his new choirboy (or "queerboy") through a keyhole—like Norman Bates eyeing up Marion Crane. Whereas these stories are especially reminiscent of Amicus, the third, Dyson and Gatiss's "The Curse of Karrit Poor," evokes a more specifically televisual manifestation of the Gothic—the Christmas ghost stories produced by the BBC between 1971 and 1978, adapted from M. R. James and Charles Dickens. With its high Gothic production values, "Karrit Poor" is a quintessentially Victorian confection, full of hansom cabs, steam trains, and magic lantern shows, the last used to narrate the origin of the eponymous curse. There are other referents, too. Some are comic—comedian Dave Allen's spookier tales and the *Ripping Yarns* episode "The Curse of the Claw"—and some are literary, such as the colonial Gothic story "The Monkey's Paw," in which artifacts from the East bring misfortune. The story provides an origin for Chinnery's deadly veterinary skills, tracing them to a curse passed to his Victorian grandfather. The malefic artifact in question is the genitalia of the maharajah's pet monkey, castrated by the ineptitude of the English colonial vet who now conspires to pass the hex to Chinnery through deceit. The story culminates in a veritable animal apocalypse when the ill-fated vet returns to London. An irresistible blend of nostalgia, atmosphere, mischief, and the BBC's ineffable capacity for "doing Victorian," "The Curse of Karrit Poor" is a labor of (particularly morbid) love and holds a special place in the hearts of the series' fans. If its evocation of deliciously spooky Christmas pasts threatens to end things on a comparatively cozy note (give or take a decapitated zebra), the framing story has other ideas: Bernice receives a Santa-suited visitor who insists on calling her "Dave"—she's *his* wife now.

The League of Gentlemen made a film in 2005 and followed it with a touring live show, but they have not worked together on television since 2002. Whereas Python seemed pressured to continue the brand name or fulfill "contractual obligations" (as a disappointing album generated under tangible duress put it), the League currently seems content to pursue solo projects or work in pairs—both Dyson and Gatiss are acclaimed writers of fiction as well as TV, and all three leads are much in demand as character actors. Pemberton and Shearsmith's *Psychoville*, currently screening on BBC2, might be the closest we get to a fourth season of the *League*, and based on the evidence so far, it can more than withstand the inevitable comparison. It continues the narrative ambition of season 3, ditches the catchphrases, but creates characters worthy of its predecessor at its best. A mother-son pairing—murderous, possibly incestuous, yet strangely endearing—is a particularly cherishable dark comic creation.

It's difficult to assess the legacy of *The League of Gentlemen* without mentioning *Little Britain*, the series that pursued the more populist aspects of the *League* (detailed and versatile character acting, infectious catchphrases, lovable grotesques), with some of the more cultish elements absent or lower in the mix (the "darkness," the narrative ambition, the immersive "world"). It's rather too easy to position *Little Britain* as *League*-lite and churlish to begrudge the way it won the hearts of a mainstream audience while the *League* sometimes alienated viewers with their more disturbing and contentious material. Nevertheless, although *Little Britain* has its own deserved place in British comic history, *The League of Gentlemen* is arguably the most fully achieved, original, and enduring British sketch comedy since Monty Python raised the bar for the genre more than thirty years ago.

Notes

1. Eco has film in mind, but the idea seems better suited to the immersiveness of cult TV.
2. The policeman's Scottish accent and name (P. C. Woodward) is just one of many references in the series to the British horror film *The Wicker Man* (1973).
3. Jeremy Dyson, interview with the author, September 10, 2007.
4. *The Fast Show* was a cult sketch show featuring a vast array of recurring characters and an equally vast array of catchphrases. One of them, "Suit you, sir!" was even uttered by series fan Johnny Depp in *The Last Ever Fast Show* (2000).
5. Specifically, "And All through the House" from *Vault of Horror* 35 (1954), which was later adapted in both the film and TV incarnations of *Tales from the Crypt*.
6. Mark Gatiss, interview with the author, September 17, 2007.

Life on Mars

Robin Nelson

Life on Mars is a British series made by the independent producer Kudos for BBC Wales.[1] Like a number of groundbreaking television programs, *Life on Mars* came to be produced somewhat by chance. Some seven years prior to production, the writers came up with the idea for a different kind of cop show with the working title *Ford Granada*. They had developed the script for what was now called *Life on Mars* to quite an advanced stage when Channel 4 summarily decided that it was too risky. By chance, the BBC had a vacant slot for an innovative cop show, and extraordinarily, Jane Tranter (BBC controller, drama commissioning) gave *Life on Mars* the green light within days. Under executive producers Julie Gardner (head of drama, BBC Wales) and Claire Parker (for Kudos), the first season of *Life on Mars* consisted of eight episodes (January–February 2006); the second season, commissioned before the first one aired, was also eight episodes (February–April 2007). *Life on Mars*, pitched as a cop show with a twist or "added depth," was finally in the right place at the right time.

According to cocreator, writer Matthew Graham, *Life on Mars* was conceived as "just your regular run-of-the-mill time-traveling cop show."[2] Since most TV cops don't travel through time, the writers may have been trying to extend the attraction of generic police series by drawing on the popularity of time travel in shows such as *Doctor Who*. But the highly popular British police series *Heartbeat* may have sparked the idea as well. *Heartbeat* is set in a regional location (the North York Moors) in the 1960s, and its sound track utilizes popular music of the time. Although the series does not make use of time traveling, its loose representation of the 1960s draws on a 1990s postmodern retro interest in that decade. *Heartbeat* can also claim to be the most enduring and successful (in terms of audience numbers) British TV drama series of all time.[3] Whatever sparked the idea, *Life on Mars* is set in Manchester (at the heart of northwest England) in the 1970s, with a sound track of popular music from that era. In its careful reconstruction of spaces and customs, it has nostalgic appeal to those who lived through the 1970s, and it parodies a popular 1970s police series, *The Sweeney*. The truly distinctive feature of *Life on Mars*, however, is the way it travels through time.

The premise of *Life on Mars* is that Detective Inspector (DI) Sam Tyler (John Simm) has regressed from the early twenty-first century to the 1970s. Although the details remain ambiguous, Tyler appears to have suffered a head injury in a car accident in 2006 and wakes up as a DI in Detective Chief Inspector (DCI) Gene Hunt's (Philip Glenister) Manchester division. Keeping his secret largely to himself—the ostensible explanation for his arrival is a transfer from another division—Tyler suffers the anguish of not knowing how he got to be where he is and whether he will ever get "back home" to the twenty-first century. The title refrain asks, is Tyler "mad, in a coma, or back in time"? This time-travel dimension and mystery contribute considerably to one aspect of the series' cult status.

Like many contemporary TV dramas, *Life on Mars* is a mix of serial and series forms—or, in my own coinage, it's a "flexi-narrative" (Nelson, *TV Drama*). It sustains some of the generic features of police series. It has a pair of detectives, Hunt and Tyler, in personal and professional conflict, though they are ultimately closely bonded. It has car chases and other physical action in which the baddies get their comeuppance. In each episode a main story arc is drawn to a conclusion, resolving the case at the top of the detectives' investigative agenda. This resolution affords the pleasure of narrative closure, which remains popular with viewers who like to know "whodunit," and it particularly suits those viewers who drop in casually for a single episode. For more regular viewers, a longer-form serial narrative, with a succession of obstacles and hooks, sustains interest over time. *Heartbeat*, besides its episode closures, creates larger serial narrative arcs, usually around the romantic or professional futures of the main characters. Indeed, the flexi-narrative mix is now common. *Life on Mars* is also a hybrid of a police-detective series (with action-adventure overtones of *The Sweeney*) and a telefantasy (from the same stable producing *Doctor Who* and *Torchwood*), with aspects of documentary realism (in the 1970s setting) and a touch of romance (in the possibility that

Sam and Constable Annie Cartwright [Liz White] might get together). What is exceptional about *Life on Mars*'s dramatic structure, however, is the increasing complexity of its long-form narrative dimension.

A key impact of the time-travel aspect of *Life on Mars* is the double perspective it invites viewers to adopt. Gene Hunt, like his *Sweeney* predecessors, hits first and asks questions later. An overt intertextual play between *Life on Mars* and *The Sweeney* is foregrounded in the imagery of the camel overcoat worn by the protagonists and the gold Ford car driven at high speed. Whereas *The Sweeney*'s hero, DI Jack Regan (John Thaw), to some extent reflects policing methods and attitudes of the 1970s, Hunt, by twenty-first century standards, is patently marked as non–politically correct, exhibiting aspects of casual racism as well as entrenched misogyny and macho aggression. Like that of his *Sweeney* progenitor Regan, Hunt's language is blunt, but his coining of incorrect catchphrases becomes almost an art form. Where Regan famously but curtly commands, "Shut it!" and "Get your trousers on, you're nicked," Hunt threatens, "You so much as belch out of line and I'll have your scrotum on a barbed wire plate." In pursuing lines of inquiry, he suggests, "We're looking for a short skinny bird, wears a big coat, lots of gob," and he observes, "She's as nervous as a very small nun at a penguin shoot." Deputy Sergeant Ray Carling and Chris Skelton serve as foils to Hunt's sharper wit, affording some Keystone Cops action in their size fourteen approach to police procedurals. Such overt comparison with *The Sweeney* and parodic differentiation make for complex viewing. The comparison reinforces a conviction of what life was like in the 1970s (even though it's an exaggeration), but measured reciprocally against the prevailing habitus of the twenty-first century.

Though Hunt is initially constructed as something of a comic caricature, the two-dimensional figure becomes more rounded by the power of Glenister's performance. In the penultimate episode, Hunt's near alcoholism as a metaphor of his conflicted personality is explained by his sense of failure at being unable to find—and save the life of—his brother. Hunt's crude but direct form of justice has held popular appeal in British drama since the consolidated state agencies outlawed direct revenge under the reign of Elizabeth I. But the popular trope is ultimately enriched in *Life on Mars* by the rounding of a familiar stock figure with a deepening character motive to produce the memorable icon Hunt has become.

John Simm might be equally applauded for the quality of his performance as Sam Tyler, whose vulnerable thoughtfulness is in marked contrast to Hunt's brash aggression. However, Tyler is not quite the "Dorothy" of Hunt's construction, since he holds his own in the action sequences and in many direct confrontations with Hunt, both physical and mental. Though their policing methods are poles apart, a mutual respect grows between the two detectives throughout the series, building up to the penultimate episode of season 2, when Sam helps get Gene out of a very sticky situation. Because of his position between two eras, however, the character of Sam Tyler was always destined to be a more complex figure than Hunt. Over and above finding himself on another planet with respect to policing methods and other aspects of culture (the lack of mobile phones, computers, databases), Sam is suffering the existential anguish of his temporal and physical displacement.

Although Matthew Graham believes that the narrative line and its motivations are ultimately clear, ambiguities remain that are important to the series' cult status. One motivation for a possible amnesiac trauma is Sam's abandonment by his father, who, if we are to believe the final episode of season 1, runs away after being caught up in some minor criminality. The significance of the loss of a father is prefigured in episode 5, in which a Manchester United football fan is killed by a fellow fan in order to incite a battle with Manchester City supporters. Sam identifies strongly with the bereaved son of the victim, ultimately finding his father's killer and giving the boy the match ticket he has taken from the killer. The repeated appearance of people from Sam's former life— he meets his mother and father, his Auntie Heather, and the mother of his girlfriend, Maya—makes family loss the prime suspect in the search for the cause of Sam's predicament.

The most puzzling narrative enigma, however, is the "sunken dream," the mystery of where Sam Tyler has come from and whether, and how, he'll "get home." As the story unfolds, no single narrative meta-arc affords an easy inferential walk. Indeed, each story strand opens up another narrative prospect. Even in the denouement, the writers have fun with the possibilities. In the final episode, Sam is led to his parents' supposed graves by Frank Morgan, where the gravestones read "Walker." Insisting that his parents are Vic and Ruth Tyler and that his surname is Tyler, not Walker, Sam spots nearby gravestones bearing the Tyler name. But these graves turn out to be dated in the 1880s, and Morgan's explanation that Sam is an amnesiac, having lost his memory in a road accident, suddenly seems not only plausible but also corroborated. Sam

Tyler (formerly Walker) is a detective from Hyde whose identity has been changed to allow him to go undercover in Manchester's A-Division to root out highly questionable policing methods. But just as it all seems to be making sense, Sam's pointed accusation that Frank himself is a figment of the imagination flips us back to the narrative possibility that Sam *is* in a coma from which he is slowly awakening. Indeed, we see him coming round, and Frank Morgan is a smug surgeon congratulating himself on his success. So the supposed "reality" of 1970s *Life on Mars* was all a dream, and Hunt was merely an imago based on the antihero of a bygone TV series.

To confirm it, Sam is a twenty-first-century DCI in A-Division, but bored out of his mind discussing the ethics of police policy with "the suits." As he tells his mother, he has lost the feeling that, according to Rasta barman Nelson (Tony Marshall), distinguishes life from its alternative. And life with Hunt, however procedurally and ethically flawed, was at least vibrant. Sam offers his apologies to his colleagues around the meeting table, makes for the roof, and takes a running jump. With Sam suspended in slow motion in midair and a fade to black as he disappears from the shot, we are momentarily left dangling on whichever narrative hook we have chosen to cling to. But we scarcely have time to mutter, "It's a cop-out, leaving future options open," before we land back in the 1970s reality of a train heist, and Sam is in yet another time frame— namely, "make your mind up" time. Will he sacrifice his colleagues to "get home" once and for all, or will he forsake his personal salvation to save them? Sam fires his pistol, shoots the villain dead, and saves the day. And, following the inevitable pub celebration, Sam is finally rewarded with a kiss from Annie Cartwright.

But, in the context of *Life on Mars*, a tinkling, romantic piano can scarcely avoid carrying an ironic overtone. Tyler's twenty-first-century attitude toward women is matched in sensitivity throughout by Annie Cartwright, constructed in part as a homely girl-next-door. But a happy ending to the romance is plausible only if other aspects of the series' treatment are overlooked. Thus, when Hunt's Ford arrives to transport the posse to yet another battle with the scumbags of Manchester, the car radio is still speaking to Sam from 2006, although the contact is fading. Sam changes the station and finds David Bowie belting out "Is there life on Mars?" Though Sam appears to have opted squarely for the vibrancy and romance of life in the 1970s, the narrative closure remains incomplete, leaving open the speculative space that is so attractive to cultists.

Life on Mars set out to be a "quality, popular" television series, and in many respects, it achieved its aim. However, as it developed, it achieved cult status, with at least some segments of the audience relating to it on a level of engagement beyond the norms of popular enjoyment. Sandvoss takes the view that *cult* "cannot be defined in textual terms but must be defined *a posteriori* in relation to consumption practices" (41). But I am persuaded by Hills's notion of an institutional interplay between "text-based, inter-text-based or audience-based definitions of cult status" ("Defining Cult TV" 522). Although fans ascribed value to the series as it progressed, *Life on Mars* has textual features that dispose it to cult status. Such a disposition has been characterized by Hills as a "hyperdiegesis" and a "perpetuated hermeneutic." The perpetuated hermeneutic involves "a central mystery that repeats familiar characteristics but whose resolution is endlessly deferred," while the hyperdiegesis involves "an internally logical, stable, yet 'unfinished' fictional world" (Hills, *Fan Cultures* 137–38).

Life on Mars illustrates both these features of telefantasy. Indeed, for one segment of the audience, the time-travel aspect of *Life on Mars* afforded such a predominant pleasure that, for these viewers, the series achieved telefantasy cult status. The sense of a TV drama carrying a special resonance for viewers often arises from the more cosmic or philosophical layers of textual significance, and *Life on Mars* affords these in the coma and time-travel angles. The text also invites speculative thinking through such features as the Open University lectures on mathematics by the strange bearded man and the BBC test card featuring Bubbles the clown and the little girl in the red dress. In particular, the girl's emergence from the test card — and, in one episode, her ghostly progress across the room to corner and dominate a fearful Tyler — suggests the production team's conscious exploitation of this provocatively mysterious aspect of *Life on Mars*. Cult readings typically pick up on, and embroider, trails of clues to a wider, perhaps more cosmic space. For those who got into the time-travel possibilities, the series offered encouragement through small but telling details: when Sam comes round in the hospital, he is on Hyde Ward, and the room number is 5612 (the phone number he has carried around on a scrap of paper throughout season 2). Even after the end of season 2, and an advance announcement that there would be no more *Life on Mars*, ambiguities remained for those who prefer the speculations of cultists.

But the series also carried a different and particular cult appeal to viewers over forty-five, for whom it involved a negotiation of the recollections of their formative years and their experiences of culture today. The producers worked to achieve a consistency of tone amid the generic hybridity of the series, and a very enthusiastic production team paid attention to details. The result was a convincing evocation of the 1970s in a mise-en-scène that had special appeal to people who grew up in that era. Among a research group of individuals aged fifty and older watching episodes of *Life on Mars*, viewers exclaimed, "I recognize that cocoa tin," "We used to have wallpaper like that," "My dad used to walk around like that with the TV aerial trying to get a better picture."[4] The test card is another case in point. In an era without daytime television, the 1970s test card was the image confronting children who switched on the television set in anticipation. The use of popular music similarly extends this sense of historical familiarity. The extensive use of Bowie's "Life on Mars" in the first episode sets up the musical device and picks up on Tyler's sense that he has "landed on a different planet." Thereafter, connections between the song lyrics and the action are left for viewers to make, and as the series develops, short refrains of a song sustain the feel of radio as a sound track to contemporary life (for those who remember the 1970s), as well as offering a lyric commentary on the action.

In sum, *Life on Mars* is a cult series because it occasioned different subsets of viewers in different ways to have a special relationship with it. In Gene Hunt, it created a distinctively attractive antihero; in its time-traveling dimension, it opened up a "perpetuated hermeneutic"; and, on a more mundane but no less effective level, it evoked the personal and collective histories of an older generation and measured them against a changed culture in the present.

Notes

1. The American version of *Life on Mars* is not addressed in this chapter.
2. Cited on the BBC's *Life on Mars* Web site. The other creators of the series were Tony Jordan and Ashley Pharoah.
3. For a history and discussion of *Heartbeat*, see Nelson, *TV Drama in Transition* 73–88.
4. This group met on October 5, 2007, as part of the author's ongoing research.

Lost

Marc Dolan

It is a commonplace of television criticism that all truly great achievements in the medium have emerged from the successful battle of a core group of brave, romantic creators against the evil machinations of multinational media conglomerates. *Lost*, however, which is one of the most creative programs in the history of regularly scheduled broadcast television, has been, from first to last, an organic product of the American entertainment industry. It even began with an entertainment executive's four-word pitch: "Plane Crashes on Island."[1]

The question, of course, is what to do with a pitch like that. With very little time to produce a pilot, Lloyd Braun, chairman of the ABC Entertainment Group from 2002 to 2004, took the idea to Jeffrey Lieber (whose major screenwriting credit prior to 2004 was his adaptation of Natalie Babbitt's young-adult fantasy novel *Tuck Everlasting*) and subsequently to J. J. Abrams (creator of, among other things, *Felicity* and *Alias*). According to the best-known version of *Lost*'s creation, it was Abrams who took Braun's bare, man-among-the-elements logline and added the series' unforgettable fantasy and science fiction elements.[2] But Braun's prior selection of Lieber as potential show runner suggests that he was purposefully seeking out writers with backgrounds in both fantasy and romance. In other words, from its inception, *Lost*—much like the American sci-fi series that would be launched in the wake of its spectacular initial success (especially *Surface* and *Invasion*)—was designed to be a peculiar hybrid: a mainstream cult show.

This is not to diminish Abrams's crucial role in the development of *Lost*. Even if Braun's idea for the show had always been premised in fantasy, Abrams made an important decision early on that undeniably distinguished the series. When first presented with the concept, Abrams couldn't see how it could work as a long-form television series. Then he shifted his focus from potential characters for the story to its possible setting. "If the island," he later remembered thinking, "wasn't just an island and if you started to look at where they were as part of the ongoing story, it started to become increasingly clear that this was a big idea." As Abrams elaborated to another interviewer: "For me, it was like looking at the show in a long term. What is the series beyond relationships such as trust and betrayal? What would give the show story tent poles that were compelling and mysterious and bigger than the obvious stuff that you see play out?" (quoted in Porter and Lavery 8, 11).

Typically, comments like these from Abrams have been interpreted as reflecting the post–*Twin Peaks*, post–*X-Files* emphasis in serialized American television on developing a so-called mythos, a larger hermeneutic puzzle whose episode-by-episode disentanglement engages potentially committed viewers enough to keep them tuning in regularly. More broadly, though, Abrams's comments reflect a larger, even older shift in American television, one that transcends the serialized-nonserialized divide: a move to supplement what David Bordwell and others have called the "classical Hollywood" paradigm of stories, based in prominently featured characters and their clear narrative through-lines, with continuing stories that are premised in environments and transforming communities (for the origins of this phenomenon, see Bordwell, Staiger, and Thompson, particularly 174–93). Despite its serialized nature, a twenty-first-century series such as *Desperate Housewives* is much more in the old character-oriented tradition of *Dallas* or *Dynasty* (or even *The Big Valley* or *Julia* before them),[3] whereas *Lost* is in the setting-oriented, departing actor–proof tradition of *Hill Street Blues* and *Homicide*, as well as more obviously fantasy-oriented shows such as *Twin Peaks* and *Buffy the Vampire Slayer*. Instinctively, Braun grasped this from the first treatment he received back from Abrams. "This, my friend," he said to one of his assistants after he finished the twenty-five-page script outline, "is *ER*" (quoted in Craig).[4]

The true irrelevance of *Lost*'s characters to its central conceit is even clearer when one considers how few of them were probably included in that initial treatment Braun approved so heartily. A subsequent fuller treatment used to cast the pilot was produced by Abrams in collaboration with Damon Lindelof in a highly accelerated fashion just before the end of the 2004 development season. Nothing in Lindelof's background (including yeoman's work on *Nash Bridges*, *Crossing Jordan*, and the Kevin Williamson–created fizzle *Wasteland*) suggested a television auteur in the making, but he and Abrams apparently bonded immediately, particularly over their affinities for a number of specific creators and texts in popular culture. Once they had figured out what sort of environment the island was, the two writers concluded that the best sort of characters to populate it were Stephen King characters. For the pilot, the most relevant King novel was *The Stand*, which supplied archetypes that inspired the characters of trusty dog Vincent, spookily pregnant Claire, and (especially) has-been rock star Charlie.[5] Walt, for his part, seems to be a clear echo of many lonely, supernaturally talented King children, particularly Danny Torrance in *The Shining*.

Although these were the characters the producers started the casting process with, they were not the characters they ended up with three weeks later. Of the fourteen regular characters featured in the opening credits of season 1, only five ended up in the pilot pretty much as they had been conceived before casting began,[6] and it was only after these fourteen regulars were cast and the principal characters reconceived that Abrams and Lindelof produced a full pilot script.[7] In doing this, they jump-started a process that is very much in the tradition of long-form television narrative: the gradual movement of characters from the authors' conception to the actors'. The longer a series goes on, the more a character becomes the property of the actor who portrays it. For instance, stars William Petersen and Kiefer Sutherland became executive producers of *CSI* and *24*, respectively, and frequently influenced plotlines in which their characters were featured. Even a self-styled television auteur like David E. Kelley, who would probably never share a producer credit with one of his leading actors, writes characters differently once he knows for whom he is writing.[8] Since the pilot of *Lost* was locked down after it was cast, that sort of writing was possible before a single frame of film was shot.

It was also possible because of the series' odd narrative structure, a feature that took both the audience and the actors by surprise from the beginning. In television, if not in film, actors are usually given a capsule biography of their characters before they start playing them. Even audience members often receive a quick exposition download in the pilot episode of a new series shortly after a character is introduced (for instance: "Yeah, he's a brilliant diagnostician, but he's never been the same since his leg went bum. Have you noticed how many pills he's pop-

Papa'iloa Beach in Hawaii, the location of the survivors' camp in *Lost*. (Courtesy of Lynnette Porter)

ping?"). On *Lost*, however, what characters say is simply that: what characters say. At their best (season 1's "Walkabout," for example), the series' infamous flashbacks work ironically, letting us see how the characters provide incomplete versions of their pasts to the others on the island. Neither the audience nor the actors know for sure what is true about the characters' lives before they crashed on the island until they see it in a flashback. In this way, not only the forward motion of the narrative that begins with the crash of Oceanic 815, but also the backward sweep of the characters' pre-island narratives, is influenced by the writers' growing sense of both the audience's preferences and the actors' abilities.[9]

Thus, as the series has continued, specific characters have waxed and waned in narrative importance, even if the overall narrative line of the series (concerning the island) has remained very close to the writers' original plan. Interestingly enough, some of the least featured characters in either flashbacks or flash-forwards have been those that remained relatively unchanged by the casting process. Boone and Shannon, the first regular characters to die, both appeared pretty much as written in the audition sides and may even date back to Lieber's original treatment for the series (Bernstein). Michael and Walt, two other relatively unchanged characters, were the next of the original fourteen regulars to depart from the series. In fact, Walt, whose departure preceded Shannon's, is the only character of the original fourteen who never received a full flashback episode of his own.[10] Claire, whose pregnancy and parenthood have been central to the island plot from the pilot forward, has remained a regular, but we have been given less access to her consciousness through flashbacks and flash-forwards compared with the other nine remaining original regulars.

Although early viewers may have assumed that they would be following a stable group of characters, it has become clear that populating the story with new people was always part of the producers' plan.[11] Indeed, the longer the series goes on, the more one can admire the general design of Lost, which is more apparent now that we are well past the midpoint of its intended narrative. (The first episode of season 4, after all, is called "The Beginning of the End.") The series' creators have repeatedly said that they meant the show to be like a video game, in that additional levels are unlocked the longer we play.[12] This metaphor is most obvious in the sense that new physical spaces are opened up at the end of each season. Many television series strike and add sets with the resumption of production after a summer hiatus, but Lost makes the discovery—and, in some cases, the literal "unlocking"—of such locations an italicized feature of its narrative.[13]

More important, and more obviously, each season introduces new levels of storytelling, what a narratologist would call new "diegetic" levels. Most of season 1's episodes present us with a regular narrative rhythm between two separate streams of time. In each episode, the on-island, post-crash narrative moves forward about a day in the foregrounded story, while we learn in an interspersed background story about a thematically relevant episode from one of the regular characters' off-island lives before the crash. Many viewers saw the flash-forwards in "Through the Looking Glass," the concluding episode of season 3, as the first break in this rhythm; however, season 2 contains its own "unlocking" of new narrative time within the larger story, as first the tail-section survivors ("The Other 48 Days," 2.7), then Claire ("Maternity Leave," 2.15), and then Michael ("Three Minutes," 2.22) have missing pieces of their post-crash, on-island stories revealed. This information fills in gaps in the story that, in some cases, we were not even aware existed.[14] In "Live

Together, Die Alone," the last episode of season 2, a fourth stream of narrative time is opened, as we learn for the first time, through flashbacks of Desmond (who becomes a series regular in season 3) about life on the island before the crash. This stream is central to several of season 3's episodes (most notably "One of Us" [3.16] and "The Man behind the Curtain" [3.20]), just as the introduction of a fifth stream of post-rescue "future" time in "Through the Looking Glass" is central to many of season 4's episodes.[15]

In a literary novel written after 1910, such jumping around in time and narrative focus require no explanation. In a network television series written after 1980, such narratological instability is permissible within the confines of the occasional "very special episode." In *Lost*, however, it comes to us in an incremental, gradually revealed fashion, one intimately tied to the castaways' own consciousnesses and quite possibly the stages of their awareness. As later episodes have made clear, this phenomenon of being "unstuck in time" is a central feature of these characters' lives. At the very least, leaving the island causes one's consciousness to become unstuck in time. In retrospect, though, we may also wonder whether just landing on the island can cause one's past to become much more palpable than mere memory. The flashes we see as viewers may very well be just as existent for all these characters (and not just for Desmond) as they are for us. Past, present, and future may seem equally "real" for these characters, even equally "present." As we are beginning to see, having one's consciousness bounced around so conspicuously and unignorably from the present to the past, from a future present back to the current moment now reconstituted as a personal but still affectable past, can easily drive one mad.

In this way, the form and style of *Lost* echo its thematic concerns. It is as far away as we can imagine from 1950s narrative episodic television, in which regular characters find themselves in an eternal present that is reset back to normal at the beginning of each episode. Decisions have consequences for these characters, and the causes and effects of specific moments in time seem equally present in their minds and thus in our viewing. Like so many pastoral environments in Western literature before it, *Lost*'s island offers the possibility of change and redemption for the characters who visit it. Memory can function as an aid or a curse to these characters in their quest for right action, depending on the spirit in which it is summoned. As Ross Douthat has observed of the series, it does not merely take place in a straightforwardly transplanted "purgatorial landscape" à la Dante or a medieval morality play; more precisely, it takes place in a purgatory that has been reconceived as a "microcosm of Western modernity," as the producers' famous habit of naming their characters for post-Renaissance Western philosophers suggests (24). In this regard, it echoes and amplifies not only Stephen King's *The Stand* but also James Hilton's *Lost Horizon*, a popular novel and subsequent film that may have influenced King's work as well. Like the stories in both these novels, *Lost*'s story is true because it is fantastic. "If you do believe," as one character warns the narrator in the first chapter of *Lost Horizon*, "it will be for Tertullian's famous reason—you remember? *Quia impossibile est*" (Hilton 18).[16]

The knowable impossibility of *Lost*'s world has been a lure for television cultists from the beginning of the series. Rambaldi fever may have been at its peak among *Alias* fans in the fall of 2004 when *Lost* premiered (heralded as *Alias*'s younger sibling, born too of Bad Robot, Abrams's well-known production company). The presence of show runner Carlton Cuse, one of the creators of *The Adventures of Brisco County, Jr.* and of ex-*Buffy*, ex-*Angel* scribe David Fury could only add to its potential cult cachet. As with *Alias*, an Internet strategy was part of the show's marketing campaign from the start.[17] One of Bad Robot's wisest decisions in this regard was to set up "The Fuselage," a site dedicated to dialogue between the show's actors and writers and those who watched it. Within weeks of *Lost*'s premiere, the Fuselage's message boards had exploded with viewer-generated threads that attempted to track the island's history, the content and source of the whispers in the jungle, and potential explanations for all the surprising connections among the characters' lives.[18]

Many of the theories proposed in these threads ended up being far more outlandish than the answers revealed in later broadcast episodes, but that made no difference. The point was the dialogue, both among fans and between fans and writers. As *Lost*'s story invites its characters to join in a community of collective action, the series invites us to join as viewers in a community of collective meaning. Indeed, to date, the show's four seasons have witnessed a fascinating contest for meaning, not between viewers and creators so much as between viewers and the network. So far, corporate parent ABC/Disney has released not only dozens of episodes and the three DVD sets that contain and supplement them but also a host of other ancillary "paratexts" and products. On the whole, fans have voted with their debit cards and Web browsers about which of these pieces they consider relevant to *Lost*'s larger puzzle. The fragmentary "Lost Experience" that circulated online between seasons 2 and 3 (with its extended elucidation of Hurley's numbers as the product of the Valinzetti equation) and the thirteen brief mobile-phone "mobisodes" (whose weekly rerelease online marked the countdown to season 4) counted for many fans. *Bad Twin* (Touchstone's badly conceived tie-in novel) and *Via Domus* (a recent video game), which appeared almost simultaneously, did not. Unlike a work of high modernist art, the "text" of *Lost* is not received by its audience in a single, holistic lump. Instead, we interpret it—and even fix it—as viewers in a linear, emergent fashion.

Despite its resemblance to *The Stand* or *Lost Horizon*, *Lost* is not a novel, nor should we consider it one. It is a television series. More precisely, it is the transmedia product of a very large twenty-first-century corporation, a product in process whose shape is nevertheless determined more by its creators and fans than by the corporation that mediates between them. Never in the history of Western civilization has corporate synergy worked to greater aesthetic effect.

Notes

1. The pitch or logline is reported in this four-word form in Porter and Lavery (8), but Lloyd Braun himself describes it as "Cast Away: The Series" in "The Genesis of *Lost*." According to Olga Craig, Braun described the potential series to Disney executives during the winter of 2004 as a cross between the Tom Hanks film *Cast Away* and the reality phenomenon *Survivor*.

2. The most canonical version of this narrative is in "The Genesis of *Lost*."

3. *Desperate Housewives* premiered on ABC the same week as *Lost*; both were important ratings successes for then-troubled ABC.

4. Braun was referring, of course, to the long-running NBC series that began in 1994 and ended in 2009.

5. This is confirmed by Lindelof's comments in "The *Lost* Book Club": "We're all pretty big Stephen King fans." But it was widely known before that. In fact, before the pilot aired on American television, Lindelof, in an interview with the Web site *Ain't It Cool News*, drew explicit parallels between half a dozen of the series regulars and their equivalent characters in *The Stand* (see "Herc Chats up Co-Creator"). For a good analysis of parallels with *The Stand* through the middle of season 2, when they were strongest, see Porter and Lavery 130–38.

6. The roles of Sawyer and Charlie, for example, were rewritten to fit Josh Holloway and Dominic Monaghan: Sawyer became southern and rural rather

than northern and urban, and Charlie was made ten or fifteen years younger than he was originally conceived. The roles of Sayid, Locke, and Hurley were specifically written for Naveen Andrews, Terry O'Quinn, and Jorge Garcia because the producers thought it would be interesting to have these actors in the show. The character of Sun was created when Yunjin Kim gave a great audition for Kate that wasn't quite right for the part as they had conceived it. This led to the creation of the character of Jin as well, to give Sun a husband to play off, ironically allowing Sun to absorb some of the original conception of Kate's character as a newlywed whose husband dies in the crash.

7. The impact of the casting was to give the project a more transnational feel than Braun or possibly even Abrams had originally intended. Since the mid-1990s, some American television producers have consciously tried to give their series more racially mixed casts, but as these initial casting choices show, the producers of *Lost* were interested in giving their series an *internationally* mixed cast. This led one scholar to call the series "most obviously an allegory of the international system [after 9/11]" (Dunn 320).

8. The most famous example of this was on *Ally McBeal*. Kelley gave John Cage, one of the senior partners of the series' law firm, a penchant for the bagpipes because he had heard actor Peter MacNicol, who portrayed Cage, play them.

9. Compare Lindelof's oh-so-steampunkish identification of Dickensian serialization as a "primitive internet" in "The *Lost* Book Club."

10. The one exception is the relatively brief scene with the birds at the end of "Special." Most of the rest of the episode centers on Michael's consciousness.

11. Indeed, many viewers balked at the introduction of the tail-section survivors in season 2 and the somehow forgotten Nikki and Paolo in season 3. However, the introduction of the Others in season 3 and of the freighter crew and passengers in season 4 were better received within the confines of the narrative.

12. See, in particular, the comments by Jesse Alexander in "The Genesis of *Lost*." For the fullest (and craziest) exploration of this analogy between *Lost* and the logic of video games, see "all_games," *Lost Is a Game.com*.

13. Although it was unsatisfying to many viewers, the fact that season 1 ended with the blowing open of the hatch was a literal emblematization of this practice. In the last moments of "Exodus," a new level is unlocked, and we enter not only the physical space of the Swan Station but also the world of the Dharma Initiative. Similar moments of spatial unlocking occur in season 3 when Sawyer is shown in "Every Man for Himself" that he and the entire Hydra Station are on a second island near the one the Oceanic 815 survivors landed on, and when the Others' barracks (formerly the property of the Dharma Initiative) are revealed in "Par Avion" behind a sonic barrier. One is tempted to say that Sayid's helicopter ride to the freighter at the end of season 4's "Confirmed Dead," which gave us our first aerial view of the island, is the ultimate moment of spatial unlocking, but at this writing, we still have two seasons and forty or fifty hours of narrative to go.

14. This is also the narrative stream in which most of the "Missing Pieces"

segments (originally produced for distribution on Verizon mobile phones and eventually posted on the series' official Web site) take place.

15. Given all the hints about the island's past, one can reasonably postulate that the next stream of time to be "unlocked" by the series' narrative will be *historical* time, the time of Jacob and the four-toed statue. This stream, we should note, cannot be reasonably accessed through the consciousness of any character we have yet encountered, with the possible exception of Richard Alpert.

16. One may even wonder whether the transformation of the series' composition across six seasons may represent a move from using *The Stand* as a narrative model to substituting *Lost Horizon* in its place. "Through the Looking Glass," which may eventually prove to be the meridian of the series' story, contains not only Jack's tragic regret at having left his paradise (an attitude very reminiscent of Hilton's Hugh Conway at the outset of his novel) but also the death of Charlie Pace (almost the last regular character on *Lost* that strongly echoes one of King's—in this case, Larry Underwood).

17. For an alternative exploration of this transmedia proliferation solely as a marketing strategy, see Walters (66–67), who examines the viral marketing of *Lost* in the context of the later marketing of Bad Robot's *Cloverfield*.

18. The message boards on the Fuselage proved more popular than those on the official ABC site because they were perceived as author run. Lostpedia (the most popular of three competing Wikipedia sites devoted to the series) also received far more hits than the official network-generated site. It was soon joined by dozens of wholly fan-generated sites, blowing up single-frame Easter eggs and deciphering sound clips.

Miami Vice

Jon Stratton

Starting in September 1984, *Miami Vice* ran for five seasons on NBC, finally ending in May 1989. By then, 107 episodes had been screened. In addition, there were four so-called lost episodes, three of which were screened in June 1989. The fourth episode, "Too Much Too Late," aired on cable's USA Network in January 1990; NBC considered its subject matter, which included child abuse, too strong. In 2006 the show was remade as a feature film with the same title, cowritten by Michael Mann and Anthony Yerkovich and directed by Mann. Both had been instrumental in the creation of the original series.

Aficionados of the series usually consider the first two seasons, and possibly the third, to be the best. Mann produced the early seasons, handing the reins over to Dick Wolf for the third. Wolf gave the series a darker and more realistic look, which he brought from his work on *Hill Street Blues* and later perfected in *Law and Order*. By the fourth season the delicate balance of image, pace, and cop show narrative had been lost. The nadir is often considered episode 7 of season 4, "Missing Hours" (which aired in November 1987), in which legendary soul singer James Brown plays an alien. However, it should be noted that this episode was written by the celebrated American science fiction author Thomas M. Disch.

Miami Vice was a cop show—but it reinvented the genre. The story of its origin is that Brandon Tartikoff, president of NBC's Entertainment Division, had an idea for a series that would combine the music and imagery of MTV (which, since its debut in 1981, had rapidly become the channel of choice for teenagers) with the narrative holding power of a cop series. By 1983, MTV had revolutionized the music business, showing that TV exposure with an appealing video could transform a single into a hit. Tartikoff is said to have written "MTV cops" on a napkin and handed it to either Mann or Yerkovich during a meeting—the story varies. Certainly, Yerkovich did the early work on the series, using the working title "Gold Coast" for the pilot and producing the first five episodes. Yerkovich was drawn to Miami as a locale because "it seemed to be an interesting socioeconomic tide pool: the incredible number of refugees from Central America and Cuba, the already extensive Cuban-American community, and on top of all that the drug trade. There is a fascinating amount of service industries that revolve around the drug trade—money laundering, bail bondsmen, attorneys who service drug smugglers." Yerkovich compared Miami with Casablanca and also described it as "a sort of Barbary Coast of free enterprise gone berserk" (quoted in Zoglin). Mann likewise explained that he "figured Miami was a perfect location for a show. . . . It was riddled with expatriates, drugs, organized crime, and was a banking center for Latin America. It had all the elements" (quoted in Janeshutz and MacGregor 14).

The show rapidly became very popular, appearing regularly in the Nielsen ratings' top-ten shows up to 1986, when its popularity began to lessen. *Miami Vice* was the top-rated cop show and comparable in popularity to the prime-time soap operas of the era, *Dallas* and *Dynasty*. The show won numerous awards, including Emmys in 1985 for Jeffrey Howard for Outstanding Art Direction and Edward James Olmos for Outstanding Supporting Actor; it was nominated for ten additional Emmys that year, including Outstanding Drama Series.

If *Miami Vice* was so popular and so successful, how can it be considered a cult show? The problem lies in the everyday usage of the term *cult*. According to Sara Gwenllian-Jones and Roberta Pearson, the term is "often loosely applied to any television program . . . that draws a niche audience" ("Introduction" ix). In other words, it is generally assumed that cult television programs cannot be popular—that is, draw a wide general audience and be of high quality (as evidenced by mainstream awards). This assumption has permeated academic discussion even as commentators have evolved other criteria to characterize cult television programs. For example, Gwenllian-Jones and Pearson imply this distinction when, listing what they consider important questions to be answered when addressing the nature of cult television, they ask: "What distinguishes 'cult' programs such as *Star Trek* and *The X-Files* . . . from other series such as *Friends* . . . , which may attract larger audiences but do not inspire significant interpretative fan cultures?" At the same time, they argue that "'Cult Television' has become a metagenre that caters to intense, interpretative audience practices" ("Introduction" x, xvi). This gives us insight into how a program might be considered both cult and popular. Matt Hills has argued that "certain films and television programs (and other media such as novels and popular music) can be defined as 'cult media' through the fact that such media texts attract passionate, enduring, and socially organized fan audiences" ("Media Fandom" 73). Such intensity does not necessarily mean that a program has a niche or minority audience. *Miami Vice* is a good example of this. As we have seen, its audience was very large. At the same time, certainly for men up to around age forty, the show offered an image of fashion and style that was intensely emulated. Indeed, as we shall see, *Miami Vice* was an important element not only in the transformation of series television but also in men's consumption practices.

At the core of *Miami Vice* are two undercover cops who work for the Miami Police Department's Organized Crime Bureau: Detective James "Sonny" Crockett (whose undercover name is Sonny Burnett), played by Don Johnson, and Detective Ricardo "Rico" Tubbs (known undercover as Rico Cooper), played by Philip Michael Thomas. Crockett is white and Tubbs is African American. In a sign of the show's political conservatism, Crockett is clearly the dominant character in the relationship—a fact legitimated narratively by having Tubbs arrive in Miami in search of the murderer of his undercover detective brother. Adding to this dynamic is the fact that Tubbs has assumed the identity of his brother and that he falsely claims to have been transferred to Miami (from New York, where he was a policeman) to hunt for his brother's killer. This situation is never cleared up, although Crockett discovers the subterfuge. Generally speaking, then, the African American Tubbs is constructed as a more problematic character than Crockett.[1]

In the first four episodes, the bureau is run by the Hispanic Lieutenant Lou Rodriguez (Gregory Sierra). Rodriguez's character is one example of the influence of the earlier cop series *Starsky & Hutch*, where the eponymous detectives' boss is the by-the-book African American Captain Harold Dobey (Bernie Hamilton). Rodriguez is killed off and replaced by Lieutenant Martin Castillo (Edward James Olmos), a very different character from his predecessor. Whereas Rodriguez, like Dobey, was a family man who had come up through the ranks, anchoring *Miami Vice* in the quotidian, Castillo is a single man with a mysterious past, including working undercover as a member of the Drug Enforcement Authority in Southeast Asia during the Vietnam War. Castillo, whose Hispanicness is always ambiguous, is withdrawn, almost monosyllabic, and highly professional. His presence in the show reorients it from the ordinary to the extraordinary, locating its concerns in threats coming from the world beyond the borders of the United States.

Four other members of the bureau are important to the show: two female undercover detectives, Gina Navarro Calabrese (Saundra Santiago) and Trudy Joplin (Olivia Brown), and two male, Larry Zito (John Diehl) and Stan Switek (Michael Talbott). Like its racial aspect, the show's gender assumptions are conservative. The Hispanic Calabrese and the African American Joplin most often work undercover as hookers, and when they are around the office, Crockett often asks them to do menial chores. Zito and Switek, seemingly of southern and central European backgrounds, provide the show's humor. They can frequently be found staffing the surveillance van, a brightly colored Bug Busters Dodge Ram with a giant-sized ant on the roof.

Although the social elements of the show were conservative, the show's form, especially its emphasis on style and its use of popular music, was radical. Tartikoff had suggested a show that connected with the MTV audience, and it was Mann's training and background as a film director that brought the stylistic gloss to the series. Mann had been a student at the International Film School in London in the late 1960s. By the time he got involved with *Miami Vice*, he had already made *Thief* (1981) and *The Keep* (1983), as well as the acclaimed made-for-television film *The Jericho Mile* (1979). In 1986 he would make the first of the Hannibal Lecter serial killer films, *Manhunter*, and would go on to become a major director in the decades ahead.[2] Mann's work as a writer on *Starsky & Hutch* linked him with the television cop genre and accounts for the similarities between the two shows. He often encouraged the use of filmmaking techniques to give *Miami Vice* a visual effect previously not considered appropriate for television series.

Complementing this was the show's preoccupation with fashion; this included both clothes and other things, from watches to guns, cars, and boats. Before *Miami Vice*, it was considered unmanly to wear stylish, fashionable clothes, but the expensive stylishness of Crockett and Tubbs was legitimated by their work as undercover cops impersonating drug dealers. *Miami Vice* was presaged by Paul Schrader's film *American Gigolo* (1980), in which Richard Gere plays a lothario framed for murder. Gere's character, Julian Kaye, has a liking for expensive and stylish clothes (the movie made Armani a household name), cars, and other items. However, from the viewer's perspective, this desire is problematized by Kaye's profession as a male prostitute. In *Miami Vice*, however, even though Crockett and Tubbs are posing as drug dealers, their "true" identities as undercover cops help legitimate their fashionable look. Reflecting a growing social shift, Crockett especially helped change American attitudes about men's fashion. In the first two seasons Crockett always dressed in pastels and, with help from Gianni Versace, created the 1980s vogue for wearing a T-shirt under an unstructured jacket with linen pants. He also helped brand the Rayban sunglasses and Rolex watch he wore. Tubbs tended to wear dark suits, often made by Hugo Boss. Such was the popularity of the men's styles portrayed on *Miami Vice* that Macy's even opened a "Miami Vice" section in its men's department. In retrospect, Crockett and Tubbs can be thought of as pioneering metrosexuals.

In *Starsky & Hutch* Starsky drove a Ford Gran Torino, but Crockett's car was, inevitably, much more up-market: a black open-top Ferrari Daytona Spyder in the first two seasons (signaling the *American Gigolo* influence, Kaye drove a black Mercedes-Benz 450 SL convertible). In season 3 Crockett was given a white Ferrari Testarossa ("Stone's War," 3.2).

The use of Miami was equally well thought out and stylish. Janeshutz and MacGregor remark: "Most of the buildings in Miami don't fit the look of the show, creating a weekly challenge to find locations which work." They quote Maria Chavez, a location manager: "One of the rules is no brick, reds or browns. We also stay away from Mediterranean architecture" (15–16). Although the show was shot in Miami, only a limited amount of the city actually looks like the Miami of *Miami Vice*. For example, as the quotation indicates, there is a lot of Mediterranean architecture in Miami, whereas *Miami Vice* constructed an image of the city as being predominantly Art Deco in design. Consequently, much of the series had to be shot in the area around South Beach, which was listed on the National Register of Historic Places in 1979 because of its fine Art Deco architecture.

Art Deco was an interwar European art and design movement. Within the mise-en-scène of *Miami Vice*, the Art Deco surroundings provide a European resonance that goes with the European style of the clothes and the cars. Because Europe is associated in American culture with stylishness, the use of Art Deco buildings reinforces the idea of the stylishness of the show. We can briefly compare this image of Miami with that generated by *CSI: Miami*, which portrays a kind of dream city of towering apartments set beside the water, a modern Venice of steel and glass. Whereas *Miami Vice*'s style has a sense of history, *CSI: Miami*'s is forward looking, reinforcing the fascination with its high-tech use of forensics to solve crimes.

The other major contribution to the stylishness of *Miami Vice* came from its use of music. The music for the show was chosen or composed by Czech-born Jan Hammer, one of the founders of the 1970s jazz-rock fusion group Mahavishnu Orchestra. Hammer's "Crockett's Theme" reached number one on the *Billboard* singles chart in 1985 and won a Grammy that year for Best Instrumental Composition. However, more important to the feel of the show was the decision to use high-profile popular music for much of the sound track of each episode rather than instrumental music composed specifically for the program. This technique was certainly influenced by the success of MTV, but again, it was indebted to *American Gigolo*, which choreographs much of the early scene to Blondie's "Call Me." In *Miami Vice*, the music normally reinforced the scene for which it was used. Each episode included three or four songs by highly regarded artists such as Phil Collins, INXS, Augustus Pablo and King Tubby, and Steppenwolf.

These features I have just outlined—from filmic techniques to the integral use of music—provided the televisual emphasis on surface, and it was this emphasis that led a number of commentators to describe the show as postmodern. Perhaps the most complete version of this thesis is Cathy Schwichtenberg's 1986 article titled "Sensual Surfaces and Stylistic Excess: The Pleasure and Politics of *Miami Vice*." Schwichtenberg developed her argument using ideas about simulation drawn from the works of French theorist Jean Baudrillard. She argues that "*Miami Vice* is hyperreal" and explains that "the map precedes the territory. *Miami Vice* is the map—the Art Deco simulacrum—that has engendered South Florida (and beyond) as a territory" (47). She ends by describing her project as "an analysis of surface pleasures" (61). Two years later, R. L. Rutsky published "Visible Sins, Vicarious Pleasures: Style and Vice in *Miami Vice*," in which he argues that "the Miami of *Miami Vice* is a fallen world, a place where the circulation of style tends to merge with the circulation of sin" (79). Like Schwichtenberg, Rutsky is concerned about the relationship between style and pleasure. He argues that *Miami Vice* is unsettling because "the vicarious pleasure of the loss of control" challenges the foundation of social order (82), which Rutsky, reworking the claim of French psychoanalyst Jacques Lacan, calls the law. Certainly, the viewer's moral relationship with the surface pleasures of *Miami Vice* is complex. The fashionable clothes, fast cars, boats, and other stylish items do not belong to Crockett and Tubbs; they belong to the Miami police force and are provided so that the undercover detectives, whose salaries would never allow them to buy such desirable commodities, can blend in with the drug dealers, arms merchants, and their ilk with whom they have to consort. It is these people who have brought this European high fashion taste to America's shores.

What made *Miami Vice* so popular? Was it the radically new, possibly postmodern, MTV-like emphasis on style and surfaces, providing the pleasures of vicarious conspicuous consumption? Or was it the conservative ideology that permeated the program, reassuring its American audience that the lawless outside world—a world seemingly saturated with drug barons, arms dealers, and bent cops—would remain outside the orderly and moral United States? In retrospect, I would have to say that it was both these things. *Miami Vice* stands today as one of the most important programs of its time, reproducing the pleasures and fears of Americans in the 1980s.

Notes

1. A discussion of the racial organization of *Miami Vice* can be found in Abalos.
2. Mann's later films include *The Last of the Mohicans* (1992), *Heat* (1995), *The Insider* (1999), *Ali* (2001), and *Collateral* (2004).

Monty Python's Flying Circus

Marcia Landy

The *Flying Circus* was indeed "something completely different," and it remains one of "the great classics of television comedy" (Wilmut 230). It used television to satirize television, along with other social institutions—medicine, psychiatry, the family, the state's administration of social life, and the disciplining of the sexual body.

The Pythons—John Cleese, Eric Idle, Graham Chapman, Terry Jones, and Michael Palin—were educated at Oxford or Cambridge and had written for and appeared in university revues before turning to television. Similarly, American Terry Gilliam abandoned academic work for a career in TV and film. Carol Cleveland's participation was critical to the success of the series. In the Pythons' experimentation with comedic form on the *Flying Circus*, no individual was singled out. No one person was the "spokesperson," the "anchorman," or the "inspiration" for the series. An examination of the scripts, the acting roles assigned, and the synchronized performances of the members reveals an equitable distribution among the group according to their various talents.

The surreal style and motifs of the series are tied to the changing character of the BBC during the 1960s, its "increasing break away from the cozy image of the 1950s" (Wilmut 57). The BBC had been a major influence in the development of radio and television in the United Kingdom and worldwide, and it was often a target of Python comedy. By 1927, under the directorship of John Reith, the BBC had evolved its identity as a "public service" institution, involving mass cultural uplift and enlightenment and setting the standards of behavior inherited from BBC radio.

One of the major transformations in the medium was occasioned by the breakup of the BBC monopoly and the establishment (mandated by the Television Act of 1954) of the commercial ITV network in 1955 under the aegis of the Independent Television Authority. The BBC underwent significant changes to compete with commercial broadcasting, while maintaining its tradition of quality. Thus the 1960s saw the emergence of new personalities and new programming formats, the most notable being *That Was the Week That Was* and *The Frost Report*, for which future Pythons wrote. The *Flying Circus* appeared during a transitional moment in British media culture, challenging both the public service legacy of BBC programming and the traditions of commercial television; it was a time of worldwide cultural transformation, opening the door to critical approaches to authority and to gendered, generational, sexual, national, and regional identity.

During the first season of the *Flying Circus*, the group experienced minimal opposition to its subject matter or language. When first embarking on the *Flying Circus*, the Pythons were told at the BBC, "Do whatever you like. Within reason, as long as it's within the bounds of common law." Increasingly, opposition was mounted from public pressure groups, politicians, and BBC administrators. Despite the BBC's "proud claim . . . that for the Corporation, censorship does not exist" (Hewison 15), indirect or self-censorship was expected. The Pythons antagonized vocal conservative and fundamentalist constituencies that were part of the growing backlash against the "permissive" society, but the series' popularity persisted.

Monty Python's Flying Circus was also a significant moment in the crossover from British to American television. The appearance of British films on U.S. television beginning in the late 1940s constituted a British ur-invasion. In the 1960s such shows as *Danger Man*, *The Saint*, *The Prisoner*, and *The Avengers* constituted a substantial second wave of British infiltration, influencing the character of American spy serials. With the advent of U.S. public television, "heritage" programming entered the American medium through *Masterpiece Theatre* and the many literary works it introduced.

The *Flying Circus* became part of that invasion. Its comedy has been linked to the Russian scholar Bakhtin's conception of the carnivalesque, a grotesque and disorderly vision of the world in which everything is inverted and altered, and nonsense reveals the tension between convention and conformity. The show's "naughtiness" is associated with bodily functions that cannot or refuse to accept official constraints, identification with animality, irreverence in behavior and action, and forms of language that disrupt reason and meaning, challenging both common and good sense. Nonsense becomes a higher form of sense manifest through body language, the inversion of linguistic categories, and distortions in reigning visual perceptions of people, places, and events.

The *Flying Circus* exemplifies two strategies characteristic of satire: "one is wit or humor founded on fantasy or a sense of the grotesque or the absurd, the other is an object of attack" (Frye 224). As in classical (Menippean) satire, the targets are "pedants, bigots, cranks, virtuosi, enthusiasts, rapacious and incompetent professional men of all kinds" (Frye 209). The grotesque quality of the characters and the situations in which they are placed in the *Flying Circus* relies on "an imaginative playing with the forbidden or the inexpressible" (Thompson, *Monty Python* 8). The sketches self-consciously and irreverently invoke drama, literature (e.g., Shakespeare, Dickens), movies (Hitchcock, Kubrick, Peckinpah), philosophy (Sartre, Kierkegaard), popular music, and painting, along with popular forms of television.

The Pythons' comedy has antecedents in British cinema. The series relied on existing forms of British comedy molded to its own ends. For example, the *Carry On* films, produced from the late 1950s to the 1970s, offered an earthy form of humor. These films were identified with a group of actors (Charles Hawtry, Joan Sims, Kenneth Williams, Sid James, Hattie Jacques) who, in satiric and slapstick fashion, spoofed revered British institutions, the army, the medical profession, classical history, patriotism, leisure life, sexual preferences, and sports. The *Carry On* series also spoofed genre forms—empire films, medical melodramas, and historical films (Jordan 312–28).

The *Flying Circus* is also indebted to BBC radio comedy, particularly the *Goon Show* (originally titled *Crazy People*), which ran from 1951 to 1960 and featured the talents of Spike Milligan (the dominant figure in the group), Harry Secombe, and Peter Sellers. The *Goon Show* was a mixture of strange characters, wordplay, and bizarre sound effects performed at lightning speed. However, while the *Goon Show* "brought situations to their illogical conclusion," the *Flying Circus* took "ideas to their logical conclusion, and then beyond that for a considerable way" (Wilmut 198).

The *Flying Circus* is an encyclopedia of comedy involving gags, slapstick, the grotesque, wordplay, and banter, and its goal is to produce a familiar world, render it strange, but ultimately and paradoxically make it recognizable. The various personas of the Pythons are central to their comedy, and they address the audience directly in their character roles and also as themselves. Direct address or its semblance is crucial to many forms of comedy. As Steve Neale and Frank Krutnik write: "Direct address to camera (in the form of a look and/or comment) and references to the fiction are just two of the most obvious—and obviously transgressive—devices used very frequently in comedies to draw attention to their artifice, to highlight the rules by which it is governed and to raise a laugh" (90).

Increasingly, the series capitalizes on and exploits the segmented character of television time. However, in its profligate "waste" of time through the disavowal, interruption, repetition, and lack of closure of many sketches, the *Flying Circus* calls attention to the continuous and indiscriminate character of time inherent to the televisual. One is always in media res, and although individual programs have their time slots, the medium absorbs all that has preceded it—radio, theater, fiction and nonfiction cinema, and the recording of live performances. Television's immediacy and liveness are often invoked in the *Flying Circus*. Through the appearance of randomness, the *Flying Circus* calls attention to the character of television as a "continuous flowing river of experience" (Smith, *Television* 2). This "flowing river" is also characterized by the segmentation of units of time and by "interruption," all of which find their way into the *Flying Circus*'s address of the medium. The format of the *Flying Circus* reveals that, unlike variety show skits, the episodes have no closure, no strong culminating punch line.

The use of animation contributes to the hybrid character of the *Flying Circus*. Although Gilliam's animation is connected to the motifs developed in the sketches, it is not mere extension or "support." The fanciful animation, like the appealing images of each of the Pythons, allows entry into a world of unreason, where time and space are disordered. For instance, the "Wacky Queen" sketch combines photographic cutouts and speeded-up motion as if a silent film were being shown at the wrong speed. The emphasis on sadistic acts by cartoon figures through images of dismemberment, decapitation, cannibalism, explosions, and various forms of physical mutilation is an invitation to contemplate a world that contradicts altruistic and benign conceptions of behavior.

In their cavalier treatment of time, the sketches reveal that the commodity television has to offer is the packaging and selling of time. In one sketch, "The Time on BBC1," a voice-over (Palin) intones: "Well, it's five past nine and nearly time for six past nine. On BBC2, now it'll shortly be six and a half minutes past nine. Later on this evening it'll be ten o'clock and at 10:30 we'll be joining BBC2 in time for 10:33, and don't forget tomorrow when it'll be 9:20. Those of you who missed 8:45 on Friday will be able to see it again this Friday at a quarter to nine." A second voice-over (Jones) says, "You're a loony," and the first voice-over responds, "I get so bored. I get so bloody bored."

In other sketches involving the BBC, the Pythons call attention to the economic dimensions of television production. They emphasize the relations between television time and monetary value through advertising, sponsorship, and reception, making it evident that "the television image is held at a pressure point between innumerable institutions—of regulation, of the market-place, of expressed and inchoate opinion" (Smith, *Television* 1). Sketches such as "Blackmail," a ludicrous treatment of quiz shows, underscore the connections between time and money, as does, more explicitly, the sketch "The BBC Is Short of Money." In "The Money Program," the presenter (Idle) announces, "Tonight on 'The Money Program,' we're going to look at money. Lots of it. . . . For it's money, money, money that makes the world go round."

The Pythons' transgressive treatment of television involves a focus on visibility: what people see, what eludes their gaze through habituation, and what might be seen differently. A technique employed by the *Flying Circus* to upset accustomed viewing responses is what Roger Wilmut calls the "format sketch." It functions by taking a familiar format, emptying the content, and replacing it "with something ludicrous" (Wilmut 198). For example, in "Hell's Grannies," a sketch ostensibly involving news reportage on crime, the rebellious criminals are not young men but old women dressed in leather, creating havoc on motorcycles, robbing, stealing, and assaulting people on the street.

Predictable television and film forms are defamiliarized, as in "The Attila the Hun Show" featuring Cleese, Palin, Chapman, Idle, and Cleveland (the token woman on the series). The linking of recognizable stock film footage (drawn from several archival sources) produces a jarring effect. Both the "epic" cinematography and the sitcom are drained of their familiar contexts and made to appear ludicrous. The sketch begins with an image of Huns on horseback accompanied by a conventional voice-over providing a pompous commentary on "the once mighty Roman Empire . . . exposed to the Barbarian hordes to the east." However, this mock epic is quickly transformed into a domestic situation comedy set in an American-style living room as Attila returns home after a day's work:

> ATTILA (Cleese): Oh darling, I'm home.
> MRS. ATTILA (Cleveland): Hello, darling. Had a busy day at the office?
> ATTILA: Not at all bad. [Playing to the camera.] Another merciless sweep across Central Europe.
> [Canned laughter.]
> MRS. ATTILA: I won't say I'm glad to see you, but boy, am I glad to see you.
> [Enormous canned laughter and applause. Enter two kids.]
> JENNY (Chapman): Hi, Daddy.
> ROBIN (Palin): Hi, Daddy.
> ATTILA: Hi Jenny, hi Robby. [Brief canned applause.] Hey, I've got a present for you two kids in that bag. [They pull out a severed head.] I want you kids to get ahead.

The eruption of such scenes in the sanitized world of sitcoms renders the familiar world grotesque. Later in the program, Attila is reintroduced in "The Attila the Bun" sketch by means of animated images of a vicious rampaging bun, unleashing even more transgressive aspects of Python humor.

The uses and abuses of language play a prominent role in most of the sketches. Often, the play on words seems nonsensical, bearing no relation to meaning. In some instances, the words are encrypted in sign language, anagrams, or syntactical distortion. In others, the interaction between two characters relies on the refusal of one to understand the other by means of confusing, deforming, or willfully misunderstanding his words. The emphasis on mutilated forms of language reinforces a major philosophical issue in the *Flying Circus:* that the illogicality or madness of the contemporary world is revealed through pathological forms of communication perpetuated through media. This "pathology" in language is manifest in "The Man Who Says Words in the Wrong Order" ("Good morning, Doctor. Nice year for the time of day") or "The Man Who Only Speaks the Ends of Words."

Many of the sketches portray commercial negotiations gone awry. In "Dead Parrot," a customer (Cleese) enters a pet shop and complains to the owner (Palin) that he has been sold a dead parrot. The owner denies that the parrot is dead. He insists that the bird is only resting, offering a psychological explanation: as a "Norwegian" parrot, the bird is homesick for the fjords. Exasperated, the customer takes the bird, dashes it to the floor, and shouts in exasperation: "This parrot is no more. It has ceased to be. It's expired and gone to see its maker. This is a late parrot. It's a stiff. Bereft of life, it rests in peace. If you hadn't nailed it to the perch, it would be pushing up the daisies. It's rung down the curtain and joined the choir invisible. It's an ex-parrot."

Another famous Python sketch is Cleese as "The Minister of Silly Walks." The choreographed and exaggerated movements ridicule the conformity that trickles down from the various government ministries. The "silly walk" also visualizes the Python concern with the captive body, emphasizing the rigidity of the back, the spastic character of each leg, one raised after the other to suggest the loss of the freedom to control movement (reminiscent of Tourette's syndrome). The sketch relies in part on its spoofing of bureaucracy, through gestures similar to those of patients in mental hospitals and indicative of the discipline and control of the gesture.

The series is also cognizant of its viewers. Woven throughout the *Flying Circus* are the "Vox Pops"—the voices of the people—representing commonsensical responses to events expressed in terms of nostalgia for bygone times and a sense of righteousness often couched in terms of good and bad taste. The "Gumby," for example, is "a brainless subhuman with rolled-up trousers, round steel-rimmed spectacles, braces, a small moustache, and a handkerchief with the corners knotted as a head piece" (Wilmut 202). The Gumbies embody the problematic character of TV as they condescend to "elevate" the "man on the street." The "Pepperpots" too, in the character of Pythons dressed as housewives, offer a domestic version of the "Vox Pops." Also playing a key role are the "letters" from disgruntled, morally offended patrons, clergymen, and military "men" (of uncertain gender). In "Apology," a voice-over reads a rolling caption, disavowing "disgusting" material: "The BBC would like to apologize to everyone in the world for the last item [Sam Peckinpah's *Salad Days*]. It was disgusting and bad and thoroughly disobedient and please don't bother to phone up. . . . And please don't write in either because the BBC is going through an unhappy phase at the moment—what with its father dying and the mortgage and BBC2 going out with men."

As time passed, the series attained cult status. In 1989 reviewer

Andrew Clifford wrote, "Twenty years on and the best of Monty Python still outshines its imitators in sheer comic inventiveness. No other comedians have inspired such a devoted, indeed virtually addicted following" (42). In 1998, at the Aspen Reunion of the group (minus Chapman, who died in 1989), the *Flying Circus* was lauded as "groundbreaking comedy and groundbreaking television . . . the group created countless quotable bits that have entered comedy history" (Weber E1).

Monty Python's Flying Circus continues to be rebroadcast, and videos and DVDs of all the episodes have been released. The series has maintained its cult status as new generations discover the Pythons. Plays and books—biographies and critical studies—appear regularly by and about the individual members of the group (as witnessed by *Spamalot*). The Pythons appear at reunions and individually on television talk shows in the United States and elsewhere. The popularity of the series internationally (for example, in Germany and Japan) contradicts the claim that comedy appeals exclusively to a national constituency, given the cultural and linguistic idiom with which it is often associated. Particularly in today's global age, the series is testimony to television's creative potential to transcend national and cultural boundaries.

My So-Called Life

Michele Byers

There is no question that *My So-Called Life* (*MSCL*) should be counted among the series we call cult TV. Like so many series that have become cult classics, it enjoyed the brief, dramatic life of a holiday sparkler, going out too fast and leaving us blinking our eyes against the spots of light left in the empty space of its absence. The cult status of *MSCL* is solidified not only by the avidness of its fans (now as then)[1] but also by the moment of its introduction into the world of popular culture. That is, *MSCL* is not only a great show, with great characters living out great stories; it is also an important marker of a massive change in the way we make and watch television.

For anyone who missed this gem of a series, *MSCL* tells the story of Angela Chase (Claire Danes), an average sophomore at Liberty High School in the Pittsburgh suburbs. The series opens with Angela's turbulent move into disgruntled adolescence as she ventures out of the middle-class life safely circumscribed by her family and dips her toes into the wider world (at least as defined by the fictional Three Rivers suburb that is her universe). This toe-dipping begins when Angela jettisons her best friend Sharon Cherski (Devon Odessa) and long-suffering neighbor Brian Krakow (Devon Gummersall) in favor of some newer, cooler friends: wild-child Rayanne Graff (A. J. Langer), gay but not-quite-out-of-the-closet Rickie Vasquez (Wilson Cruz), and the cutest boy to ever lean against a locker, Jordan Catalano (Jared Leto). This change causes endless frustration to the Chase parents, Patty (Bess Armstrong) and Graham (Tom Irwin), who are going through growing pains of their own.

MSCL has an important pedigree. Marshall Herskovitz and Ed Zwick were looking to follow up their real yet cerebral hit *thirtysome-*

From left: Angela Chase (Claire Danes), Rickie Vasquez (Wilson Cruz), Rayanne Graff (A. J. Langer), and Brian Krakow (Devon Gummersall) talk in front of their lockers in *My So-Called Life*.

thing. Writer Winnie Holzman was up and coming. ABC was looking to them to create something brilliant to contribute to its winning family lineup. But what was finally laid on the table didn't quite fit the bill. As Holzman writes, ABC kept asking: "Who is this for?" (2). The question makes sense: *MSCL* wasn't really a family drama, but it wasn't really a teen series either. It was trying to be both, or, rather, the network was trying to make it into both. The network was reluctant to bank on a teen demographic—especially one that placed so much weight on teen girls—so it continually exerted pressure on the series' writers and producers to give the family and adult dramatic arcs more airtime (Murphy 167). Given the realities of the 1990s, this was not particularly remarkable. And although it would probably be a different story today, we cannot know whether anything could have saved the series in the end.

In the early 1990s, American television was moving from what was still basically a tripartite network system to something infinitely more complicated and fragmented. Under the old system, executives were still looking for massive, broad-based audiences cobbled together from as many demographic segments as possible; niche marketing and the recognition of teens (especially teen girls) as a key group was still a few years off. In this way, *MSCL* was, like many works of genius, a little too far ahead of its time. It was a bit too early to cash in on the mainstreaming of grunge and riot grrrl culture, as evidenced by its superb use of indie bands such as Bettie Serveert ("Father Figures," 1.4), Juliana Hatfield ("Other People's Mothers," 1.10; "So-Called Angels," 1.15), Urge Overkill ("Life of Brian," 1.11), and Buffalo Tom ("Why Jordan Can't Read," 1.7; "Self-Esteem," 1.12). It was a bit too early for the heavy stunting that would become a staple of television in the 2000s with the growth of reality TV. But it was hinted at in episodes such as "Halloween" (1.9), where Angela appears to go back in time when she dresses up in 1960s garb and finds herself in pursuit of a troubled boy who supposedly died at Liberty High on Halloween night 1962, and "So-Called Angels" (1.15), the Christmas episode where Angela and Patty learn life lessons from a street kid (played by Juliana Hatfield) who, we later learn, is already dead, having frozen to death. Most of all, it was too early to bank on the idea that teen girls were a worthwhile market in their own right, something that would become all too evident with shows that followed, such as *Buffy the Vampire Slayer*, *Popular*, and *Veronica Mars*.

MSCL was slated to air in the 1993–1994 season but wasn't actually broadcast until the late summer of 1994. By February 1995 it was gone. That is, the first season was over, but the show's status remained uncertain. Then, in an unusual move, ABC licensed *MSCL*'s nineteen existing episodes to MTV, where it ran consistently until 1997, two years after its official cancellation. The transfer of affiliation never did a lot for *MSCL*'s ratings, but those ratings meant something entirely different in these two televisual spaces. MTV was hip and youthful, and *MSCL* added a different (but perhaps contiguous) discourse of realism to that already offered by the still new *Real World* (which debuted in 1992). In the twelve- to thirty-four-year-old niche that MTV craved, *MSCL* never failed to deliver. In a way, the series didn't find a real home until it left ABC.[2]

Something else was happening in 1995. At about the same time *MSCL* was fighting a losing battle to stay afloat on ABC,[3] Time Warner (as the major stakeholder) was launching a new venture—a television network (sometimes referred to as a "netlet") known as the WB. The WB took a couple of years to find its footing, but it eventually did so with *Buffy the Vampire Slayer* in 1997.[4] *Buffy*, like *MSCL*, was the critics' darling. It created avid fans. It had a wide Web presence in the relatively early days of such things. Despite the fact that *Buffy*, on one level, concerned itself with vampires, slayers, and demons—not to mention Southern California—like *MSCL*, it was heralded for its great realism in representing adolescence and the human condition.[5] There was yet another similarity: *Buffy*'s performance in the ratings game was less than stellar, garnering between 4 million and 6 million viewers for an average episode. But the game itself had changed. Those 4 million to 6 million viewers were enough to make *Buffy* the linchpin of the WB's fledgling lineup—virtually none of its shows had as many as 8 million viewers—whereas *MSCL*'s roughly 10 million viewers had seemed to spell disaster for ABC just a few years earlier.[6]

Given how much the critics seemed to like *MSCL*, some people wondered why so few viewers tuned in. The inimitable Joss Whedon ("Reality TV" 5–6) gives us a hint in his contribution to the 2007 DVD box set:

> While [*Beverly Hills, 90210*] dealt with issues, they were the sort of issues grown-ups think kids should be worrying about, not what they actually were. And while it ruled the airwaves and began the aging down of the television landscape ... something came and went, like a flash of gold at the bottom of a riverbed that's gone by the time you pan for it. The show I had dreamed of, only better, far better than my little dreams. I saw the ads, knew the Zwick, Herskovitz pedigree, anticipated it with glee. And when the pilot aired, idiotic America turned the show right off. And so did I. My shame is not small. . . . I have pined for reality and when someone showed it to me I passed.

In fact, *MSCL*'s closest predecessor was not *90210*. In my view, the series is much closer to the late 1980s Canadian teen series *Degrassi Junior High* (later *Degrassi High*), another show a lot of people overlooked. *Degrassi*, like *MSCL*, was lauded for its depiction of the tumultuous lives of average teens. Although the series are distinct in many ways, both are set apart from others of their ilk by their authenticity in depicting teens. Both captivated viewers not by showing them fantasy worlds but by offering them glimpses of lives very much like their own. And for some, this authenticity was just too close for comfort: we see "reality" and, like Joss, we pass.[7] But not everyone passed. There were, after all, those 10 million weekly viewers who were devastated when *MSCL* was pulled prematurely. The series had a strong Web presence that helped its fans mobilize to try to overturn ABC's cancellation—something that happens a lot more frequently today. Steve Joyner and his Operation *Life* Support (a grassroots, Web-based organization that tried to save the series) did, however, help bring *MSCL* and its devoted fans to the attention of the wider world.

Through the all-too-brief nineteen episodes of *MSCL*, we follow Angela Chase's vacillations between her old life and her potential new ones, between the safety of childhood and the looming unknown of adulthood, between the mainstream that is her birthright and the marginal worlds she is intrigued enough to visit. And it all begins with her hair. Perhaps the most enduring image from the series is Angela dyeing her hair a lovely "Crimson Glow" and intoning in the seriousness that is surely a hallmark of adolescence: "School is a battlefield, for your heart. So when Rayanne Graff told me my hair was holding me back, I had to listen. 'Cause she wasn't just talking about my hair, she was talking about my life." The use of voice-over narration is one of the central elements of the series' style. Usually it is Angela's voice we hear, as she takes us through the emotional landscape we have traversed with her in the course of a particular episode.[8] Voice-overs are used in a more stunting fashion by Brian ("Life of Brian," 1.11) and by Angela's little sister Danielle (Lisa Wilhoit; "Weekend," 1.18),[9] but usually Angela provides us with the key.

MSCL distinguishes itself through the choices it makes in terms of character and narrative arc; in these ways, it is also more like *Degrassi* than *90210*. Angela's supposed averageness is a good example of this. In "Self-Esteem" (1.12) the students read Shakespeare's Sonnet 130, and Brian interprets the writer as loving his mistress because "she's not just a fantasy. She's got like—flaws. She's real."[10] Angela's realness is conveyed in a variety of ways: she gets pimples, she often wears the same baggy overalls and plaid shirts, she doesn't command a lot of male attention (except from the nerdy Brian), she's bad at math, she makes bad (but not monumental or irreparable) choices. *MSCL* also distinguishes itself by being one of the first shows, if not *the* first, to have a gay teen in a key, ongoing role: Wilson Cruz as Rickie Vasquez.[11] Like many of the series' issue-oriented arcs, Rickie's struggle to come to terms publicly with his sexual orientation is integrated into the broader series rather than introduced as "very special" episodes featuring "very special" guest stars.

This way of tackling of social issues—that is, making them problems of the core cast rather than of special guest stars—is a cornerstone of

MSCL. In one short season the series deals with its fair share of issues: guns in school ("Guns and Gossip," 1.3), parental infidelity ("Father Figures," 1.4), illiteracy ("Why Jordan Can't Read," 1.7), drug and alcohol abuse ("Other People's Mothers," 1.10), homelessness and child battery ("So-Called Angels," 1.15). But in many ways, *MSCL* really distinguishes itself by its treatment of more mundane social issues and observations: Angela, passing her father on the way from the shower to her room wearing only a towel and observing, "my breasts have come between us"; Brian slowly riding his bike in circles in front of Angela's house; Angela realizing that Rayanne has slept with Jordan, that her good-girl former best friend isn't a virgin, that it was Brian who wrote the beautiful letter she had so hoped was from Jordan. In my mind, the beauty of these episodes is in the way they threw me—painfully, delightfully—back into my fifteen-year-old body, my fifteen-year-old self.

Angela paved the way for a lot of TV heroines who came after her. They are a disparate lot—Buffy Summers, Joey Potter, Felicity Porter, Veronica Mars, Lindsay Weir—but they share a particular brand of mythic normality that they either embody or crave. For many viewers, this means that these characters either are or wish they were like us. The stars had to be in precisely the right alignment for the emergence (even fleetingly) of a series like *MSCL*, but its legacy lingers on and on.

Notes

Although the material here is original, some of it is similar to what appeared in my essay included in the 2007 *My So-Called Life* DVD box set.

    1. It is especially popular with girls, which was seen both as a blessing and as partly responsible for the show's eventual demise. For more on this, see Murray; Murphy.

    2. For a more extensive discussion of this shift from ABC to MTV, see Murphy. In Canada, the series ran on Showcase.

    3. For a discussion of this type of mortality metaphor in relation to *MSCL*, see Diffrient.

    4. The WB followed this up by courting the teen audience formerly dominated by FOX with series such as *Dawson's Creek*, *Felicity*, *Roswell*, *Popular*, *Smallville*, and *One Tree Hill*.

    5. There are many articles that discuss this aspect of *Buffy*. For one good summary that came as the series went off the air, see Stafford.

    6. It's not surprising that *Buffy* had a little something of *MSCL* in its gene pool. Joss Whedon has admitted that he saw the show as a "benchmark," describing *Buffy* as the progeny of *The X-Files* and *MSCL* (see Lavery, "Afterword" 211–16).

7. See, for example, Shalit.

8. Several people have pointed out that Angela follows the pattern of the "unreliable" narrator, more familiar from the realm of literary fiction. Angela's observations about her own life and the lives of others, we are cautioned, should be taken with the proverbial grain of salt. This unreliable quality, however, reinforces rather than disrupts the series' feeling of authenticity. See, for example, Bell.

9. Shifting the focus in this way also highlights the particular partiality of Angela's voice-over perspective, which is familiar to viewers.

10. This brings us back to the unreliable narrator. Although we know that Brian is thinking about Angela as he responds, this requires us not only to accept his words (that Angela is "real") but also to accept that these words make sense when spoken in relation to the gorgeous Claire Danes.

11. For an insightful discussion of this, see Battis, "My So-Called Queer."

Mystery Science Theater 3000

Robert Holtzclaw

Poor, unlucky Joel Robinson. A hardworking custodian at Gizmonic Institute, he is seized by his diabolical bosses and rocketed into space. As if that isn't traumatic enough, once in orbit he is forced to watch really bad movies while his villainous captors monitor his mind and his reactions. Their demonic goal? To determine the effects of horrible films on a person's stability and, ultimately, sanity, as part of their plot to take over the world. Joel's only hope for survival is to poke fun at the movies and banter back at them in an attempt to weaken their power to destroy his mental fortitude. Such is the premise of *Mystery Science Theater 3000* (*MST3K*), which ran for almost 200 episodes over an eleven-year period (1988–1999).

Background, Awards, and Recognition

After beginning as a very low-budget local production for independent television station KTMA Channel 23 in Minneapolis–St. Paul, *MST3K* moved to the national cable network Comedy Central (originally known as the Comedy Channel) from 1989 to 1996 and then to the Sci-Fi Channel until its cancellation in 1999. Along the way, *MST3K* received eight Cable Ace Award nominations (for Best Comedy Series, Best Writing, and Best Art Direction) and two Emmy nominations (for writing) during its run. Additionally, the program received a prestigious Peabody Award in 1993; the award citation referred to *MST3K* as "an ingenious eclectic series" that references "everything from Proust to *Gilligan's Island* [and] fuses superb, clever writing with wonderfully terrible B-grade movies" (Peabody Awards).

A decade after its cancellation, memory of the series endures. Recent indicators of its continued cultural presence and significance include recognition in two mainstream periodicals. In August 2007 *Time* magazine published "The 100 Best TV Shows of All Time." In that alphabetical (unranked) list, *Mystery Science Theater* can be found alongside such classics as *All in the Family*, *I Love Lucy*, *The Sopranos*, and *Seinfeld*. In its appreciation of the series, *Time* notes: "This basic-cable masterpiece raised talking back to the TV into an art form. . . . It filled the snarky role of blogs before blogs existed. From the vantage of *MST3K*'s lonely Satellite of Love, pop culture was hell, and heaven too."

Also in the summer of 2007, *TV Guide* released its revised list of the top thirty cult shows ever. In defining the term *cult*, the magazine alluded to such qualities as the fervency of a program's audience support, the degree to which its language and catchphrases enter the audience's vocabulary, fans' determination to amass collectibles and memorabilia, and conventions at which like-minded souls can congregate and share their passion. *MST3K* was ranked at position thirteen, between number twelve *Pee-Wee's Playhouse* and number fourteen *Battlestar Galactica* ("*TV Guide* Names the Top Cult Shows Ever"). (For the record, *Star Trek* finished first.) Although this represented a drop of two spots from its position in the original 2004 *TV Guide* list (newcomers *Jericho* and *Lost* slid in above it), *MST3K*'s lofty ranking among all the programs in television history indicates its entrenched position in the pantheon of cult television. And based on the aforementioned *Time* recognition, it holds a noteworthy place in the world of television in general as well.

The Nature of *MST3K*'s Appeal

We now return to poor, unlucky Joel Robinson, marooned, against his will, in space. With no human (or animal) companionship, his loneliness and his creativity compel him to find sufficient materials on his spaceship prison to construct four robots to keep him company through the endless days, nights, and lousy movies: Tom Servo (who looks like a gumball machine), Crow T. Robot, Gypsy, and Cambot. His new friends Tom and Crow join Joel in the screening room each time the mad scientists force him to watch a terrible film. The three of them fight the increasing sense of depression and desperation brought on by the onslaught of lame scripts, bad acting, and vile cinematography by yelling back at the movie screen, ridiculing the actors, the dialogue, and

Their pain was our pleasure: Joel Robinson (played by Joel Hodgson) with Crow T. Robot (left) and Tom Servo (right), space captives and hosts of *Mystery Science Theater 3000*.

anything else they can think of to stave off the effects of continuous exposure to terrible films.

In a sense, *MST3K* engages viewers on three distinct (but related) levels: (1) the perverse allure of the rotten movies themselves, a who's who of low-budget, incomprehensibly scripted, delusions-of-grandeur-laced disasters; (2) the rapid-fire commentary of Joel, Tom, and Crow as they watch the movies, riffing on what they see and hear in a scattershot barrage of popular culture references to other movies, television programs, politics, sports, and numerous other topics; and (3) the story of the space captives themselves (and their evil captors on Earth), developed episode by episode until each of the robots has a personality of its own, in addition to the character of Joel and, later, his replacement in space, Mike Nelson.

What is it about human nature that makes people (some of them, anyway) enjoy suffering through egregiously bad pieces of "entertainment"? Many people, it seems, have a perverse love for horrible songs, insufferable television shows, and, perhaps most of all, grade-C (and lower) movies. There is no humor like the unintentional humor of movies that strike the funny bone even as they aim for drama or the grandiose treatment of eternal themes; that aim for suspense and tension but collapse into unintended absurdity. *MST3K* provides a parade of such creations, as well as movies that actually attempt to be funny, fail miserably, and then transform into a different kind of comedy based on abject failure itself. Only a special breed of cinematic misfire is worthy of the *MST* treatment, yet somehow, the program found almost 200 examples. It's not enough to be bad—the movie must be so bad that it circles back around and becomes enjoyable precisely because of its own (lack of) merit. Thus the movies themselves, even without the sarcastic remarks of Joel or Mike and the robots, are part of the reason for *MST3K*'s cult success.

But the commentary of these orbiting space prisoners to defend against the attack of the rotten movies is most assuredly a key component in *MST3K*'s cult success as well. The retorts come at a breakneck pace, with more than 500 jokes or wisecracks per ninety-minute episode (Hidalgo). Some of the comments are extremely abstract and perhaps indecipherable in their connection to the material onscreen, while others are quite literal and even childlike in their elementary nature (making fun of someone's appearance is a favorite tactic). Not all are laugh-out-loud funny, but the batting average is quite high, and attempting to figure out the sometimes tenuous correlation between the caustic remarks and the action onscreen is part of the fun. Whether the joke falls flat or needs more thought to be understood, time is tight because the next free-associating observation will most likely be launched in a matter of seconds. Viewers get a feeling of accomplishment when they figure out some of the more obscure references, as well as a feeling of kinship in listening to the sarcastic comments. We have all yelled back at the television or perhaps muttered something to our moviegoing companions in response to a particularly inept scene or line of dialogue. As Joel Hodgson (the actor portraying Joel Robinson) said in an interview, "It's about liberty, in a small, goofy way" ("Epilogue")—the freedom to talk back to the screen and let the movie know that you know it's mediocre at best and that you can project your own enjoyment into the narrative to compensate for what the film has failed to provide.

Although each episode can easily stand alone, since it's built around a separate movie, *MST3K* also has the appeal of a continuing television series in the sense of character development and cross-episode referencing. Through the conversations and skits that run between movie-viewing segments in each episode, regular viewers come to know the distinct personalities of Joel, his robot pals, and the villains on Earth, including Dr. Clayton Forrester, Frank, and, later in the series, the equally evil Pearl Forrester and her associates. When Joel Hodgson decided to leave the program in 1993, his character was able to exit the spaceship thanks to an escape pod discovered in a box of "Hamdingers," and he was replaced by new captive Mike (played by Mike Nelson). Mike brought a somewhat different interpretation to the character of a human space captive, and his persona was developed through the second half of the series' run. Thus viewers are treated to a separate movie and narrative each week while simultaneously spending time with familiar characters whose personas develop as the series unfolds.

In addition, some of the characters' comments as they watch the dismal movies are actually references to earlier episodes of the program and earlier bad films they have seen. A particularly ridiculous line of dialogue, for example, may be recalled by the characters and shouted at the screen during a movie viewed several episodes (or years) later, and some characters from earlier movies reappear (played by *MST* personnel) in later skits. Recognizing these references to earlier episodes is yet another way that loyal viewers feel "in the know" and another way that *MST3K* transcends the concept of single-episode stand-alone movies and becomes more like a continuing comedy-adventure series. This concept of "insider knowledge"—a legacy or blueprint to a show that makes certain elements fully understandable only to regular viewers—is a key component in the development of cult status.

Somehow, the creative team behind *MST3K* was able to find almost 200 movies (along with some memorably awful short films) worthy of being featured on the program. Although that was very good news for fans, it also points out, somewhat disturbingly, the vast and boundless depths of available material, and had the show continued even longer, there would have been no shortage of movies out there waiting to be ridiculed. As *MST* actor-writer Mike Nelson noted, "You think the series is done, you think you've had it, and then a movie like *Hobgoblin* shows up and injects new life into the show. Or a new death, depending on how you look at it" (Wolk).

Although every devoted viewer has his or her personal list of must-see episodes, certain films have emerged as consensus examples of *MST3K* at its best. The formula for a classic episode is easy to describe but harder to capture: one part truly horrible movie; one part particularly inspired commentary from the three viewers (Mike or Joel and the two robots) seen in silhouette in the bottom right-hand corner of the screen; and one part especially manic and absurd sketches, parodies, and battles between good and evil during the segments between the featured movie. Among the episodes with the most devoted followings are those featuring the movies *Manos: The Hands of Fate*, *The Amazing Colossal Man*, *Teenage Caveman*, *Attack of the Giant Leeches*, several in which the creature "Gamera" fights an array of evil monsters, *Swamp Diamonds*, *I Accuse My Parents*, and *Sidehackers*. Although most of the movies had, at least ostensibly, science fiction or horror themes, *MST*'s choices also included (purported) comedies, dramas, and even, in its final season, *Hamlet*.

After nearly 200 episodes, the program's cancellation was still met with widespread sadness among its many devoted fans. Actually, *MST3K* was canceled twice: in late 1995 Comedy Central announced that it would drop the show, stating that "seven years is a long time for any show. The ratings have been declining for awhile" (Svetkey, "R.I.P."). Reaction was as extreme and dramatic as the show itself: "Oh, the tragedy! Oh, the humanity!" Benjamin Svetkey wrote in *Entertainment Weekly*. "In what could turn out to be the most notorious cancellation since NBC axed *Star Trek* in 1969, Comedy Central has pulled the plug on *Mystery Science Theater 3000*, the cult hit that's been skewering bad movies for more than seven years." A few months later Svetkey was still not over the shock; he began his short piece about the video release of three *MST* episodes with this heartbreaking reminder: "Some tragedies are so shocking, the horror resonated forever: the crash of the *Hindenberg*. The sinking of the *Titanic*. The cancellation of *Mystery Science Theater 3000*. Who can forget that dark day last December when Comedy Central pulled the plug on the cult TV series?" ("Theater of the Absurdists"). In one of the earliest examples of fan-initiated attempts to rescue a canceled series (now more common with such programs as *Jericho*), *MST* loyalists took advantage of the rapid growth of the Internet to launch Web-based write-in campaigns to save the show, as well as to collect funds to pay for a full-page advertisement in the influential entertainment publication *Daily Variety*. Fortunately, the show was picked up by the Sci-Fi Channel, where it ran for three more seasons before its second cancellation in 1999.

Beyond the Television Series

The mid-1990s saw the attempted expansion of the *MST* domain on several fronts: in 1996 Universal Studios released *Mystery Science Theater 3000: The Movie*, in which Mike and the robots are forced to endure a screening of *This Island Earth*. Through the years, many of the series' television episodes have been released on DVD as well. Two official fan conventions have taken place in Minnesota, sponsored by *MST*'s production company: the first, ConventioCon ExpoFest-A-Rama, was held in 1994, followed by ConventioCon ExpoFest-A-Rama 2: Electric Bugaloo in 1996. The same year saw the release of a book entitled *The Mystery Science Theater 3000 Amazing Colossal Episode Guide*, which, as its title proclaims, is a thorough recounting of the series up to that point, complete with episode summaries and assorted additional interviews and facts. *MST3K* also maintains a strong Web presence (mst3kinfo.com and mst3k.com are good starting points).

In recent years, several of those involved with *MST* have embarked on somewhat similar projects, including Mike Nelson's Web site RiffTrax, which features *MST*-style audio commentaries to accompany the viewing of more recent movies (including *Terminator 3* and *Eragon*). The Film Crew is another Nelson project in which he, Kevin Murphy, and Bill Corbett (the voices of robots Tom and Crow) riff on older movies (with the movies provided as well, unlike RiffTrax). In late 2007 Joel Hodgson also unveiled his new *MST*-esque venture, Cinematic Titanic, in which he joins with other former cast members to once again heckle the screen while viewing bad movies. Thus, although the formats and personnel are not quite the same as they were during *MST3K*'s run, the concept is still very much alive.

The Cosmic Significance

In his 1997 book *Interface Culture*, Steven Johnson looks briefly (as part of a larger argument) at television programs that derive most of their content from other programs rather than generating it themselves, and he examines how this type of programming serves both to contextualize and to provide a spin of sorts on the material it presents. Johnson addresses the rise of "self-referential commentary shows" on television, such as *Talk Soup* (now known as *The Soup*) and *MST3K*, and he rejects the notion that these heavily ironic programs are simply repackaging and feeding off the material of other programs, asserting instead that they are "information filters—data making sense of other data" (32). Viewers have the option of watching the actual source material or, instead, watching it through the filter of the *MST* crew or the host of *Talk Soup*, or even watching music videos through the "filter" of *Beavis and Butthead*. Johnson sees *MST3K* and others like it as part of television's attempt to provide some sort of order or context for the "bewildering sensory overload of the contemporary mediasphere" (Rosenberg, "Interface This"), although he asserts that television's attempts are mostly "clumsy, two-dimensional" and that the real future of such endeavors lies on the Web and beyond (Johnson, *Interface Culture* 38).

Johnson's book was published during the height of *MST3K*'s television run, and his ideas help place the program in a somewhat broader context. Beyond its clear possession of the qualities that mark it as a cult television show, *MST* is also part of the late-twentieth-century growth of postmodern, self-referential programs that spin their material through a popular culture blender and provide meta-commentary on their ostensible subjects, on themselves, and on the media by which they are disseminated. This represents a lot of layers of meaning to place on a show with robots and B movies at its core, but it is a burden that Joel, Mike, Tom, and Crow can carry with ease. *MST3K* is fun, fast, and silly, and it is an insightful reflection of its time and place as well as a program that transcends those parameters. Along with the qualities discussed earlier, these features mark it as true cult television.

The Prisoner

Douglas L. Howard

Before people were ever lost on the island or caught up in the Matrix, before the truth was out there, before *The Truman Show*, *Nowhere Man*, *Twin Peaks*, or *Burn Notice*, there was *The Prisoner*, Patrick McGoohan's short-lived 1960s series that continues to capture viewers' imaginations and influence network television and feature films alike. For almost forty years, critics and fans have been trying to make sense of exactly what they saw onscreen when the thunder crashed and McGoohan's Lotus 7 sped down the highway for the final time. Was it a science fiction show? Was it a spy thriller? Was it a subversive political commentary? Or was it an allegory about the struggle of the individual against the armies of social conformity? Like Number Six himself, the show's brief run has perhaps provoked more questions than it answered, leaving viewers to perpetually chase down its hidden meanings and come to their own conclusions where the stoic former spy provided none. Fans have formed (and continue to form) a variety of clubs, Web sites, and discussion groups dedicated to analyzing and deciphering the series.[1] Robert Sellers even calls it "television's greatest ever cult show" (54). But within its many mysteries and its inherent ambiguities, *The Prisoner* is also an eerily prophetic vision of the postmodern world, with its encroaching military-industrial complex and its invasive technologies, a vision that still speaks to us as we examine the cold steel doors in our own domestic cells.

The Prisoner was born from the Cold War and the cultural fascination with the spy genre in the early 1960s. With the success of Ian Fleming's James Bond novels (and later the iconic motion picture adaptations), among others, the television networks began crafting spy series of their own, including *The Man from U.N.C.L.E.*, *I Spy*, *The Wild*,

Wild West, and *The Saint.* One of the first shows of this type, *Danger Man,* was a half-hour British creation that debuted in England in 1960, "two years before the first Bond film" (Sellers 41), and aired in 1961 in the United States on CBS. *Danger Man* starred Patrick McGoohan as John Drake, a NATO agent who was frequently called on to deal with matters of international security. Although it was canceled in the United States the same year it began (it lasted in England until 1962), Incorporated Television Company (ITC) and its head Lew Grade were convinced that, given the growing popularity of the genre, it could be reworked to appeal to American audiences.

Grade also strongly believed in the marketability of his star. McGoohan had actually been offered the role of James Bond before Sean Connery, but he turned it down "on moral grounds" (Langley 83); Bond's scripted trysts with women conflicted with McGoohan's conservative Catholic upbringing. With a new one-hour format and with Drake now working for the British government's M-9 agency instead of NATO, *Danger Man* returned to British television in 1964 and was given a catchy new Johnny Rivers theme song.[2] ITC repackaged the series as *Secret Agent* when it began its run on CBS in 1965. Although Drake's new adventures and the new format fared much better than the original, the series was canceled a little over a year later, in part because it "was no longer different enough from [other] American programs" (Miller, *Something Completely Different* 42), and it had to compete for viewers with the other spy shows in the network lineups. Sellers, however, suggests that the real reason behind the show's cancellation had more to do with McGoohan himself: he had "grown bored with Drake and wanted out" (54). By most accounts, as McGoohan was getting more and more disenchanted with *Danger Man/Secret Agent,* he was already planning his escape and plotting out *The Prisoner.*[3] Based on his continued faith in his star, Grade was more than willing to support him in another show, so in 1967 (1968 in America), *The Prisoner* was released.[4]

The Prisoner focuses on the trials and tribulations of a former British agent who no sooner resigns from government service than he is abducted and taken to the Village, a secret seaside community for scientists, agents, and government officials who "know too much." (As the first Number Two tells him, "the information in [his] head is priceless," and inasmuch as he "is worth a great deal on the open market," he poses a significant security risk to both sides.) Like the other residents in the Village, McGoohan's character is, upon "Arrival" (the title of the first of seventeen episodes),⁵ immediately reduced to a number (Number Six) and is thereafter subjected to a variety of insidious physical and psychological torments designed to break him down and provide his captors with what they desire most: information.

With a few notable exceptions, each week Number Six squares off against a new Number Two, a new jailer with a different plot to trick or unnerve him and a different plan to reveal the truth behind his resignation.⁶ Although Number Six asserts that they will never break him and that he "will not be pushed, stamped, filed, indexed, briefed, debriefed, or numbered" ("Arrival"), almost all the Number Twos confidently maintain that they will, in the end, get what they want from him "by hook or by crook." In some cases, as in "A, B, and C," "The Schizoid Man," "A Change of Mind," and "Living in Harmony," they resort to brainwashing, drugs, and mind control to make Number Six cooperate and confess. In others, such as "The Chimes of Big Ben" or "Many Happy Returns," they convincingly let him believe that he has escaped, only to return him to his "prison" in the Village and restart the struggle. And through it all, the real presence behind Number Six's imprisonment, the puppet master, Number One, remains a mystery.

While *The Prisoner*, like its jaunty Ron Grainer theme music, carries overtones of the spy thriller—from its former *Danger Man/Secret Agent* star to its weekly assortment of unscrupulous villains and its high-tech gadgetry—it clearly departs from (and responds to) the genre. For one thing, McGoohan's agent, unlike James Bond, Napoleon Solo, John Steed, and many other spies with ultracool names, is never named—a fact, as Jeffrey Miller notes, that has controversially led viewers of both *Danger Man/Secret Agent* and *The Prisoner* to "plausibly assume that some form of intertextuality was in play" (43) and that Drake is Number Six.⁷ Whereas Bond, the *Mission: Impossible* team, and even Drake himself go undercover and assume other identities to accomplish their missions, this prisoner fights to maintain his identity, particularly in episodes such as "The Schizoid Man" and "Do Not Forsake Me, Oh My Darling," when he suddenly appears to be someone else. Bond's 007 designation has special meaning and value (EON's recent James Bond reboot, *Casino Royale*, shows viewers exactly what he must go through to earn his "license to kill"), but McGoohan's character wants nothing to do with his "Six."⁸ Throughout the series, he has only contempt for the number because it represents an attempt to rob him of his individuality, just as he actively rejects his captors' efforts to make him conform to the

Number Six (Patrick McGoohan, left) resists another attempt at mind control in "The General."

rules and regulations of the Village. As he dramatically asserts at the start of almost every episode, "I am not a number. I am a free man!"

And whereas so many spies, both on television and in film, pride themselves (like Bond) on attracting the company of beautiful women, McGoohan's protagonist, by contrast, largely refuses (like *Danger Man's* Drake) to allow himself to get close to anyone. Even when a black female cat takes a liking to him in "Dance of the Dead," he is quick to make his feelings clear: "Never trust a woman," he tells Mary Morris's Number Two, "even the four-legged variety."[9]

Perhaps the central difference, though, between *The Prisoner* and so many other spy films and series both before and after it is that McGoohan's agent frequently fails. From Dr. No to Hugo Drax, Bond almost always foils the best-laid plans of his nemesis and typically kills him in the end. His superspy descendants, from Solo and Steed to Jason Bourne (who also deals with questions of identity) and Ethan Hunt, generally follow suit. But for all his determination and resourcefulness, Number Six often finds himself at the mercy of Number Two and the forces behind his incarceration, whoever they might be. When he cleverly uses the psychology behind the Village's "human chess game" to identify the other prisoners and plan an escape in "Checkmate," for example, his co-conspirator, the "Rook," betrays him to Peter Wyngarde's Number Two because, in assuming the role of leader in this plot, Number Six also assumes the "air of authority" of a Village guardian. Similarly, after making his way into a secret back room in the town hall at the end of "Dance of the Dead," he violently dismantles a teletype machine in yet another attempt to disrupt the order in the Village and defiantly vows to Morris's Number Two that she "will never win." No sooner does he get these words out, however, than the machine miraculously begins typing again, a sign of just how powerful, persistent, and perpetual the Village's "machinery" and all its sinister forces truly are.[10]

Regardless of how well he fares against the Number Two in question—for instance, by preying on the paranoia of Patrick Cargill's sadistic Number Two in "Hammer into Anvil," he pushes his jailer into a nervous breakdown, and after their pitched psychological battle in "Once upon a Time," Leo McKern's Number Two drops dead—Number Six still finds himself in the Village as the episode comes to a close. He never comes away with definitive answers to the questions he poses to each new Number Two at the start, questions that become his burden as captive (and Number Two's as jailer), just as they become the audience's in watching.[11] Thus, even in his moments of success, he fails within the scope of the larger narrative. Alain Carrazé and Hélène Oswald go so far as to call him "the eternal loser," a description driven home visually at the end of each episode "with symbolic bars closing on his face" (33). According to *The Prisoner Video Companion*, ITC head Lew Grade was initially "skeptical" of the concept of the series precisely because he feared "that viewers would revolt at the idea of their hero failing week after week" (*Complete Prisoner*). Yet Number Six's failure and his consistent rebellion in spite of that failure, as well as what Matt Hills calls the show's "endlessly deferred narrative" (*Fan Cultures* 134),[12] are part of what makes *The Prisoner* so compelling and have contributed to its cult status. Where other spies and other television heroes operate under the premise of weekly success, McGoohan's prisoner is hardly so lucky, and he continues to stand out, in his defiance, against the landscape of predictable dramas and formulaic thrillers.

As a modern-day nightmare or a horrific political allegory, *The Prisoner* has often been compared to the works of Franz Kafka or George Orwell,[13] perhaps because the ambiguous nature of the narrative and the metaphoric nature of the plots immediately lend themselves to such larger readings. Whether Number Six is Drake or not, his deliberate lack of a name on the show makes him a universal figure. As Chris Gregory notes, the name of McGoohan's production company, Everyman Films, "was a reference to an allegorical medieval morality play [*Everyman*] and pointed to the kind of role McGoohan would play" (29). And even though his experiences are largely restricted to the Village—with its iconic visual imagery, its multicolored capes and umbrellas, its aversion therapy rooms, its penny-farthing bicycle logo, and its menacing, spherical, white Rover—the Village does not appear to exist in a fixed location. Nadia tells Number Six that the Village is in Lithuania, "thirty miles . . . from the Polish border," in "The Chimes of Big Ben," but he and his colleagues deduce that it is off the "coast of Morocco, southwest of Portugal and Spain," in "Many Happy Returns." *The Prisoner Video Companion* adds that "the Village [also] appears to be at the end of a tunnel leading to the A20 [highway] in Kent," just outside of London, in "Fall Out" (the final episode), where the specific location shoot is identified as Portmeirion, in northern Wales (*Complete Prisoner*). Essentially, the Village is in all these locations and none of them. Christian Durante explains the allegory bluntly: "We are living in the village. And we are numbers—from our social security number to one of our credit card numbers" (Carrazé and Oswald 20).

Number Six's struggles in the Village thus microcosmically typify the struggles of the individual in a society that increasingly demands conformity and mercilessly attempts to bend all individuals to fit into its social constructs, subscribe to its psychological norms, and commit to its bureaucratic institutions. The episode in which Number Six is encouraged to run for the office of Number Two, "Free for All,"[14] becomes a commentary on democratic elections and the political process as it exists today. Although he initially runs with the intention of using his position to free his fellow prisoners, Number Six's platform is handed to him by the local newspaper, and he is literally brainwashed into a more "Village-friendly" candidate, spouting a sanitized rhetoric in keeping with the philosophies of his captors and promising the community "that their interests are very much [his] own." He cannot speak his mind; rather, he is forced to say what the Villagers and the Village administration want to hear—a pointed statement about the illusory nature of contemporary democracy and how it too has become a prison of a different sort. "A Change of Mind," in contrast, addresses the question of rebellion and antisocial behavior as a cause for public concern. When Number Six is labeled "unmutual" by the Village Welfare Committee for his continued refusal to take part in the community, the other Villagers shun and ostracize him, and he is finally sentenced to "social conversion" therapy and seemingly lobotomized for his crimes. Reminiscent of the way that the community is called on to carry out his death sentence in "Dance of the Dead," the community here, in its inability to accept the rights of the individual, again appears as an angry mob, which Number Six is able to turn to his advantage and against the scheming Number Two. Even CBS was aware of and sensitive to the possible political meanings of these allegories. It pulled "Living in Harmony" from its original run because it felt that a story about a sheriff who refuses to carry his gun could, in Gregory's words, "be interpreted as . . . encouragement to the 'draft dodgers' and the anti–Vietnam war movement" (147).

Long before David Chase went to France to avoid the backlash from the final episode of *The Sopranos*, Patrick McGoohan "took his family to Switzerland" because "he had been forced to go into hiding" after the "fallout" from the final episode of *The Prisoner* (Langley 189). Many viewers and some of the show's creators had expected the series to end conclusively, according to Wesley Britton, like "a version of *Goldfinger*" (107), with answers to all the questions it had posed over the preceding sixteen episodes. McGoohan, however, had other ideas. He rebelled, "Six-like," against a more formulaic ending and turned the final episode into a metaphoric abstraction set against the backdrop of Number Six's release and the end of the Village. In the process, he also created what Sellers describes as "the most controversial television denouement ever" (134).

Having survived Number Two's "ultimate test" in "Once upon a Time," Number Six is taken before a masked, hooded underground assembly, where he is freed from the burden of his number and praised for "gloriously vindicat[ing] the right of the individual to be individual." The president of the assembly offers him the option of leading them or leaving, but the former Number Six chooses to confront Number One, who turns out to be an insane version of himself. (As McGoohan himself later explained, "The greatest evil that one has to fight constantly every minute of the day until one dies is the worser part of oneself" [Langley 232].) Initiating an apocalypse of sorts,[15] McGoohan's "Individual" pushes the button that ignites Number One's rocket, which forces an immediate evacuation of the Village and destroys the Rover. He is driven back to London, along with fellow "revolutionaries" Number Forty-eight and Leo McKern's miraculously revived Number Two, and winds up at his flat with the Butler, who now dutifully serves him.[16] In the final scene, the series ends as it began, with McGoohan racing down the highway in his Lotus 7, beginning the fight to maintain his individuality all over again.[17]

For all the controversy surrounding the last episode, *The Prisoner* continues to be a cult classic, perhaps because its political allegory and its disturbing visions of science, psychology, democracy, the legal system, and the community as they are brought to bear against the individual speak so clearly and so prophetically to what has become the prison of this postmodern world.[18] In considering the current state of "hyperreality" in this age of advanced technology and mass media, Jean Baudrillard suggests that "we already live out the 'aesthetic' hallucination of reality"; "the map . . . precedes the territory," and "perhaps only the allegory of the Empire remains" (146, 166). Knowing only that the forces of his capture are out to break him, Number Six can never know the reality behind the prison, since the simulacra, the allegory, the hallucination have become everything for him (and us) and are all that is left. Even in those moments when he returns or thinks he has returned to London, he can never truly relax because, in this increasingly paranoid scenario, he never knows whether he is involved in yet another plot or stepping into yet another trap. As he angrily tells his superior, the Colonel (who is, in fact, working for Number Two), in "The Chimes of Big Ben," after apparently escaping from the Village, he came back "home because [he] thought [it] was different." In the last episode, after he has left the Village and is once again driving his car through the streets of London, the word "prisoner" still appears over his car and still identifies him and his situation amid the bustling city streets. As we now step out into a world of satellite surveillance (according to the *Guardian*'s Mary Bowers, London is "the most surveilled city in the world"), Web cams, cell phone cameras, and worldwide Internet coverage, individual privacy and personal freedom have never seemed more at risk, and the Village has never seemed more populated. And inasmuch as the postmodern condition has divided us into fragmented identities,[19] the likelihood of "Six" being "One" and of finding our own worst enemies within ourselves seems all the more possible. So ultimately, *The Prisoner* may be an existential 1960s fairy tale of sorts, but like the best television shows, it dares us to look beyond the screen and confront the darker truth as we lock the front door and turn out the light: there is no escape.

Notes

1. Most notably, Six of One: the international *Prisoner* Appreciation Society, has been "recogniz[ing] each individual member's right to interpret the series in his or her own way" for the past thirty years and continues to hold annual conferences in Portmeirion, Wales, where the series was filmed.

2. As Wesley Britton points out, the new theme song "'Secret Agent Man,' with its distinctive guitar hook, became the definitive spy theme, reaching number three on the charts in March 1966" (97).

3. Although Roger Langley states that the question of when McGoohan had the idea for *The Prisoner* and whether it prompted him to leave the show "will [never] be ... satisfactorily resolved," he believes that, based on the short gap between the end of the first show and the production of the second, "McGoohan had been hatching his plan for the 'sequel'" all along (100). One of the other controversies surrounding the creation of the show is who came up with the idea. Although the inspiration for the series is generally attributed to McGoohan—production manager Bernie Williams, for example, maintains that the series "was basically in Patrick's head" (*Complete Prisoner*)—writer and assistant editor Ian Rakoff notes that *Prisoner* script editor George Markstein claimed that "he'd been cultivating the idea since he'd worked for Britain's Intelligence Service during the Second World War" (55).

4. In spite of McGoohan's disenchantment, *Danger Man/Secret Agent* certainly provided a degree of inspiration for his new show. The first episode of *Danger Man*, "View from the Villa," was actually filmed in part in Portmeirion, the location shoot for the Village. Another episode, called "The Prisoner," deals with Drake's attempt to free a man from an embassy in a foreign country. In a third, "Colony Three" (2.3), Drake infiltrates a communist spy camp designed like a British village. As one of the Soviet agents tells him, in a line that could have come straight from *The Prisoner*, "Once people enter Colony Three, they cease to exist."

5. According to Tony Williams, "The initial idea was to shoot thirteen episodes with a production break, then return to complete a probable season of another thirteen" (68). But as Sellers explains, production became "increasingly more expensive and bewildering [and ITC head Lew] Grade decided McGoohan's number was finally up" (134), calling for an end to the show with

the seventeenth episode. Looking back, McGoohan later stated that "seven episodes would have been the ideal number" (Carrazé and Oswald 8). Even the order of the episodes has been a matter of controversy, with *Prisoner* purists, fans, and critics arguing for a variety of different configurations in an attempt to (re)construct the show's "intended master narrative." Part of this controversy comes from differences among the production schedule, the intended order (if McGoohan and the show's creative team did, in fact, have a specific one in mind), and the original televised order. Since the series was in production as it was being aired, Chris Gregory notes that some episodes may have been "shown earlier than intended due to them being completed first" (20n). Adding to this confusion, "in the UK and in some other countries, a different order of episodes was adopted" (Langley 321). But Langley suggests that, within the scope of the larger narrative, the actual order may be irrelevant, "as long as *Arrival* comes first, with *Once Upon a Time* and *Fall Out* at the other end" (321). In light of this debate, I have opted to identify episodes by name only.

6. Leo McKern's Number Two appears in "The Chimes of Big Ben" and "Once upon a Time." Colin Gordon's Number Two returns for "The General" after failing in "A, B, and C." McKern's Number Two also appears in "Fall Out," as does Kenneth Griffith, who plays Number Two in "The Girl Who Was Death" and is the president of the hooded assembly in the final episode, but in both cases, they no longer serve as Number Six's antagonist.

7. As *The Prisoner Video Companion* notes, there are compelling arguments for this connection: "[Script editor] George Markstein has stated for the record that [this was the case]," and Number Six's contact Potter in "The Girl Who Was Death" "was also a confidante of Drake's in *Danger Man/Secret Agent* . . . and was played by the same person in both series" (*Complete Prisoner*). Sellers explains that McGoohan always contested the claim of a connection between the two series, although the actor may have had good legal and financial reasons for doing so: "If he had admitted it, his old *Danger Man* boss, producer Ralph Smart, might have sued, seeing that he and he alone owned the rights to the character" (Sellers 138).

8. The exact meaning of McGoohan's number and its significance on the show is yet another matter of critical debate. Not only is "6" one less than James Bond's "7," but it may also refer to the "devil" and "666," "the number of the beast" (*Complete Prisoner*). Amid the apparent (but illusory) peace of the Village, Number Six consistently rebels, refusing to fit in or behave. Number Six's "infernal" contempt for the Village, however, also contrasts with his role as "modern day prophet" in the series: "like all the Biblical prophets before him, he rebel[s] against norms of society" (*Complete Prisoner*). In terms of the use of numbers on the show in general, Langley refers to the possible influence of the 1965 James Bond film *Thunderball*, in which "enemy agents have numbers instead of names . . . and the person in control is 'Number One'" (100). Like the mysterious Number One in *The Prisoner*, the identity of this central villain is largely kept secret in the film (although he is revealed as the maniacal Ernst Stavro Blofeld in the 1967 follow-up *You Only Live Twice*).

9. As Jeffrey Miller notes in his discussion of Drake's morality in *Danger*

Man/Secret Agent, although women find him attractive, "a look was about all they might hope for in return" (40). M. Keith Booker agrees that "the Prisoner is no Bond," inasmuch as "he seems entirely celibate and does not even appear to like women very much" (75). Gregory points out that "in the Village sexuality appears to be almost completely repressed," a state that "appears to emanate directly from McGoohan himself" and reflects his almost "puritanical" attitude (201).

10. Alain Carrazé and Hélène Oswald believe that Number Six's state of imprisonment at the end of this episode never seems "so hopeless" (116).

11. As Number Six is reminded by Number Two Hundred and Forty in "Dance of the Dead" (and throughout the series), "Questions are a burden to others; answers a prison for oneself."

12. Hills explains that the "'endlessly deferred narrative' typically lends the cult programme both its encapsulated identity and its title." Rather than "revolting" viewers, they are drawn in by the lack of resolution (or the future promise of it) and intrigued by the story line, "which continues without end" (*Fan Cultures* 134).

13. A number of critics have made these literary connections. Brian J. Woodman believes that the show "deals with very Orwellian themes" (941), Roland Topor compares *The Prisoner*'s world to "Huxley's world, but also that of Orwell, Kafka, Lewis Carroll, Ambler, and many others" (Carrazé and Oswald 10), and Chris Gregory describes how "the series . . . moves towards a more Kafkaesque 'psychological allegory'" (61). Tony Williams suggests that Alexis Kanner's "Number Forty-eight" in the last episode also works as "an inverse of 'Nineteen Eighty-Four'" (71).

14. The multiple meanings of this phrase work well here. The election itself implies that the Village is inherently democratic and that Number Six is attempting to make the Village "free for all." But inasmuch as this phrase can also refer to a chaotic brawl, Number Six's candidacy becomes part of yet another Village scheme against him, and on more than one occasion he finds himself fighting against other Villagers in an attempt to escape.

15. Given the apocalyptic imagery at the end of "The Chimes of Big Ben" and the playful recurrence of "pop" in the series, *The Prisoner Video Companion* notes that if "the control room in 'Fall Out' [is] the area to launch a nuclear strike [then] Number Six does press the button" (*Complete Prisoner*). In this regard, the title "Fall Out" itself can also refer to the radioactive consequences of a nuclear explosion and the possibility of a nuclear holocaust.

16. Considering the symbolic significance of these characters, Langley suggests that Number Forty-eight is "youth in rebellion against the establishment," McKern's Number Two is a "former trusted member of the establishment who . . . is being made by authority to pay for his failures," and the Butler "represents the little men of every community, prepared to follow faithfully, like sheep, any established leader" (175).

17. This return to the beginning of the series illustrates what Piers D. Britton and Simon J. Barker call the "clearly defined cyclical aspects [of] the narrative" (115), and it connects to the show's general preoccupation, on both a narrative and a visual level, with "the circle/sphere motif" (114).

18. In examining *The Prisoner* as a "cult," Gregory agrees that "one stimulus" is "the increasing resemblance of the 'world' to the 'Village'" (197).

19. Douglas Kellner explains that, in the postmodern view, "the autonomous, self-constituting subject . . . is fragmenting and disappearing, due to social processes which produce the leveling of individuality in a rationalized, bureaucratized and consumerized mass society and media culture" (233). Thus, within the spirit of the series, the postmodern condition makes prisoners of us all.

Quantum Leap

Lynnette Porter

In February 1996 I attended what I assumed would be one of the last *Quantum Leap* (*QL*) fan conventions. The North Hollywood, California, Leap Con boasted appearances by many actors (including Daniel Roebuck, better known for later roles on *Nash Bridges* and *Lost*) who had played memorable but often only one-episode roles on the NBC series. The crowd enjoyed chatting up the actors and hearing what it was like to make their episodes. But they were really waiting for one man: Scott Bakula.

The actor is so closely identified with his TV character that one of the first lucky ones to address her idol mistakenly called him "Sam." Bakula cocked an eyebrow and feigned annoyance but then launched into another amusing tale about life as Dr. Sam Beckett. Whether as Scott or Sam, the man attracts loyal fans who regularly leap through space, often traveling hundreds of miles to see him. More than a decade later, fans were planning a leap back in time — a highly anticipated 2009 *Quantum Leap* convention to reunite "leapers" and actors on the series' twentieth anniversary. Although Bakula admitted in 1996 that his leaping days were likely over, even if Universal developed a new series, Beckett's loyal fans ensure that his adventures will continue.

In 2007 *TV Guide* ranked *Quantum Leap* number nineteen on its list of Top Cult Shows Ever ("*TV Guide* Names"). Its compelling stories, fine acting, and sympathetic characters inspired fans' cultlike devotion. *QL*'s fandom originated during the "dark ages" of paper newsletters mailed to subscribers and letter-writing campaigns, but it has evolved in the Internet age into Web sites full of discussion boards, fan-fiction archives, media tributes, interviews, and news. Leapers have not only embraced the TV series and its actors but also developed tightly knit communities that raise money for charity—a very "Sam"-type activity.

Quantum Leap debuted on NBC in March 1989 and broadcast its finale in May 1993. Though never a ratings blockbuster (surviving an early cancellation because of an effective fan letter-writing campaign), it quickly endeared itself to audiences and critics because, as critic Howard Rosenberg observed, it "ranks among the boldest, freshest and most-entertaining dramatic series on TV." Bakula won a Golden Globe in 1992; Dean Stockwell (Al) took home a Golden Globe as best supporting actor in 1990. The series won five technical Emmys and garnered nominations or awards from the Academy of Science Fiction, Fantasy, and Horror Films; American Cinema Editors; American Society of Cinematographers; Directors Guild of America; and Viewers for Quality Television, among others.

Beginning in the early 1990s, while the series was still on the air, *QL* spawned other creative endeavors. Between 1990 and 2000 twenty novels were published. Ace Books and later Boulevard/Berkeley Boulevard published the majority in the United States; Corgi and then Boxtree published a few original and some retitled U.S. books in the United Kingdom, where *QL* was shown on BBC2. A series of thirteen Innovation comics between 1991 and 1993 featured stories and news about the series and its actors. Because of Bakula's pre-*QL* stage roles—often in musicals such as *Romance, Romance,* for which he was nominated for a Tony—fans became interested in his singing career. *QL*'s sound track CD, featuring Bakula singing "The Impossible Dream," was a big hit with fans. Episodes on tape and DVD (the season 5 DVD set arrived in 2006) continue to sell well.

The Basics of Leaping

The series' pseudoscientific premise initially categorized *QL* as science fiction. In the pilot episode, physicist Sam Beckett tests his time-travel accelerator chamber when Project Quantum Leap (PQL) is about to be shut down. According to the introductory narration, "Dr. Sam Beckett stepped into the Quantum Leap accelerator ... and vanished! He awoke to find himself trapped in the past, facing mirror images that were not his own, and driven by an unknown force to change history for the better." Sam's version of "string theory" hypothesizes that he can leap within his own lifetime. Time is like a string looped in one's hand: one end represents birth and the other death; the points at which the string crosses itself form a connection to travel out of sequence from one moment to another. Unfortunately for Sam (and for his friend and project monitor Admiral Al Calavicci), the accelerator wasn't quite ready; Sam can't return home or control his leaps. (Later episodes turn philosophical: is God, fate, Sam, or something or someone else controlling Sam's journey?)

When Sam "leaps" into another person, usually just before some crisis point, that person conveniently leaps into PQL's waiting room. The audience sees Sam as the character with whom he has switched places, but the character's friends and family see the person they know. Sam realizes what he looks like and who he has become only when he looks into a mirror. He "makes right what once went wrong" while quite literally viewing the world through someone else's eyes. Televisually and metaphorically, *QL* holds a mirror to more than forty years of U.S. sociopolitical history.

One of *Quantum Leap*'s strengths is its ability to place Sam in a new time and place in every episode, as well as its ability to feature different genres. Thus he can plausibly become involved in such diverse scenarios as tearful family dramas, murder mysteries, romances, and even musicals, such as the *Man of La Mancha*–themed episode "Catch a Falling Star" (2.10). This flexibility elevates *QL* from a simple time-travel sci-fi series like *The Time Tunnel* and allows it to become a platform for multigenre storytelling. *Quantum Leap* set a new standard for time-travel adventures, one that newer series, such as NBC's short-lived *Journeyman*, have so far failed to reach.[1]

Although leaping "Swiss cheeses" Sam's memory, leaving inconvenient holes in his knowledge, he is supported by the intrepid PQL staff, including hybrid computer Ziggy and Sam's devoted human colleagues. *Quantum Leap* emphasizes family ties and deep friendships that can withstand crises and separations; the characters into whom Sam leaps, as well as Sam, his friends, and family (including the wife he doesn't remember leaving behind), tell memorable stories. In particular, fans like the chemistry between Sam/Bakula and Al/Stockwell. Although Sam and Al cannot physically touch—Al is, after all, only a hologram in Sam's world—their touching friendship makes this series a highly memorable buddy road trip.

Leaping among Perspectives

A hallmark of a cult series is its ability to tell stories from a new or unusual perspective. Sam and Al present divergent viewpoints when confronted with ethical dilemmas. Because of their different backgrounds and experiences, plus a generational gap, they often approach controversial topics from opposing starting points. QL "pits an epic hero [Sam] and an anti-hero [Al] against the wrongs that have been done in past lives. The ethical stance of the show is liberal egalitarianism in response to racial issues, women's rights, gay rights, animal rights, and the rights of the disabled and the aged. . . . [Sam] is a moral man faced with often conflicting dilemmas. . . . Al is a more fallible human being who, while often moved by the plight of others, operates on situational ethics" (Wiggins 116). Whereas straight-arrow Sam is monogamous, book smart, and open-minded, womanizing Al bases his responses on life experiences gained from a rough childhood and the military. When Sam tackles issues such as homosexuality in the military, he and Al initially disagree and fail to find common ground but eventually come to understand the other's perspective. Throughout the series, the audience watches Sam and Al's friendship deepen as they discuss controversial topics; if they can bridge such a gap, viewers may reason, so might we all.

During five TV seasons, Sam switches gender several times, leaping into the lives of an unwed pregnant teen ("8 ½ Months," 3.12), a sexually harassed secretary ("What Price Gloria?" 2.4), and a rape victim ("Raped," 4.6). Sam's reactions to a range of women's issues, including motherhood, sexism, rape, and women's liberation, force Al to face facts about his own sexuality. In "What Price Gloria?" Al is attracted to the body of the woman Sam has become; in "Dr. Ruth" (5.14), sexologist Dr. Ruth Westheimer helps Al explore the reasons why he is obsessed with women.

Sam also provides a voice for disenfranchised groups and makes viewers aware of current and past injustices. This gives audiences a character to root for, and it lets them see life from some very different perspectives. For instance, Sam experiences discrimination when he leaps into an African American chauffeur in the segregated South ("The Color of Truth," 1.6). During a leap into a young man with Down syndrome ("Jimmy," 2.8), Sam learns what it's like to be mentally challenged—a very different perspective for the boy genius–turned–theoretical physicist. Nevertheless, genius Sam has never had a job interview, so both he and Jimmy deal with the anxiety of getting that first job. Sam leaps into the life of a blind pianist ("Blind Faith," 2.5) and fears he won't regain his eyesight. He helps a deaf woman achieve her goal to be a dancer ("Private Dancer," 3.14). Using one's abilities to the greatest extent possible is a recurring theme.

In a controversial leap ("The Wrong Stuff," 4.7), Sam even becomes a crash-helmet test chimpanzee in a scientific testing facility, an episode that generated such controversy that, as one critic put it, "You could hear the screams from Hollywood" (Read D8). This episode led to a great deal of discussion about animal rights, and an issue of *Laboratory Primate Newsletter* even addressed the episode (Harper). Although audiences might have laughed at seeing Sam dressed in a diaper and confined to a cage, Bakula (and the scriptwriters) succeed in making the chimp's plight understandable and invoking sympathy. Some characters make the case for animal testing to help protect humans, but others side with the chimps.

Audiences' perceptions of the past are often influenced by TV portrayals of historic events, and *Quantum Leap* regularly provided windows into difficult periods in U.S. history. Especially during its final season, these history episodes, dealing with events such as JFK's assassination, became prime-time events. Although Sam's sometimes awkward introductions to famous people (e.g., Elvis Presley, Marilyn Monroe, Lee Harvey Oswald) may have made season 5 painful for some fans, the series' first four seasons emphasized "little moments" in a character's personal history that coincided with flash points in U.S. history.

QL reminded viewers of important social issues. Sam idealistically believes that one person can change history (or the world) for the better. He grew up in the turbulent 1960s and became a government-funded physicist in the 1980s. At the time the series debuted, Scott Bakula was an attractive, articulate, thirty-four-year-old actor well suited to represent his generation, which was also a large percentage of the audience. Sam's philosophy was consistent with that of many thirty-somethings who grew up during the 1960s and wanted to "right what once went wrong." Those who recall Bill Clinton's first inaugural party might remember the confidence and exuberance of young Democrats in the early 1990s; Sam's idealism fit well in that era.

Although the political climate of the early 2000s is much different from that of the *QL* years, the series' message is still relevant, especially to young viewers who see Sam as a role model (and to their parents, who watched first-run episodes and still admire Sam's lack of cynicism in the face of crisis). In the politically conservative 2000s, *QL* offers an activist worldview seldom seen on network television. *QL* was a voice for its time, but its themes of respect, love, and friendship are timeless.

Leaping into the Next Millennium

Every cult TV series needs at least one good conspiracy theory. *Quantum Leap*'s involves the series' last onscreen image, the haunting message: "Dr. Sam Becket never returned home" ("Mirror Image," 5.22). This was an emotionally shattering statement for fans who longed for Sam to come home for good, but it also introduced a "secret code": Sam's last name was misspelled. Fans didn't buy the idea that a postproduction typo would be broadcast in the final moments of the series' last original episode. Conspiracy-minded fans then concocted a variety of alternative endings: Sam did return home, and more adventures would be forthcoming; a pseudo-Sam continued to leap, but "our" Sam returned home; the final leap was a mistake—almost a Bobby Ewing in the shower on *Dallas*-type ending—set up to allow Sam to make Al's world right (by changing history so that his long-term captivity as a Vietnam prisoner of war didn't destroy his marriage to his true love, Beth). In any of these proposed scenarios, Sam achieves a happy ending instead of what non-conspiracy-minded fans think is just a terribly sad conclusion to an upbeat series.[2]

Whether motivated by the conspiracy theory or just by a reluctance to let Sam go, fans continue to write new adventures for *QL* as well as discuss the old ones. Fan sites with names such as "Al's Place" and "Project Quantum Leap" are still active,[3] and the archives of fan fiction now span more than twenty years of storytelling. After the 2009 reunion, *QL* is likely to see a resurgence in fan activities.

In 2002 the Sci Fi Channel announced a forthcoming *Quantum Leap* movie, possibly leading to a new series ("New *Leap*"). The proposed script was rumored to introduce a new leaper (or possibly several); fans thought that Sam's daughter, Samantha, conceived during a particularly memorable multiple-episode story arc ("Trilogy," 5.8–5.10), might be the new "Sam Beckett." Although that film never materialized, a new *Quantum Leap* is still possible. According to Leap Back convention planner Brian Greene (personal e-mail), in 2007, writer-producer Deborah Pratt (also a *QL* actor and former spouse of *QL* creator Donald Bellisario) was "in talks with Universal to produce her *Quantum Leap* feature film script." With the recent interest in film adaptations of other once-loved TV series (e.g., *Get Smart*, *The Dukes of Hazzard*) and TV's "reimagined" versions of *Battlestar Galactica* and *The Bionic Woman*, Sam Beckett may yet make that *Quantum Leap* onto the big screen.

Notes

1. Comments such as "It doesn't look like it'll ever be a *Heroes* or a *Quantum Leap*" were, unfortunately and perhaps unfairly, written in reviews of *Journeyman* (Elfman).
2. The misspelling and the sad ending to this beloved series continue to be analyzed in reviews and news (Tircuit).
3. Pam's Quantum Leap Page was one of the earliest and best fan sites. It morphed into the current BakulaNews.com as Scott Bakula's career moved past *QL* into stage, film, and new TV projects, including *Enterprise*. BakulaNews.com, however, still remains linked to the older site and updates fans about *QL* actors' projects. See http://www.mindspring.com/~pashworth/scotsite.html.

Red Dwarf

Dee Amy-Chinn

Red Dwarf was the most successful and long-running comedy on BBC2.[1] First broadcast on February 15, 1988, the show was celebrated ten years later at a *Red Dwarf* night hosted by Jean-Luc Picard himself, Patrick Stewart, a die-hard Dwarfer. The content of that evening stands as testimony to *Dwarf*'s achievement of cult status, demonstrating many of the key features—quizzes, trivia, shared expertise—of cult TV (Gwenllian-Jones and Pearson ix). The evening began with a spoof of the then-popular *Can't Cook, Won't Cook,* in which the cast was challenged to cook chicken vindaloo (a mouth-burningly hot curry)—the favorite dish of lead character Dave Lister. The *Dwarf* version was billed as *Can't Smeg, Won't Smeg* (*smeg* being a generic term of abuse on the show, as in "smeg-head").[2] This spoof had added resonance for fans, as *Can't Cook, Won't Cook*'s regular host, TV chef Ainsley Harriot, had made a well-disguised appearance as the Gelf Chief in *Dwarf*'s season 6 episode "Emohawk—Polymorph II" (6.4). This was followed by a *Dwarf*-themed version of another popular BBC show, *University Challenge,* whose cast members lost (not surprisingly) to a team of *Dwarf* fans. Then *Red Dwarf A–Z* saw famous fans (including Stewart, Stephen Hawking, and Terry Pratchett) focusing on different aspects of the show. The evening concluded with a screening of the Emmy Award–winning episode "Gunmen of the Apocalypse" (6.3).

Red Dwarf's fifty-two episodes were broadcast between 1988 and 1999—a generally infertile period for science fiction on British television. The heyday of British science fiction was the 1960s and 1970s; by the 1980s, the bigger budgets and more advanced special effects of American film and television had made U.K. efforts seem rather out-of-date (Cook and Wright 15). Indeed, the jewel in the crown of U.K. sci-fi, *Doctor Who*, was canceled in 1989. The British approach was to abandon serious sci-fi programming and combine the genre with comedy, inspired perhaps by the success of Douglas Adams's *Hitchhiker's Guide to the Galaxy* (1981). *Hitchhiker's* had its origins in a BBC radio show, and *Red Dwarf* has a similar origin story. The concept started out as a series of sketches—"Dave Hollins: Space Cadet"—broadcast as part of Radio 4's mid-1980s series *Son of Cliché* and written by *Dwarf* show runners Rob Grant and Doug Naylor (Howarth and Lyons 2–3). The two main characters in four of the five sketches were Hollins and a computer named Hab (a reference to *2001*'s HAL). Hab was voiced by Chris Barrie, who would go on to play one of the central characters in the TV version. Numerous other sci-fi influences can be detected in *Red Dwarf*—most notably the films *Dark Star* and *Alien*; the series as a whole is littered with references to classic films.

Red Dwarf is set about 3 million years in the future. The first episode (ironically titled "The End") introduces the audience to the crew of the Jupiter Mining Corporation spaceship *Red Dwarf* and the show's central character, Dave Lister, "a curry-loving slob" (Charles, "Launching *Red Dwarf*"). Lister is the lowest-ranking member of the crew, and the early shows are built around his antagonistic relationship with his pompous and officious boss (the crew's second lowest-ranking member), Arnold J. (for Judas) Rimmer.[3] During the course of the episode, Lister is faced with a choice: give up his pregnant cat Frankenstein (it is against corporation regulations to have unquarantined animals on board), or face eighteen months in the ship's stasis chamber while the crew completes its tour of duty. Lister opts for stasis. However, an accident—caused by Rimmer—results in a radiation leak that kills the entire crew, and it takes the aforementioned 3 million years for the radiation to subside to a level at which Holly, the onboard computer, can set Lister free. Although he is the last man alive, Lister is not alone. The ship has the facility to support one hologramatic life-form, and Holly chooses Rimmer as the person most likely to keep Lister sane. There is also the Cat, a humanoid creature that evolved over the millennia from Frankenstein. These three form the basis of the *Red Dwarf* crew for all eight seasons (although Rimmer is absent for part of season 7). Season 3 sees the team joined on a full-time basis by sanitation mechanoid Kryten. Holly—a key component of the early shows (and she undergoes a "sex change" between seasons 2 and 3 when Hattie Hayridge replaces Norman Lovett)—is absent in seasons 6 and 7. The final two seasons introduce a central female character—Kristine Kochanski—and (for season 8) the resurrection of the full *Red Dwarf* crew.

There are plenty of classic sci-fi elements to the show, and this contributes to its cult status. But for most fans, this takes second place to its (laddish) humor, and the show's commissioning editor, Peter Ridsdale Scott, has stated that, first and foremost, *Red Dwarf* is a comedy. The writing team of Rob Grant and Doug Naylor (often credited under the single name Grant Naylor) came from a comedy background, having worked together on several radio and television projects.[4] Key cast members also had strong comedy backgrounds. Chris Barrie, who played Arnold (and his parallel universe counterpart Ace) Rimmer, was a voice artist who had worked with Grant and Naylor on *Spitting Image*.[5] Norman Lovett, who took the role of the computer, was a stand-up comedian who had originally auditioned for the role of Rimmer. The role of Lister went to punk poet Craig Charles, who, in his own words, "had no acting experience whatsoever" ("Launching *Red Dwarf*"). Charles decided to audition for the part after producer Paul Jackson sought his advice as to whether the character of the Cat (played by black British actor, singer, and dancer Danny John-Jules) might be considered racist in the politically correct 1980s. With the hiring of Charles and John-Jules, two of the leading characters in the show were black, yet *Red Dwarf* avoided casting any critical spotlight on racial issues (Malik 100).

Although race may not be important to the dynamic of *Red Dwarf*, class is. Elyce Rae Helford notes that Lister and Holly are working class and are privileged over the more middle-class Rimmer—a self-acknowledged coward who nevertheless aspires to officer status. Working-class masculinity receives a further boost in later seasons when contrasted with the middle-classness of Kristine Kochanski (Helford 243, 250; see also Charles, "Dwarfing USA"). This focus may be seen as a hallmark of the show's "Britishness," drawing on an apparent obsession with class distinctions. There are other forms of caricature as well. Lister is the archetypal antihero slacker who is, at his core, a decent person with a commitment to doing the right thing, making him easy for the target audience to identify with. His nemesis, Rimmer, is pompous, officious, and arrogant (and a real-life failure whose incompetence led to the accident that caused the death of the crew). The Cat, ostensibly nonhuman, also draws on a particular subcultural form of black masculinity, with his zoot suits, narcissism, and attitude.[6]

In addition to acting as a counterpoint to representations of masculinity, the addition of Kochanski in season 7 disrupts the all-male alternative family bonds that have developed between the key characters over the first six seasons. Indeed, it has been argued that the show fits into the genre of comedy that focuses on the surrogate family (with all the tensions that entails), linking *Red Dwarf* with the British sitcoms *Father Ted* and *Men Behaving Badly* (Mills, *Television Sitcom* 44). The similarities between *Red Dwarf* and *Men Behaving Badly* are not restricted to the surrogate family: *Red Dwarf* might be described as men behaving badly in space. Reviewing the show on TV.com, paul001 highlights its "ladishness," describing it as "the classic British comedy [about] the last human (Dave Lister) who just wants to eat curry, drink beer and get laid. A cat that has become humanoid that just wants to sleep, eat fish and get laid. A hologram that is so cowardly that he's never been laid." A desire for curry (at least on the part of Lister) and sex (or, rather, the lack of it) are themes that dominate the humor of the show, alongside issues surrounding Lister's poor personal hygiene (Howarth and Lyons 8). Indeed, one of Craig Charles's criticisms of the failed U.S. pilot version of the show was that it was too clean and had "no grunge" ("Dwarfing USA").

That said, there are considerable variations across the seasons in terms of setting, theme, and production values. Seasons 1 through 5 are set on *Red Dwarf* itself, although from season 3 onward, the production values are much higher and the action moves beyond the ship. For seasons 6 and 7 the crew is left with only the much smaller *Starbug*, making for a more intimate setting. By season 8 the *Red Dwarf* ship is back, along with an expanded cast. The general consensus is that the departure of Rob Grant at the end of season 6 led to an overall decline in the quality of the scripts. If awards are the measure of quality, then season 6 marks the high point of the show: it won the British Comedy Award for Best BBC Comedy Series and an International Emmy for "Gunmen of the Apocalypse" (6.3). The documentary that accompanies the DVD of season 6 notes its departure from the earlier format, with a new look for the characters, better special effects, and very strong scripts. Craig Charles has commented that this season has some of the funniest episodes ("Starbuggers"). On the negative side, a long-running rift between Charles and Chris Barrie meant that it featured less interaction between the characters and, at times, threatened to become "a monster of the moment marathon" (Gibron).

Critical acclaim aside, if one particular episode has to be selected to epitomize the blend of sci-fi and comedy that made the show such a hit, the fan favorite is undoubtedly "Quarantine" (5.4).[7] It opens with the crew landing on a deserted ice planet and discovering an abandoned research center. Tensions among the crew lead to Rimmer's return alone to the *Red Dwarf*. The center's one survivor is the hologramatic incarnation of one of the scientists working on "positive viruses," who has become infected with a "psychopathic holo-plague." On their return to the ship, Rimmer puts his fellow crew members into quarantine, but it turns out that the only one infected is Rimmer himself. The result is a psychotic Rimmer—dressed in a red and white gingham dress, complete with bonnet and blond plaits and his friend Mister Flibble (a psychotic penguin glove puppet)—chasing the crew until, making use of the positive "luck virus," Lister acquires all the items necessary to neutralize Rimmer's infection.

Despite its success and its cult status, the show's production history was not without problems. The pilot was written in 1983, but lack of interest from the BBC meant that the show was not commissioned until 1986, and filming of the first season was hampered by an electricians' strike (Howarth and Lyons 60). The breakup of the writing team, with Rob Grant departing to pursue his own projects, meant that there was a three-year hiatus between seasons 6 and 7 and an additional two-year gap before season 8 was screened in early 1999. Easter 2009 was the screening of a new three-part *Red Dwarf* special, but the episodes received mixed critical reviews, and further commissions seem very unlikely. It also seems fair to say that the humor that characterized *Red Dwarf* has been superseded by comedies with darker undertones, such as *The League of Gentlemen*. And the successful revival of *Doctor Who* has changed the landscape of British television science fiction.

Red Dwarf does not regularly appear on British television. The laddish BBC cable channel Dave screened episodes (mostly from season 6) on February 16–17, 2008, to mark *Dwarf*'s twentieth anniversary, and fans have ample material to fall back on. All the seasons have been released on DVD, each with an impressive "extras" package that includes commentaries by cast members and fans, deleted scenes, outtakes and "making of" documentaries. Bill Gibron gives high praise to the additional material, claiming that "you [can] end up with your very own *Red Dwarf* encyclopedia." Supplementing this are four novels written by Grant or Naylor or both: *Infinity Welcomes Careful Drivers* (1989), *Better Than*

Life (1991), *The Last Human* (1995), and *Backwards* (1996). Finally, the interactive DVD game *Beat the Geek* was issued in 2006.

I leave the final words on this show to Gibron: "[*Red Dwarf*] is one of the best-written, most wonderfully acted sitcoms of all time.... It took a premise that shouldn't have worked (sci-fi show), tossed in a cast of relative unknowns, mixed in a little complicated plot lining, and garnished with a big fat helping of humor.... From the pitch-perfect performing to the clever writing and direction, it is a show that leaves a lasting impression once it has been experienced." Is this not the very definition of cult TV?

Notes

1. http://www.galactic-guide.com/articles/9R15.html. The final season attracted an audience of more than 8 million viewers.

2. The word derives from *smegma*—a substance that accumulates under the foreskin of uncircumcised males.

3. In keeping with the show's humor, the name carries connotations of arse-licking.

4. Howarth and Lyons note that Grant and Naylor worked on *Carrott's Lib* and *Spitting Image*. In the documentary accompanying the season 1 DVD, *Red Dwarf* producer Paul Jackson notes that he worked with both writers on *Carrott's Lib* and *Three of a Kind*, as well as working with Craig Charles on *Saturday Night Live*.

5. Barrie went on to play the lead role in the BBC sitcoms *The Brittas Empire* and *A Prince among Men*.

6. See Cosgrove for a detailed analysis of the subcultural meaning of the zoot suit. In the documentary accompanying the season 1 DVD, Danny John-Jules (who plays the Cat) discusses attending the audition "in character," wearing his father's wedding suit, which he describes as a "zoot suit."

7. Based on fan ratings at http://www.tv.com/red-dwarf/show/132/reviews.html?flag=3&tag=subtabs;ep_review and http://www.imdb.com/title/tt0094535/usercomments.

Roswell

Stan Beeler

Roswell appeared on American television during a period in the life of the nation (1999–2002) that paralleled the coming-of-age represented by this teen drama. This coincidence of *Roswell*'s young-adult themes and a "new world" ushered in by the cusp of a new millennium, the Columbine incident,[1] and the events of September 11, 2001,[2] may be why the series has such a strong impact on its audience and why *Roswell* garnered the obsessive viewers that characterize cult television. For example, on Facebook, "Everything I Need to Know I Learned from *Roswell*" is an ingenuous mixture of humorous, political, and personal insights referenced by events in the series ("Ultimatums are bad," "The FBI is not our friend," "Don't get romantically involved with an ex"). *Roswell*'s great strength is that it presents its target audience with characters and situations easily applicable to their own turbulent lives in both a micro and a macro sense.

The series was developed by Jason Katims for FOX Television from a series of young-adult novels by Melinda Metz.[3] It aired on the WB network for two seasons before it was packaged with *Buffy the Vampire Slayer* for its third and final season on UPN. Despite a series of vigorous campaigns by its fans, including sending thousands of bottles of Tabasco sauce to WB, UPN, and FOX network executives,[4] *Roswell* was eventually canceled because of its chronically weak Nielsen ratings.

Katims, though an experienced developer of youth television, had never attempted the science fiction genre before, and the initial season of *Roswell* reflected his background, focusing on the love story between a human girl and a boy from the wrong side of the galaxy. The second season began to explore the science fiction premise more thoroughly with the introduction of *Star Trek* alumnus and future *Battlestar Galactica* reimaginer Ronald D. Moore as co-executive producer of the series.[5] The tension between the character-driven love story and the strong science fiction elements led to a thematic interaction that may well have been the key to the series' success as a cult favorite. *Roswell* serves as a powerful metaphor for personal histories and as a reference point not only for its contemporary audience but also for a whole new generation of young adults who have watched the show in reruns or on DVD.[6]

In an interview with *Science Fiction Weekly*, Katims reacts to a description of *Roswell* as a "combination of *My So-Called Life* and *The X-Files*":

> That characterization is great as far as I'm concerned. I feel like it's a series that has both a really strong SF element to it, and also characters who are rich and diverse and three-dimensional. And we as writers approach it by trying to service both things.... We do so by integrating the two genres as much as possible, so we don't feel like, "Now we're going write an SF scene, now a relationship scene," but that both of those are melded and activated at once.... What I like about it is that the SF element of the story and all of the mythology and the danger that they're in all gives you a lot of great story stuff to play. But the fact that we get connected to and invested in the characters humanizes the stories so that they become emotional as well.

Although Moore's considerable experience as a science fiction writer was a balancing force to Katims's more humanist leanings, Moore fully supported the series' more character-driven tone.

On one level, *Roswell* is the story of three alien teenagers and their human friends coming of age at the beginning of the twenty-first century; on another level, it is a variation on the theme of Romeo and Juliet re-created in serial TV format—a format that, by its very nature, precludes a tragic ending. The series begins as Liz Parker (Sheri Appleby), a waitress in her parents' kitschy, alien-themed diner in Roswell, New Mexico, is accidentally shot by a pair of strangers and then brought back from the dead by a half-alien schoolmate, Max Evens (Jason Behr). This encounter develops into a romance that lasts—with some ups and downs—throughout the course of the series. Max reveals to Liz that he and his sister Isabel (Katherine Heigl) and their close friend Michael

Guerin (Brandon Fehr) have been hiding their true origins since their adoption by unsuspecting human families fourteen years earlier. The alien backstory is gradually revealed over the course of the series: four members of an alien royal family were sent to Earth; three have remained in Roswell, and the fourth, Tess Harding (Emilie de Ravin), returns to Roswell in season 2.[7]

Unlike many other cult series of the genre, the science fiction aspect of *Roswell* has not resulted in a highly developed mythology. Nor does the series attract fans who spend endless hours exploring the intricacies of the alternative reality developed by the writers. What is important to the *Roswell* audience is that Liz and Max are in love and their peculiar social situation prevents them from having a normal relationship. In "The End of the World" (2.5) Liz reflects on the similarities between her situation and Shakespeare's play: "OK, I just reread 'Romeo and Juliet,' and you know, the first thing that I realized is that isn't even the title. It's called 'The Tragedy of Romeo and Juliet.' They die."

The problems experienced by the "star-crossed lovers" Max and Liz are paralleled in the equally difficult relationship between Michael and Maria DeLuca (Majandra Delfino). This secondary alien-human love story is often played for comic effect, much like servants' love affairs in classical romantic farce. Although Isabel's nascent relationship with Alex Whitman (Colin Hanks) comes to a tragic conclusion when he is killed by Tess, her marriage to Jesse Ramirez (Adam Rodriguez) is fraught with difficulties that are often used as the basis of humor. "I Married an Alien" (3.11) is an elaborate intertextual reference to the sitcom *Bewitched*, with Isabel in the role of Samantha Stevens (Elizabeth Montgomery) and Jesse as the long-suffering Darren Stevens (Dick York, Dick Sargent).

Although *Roswell* never had the kind of ratings that would make it the subject of extensive popular commentary, it engendered a respectable amount of critical discussion. There are numerous articles concerning the series' impact, both directly and as the focus of Internet discussion groups. Miranda J. Banks presents *Roswell* as a paradigmatic example of a "teen male melodrama" characterized by "a new television hero who is motivated to action by enlightened dreams for an equal partner, emotionally fulfilling relationships and a sense of duty to his community" (18). Although *Roswell* is definitely a melodrama in the classic definition of the word—a drama that uses music to enhance the emotional impact of key scenes—Max Evens, the teen male lead, is not the sole focus of the action. *Roswell*, like most serial television, is an ensemble piece that provides its audience with a number of central figures who take turns serving as the dramatic focus in single episodes and in multiepisode plot arcs. For instance, Liz Parker's experience is clearly central to the structure of the series. Undoubtedly Max's goals usually fall within the parameters of enlightened twenty-first-century masculinity, but one can easily argue that this is most prominent in episodes that focus on his beloved Liz. Episodes such as "Busted" (3.1), in which Max convinces Liz to accompany him in an armed robbery of a convenience store, hardly portray him as overly concerned with an "emotionally fulfilling relationship." Nor is Max's ambivalent relationship with Tess particularly emotionally fulfilling. In fact, the situation that evolves—Tess, Max's wife in his previous alien life, steals away their son—puts Liz in the role of a second wife in the matrix of a much more mature relationship.[8] Although this narrative line in no way excludes *Roswell* from the time-honored category of melodrama, it calls into question the statement that "on television the text always privileges the thoughtful, more obedient boy" (Banks 19). In this aspect of the plot it is clear that Liz has taken over the function of the melodramatic heroine, attempting to live with a decidedly uncomfortable situation to accommodate her beloved.

The plot structure of *Roswell* is, as mentioned earlier, more of an ensemble melodrama than a "teen male melodrama," and acts of self-sacrifice for the greater good of the family are just as common among the female characters—Liz, Maria, and Isabel—as they are among Max, Michael, and Alex. Banks's assertion that "the action of the narrative, as well as the fate of all the characters . . . revolves around a central teen male" (19) is not completely accurate for this series. In fact, the narrative is symmetrically balanced, with the Max-Liz relationship providing the primary focus that is mirrored in the relationships of the other human-alien pairs.

Banks is correct, however, in her assessment that *Roswell* epitomizes the traditional melodrama in its use of contemporary pop music to enhance the emotional impact of the narrative. Moreover, it augments pop music with the effective use of cinematography to drive home the bittersweet emotions of the primary characters. For example, Max and Liz are constantly filmed viewing each other through rain-streaked windowpanes—the pathetic fallacy of nature's tears combining with the tight framing of the casement to drive home the restrictions of their circumstances. When Max and Liz kiss, a montage of childhood memories alternating with the vast reaches of space replaces the usual soap-opera cliché of an extreme close-up. These visual enhancements of the narrative are extremely effective and go far beyond the traditional limitations of narrative television.[9] *Roswell* demonstrates that, as the technology of television improves, it can draw on the visual language of cinematography in ways that would have been impossible only a decade earlier.

In contrast to Banks's characterization of *Roswell* as melodrama, Neil Badmington uses the series as a focal point for musings on the concept of posthumanism: "Could it even be that the alien-ated youth opens up a space in which to rethink the relationship between the human and the inhuman?" (167). To Badmington, the primary significance of the series is the metaphorical relationship between teenagers and educational institutions. When Roswell High's characters—both human and alien—refuse to take the edicts of education as a given or when they engage in a game of trickery with the established authorities, they are rebelling against the cultural institution of humanism; they are all alien. When Badmington suggests "that close encounters with beings from other worlds might actually be good for us, and the real enemy is more likely to be the American government" (166), he foregrounds the rebellious aspect of youth culture so prominent in *Roswell*'s story lines. Badmington appears to be impressed by the fact that *Roswell* reflects a disillusionment with accepted modes of thinking about family, government, and education. *Roswell* "offers a radical challenge to traditional ways of understanding who 'we' and our 'others' might be" (Badmington 173).

The series is about growing up, and it reflects a nation that is growing up as well—a nation that has begun to realize that it is not alone in the world and that there are many others who may not wish it well. *Roswell* is not only an extended tale of teenage love; it is also a story of disillusionment and the acceptance of responsibility. *Roswell* is a cult object because it is a cautionary tale that fans can apply to their own experience. As Facebook so succinctly puts it, "Everything I Need to Know I Learned from *Roswell*."

Notes

1. Max's impromptu valedictory speech at the graduation ceremony in the final episode of season 3 lends some validity to Murray Forman's comments on

Roswell's post-Columbine representation of the power differential between the "cool" students and those of lower social status. Max says:

> I'm a member of that group of outsiders. I always knew I was different, and for a long, long, time all I wanted was to be another face in the crowd. But in the end, it wasn't possible. I guess it never was. So from now on, I'll just concentrate on being who I really am. Some of you might not like that. Some of you might even find that frightening, but that's not my problem any more. I have to be who I really am and let fate take care of the rest. So, thank you, Roswell. Thank you for letting me live among you. Thank you for giving me a family. Thank you for giving me a home. ("Graduation," 3.18)

2. Louisa Ellen Stein's article highlights the connection: "Looking at *Roswell* fans' discourse after 11 September reveals not only that fans are committed to the ideals of their favourite program, but also how they apply those ideals to their behaviour in online interactions and in their understanding of their lives in general, in experiences that move beyond the specific programs that they gather online to discuss" (473).

3. The ten Roswell High novels by Metz were published between 1998 and 2000, beginning with *The Outsider*. The characters' names were somewhat different in the novels, and the books were aimed at a younger audience than the series. In 2002 Metz wrote an episode of the television series entitled "A Tale of Two Parties" (3.10).

4. All the alien characters in *Roswell* have a taste for Tabasco sauce sprinkled liberally on sweet foods because they acquired a preference for strong flavors while getting used to their human bodies.

5. In an interview with the BBC, Katims presents his approach to the mixture of genres in the series:

> First of all, my background is very much in more character driven stuff, relationship driven stuff, and I've never really worked in the science fiction genre at all. So for me a lot of this was the learning experience of getting involved with that world and also coming to discover the possibilities and loving that aspect of the show.
>
> For me it started out more from a character perspective and then we started to introduce more of the science fiction elements as I became more comfortable with that. We just tried to as much as possible combine the best of both worlds.
>
> I feel the show is at its best when it is rooted in some universally relatable theme, something very human in fact, and we use the science fiction premise of the show as a way to differentiate it from other things that are out there. To add to this world something magical.

6. The *Roswell* groups on Facebook seem to confirm this, as their membership is evenly divided between high school students and university undergradu-

ates. Given that the series ended in 2003, this means that current high school students probably encountered *Roswell* after its initial broadcast.

7. Max is the king, Tess is his wife, Michael is the military enforcer, and Isabel is the king's sister who has betrayed the group to their political adversaries. The series plays these predetermined roles against the new lives and loyalties the teenagers have developed on Earth: Max finds a new love interest, Isabel develops a sense of loyalty to the group, Tess becomes the betrayer, and Michael loses—to some extent—the aggressive military focus of his former life.

8. Although *Roswell* is first and foremost a teen drama, the Max-Tess-Liz love triangle provides a plot element that speaks to a more mature audience. It is possible that the writers expected the young-adult audience to have experienced this sort of situation through their parents.

9. Forman compares *Roswell* to the production aesthetics developed by Chris Carter for *The X-Files*, including "muted lighting, unorthodox camera angles and shot framing, restrained or affectless acting styles, and a moody soundtrack" (79).

The Simpsons

Jonathan Gray

In July 2007 *The Simpsons Movie* opened to much fanfare: across the United States and Canada, twelve 7–Eleven convenience stores were converted into Kwik-E-Marts, and the multiple Springfields were invited to take part in a video contest to determine which would be the "real" Springfield and host the premiere of the film, which grossed $74 million its opening weekend. Meanwhile, in November 2007, the *Simpsons Game* was released for various video consoles; a British entrepreneur began a business that hired Kenyan soapstone carvers to fashion *Simpsons* characters; and, back on television, *The Simpsons* began its nineteenth season on network television. Few if any television shows have commanded the viewership and cultural power of *The Simpsons*.

Cult TV of Homeric Proportions

Only somewhat hyperbolically, Chris Turner notes that "if there is a common cultural currency, it's got Homer Simpson's picture on it" (10). A 1999 Roper Starch Worldwide study found that 84 percent of Americans could identify the Simpson family members, and in 2002 the Oxford dictionary officially added Homer's "d'oh!" to the English language. Indeed, given *The Simpsons*' success and place in the cultural mainstream, some may question its inclusion in a collection about cult TV shows, since it may seem to represent the opposite of cult. Nevertheless, it has never cracked the Nielsen ratings' annual top twenty, and even when it boasted higher figures in its early years, it was heavily criticized by politicians and moral crusaders alike, surrounded by the air of a countercultural provocateur. Furthermore, its snarky, edgy attack on American life, values, and media have made it a cult favorite, and many other cult comedy shows followed in its footsteps. Thus, even though seemingly dressed in mainstream garb, and despite its role as a flagship program of News Corporation's media empire, *The Simpsons* has enjoyed cult status for much of its life and has even played the role of cult grandfather to shows such as *South Park* and *The Daily Show with Jon Stewart*.

The Simpson family was originally created by Matt Groening, a cartoonist who had already made waves with his *Life in Hell* syndicated strip, featuring several odd bunnies and the gay fez-wearing couple Akbar and Jeff. Groening's work and his wry parodic-satiric sensibility were then applied to the Simpson characters for *The Tracey Ullman Show*, where they appeared in shorts on Ullman's variety program on the fledgling FOX network from 1987 to 1989. The shorts all took aim at the perfect nuclear family image that was so common in the 1980s, when *Growing Pains, Family Ties,* and *The Cosby Show* reigned supreme over prime time. Father Homer, mother Marge, son Bart, daughter Lisa, and baby Maggie interacted as real families do, not as perfect sitcom families do; they fought, they worried about death, and so forth. The Simpson family shot to popularity, leading FOX to green-light a half hour Christmas special for the end of 1989, followed by the premiere of *The Simpsons* in early 1990.

The Simpsons' early days saw considerable controversy and press. In an effort to force its way onto American television as the fourth network, FOX programmed with a countercultural sensibility, offering such programs as the black variety show *In Living Color*, the frequently offensive *Married . . . With Children*, its now signature gaudy reality shows, and the anti-Cosby *Simpsons*. Certainly, many cultural commentators paired *The Simpsons* with *Cosby*, especially when FOX boldly placed the former up against Cliff and Clair Huxtable and their kids in the prime-time schedule. While Cliff made funny faces and solved all problems, Homer throttled Bart, and Lisa solved all problems; while Rudy offered cuteness on top of cuteness, Bart talked back to teachers and other adults; and while Clair balanced five kids, a huge house, and a job as a lawyer with endless good humor, poor Marge tried her best but teetered on the edge of sanity. And so a war was declared by many in the press (and by many viewers) between the mainstream, upbeat, "family values"–rich depiction of the Cosbys—one that had existed on television largely unchanged since the 1950s with *Father Knows Best* and

Leave It to Beaver—and *The Simpsons'* cynical disbelief in perfection and its embrace of dysfunctionality. Groening refused to give adults the unquestioned authority and wisdom they enjoyed in countless other sitcoms and *Walton*-esque family dramas. Instead, Bart becomes the hero of the show, complete with his flagrant disregard for rules. Lisa, too, constantly shows up the ignorance and incompetence of her elders, many of whom are obstacles to her development, not helpers. To many of its early fans, *The Simpsons* was a breath of fresh air, always ready with a wicked undercut to any moral platitude and unconcerned with ending each episode happily.

A Show About Shows

Through the final shot of its opening credits—in the frame of the family's television—*The Simpsons* makes it clear that it is a show *about* television, our current media age, and their many foibles (see Gray, *Watching with* The Simpsons). Thus, while mocking American family sitcoms, it also takes regular potshots at advertising, the news, and all manner of other media genres and horrors, especially through the characters of pretentious newsman Kent Brockman, hack children's entertainer Krusty the Clown, and washed-out actor Troy McClure. Brockman runs an infotainment news program called *Eye on Springfield* that has aired six-part specials on the history of the bikini, is easily influenced by corporate ownership, and is prone to spectacularize all news (such as when he opens a report on a child uprising at Kamp Krusty by noting, "Ladies and gentlemen, I've been to Vietnam, Afghanistan, and Iraq, and I can say without hyperbole that this is a million times worse than all of them put together"). On Krusty's show, the chain-smoking, burnt-out clown sets up sidekicks for pratfalls and screens the hyperviolent cartoon *Itchy and Scratchy*. McClure, meanwhile, has a dubious acting résumé that includes films such as *Good Time Slim, Uncle Doobie, and the Great 'Frisco Freak-Out* and instructional videos such as *Alice's Adventures through the Windshield Glass*.

Another appeal of the show is its wry treatment of guests. As the show grew in popularity, and as it started to include guest stars voicing either themselves or characters, *The Simpsons* became *the* place to be on television. Over its lifetime, *The Simpsons* has hosted former British prime minister Tony Blair, scientist Stephen Hawking, novelist Jonathan Franzen, artist Jasper Johns, movie star Glenn Close, musicians The

Ramones, sports star Magic Johnson, and many others. It has also caricaturized numerous other public figures, including presidents George H. W. Bush and Gerald Ford and California governor Arnold Schwarzenegger (the last in the personage of Springfieldian action star Rainier Wolfcastle or the illiterate President Schwarzenegger in *The Simpsons Movie*). Frequently, the price of admission to the show has been an openness to being mocked or at least cajoled somewhat. Tony Blair, for instance—who appeared while he was still prime minister, no less—is mistaken for bumbling fool Mr. Bean by Homer and is depicted as fawning to foreigners, fashioning himself as a James Bond figure. Jasper Johns appears as a kleptomaniac, while Jonathan Franzen and author Michael Chabon carry out a childish rivalry throughout their guest appearances. In such a manner, *The Simpsons* allows room for playing with public image, taking some shine off its guest stars.

Most impressively, though, throughout its long tenure on American prime-time television, *The Simpsons* has remained one of the few programs willing to regularly attack advertisers. Springfield has shown us a children's beauty pageant sponsored by Laramie cigarettes and beer ads placed on a cable network for the unemployed; Krusty the Clown regularly abuses his place as a beloved children's entertainer to hawk his wares—including Krusty Chew Goo Gum-Like Substance, which contains spider eggs and the hantavirus, and the Krusty Brand Pregnancy Test, which warns of possibly causing birth defects. Moreover, in individual episodes advertisers have taken over the school and the church, and a Halloween "Treehouse of Horror" special has seen Springfield's oversized ad mascots come alive and terrorize the town. Referring to this last event, Brockman warns viewers: "Even as I speak, this scourge of advertising could be heading towards your town. Lock your doors. Bar your windows. Because the next advertisement you see could destroy your house and eat your family"—at which point *The Simpsons* cuts to a commercial break. Meanwhile, most corporations in Springfield are evil and callous, personified most obviously in the character of nuclear power plant owner Montgomery Burns. Burns can kill plants with his touch, runs a dangerously unsafe plant that is responsible for Springfield's fish having three eyes, and exhibits a disregard for human life matched only by his thirst for yet more cash. Although (as discussed later) *The Simpsons* has itself become a veritable advertising powerhouse and economic dynamo for its parent News Corporation, it has also proved a rare oasis for the critique of rampant consumerism and corporate America. Not only does the show depict corporate America run amok; it also shows little resistance. Lisa and sometimes Marge provide the lone voices of resistance, while Homer keeps buying what he's told to buy and relishing with glee all pop culture fads.

As the show became firmer on its feet it exhibited a willingness to take on its own corporate parent, frequently mocking FOX, News Corp, and CEO Rupert Murdoch. For instance, in one episode Homer places an ad on public-access television and exclaims, rich with double meaning, "We may be on a crappy channel, but the Simpsons are on TV!" Following the advent of FOX News Channel, with its overt conservative bias, the show has needled its owners for their shameless partisanship. Thus, in a 2005 episode the FOX News truck arrives at a news circus with a huge Bush-Cheney '04 banner displayed, victoriously playing Queen's "We Are the Champions." *The Simpsons* enjoys an almost unique contractual freedom in Hollywood—a "no notes" policy, brokered by producer James L. Brooks due to his past sitcom success (Leopold); hence, barring cancellation, FOX is powerless to change the show's content.

George H. W. versus Homer J.

The Simpsons' boldness in tackling advertisers, corporations, and News Corp built over time, as did its cult following based in part on these qualities. Early episodes, for example, focus primarily on familial politics. However, if *The Simpsons* wasn't on Americans' cultural radar in its first few months on the air, President George H. W. Bush soon ensured that it would be. In the run-up to the 1992 elections, he and Vice President Dan Quayle used the show as a symbol of what was wrong with American family values. In his State of the Union address, Bush argued, "We need a nation closer to the Waltons than the Simpsons." Thus the show was dragged into the political arena, as conservatives were invited to avoid it and progressives were invited to identify with the show's depiction of the real America. With one speech, Bush ensured the cult status of *The Simpsons* and the value of being a *Simpsons* fan. For its part, *The Simpsons* fought back when, preceding the airing of "Stark Raving Dad" in 1992, the family watches Bush's declaration on television and Bart observes, "Hey, we're like the Waltons. We're praying for the end of the depression too."

Meanwhile, Bart found himself in many a moral crusader's crosshairs, with his "eat my shorts" catchphrase and the phenomenal sales of his "Underachiever and Proud of It" T-shirts. As Laurie Schulze notes of the T-shirts, "Bart has managed to turn the tables on the system that's devalued him and say, 'In your face. I'm not worthless, insignificant, or stupid. If you want to label me an underachiever, I'll turn that into a badge of courage and say I'm proud of it'" (quoted in Brook 178). Thus *The Simpsons* had become shorthand for a minor rebellion against Bush Sr., against conservative moral policing, against parental authority, and against a legacy of goody-two-shoes television. In the early 1990s *The Simpsons* rocketed to success with college students in particular, and it played in dorms across the country to great acclaim. As Peter Parisi notes, Bart's countercultural cachet even resulted in a short-lived "Black Bart" moment, wherein Bart became a cultural icon in African American youth culture. To this day, *The Simpsons*' iconic status is rivaled by few other television programs. It has become a veritable bible of recent popular culture, its quotations and events a frame through which many fans view and make sense of the world around them.

The Simpsons' parodic and satiric attack on notions of the perfect America soon struck an international chord too. To Americans, *The Simpsons* may have simply represented a negation of prevalent images on prime-time television, or perhaps small-town America, but when it was broadcast overseas, audiences saw the show as illustrating the "real" America, complete with rampant commercialism, a feckless school system, corporate and governmental corruption, and familial strife. As much as Bart was a cause for cultural concern at home in America, and as much as he took center stage in the early seasons, soon Homer came into his own, a wonderful caricature of a dumb American. Homer drinks and eats too much, knows very little that can't be learned off a cereal box, isn't registered to vote, and is constantly screwing up, yet he seems oblivious to his own failures. He is someone we love because he fails, thereby validating failure as an acceptable option. Homer is a veritable antihero, like his son Bart. He also offers non-Americans an image of an ignorant American, infatuated with any commercial trend and laying claim to great power and authority, yet never justifying it with his behavior. It is no wonder, then, that the cult of *The Simpsons* grew at a particularly rapid rate in Canada, the United Kingdom, Ireland, Australia, and other frequent recipients of America's more over-the-top, flag-waving programming. As I found when researching audiences' responses to the show's parody and satire, many around the world love the show because of its satire on modern American television and values (see Gray, "Imagining America"). Hence, for much of the 1990s and early 2000s, *The Simpsons* ruled British television, regularly capturing a spot in the British Audience Research Bureau's top ten (similar to the American Nielsen ratings) with new episodes and occupying much of cable and satellite channel Sky One's top ten.

Springfield and Beyond

As suggested earlier, arguably more than has any other television program, *The Simpsons* has overflowed from television to merchandise, movies, computer games, high-end and low-end toys, comics, CDs, DVDs, and so forth. Most reports suggest that Matt Groening's key role is now one of corralling, coauthoring, or vetting the show's seemingly endless ventures into everyday life. Although the show has seen its fair share of Ralph Wiggum key chains, dancing Homer dolls, and other humdrum items, the show's cult ethos is alive and well in other merchandise. The 2007 *Simpsons Game*, for instance, is chock-full of computer game parodies, with inside references aplenty and even a collection of videogame clichés pointed out by Comic Book Guy as the player encounters them. One can also buy Krusty Seals of Approval to place on anything, as might Krusty himself. And when those twelve 7–Elevens were turned into Kwik-E-Marts, they were filled with signs reading "Buy 3 for the price of 3," "Buy today's pastries at tomorrow's prices," and so forth. Thus, as in the television show itself, *Simpsons* merchandise balances being an unmitigated sellout with its cult, snarky, anticonsumerist message.

To many, categorization as "cult television" requires placement outside the mainstream, only marginal economic success, and nothing close to *The Simpsons*' merchandising preeminence. Thus, *The Simpsons* might appear to be the antithesis of most programs included in this collection, being one of global television's more successful shows and a financial and merchandising powerhouse for Groening and News Corporation alike. But *The Simpsons*' ethos and message have remained countercultural. In 2010, twenty-three years after it premiered on *The Tracey Ullman Show*, it is admittedly less able to shock viewers than it once was. It is now more of a known entity whose edginess has been one-upped by many of its cable television colleagues. However, *The Simpsons* is still a rarity in cult television: it offers a cult message and sensibility in a mainstream package. And its success at pulling off such a balancing trick has had considerable influence on the subsequent development of comedy on American television and on many of those cable colleagues. *South Park*, *King of the Hill*, *Family Guy*, *The Daily Show with Jon Stewart*, *The Colbert Report*, *The Boondocks*, and numerous other parodic-satiric shows of the last ten or more years have learned a lot from *The Simpsons*, solidifying its place not only as a cult television program but also as a cult television grandparent. And yet the show keeps going, perhaps echoing Grampa Simpson's sentiment, expressed in "Homer's Triple Bypass": "They say the greatest tragedy is when a father outlives his son. I have never fully understood why. Frankly, I can see an up side to it!"

South Park

Jason Jacobs

Matt Stone and Trey Parker's *South Park* is one of the more notorious examples of the success of adult animated television series over the past decade. Its popularity on Comedy Central, in syndication, and as an international export, as well as the regular controversies it provokes, means that it has attracted a considerable amount of critical, academic, and media attention. Indeed, its influence even reached the political sphere, with conservative blogger Andrew Sullivan coining the phrase "*South Park* Republican" in 2001, which was widely adopted by other commentators (see, for example, Anderson).

Stone, the son of a college professor, and Parker, the son of a geologist, met at the University of Colorado–Boulder in the early 1990s. Stone was majoring in mathematics and film, and Parker was majoring in music in the hope of scoring movies one day. Music continues to be a vital component of their comedy identity, and *South Park* is unthinkable without its distinctive scoring and superb original songwriting. One of their early projects together was a musical version of the life of Alfred Packer, the first American to be convicted of cannibalism (released in 1996 as *Cannibal! The Musical*); they also made a short 8mm animated film using paper cutout characters depicting four small boys who build a magic snowman. In *The Spirit of Christmas* (1992)—aka *Jesus vs. Frosty*—Frosty the snowman turns out to be a psychopathic monster who kills one of the boys (Kenny). The others recruit Jesus, who kills Frosty with his halo. When a FOX executive saw the film in 1995, he paid Stone and Parker $2,000 to make him a personal video Christmas card version. That version, *The Spirit of Christmas* (1996)—aka *Jesus vs. Santa*—is more recognizably the forerunner of *South Park* and features what were to become the main characters of the series: four nine-year-old boys who use frequent obscenities and seem to have an incongruously adult perspective on events around them. The notoriety of the video card in Hollywood circles eventually brought Stone and Parker a number of offers, but it was the Comedy Central network that eventually secured their talent, and the first episode aired in August 1997. At the time of this writing, the show has run for twelve seasons, and the creators are contracted to produce more until at least 2011.

South Park's zany title sequence is indicative of the interests, character, and range of the show. The sequence foregrounds the manufacture of the central characters—we literally see them being cut out and assembled from simple shapes and colors. This allusion to the early learning activities of children, such as cutting and pasting, constructing collages, and using bright paints and crayons, is juxtaposed with the slightly sinister music, a blend of hillbilly bluegrass and alternative rock, with vocals by Primus's Les Claypool. His monotonous drawl hints suggestively at the town's promise as a place to "unwind," but this is in direct tension with the seemingly innocent shout-singing of the children: "Friendly faces everywhere." Of course, this is hardly as innocent as it seems, since the children appear to be parroting the banal language of a local tourist agency ("ample parking day and night"), albeit one that is processed through the particular consciousness of the child (Cartman's line continues, "people spouting howdy neighbor," while Kenny's contribution is sheer, if muffled, obscenity: "I love girls with big fat titties. I love girls with deep vaginas"). The figuring of the children as manufactured puppets points to a recurring theme of the show: the vast and inexhaustible suggestibility, gullibility, and availability of the town's inhabitants to fads, trends, ideologies, bigotries, and fashions of every kind, including reverse defecation, sexual and racial bigotry (often with bizarre reversals and twists), and widespread addiction to computer games.

The title sequence typically foregrounds the four main characters—Stan Marsh (dark blue hat, voiced by Parker), Kyle Broflovski (green ushanka, voiced by Stone), Eric Cartman (light blue hat, Parker), and Kenny McCormick (orange hooded parka, Stone). As in the traditional sitcom, these nine-year-olds are usually at the center of each episode. The fact that Kenny is killed and resurrected reflects and underscores the point made in the title sequence that this is a flexible world re-created anew each week. But it also highlights the absurdity of one of the key oddities of the sitcom genre: its weekly reset of the "sit." After Kenny appeared to be permanently dead at the end of season 5, the three remaining boys were joined in season 6 by Butters Stotch, an intensely nervous but nevertheless optimistic figure who was born, appropriately enough, on September 11 (Kenny returned the next season). In any case, the show's narrative interests are not hostage to its central characters, and they may be sidelined or abandoned in certain circumstances.

Since the show is about a place rather than the group, it can draw on a wide range of minor characters both for local color and for story stimulation. The show has many recurring characters, the most iconic of which include the schoolteacher Mr. (later Mrs.) Garrison; Chef (voiced by Isaac Hayes); schoolmates such as Timmy, Jimmy, and Token; and family members Randy (Stan's father) and Sheila (Kyle's mom). There are also standard generic figures such as the town cop, Officer Barbrady, as well as a number of bizarre characters that have recurring appearances, such as Mr. Hankey, a festive talking piece of excrement with a penchant for song (something shared by many of the characters), and Towelie (voiced by comic writer Vernon Chatman), a high-tech military towel who enjoys getting high. Santa and Jesus also make regular appearances, as do various heads of state.

One of the joys of *South Park* is its pitiless depiction of celebrities and other public figures. Stone and Parker are on record as hating celebrity actors who imagine that their fame provides them with political insight, a view admirably articulated in their 2004 marionette movie *Team America*. Over the years the show has parodied and pilloried a vast number of celebrities of all kinds, including actors (Tom Cruise, Mel Gibson, George Clooney), singers (Barbra Streisand, Jennifer Lopez, Phil Collins), bands (Korn, Fleetwood Mac), models (Paris Hilton), sports and TV personalities (Michael Jordan, Steve Irwin, Bill O'Reilly), politicians (Hillary Clinton, Jesse Jackson), scientists (Richard Dawkins), and serial killers (Ted Bundy, Jeffrey Dahmer).

Its range of setting, character, and reference to the contemporary world of current affairs and popular culture provides *South Park* with a very flexible resource for its storytelling. Similarly, the style of its comedy indicates several broad influences; particularly apparent are aspects of the underground comics movement of the late 1960s and some of the pseudonihilistic and carnivalesque trends in American alternative music of the 1990s. There is also a clear inheritance from television animated comedy series such as *Beavis and Butthead* and *The Simpsons*. However, a major inspiration for the visual style and overall tone of the show is the British sketch show *Monty Python's Flying Circus*, which the young Stone and Parker watched as PBS repeated it late in the evening during the 1980s. Terry Gilliam's bizarre cutout animation sequences, which have a surreal but emotionally dark tone, are an obvious influence. Although *South Park* largely eschews the surreal, it incorporates Gilliam-style cutouts and uses their flexibility to create sudden comic movements (such as squashing or flying) and basic lines and shapes to express emotion and attitude. Gilliam was also one of the first to realize the impact of occasional stillness in his animation, something that is used to fabulous comic effect in *South Park*. Cartman's character is frequently given extremely simple, or merely static, facial expressions that are strongly resonant of his feelings—for example, his immediate expression upon being told that Kenny's life-support machine will not be switched off in "Best Friends Forever." Another example: the minor addition of a parting in Cartman's hair is richly expressive when he attempts to "be good" and bring Christmas to the children of Iraq ("Red Sleigh Down"). Like Gilliam's work, *South Park*'s visual style offers what at first glance appears to be a basic, do-it-yourself aesthetic of simple construction but that also implies significant artistic control and accomplishment.

Although the popular reception of *South Park* has sometimes been mixed, academic reception has been almost exclusively positive. Jason Mittell describes it as "some of the most clever and sophisticated satire of its era" (2144), and it has inevitably become part of the " . . . and *Philosophy*" series of books. Some have noted the show's postmodern qualities, pointing to its rich allusions to film, music, and television; its cynical irony; and its other forms of intertextuality. Toni Johnson-Woods describes it as "the postmodern pastiche par excellence" (xi). Of course, these postmodern features can be found in many television shows made since the late 1980s, and on their own, they do not make the show distinctive. *South Park*'s identity is idiosyncratically tied to that of its creators, much more so than most other shows. This tends to mean that the quality of episodes is mixed, in contrast with *The Simpsons*, which, with a larger team of writers, is much more consistent in its quality. It also means that several themes—such as censorship, disability, sexuality, personal and political hypocrisy, and the neglect, equalization, and abuse of children—have a recurring prominence throughout the series. Each of these, as well as others, can be mobilized, usually in relation to a current event or issue that Stone and Parker want to address. In this way, even though it is a narrative fictional show, *South Park* resembles current-affair satirical chat shows such as *The Tonight Show with Jay Leno* and *The Daily Show*.

Like these shows *South Park* feeds on topicality, frequently incorporating recent issues, themes, and events into an episode. This is made possible by a tight production pattern, whereby Parker and Stone are able to write, direct, and edit an episode within a week, allowing them to be responsive to current events. Indeed, one of the attractions of the show is the anticipation of what the "*South Park* take" on an issue might be. A good example of this is the approach to the Terri Schiavo case in 2005. Schiavo, who had been hospitalized in a vegetative state since the early 1990s, was the focus of a complex series of legal and political disputes between her husband and the rest of her family that centered around whether she should continue to receive life-supporting care. The week her feeding tube was removed, Parker and Stone began writing the episode "Best Friends Forever," in which Kenny is hit by a van and left in a persistent vegetative state. Cartman wants Kenny's feeding tube removed because that would mean he could have Kenny's Playstation Portable (PSP); unsurprisingly, Kyle and Stan campaign to keep him alive. When Kenny's final wishes are revealed, his note instructs, "Don't ever show me in that condition on national television." Rather than take one of the two obvious sides in the Schiavo case, Stone and Parker point to the degrading nature of the coverage itself. The episode aired the day before Schiavo died and won an Emmy for Outstanding Animated Program.

Although it can respond with rapidity to events, the show also finds interest in less dramatic but nonetheless prominent trends in the cultural imagination. For example, the popularity of online games, especially the MMORPG (massively multiplayer online role-playing game) *World of Warcraft*, was addressed in the season 10 episode "Make Love Not Warcraft." The skill and pleasure of this episode lie in the deft way it addresses and draws on two different cultural competences: knowledge and experience of the world (characters, history, traditions, events) of *South Park* and a similarly rich knowledge and experience of the *World of Warcraft*. In a *machinima*-style rendering of the game world (machinimas are movies, usually short, made using game engines), we see Kyle, Stan, Cartman, and Kenny playing their fantasy characters, and to avid WOW players, it seems entirely appropriate that Cartman's character is a red-headed dwarf warrior (or "tank"). The narrative explicitly mocks online gamers' devotion and "waste of a life" as they invest massive amounts of time doing trivial and repetitive things such as killing boars to earn experience points. The episode ends with the boys still playing together, but after months of effort, they are grotesquely fattened and pimpled creatures. The pleasure of recognition and acknowledgment—the rewards of fandom for gamers and viewers alike—is central to the cult status of both game and show. There is also the sheer aesthetic kick of seeing familiar characters from one cartoon medium transposed to the equally artificial medium of gaming.

South Park is generous with the range of attention it pays to the various characters; however, it is fair to say that Cartman is most central in terms of providing narrative energy and drive. Kenny's role, though occasionally central (e.g., "Major Boobage"), varies between that of observer and victim. Kyle and Stan tend to react to the egregious behavior of Cartman or others; the pair may also provide a relatively stable moral baseline (sometimes opposing each other), which stimulates ensuing patterns of conflict and resolution. Kyle in particular seems to possess a stronger and more reflective moral outlook than the others (Devlin 87–94). For example, he is forced to reexamine his faith in the goodness of God after Cartman inherits a million dollars and opens an amusement park ("Cartmanland"). Kyle's questioning of his faith is rather conventional in itself, but the humor derives from its stimulus—the fact that Cartman astutely anticipates how frustrating it will be for Kyle and actually advertises the park on television *just* to annoy his friend.

In contrast to the others, Cartman has a far richer history on the show—paradoxically, a product of his shallow, brutal, and cruel selfishness. It is hard to imagine a more chilling sight than Cartman licking the tears from Scott Tenorman's eyes and crooning with delight after he has tricked him into eating his own parents: "Yes! Let me taste your tears Scott! . . . Mm your tears are so yummy and sweet!" ("Scott Tenorman Must Die"). Yet it is precisely the grim, tickling perversity of that horror that makes it so funny. Cartman's appeal is hardly puzzling, however. Although he is selfish, cruel, and manipulative, because of his odd size and shape, he strikes a simultaneously comic and pathetic figure; he can be both sentimentally naïve and demonically cunning. His childish ignorance of some matters should not disguise the fact that in some ways he embodies a very adult kind of character: the narcissistic consumer. His enthusiasms and desires—for products such as the PSP or Wii—are single-minded and total, as is his bigoted suspicion of various groups (hippies, Muslims, Jews, people with ginger hair).

In Cartman we see another aspect of the significance of *South Park* and one of the reasons it has accrued such a cult following: the way the show can relatively easily approximate the subjectivity of a child with that of an adult. Various scholars have pointed out, in different ways and at different times, the infantilization of Western society. One way to calibrate this is to look at the increasing prominence of ever-younger children represented and catered to by popular culture over the past thirty years. An economist might point to the growth of industry attention to this demographic as a result of its augmented buying power, but this only seems to beg the question. The problem, as *South Park* illustrates, is not so much that children are more important but that adult subjectivity is increasingly addressed—by governments, by advertisers, by employers—as childlike. Perhaps this is one way to understand the attribution of conservatism to a show that derives a great deal of its comedy from the depiction of infantile behavior that is particularly resistant to the enforcement of paternalistic behavioral and moral codes. Judith Kegan Gardiner, in an interesting take on the film *South Park—Bigger, Longer, and Uncut* (1999), notes that its "ebullient and vividly corporeal perversities" evoke French feminist Hélène Cixous's concept of *écriture feminine*, a subversive and disruptive practice of writing that resonates with the logic, rhythms, and destabilized order of desire and the body. As Gardiner points out, while Cixous insisted that this practice was necessarily feminine, *South Park* points to a strongly masculinized form of disruption (57).

This potent current of energy was released in the late 1990s, and anyone who saw the first season in 1997 surely realized—some with considerable gratitude—that what many considered "shocking comedy" in the past was merely a crustier slice from the same pie. Although it has become a cliché to talk of bringing anything "to a new level," the sight of a vast alien probe sliding in and out of a boy's ass ("Cartman Gets an Anal Probe") stimulated many to realize that they had been somewhat shortchanged in the comedy stakes over the past few years. It brought to life an observation made by nineteenth-century Swiss novelist Gottfried Keller, who stated, "The bohemian petit bourgeois is not a bit wittier than the solid citizen" (quoted in Lukacs 105). The compassionate wit of *M*A*S*H*, the infantile agonizing over trivia in *Seinfeld*, even the mostly comforting brilliance of *The Simpsons* seem tame by comparison. As Trey Parker put it on the *Charlie Rose Show*, "The people screaming on this side and the people screaming on that side are the same people, and it's OK to be someone in the middle laughing at both of them."

Ultimately, *South Park*'s success is based on two major assets: its fascination with and utter contempt for the infantile narcissism of contemporary culture and politics, and its ability to articulate this contempt in a way that is always distinctive and often hilarious. As purely a medium to express the aggressive, vulgar disdain of its creators for the shameless hypocrisy of a world that offers endless self-righteous justification for grand values, visions, and ideas that are little more than ephemeral public relations bullshit, *South Park* is perfect.

Acknowledgment

I would like to thank Jim Harris and Jason Wilson for their suggestions.

Stargate SG-1

Angela Ndalianis

Stargates and interplanetary wormhole travel, interstellar wars, galactic warlords controlled by parasitic evil aliens, mercenary android replicants bent on annihilating anything in their path, wisecracking ex-MacGyver hero extraordinaire—this is the world of *Stargate SG-1*. It ran for ten seasons, outlasting *Star Trek* and *The X-Files* as the longest consecutively running U.S. science fiction–fantasy series on television (its 214 episodes outperforming *X-Files*' 202). Created by Jonathan Glassner and Brad Wright, the show first aired on Showtime in 1997 and migrated in 2002 to the Sci-Fi Channel for its final five seasons. Produced by Metro-Goldwyn-Mayer, the series was filmed in Vancouver and was based on the 1994 science fiction film *Stargate*, written by Dean Devlin and Roland Emmerich and directed by Emmerich, of *Independence Day* (1996) fame. When the Sci-Fi Channel announced on August 21, 2006, that the show wouldn't be returning for an eleventh season, fans were outraged, signing petitions and attempting to pressure the executives to reverse their decision—but to no avail.

The enormous impact of the series is indisputable. It generated a highly successful spin-off series, *Stargate Atlantis*, which included crossover story lines, and an additional series—*Stargate Universe*—appears to be in the cards for 2009. As is typical of many cult shows nowadays, the corporate generator of *Stargate SG-1*, MGM, has been quick to recognize the show's marketing, serial, and cross-media potential. In addition to the TV spin-offs, following in the footsteps of *Star Trek*, the mother of all science fiction classics, the *Stargate SG-1* franchise has launched into films, albeit on DVD (one of the primary modes of engagement for cult TV fans). *Stargate: The Ark of Truth*, released in March 2008, provided the much-awaited conclusion to *Stargate SG-1* and the battle with the Ori, who not only have great power and exist on a higher plane but also use their human prophets as nightmarish versions of door-to-door Bible bashers on a galactic scale. This was followed in July 2008 with the release of *Stargate: Continuum*. Add to this the animated TV series *Stargate Infinity*; the role-playing, trading-card, and computer games (*Stargate SG-1 Roleplaying Game, Stargate Trading Card Game, Stargate Worlds,* and *Stargate SG-1: The Alliance,* which was eventually pulled from production); the tie-in novels published by ROC and Fandemonium Press; and the comics published by Avatar Press, and fans were given a healthy franchise with which to satisfy their ever-increasing appetites.

Like its film predecessor, the series is best categorized as "military science fiction" in the tradition of shows such as *Battlestar Galactica, Space: Above and Beyond,* and, to a certain extent, *Farscape, Babylon 5,* and the *Star Trek* franchise (although the latter are not always engaged in interstellar conflict that involves military intervention). The Stargate is a sophisticated and highly advanced piece of alien technology that makes interplanetary space travel possible through the creation of a wormhole teleportation system that connects to thousands of locations across the galaxy (rather than the singular location of Abydos, which the film focused on). Generating its own mythology by rewriting centuries-old human mythologies—Egyptian, Norse, Aztec, Greek, Arthurian, Roman—the series takes these myths and "reboots" them as scientific fact.

In a story that would make Erich von Däniken proud, the series' premise relies on the fact that the sources of these myths were aliens who had, at some time in humanity's past, based themselves on Earth before trekking off with their human slaves and followers to find other planets to conquer. But these are a particularly fiendish type of alien: the snakelike Goa'uld use humans (or Tau'ri) as hosts, invading their brain stems and spinal cords to take over their identities. Realizing that the Jaffa race can act as receptacles to nurture and raise their young until they are ready for transfer as sentient adults into human hosts, the Goa'uld enslave the Jaffa and set themselves up as a strategically dispersed system of warlords throughout a galaxy that they rule (falsely) as gods. When a Goa'uld (other than Ra, who appeared in the film) enters the nonoperational Stargate base through the gate and kidnaps a female officer (killing the rest), the Stargate Command military base is brought back into action, and SG teams—beginning with SG-1—are formed to defend humanity and to explore the mysteries, other civilizations, and potential threats that lie beyond the gate. The generic context opens thematic issues that are typical of science fiction: technological advancement and militaristic power become the means to explore gender equality, religious belief systems, scientific rationalism, racism and cultural difference, eugenics and biological tampering, mind control, mortality and immortality, the destruction of nature and the creation of artificial life, and a wealth of other complex philosophical and political issues that are familiar to the science fiction genre.

The show's main players are Richard Dean Anderson as the esoteric, old-school hero-type Jack O'Neill, the SG-1 leader for the first eight seasons. When O'Neill moves offscreen (making only occasional appearances) to perform top-secret duties for the Stargate program, he is replaced by Ben Browder (of *Farscape* fame) as the new SG-1 leader, Cameron Mitchell, in seasons 9 and 10. Amanda Tapping plays the team's genius-scientist Samantha Carter; Christopher Judge is the wonderfully stoic alien Jaffa Teal'c; and Michael Shanks plays the controversial archaeologist Daniel Jackson, who unveils the purpose and function of the Stargates and is replaced on the SG-1 team in seasons 6 and 7 by the alien scientist Jonas Quinn, played by Corin Nemec. Add to this scene-stealer Claudia Black (also from *Farscape*), who plays Vala Mal Doran, another alien addition to the SG-1 team during seasons 9 and 10, and throw in Stargate commanders George Hammond (Don S. Davis) and Hank Landry (Beau Bridges) and numerous other regulars, and we have the narrative machine that drove *Stargate SG-1* for a decade.

I admit that I wasn't a *Stargate SG-1* fan initially. As a sci-fi fiend, I don't remember why the series' initial broadcast on Channel 7 in Australia didn't grab my attention. Then, everything changed. Late-night viewing on the cable station TV1 (and later the Sci-Fi Channel) drew me in every night of the week: 12 A.M.—the witching hour—became *Stargate SG-1* happy hour. I think I started watching during season 3, and I soon sought out the first three seasons on DVD and discovered with glee that season 4 had already been released in the United Kingdom. These were my pre-download-savvy days, and like an addict, I'd wait anxiously (due to delayed televising in Australia, sometimes up to a year!) for my next fix. This frenzy was fostered by the discovery that a friend of mine—let's call him Simon—had become hooked in a similar way. So Simon and I would lie on our respective couches three or four suburbs away from each other and text messages about what we were watching. Then, every week or so, we'd meet up and "debrief" over a baker's dozen worth of coffees, recounting special episode moments—from the more epic drama and mayhem caused by the various villains such as the Gou'ald, the old-school Replicators (before they figured out how to mimic human form), and the Ori (who, admittedly, paled by comparison to the others and to *Stargate Atlantis*'s master-class villains, the Wraith) to the magic encapsulated within the little details, especially the O'Neill and Teal'c exchanges, which grew better and better with time. Then with season 6 came the downloads. Through the wonder of technology (and fans), episodes would appear on my computer soon after being broadcast in the United States, and I'd pass them on to Simon. These exchanges felt like we were participating in some illegal drug deal—I'd get my fix, then he'd get his fix.

As Gwenllian-Jones and Pearson convincingly argue, its serial nature is one of the primary traits that distinguishes cult television from cult film. Furthermore, the conditions, secret ingredients, and magic potions that generate the cult experience can become dramatically amplified by the serial logic of television and, in the process, attract audiences that "inspire significant interpretive fan cultures" (x–xi). Certainly, given its reliance on the series format since its inception, the television medium is conducive to serial narrative structures. So why aren't all television series cult phenomena? Any definitive answer to this question is sure to get me into hot water, so I won't even attempt a response. It's more productive to consider why a show like *Stargate SG-1* has achieved a cult following. Yes, serialization is a key aspect of the series, with combinations of single-episode stories and complex story arcs interweaving with increasing complexity as the series progresses. Television's power comes from its capacity to infiltrate the privacy of our home; through the initial broadcast, DVD viewing, and downloading, we can engage in the ritual-like viewing and re-viewing that allow the intricate story lines and developing character identities to enter our lives further. But these are particular kinds of characters and story lines. Richard Dean Anderson's other star vehicle, *MacGyver*, may be the thing that blows Patty and Selma Bouvier's trumpets on *The Simpsons*, but for me, it's Jack O'Neill who rings my bells. Unlike the darker, depressed, man-of-no-words Kurt Russell version of O'Neil in the movie, Anderson's O'Neill may be a man of few words, but those that come out of his mouth are the kind you want to cryogenically freeze and keep forever. As O'Neill himself reflexively clarifies, "That's O'Neill with two *L*s. There's another Colonel O'Neil with only one *L*, he has no sense of humor at all" (2.9). O'Neill is the master of witty and sarcastic exchanges with other characters:

> MARTOUF: You are familiar with the way Sokar has assumed the persona of the entity known as the Devil?
> O'NEILL: Yeah. A bit pretentious, don't you think? ("Jolinar's Memories," 3.12).

He is prone to utter those oh-so-special one-liners, such as when he tells the evil Gou'ald: "You finished that sentence with a preposition! Bastard!" ("The Other Guys," 6.8). And there are the endless references to *The Simpsons*.[1] There are so many "O'Neillisms," in fact, that entire Web sites are dedicated to them.

The serial nature of TV shows such as *Stargate SG-1* encourages a growing familiarity with our favorite characters that isn't possible in film. Serialization is also the primary vehicle that encourages the rampant meta- and intertextual logic that drives these series.[2] Like the convoluted mythologies generated by the fictional universes of *Star Trek* and *The X-Files*, *Stargate SG-1* introduces audiences to a layered mythology— one that borrows shamelessly from familiar "real-life" mythologies and transforms, rationalizes, and transposes them onto alien creatures and the worlds they inhabit. The Goa'uld System Lords Apophis, Anubis, and Osiris—to name but a few—recall Egyptian gods and mythologies. Other Goa'uld claim Greek (Cronus, Aries), Phoenician (Ba'al, Moloc), Shinto (Amaterasu), Celtic (Camulus, Mórrígan), Hindu (Kali, Nirrti), and Babylonian (Marduk, Ishkur) mythological connections. With the defeat of the Goa'uld in seasons 8 and 9 comes a new threat, the Ori (whose concern with spirituality recalls the African belief system of the Yoruba). The show's writers also turn to Arthurian legends, and we witness the appearance of both Merlin and Morgan le Fay. The latter also happen to be "Ancients," incredibly advanced technological beings and descendants of the Earth's Atlantians who, like the villainous Ori but with more virtuous purpose, have ascended to a higher plane of existence. Add to this mix the good-guy aliens the Asgard (whose origins are overtly linked to Norse mythology) and the evil Replicators (mechanical bugs that reproduce by ingesting technological matter—the contemporary mythological stuff of sci-fi–horror), and we have not only a postmodern web of enmeshed narratives but also a truly galactic network of mythological forces at work. It's all in the detail, and ten years of *Stargate SG-1* presented audiences with a lot of detail.

Serialization promotes a shift away from strict linearity, and over time, certain narrative strands may be revisited by writers so that "multiple backstories" and "parallel histories" can be established (Gwenllian-Jones and Pearson xii). For the fan, part of the joy comes from seeing these intricate narrative webs develop, intersect, alter, and become more dense and labyrinthine. Another part of the joy comes from being able to revisit and make connections between certain narrative paths across episodes, seasons, series, and crossover series such as *Stargate Atlantis*. As Gwenllian-Jones and Pearson explain, intertextuality, metatextuality, and self-referentiality in cult television "combine to draw viewers into intense imaginative and interpretative engagement with the series" (xv). Add to this fan-based story extensions found on Gater Web sites such as *GateWorld* (http://www.gateworld.net/), *Heliopolis* (http://www.sg1-heliopolis.com/), *Alpha Gate* (http://www.thealphagate.com/), *Stargatefan* (http://www.stargatefan.com/fiction/), and *Area 52: The HKH Standard* (http://www.area52hkh.net/), and the metatextual universe becomes even vaster.

Admittedly, I never got into the fan fiction, and although I love the sense of mastery that familiarity with *Stargate SG-1*'s narrative continuity brings, the episodes that offer me the greatest delight are the self-reflexive, comical, parodic ones that operate as if possessed by a mysterious "O'Neillism" virus. There are many of these little gems. "The Other Guys" (6.8) introduces us to three nerdy scientists. One of them, Felger, worships SG-1 and, in particular, O'Neill and Teal'c; another, Coombs, is a *Star Trek* fan who can't understand how Felger can consider himself a scientist and not "worship at the altar of Roddenberry." These scientists decide to "save" SG-1 from the evil clutches of the Goa'uld, and during their adventures they manage to parody the conventions of small-screen science fiction; needless to say, *Star Trek* takes a hammering.

Another favorite is "Wormhole X-Treme!" (5.12), an episode that "does a Shakespeare" by presenting the viewer with a TV show within a TV show. SG-1 discovers that a new TV show—*Wormhole X-Treme* ("Research says that shows with 'X' in the name get higher ratings")—is about to hit the screens, and its narrative premise and main characters are suspiciously like those at Stargate. In this episode, *Stargate SG-1* producers, directors, and crew members all play versions of themselves, and the television production, distribution, and exhibition process is mercilessly parodied by the very individuals who work on the series. In addition, we're introduced to the series-within-a-series actor Nick Marlowe (played by Michael DeLuise), one of the masterpiece characters of any series ever. Combining the personas of Jack O'Neill and Captain James T. Kirk, Marlowe plays *Wormhole X-Treme*'s Colonel Danning in a performance that is sheer comic genius.

In the award-winning episode "200" (10.6), the movie adaptation of the shelved television show *Wormhole X-Treme* is planned, and members of the SG-1 team pitch their own versions of such a film. Martin, the show's producer, suggests a *Thunderbird*-style program in which SG-1 members appear as marionettes; Cameron Mitchell favors a zombie invasion in the tradition of Romero's *Living Dead* films; Carter posits a mission that sees O'Neill become invisible (thus reflecting the actual absence of O'Neill/Anderson from the series); Teal'c offers a noir imagining of himself as a private investigator; and, after having her *Gilligan's Island* pitch rejected, Vala provides two fabulous reimaginings of the SG-1 team as the main characters from *The Wizard of Oz* (1939) and *Farscape* (the cult TV show that Claudia Black and Ben Browder appeared in prior to *Stargate SG-1*—but this time with Black playing Aeryn, Browder as Stark, Teal'c as D'Argo, Daniel as Crichton, and Thor as Rygel).

To do any of these episodes justice, I would have to describe every minute detail and the effect these details had on my viewing experience. But even if I could describe these sensations, perhaps the spaces that hold the indescribable are where the cult experience is to be found.

Notes

1. In the episode "Citizen Joe," Dan Castellaneta, the voice of Homer Simpson and Jack O'Neill's hero, finally appears as Joe Spencer, a barber who begins having visions of SG-1 missions.

2. On television and serialization, see Hammond and Mazdon's collection *The Contemporary Television Series*.

The *Star Trek* Franchise

Rhonda V. Wilcox

The opening voice-over by Captain James T. Kirk (William Shatner) intones: "These are the voyages of the starship *Enterprise*. Its five-year mission: To explore strange new worlds. To seek out new life and new civilizations. To boldly go where no man has gone before." The enterprise of Gene Roddenberry's *Enterprise* was both shorter and far longer than five years. The original series was canceled after three years (1966–1969), but now, more than forty years later, we are still talking about and seeing Roddenberry's world of *Star Trek*. In addition to the five *Star Trek* series and eight movies that have been made, another *Star Trek* movie (a prequel) has just been produced by *Lost* cocreator J. J. Abrams.

Certainly *Star Trek* is one of the quintessential examples of cult television and the template for much of the fan-series interaction that followed. An intense letter-writing campaign by fans saved the show from cancellation after its second season, providing a show-saving model for subsequent series. In the years after *Star Trek*'s cancellation, fans were not content with multiple re-viewings of beloved episodes in syndication: they wrote their own stories (fan fiction), continuing the adventures of the *Star Trek* characters, and exchanged them in fanzines or sometimes, before the Internet, just mimeographed sheets; they drew portraits of the characters (see Trimble 17–31); they sewed facsimiles of the costumes; they sang fan folk songs (filk); they gathered for face-to-face meetings (see Bacon-Smith; Jenkins, *Textual Poachers*). Their enthusiasm was such that in 1979 the first *Star Trek* movie, *Star Trek, The Motion Picture* was released by Paramount, followed by *Star Trek: The Wrath of Khan* (1982), *Star Trek III: The Search for Spock* (1984) and *Star Trek IV: The Voyage Home* (1986). Then in 1987, *Star Trek:*

The Next Generation broadcast the first of its seven years of episodes, to be followed by *Star Trek: Deep Space Nine* (1992–1999), *Star Trek: Voyager* (1995–2001), and *Enterprise* (2001–2005; retitled *Star Trek: Enterprise* in 2003). Meanwhile, a whole industry of *Star Trek*–based novels, games, and paraphernalia (lunch boxes, action figures, clothing, toys) continues unabated—not to mention the fact that in the real world, a NASA space shuttle was named *Enterprise* at the urging of fans.

What accounts for the intensity of this response? And why does it endure? *Star Trek* stands at the intersection of art and society. To expect to fully explain such a phenomenon would be hubris indeed; many of us who write seriously about television have been enjoying and struggling through the contemplation of *Star Trek* for more than forty years. But certainly understanding must begin with the original series.

Star Trek

Gene Roddenberry's *Star Trek* was born in the tradition of Rod Serling's *The Twilight Zone*—a science fiction–fantasy series that gives a symbolic presentation of social issues. The fact that the social issues are hidden reduces the likelihood of economically based objection from sponsors, networks, and production companies, and the interpretation of symbolism involves the audience in a pleasurable intellectual exercise. Audiences who agree with the thematic thrusts of the series have already become more engaged than the typical television viewer because they have thought through the symbols to the meaning (or, more precisely, *a* meaning, since interpretations vary). Thoughtful viewers can also appreciate the maturity of vision that means that (again, like *The Twilight Zone*) the ending of an episode is not always happy: the wedding interrupted at the beginning ends with the funeral of the groom-to-be ("Balance of Terror"); the beautiful young Shakespearean actor is discovered to be a murdering madwoman ("The Conscience of the King"); Kirk's soul mate must die in Harlan Ellison's "City on the Edge of Forever"; the adolescent "Charlie X" must be returned to the disembodied Thasians, the poignant memory of his "I want to stay" echoing in our ears. These moments of sorrow help to earn the overall positive thrust of the series. Roddenberry, a former navy pilot, loved the idea of exploration, both physical and intellectual, and he grounded that general theme in his largely hopeful future world—neither utopian nor dystopian: "I like to think that there always are ... possibilities," to quote Kirk citing Spock (*Star Trek II*).

Some of the possibilities presented themselves in the crew: an Asian man, an African American woman, a Russian (despite the Cold War), a Scot, a southerner, a half-alien, and a middle-American white male. In 1966 this combination itself presented a strong symbolic assertion of the value of diversity. In fact, the term is used directly: the honored IDIC symbol of Vulcan stands for "Infinite Diversity in Infinite Combinations" ("Is There in Truth No Beauty?"). Oscar-winning actress Whoopi Goldberg has spoken of the importance to her (as an African American youngster) of seeing the beautiful Nichelle Nichols (who later worked in public relations for NASA) as Uhura, an officer on the bridge of the ship and even, on rare occasions, in command. The real astronaut Dr. Mae Jemison, the first African American woman in space, indicated her inspiration when she appeared in *The Next Generation* episode "Second Chances" and posed on the set with Nichols (Reeves-Stevens and Reeves-Stevens 187).

The episodes of the series confront social issues such as overpopulation, racism, the role of computers, war (again and again, war, during the Vietnam War), and class and socioeconomic differences. "The Cloud-Minders," for instance, examines the idea of the stratification of classes based on environmental conditions: the upper classes live in the clouds of Stratos, while the (literally) lower classes suffer impaired intellectual development (caused by "zienite gas"). In "Let That Be Your Last Battlefield," aliens Lokai, who is black on the left side and white on the right, and Bele, who is black on the right side and white on the left, fight viciously over Bele's assumption of racial superiority—a bitter parody of racism in a world that had just lost Martin Luther King Jr. In "The Omega Glory," descendants of people from the United States ("Yangs") engage in battle inspired by the distorted words of the U.S. Constitution, used as a talisman but with no understanding of their true meaning. It seems the applications of the social themes of the original *Star Trek* are not limited to the 1960s.

But these ideas would have been mere pedantry without their incarnation in living characters. Indeed, the central idea of the acceptance of difference is made real in the characters' relationships. The main three—the devoted, choleric, and humanely emotional physician Dr. Leonard "Bones" McCoy (DeForest Kelley); the half-Vulcan, half-human science officer Commander Spock, for whom logic is not just a value but a cultural imperative; and the energetic young starship captain who balances between the two, James Tiberius Kirk of the United Federation of Planets—not only talk about thematic issues but also represent difference by their natures (as do the supporting characters).

A first-season episode called "The Corbomite Maneuver" (written by Jerry Sohl) is especially effective in conveying the characters' qualities. When a silent red-alert light goes on while McCoy is giving Kirk his quarterly physical, the doctor simply ignores it, to the manifest irritation of Kirk, who then leaves. "If I jumped every time a light came on around here, I'd end up talking to myself," says the doctor, alone in the sick bay. As for Spock, we see him interacting with young Lieutenant Dave Bailey, who asserts, "Raising my voice back there doesn't mean I'm scared. . . . It means I happen to have a human thing called an adrenaline gland." Spock's response: "Hmm. Does sound most inconvenient, however. Have you considered having it removed?" ("Try to cross brains with Spock—he'll cut you down every time," dryly advises helmsman Mr. Sulu [George Takei].) And Uhura's body language during a later meeting conveys her extreme boredom with the tense young Bailey.

This episode not only establishes character traits, however; it also demonstrates the ways these very different people coalesce into solution. When an alien holds the ship captive and informs the crew of their imminent demise, Bailey cracks under the strain (as McCoy had warned he might). After a variety of failed attempts to secure their release, Spock tells the captain, "In chess, when one is outmatched, the game is over. Checkmate." Identifying himself with the game of intellectuals, Spock, in effect, gives up. In the midst of the countdown to their doom, McCoy goes to the bridge to ask that Kirk soften his report on Bailey; otherwise, he'll put in the record that Kirk disregarded his warning—"and that's no bluff." "Any time you can bluff me, Doctor . . . ," the captain almost shouts. And then, quietly, as the camera moves from face to face, the solution comes to him: "Not chess, Mr. Spock—poker." This very human solution takes brains, courage, and control of one's emotions in a crisis. The captain bluffs his way out of the threat by inventing, on the spot, a substance—Corbomite—that explodes whenever the vessel is attacked. When the alien backs down, Spock notes, "A very interesting game, this poker." Kirk responds, "It does have its advantages over chess." And McCoy, with sharklike geniality, adds, "Love to teach it to you sometime." The episode ends with the discovery that the alien had simply been testing the *Enterprise* to ensure that its assertions and records of peacefulness were not merely deceptions; destruction was never the intention. And so their ability to get along with one another recapitulates their ability to deal with the foreign, the Other, in a larger world. Both language and looks transmute aggression into play. The joy of this playfulness and the hope of good sense prevailing in human interactions are surely part of the enduring appeal.

It must be noted that this success in representing human interaction comes in part from the actors' effectiveness as well as the writing I have so liberally quoted. William Shatner has been charged with overacting, but his long career (including recent Emmy Awards) confirms his skill; except for a few scenes, he commands the screen for both dramatic and humorous moments. Leonard Nimoy's Spock was, if anything, even more successful, to the point that it was difficult for this gifted actor to escape the role. Part of the success was, of course, due to the nature of the character. The second season opener, "Amok Time," was penned by noted science fiction writer Theodore Sturgeon, and in it we learn that the Vulcan repression of emotion results in a correspondingly fierce mating cycle every seven years. This idea of the divided character was very appealing to modern people, who had to force themselves to behave with restraint in their workaday worlds and might very much enjoy an excuse to break loose. Spock's hidden emotions had also been effectively displayed in the first season's fourth episode, "The Naked Time," in which most of the regular characters' inhibitions are released after contact with an alien contagion.

That episode, like "The Corbomite Maneuver," is also noteworthy for the camera work of Jerry Finnerman. Throughout the series, Finnerman's work literally illuminates the characters and enhances their Romantic boldness and beauty. In "The Naked Time," however, one shot in particular is used to eerie effect. As Nurse Christine Chappell (Majel Barrett, later Roddenberry's wife and the computer voice of future *Star Trek* series) confesses her secret love to Spock under the effect of the contagion, an extreme close-up of Nimoy's face—with his green-undertoned skin and pointed ears—highlights his alienness. It is not a beauty shot but an emotionally revealing one. The later climactic shot—pulling back from the people on the bridge, overlaid by the motion of the stars rushing back too—is a simple but extremely effective visual for the dangerous whiplash in time that crowns the episode. The symphonic emphasis of the music at this point is an important element of the scene. The musical score provided by Alexander Courage is part of the emotional cuing throughout the series—not just the (by now) internationally known fanfare of the series' theme but also the supporting tracks throughout the show (many of which can be hummed by fans). The special effects may have been bargain basement, but other elements of the series combined successfully to create the believable world of emotion and thought inhabited by these memorable, flawed, admirable people.

Having mentioned the characters' flaws, perhaps it is best to acknowledge some of the series' flaws as well. It has been accused of imperialism: although the Federation's "Prime Directive" asserts that they should not interfere with less advanced societies, the *Enterprise* crew breaks that directive again and again. Other weaknesses have to do with race. Comedian Franklin Ajaye famously asked why, on *Star Trek*, the black guy always gets "cubed." Although the series was a beacon of progressive thought in some ways, it was also a creation of its time. So it is perhaps not surprising that in the episode "The Ultimate Computer," the character of the brilliant, Nobel Prize–winning black scientist Dr. Richard Daystrom has a nervous breakdown: not only did he insult Captain Kirk, but he also suffered from the extratextual stress of being a token. However, it is still refreshing to recognize that the character is allowed to live outside perfection and is given the humanity of having such a breakdown—a sophisticated sort of misery. As for Ajaye's specific image of "cubing" the disposable character, in the episode "By Any Other Name," two minor characters are actually turned into cube shapes: a black male and a white female. In their cubed form, one is crushed. It is worth noting that the one returned to human form is the black male; the "handful of dust" is the female.

Long ago, Karin Blair wrote of the "Disposable Female" in *Star Trek*. It is true that Captain Kirk and, on occasion, Spock and McCoy fit the Jewett and Lawrence pattern of the American Monomyth—a hero who sheds women as he goes. It is also worth remembering that, though forced to relinquish the idea, Roddenberry wanted to have the captain's second in command played by a woman (Whitfield 128). And in terms of race, one should not forget that *Star Trek* gave us the first interracial kiss on TV, between Kirk and Uhura ("Plato's Stepchildren"). True, the kiss was forced on them by aliens—they were, after all, not lovers but comrades, part of the family of shipmates. But the kiss was also forced on them by Roddenberry. The series was not immaculate in terms of racism or sexism, but it was certainly progressive. Like the characters, the series was flawed; like the characters, it was also heroic.

Star Trek: The Next Generation

Star Trek: The Next Generation (TNG) very easily could have been a pallid copy of the original. And indeed, in the first season its characters spent a fair amount of time standing about looking nobly upward. But even from the start, it had a flavor of its own, mixed with foundational elements from the earlier series. As *TNG*'s Dr. Beverly Crusher (Gates McFadden) states in "The Naked Now": "I made this a broader-based remedy, I hope, but it's still very close to the formula from the old *Enterprise*."

The signature difference that marks each of the *Star Trek* series can be found in the captain, who embodies the series' central attitudes. Jean-Luc Picard is another white male, but rather than being young and headstrong, he is significantly older — by appearance, at least in his fifties — intellectual, and, not to put too fine a point on it, bald. Shakespearean actor Patrick Stewart was proposed by original *Star Trek* co-executive producer Robert Justman and *TNG* co-executive producer Richard Berman and was eventually accepted by Roddenberry (Reeves-Stevens and Reeves-Stevens 295–97). Stewart's Picard is a lover of literature, classical music, and archaeology — a man passionate about matters intellectual.

As for the crew overall, they are more of an ensemble of equals in terms of screen time. In many ways, the qualities of the first series' crew seem to be divided among the members of the second crew (Wilcox, "Shifting Roles"). Spock's extreme logic goes to the android Data (Brent Spiner), while the Vulcan's telepathic abilities are inherited, in modified form, by the half-Betazed empath Troi (Marina Sirtis). McCoy's role as healer of both body and mind is taken by the psychologist Counselor Troi and the physician Dr. Crusher. Although Kirk's love of exploration is shared by Picard, his other love interests devolve on Riker (Jonathan Frakes), the tall, young first officer, clearly intended as the romantic lead. Spock's role as the outsider accepted on the bridge can be seen in more than one character: not only the android Data but also Klingon Starfleet officer Worf, who was raised by humans. The idea of incorporating — in some ways, assimilating — the enemy is a recurring *Star Trek* theme, but *TNG* makes sure to show the value of Worf's retaining his own culture. The producers chose African American Michael Dorn to play Worf. African American actor Levar Burton, widely known for his role in *Roots*, plays another officer who does double duty in representing diversity; his character, Chief Engineer Geordi LaForge (named for a *Star Trek* fan), is blind and perceives the world differently, through special sensors. An even higher-profile African American actor requested to join the cast in the second season: Whoopi Goldberg. She plays Guinan, the bartender who shares some of Counselor Troi's functions but is also an alien with a special sense of time—a woman of wisdom whom even Captain Picard obeys when she asserts her view ("Yesterday's Enterprise"). Her Wife of Bath hats add to her feminist presence (Wilcox, "Goldberg"). In short, this second *Enterprise* crew once again conveys the message of complex diversity.

The major enemies or opponents encountered by the *Enterprise* also define the series. In the first season the Ferengi are introduced, a species clearly meant to mock the 1980s culture of greed depicted, for example, in the movie *Wall Street*, released the same year *TNG* began broadcasting. The Ferengi seem more laughable than fearsome. That certainly cannot be said of the series' most famous enemy species—the Borg, a hive mind of astonishing technological sophistication and frightening intellectual and physical conformity. This all-white conglomerate exists, in their words, to "assimilate" others, absorb production, and extend their own reach, in a ghastly representation of economic and cultural imperialism. At least thematically, the series certainly comes to grips with an issue that had plagued the 1960s show. That issue of assimilation and imperialism is addressed most vividly when the captain is temporarily taken and becomes "Locutus of Borg," the Borg's voice—an entity the younger crew members must reject. The Borg are introduced by a recurring character created by Roddenberry: Q, a member of the Q Continuum, is omnipotent (almost), judgmental, childlike, puckish in humor, and always good for a plot device or a philosophical conundrum. Vibrantly played by actor John de Lancie, he sometimes faces off with Goldberg's Guinan and ends up seeming to be Picard's friend (not to mention more or less dating Picard's ex).

Another distinguishing quality of *TNG* is its tendency toward the metatextual—a tendency furthered by the inclusion of the holodeck, a twenty-fourth-century variation on the play-within-a-play. Using the holodeck, crew members can program three-dimensional, interactive fictional worlds for exercise or entertainment. Picard's enjoyment of genre literature, specifically 1940s noir detective fiction, is showcased in "The Big Goodbye," a first-season episode that won a Peabody Award. One of the most widely admired episodes of the series, the sixth season's "The Inner Light," has Picard mentally living, in half an hour, the entire lifetime of a man from a drought-stricken planet. The now-dead inhabitants of that world had chosen this extraordinarily vivid way of passing on their story. Picard is left with poignantly real memories of a wife and children and with a touch of the music of that life—the ability to play a song flute that it had taken him years to master. The episode is, in a sense, a depiction of the role of fiction—a living story that allows us to share the lives of others—just as *Star Trek* itself does. Then there is the mental asylum–political prisoner story "Frame of Mind," Brannon Braga's variation on a Tom Stoppard play that had been performed by a touring company comprising *TNG* actors—yet another exploration of the nature of appearance and reality, of the worlds we construct in our minds. And what better show than *Star Trek* to consider such a contest of realities? (Wilcox, "Unreal TV" 211–12).

Of course, the series does not require metatext to be thoughtful. The original's "Corbomite Maneuver" tale of benign testing by a powerful stranger is transmuted, in "Where Silence Has Lease," to a meditation on death in, quite literally, the face of a *2001*-like star child–gone–dark creature who registers on their instruments as nothing—"a damned ugly nothing," as LaForge puts it. Once again, there is the idea of a "bluff" in the face of danger, but this time the danger is genuine. Picard has ordered the ship to self-destruct rather than let "Nagilum" explore the varieties of death by killing half his crew. But "was he bluffing?" asks Riker. With this captain and this series, death seems a bit more real. This grimmer worldview is also reflected in the death of one of the major characters in the first season—Security Chief Tasha Yar, played by Denise Crosby. Crosby had asked to be released from the series, tired of spending most of her time echoing Uhura ("Hailing frequencies open, Captain"). But external cause notwithstanding, the series makes the death of the character count, with many subsequent references to her loss.

There are not only philosophical responses to death but also thoughtful perspectives on communication. Whereas the original's "The Devil in the Dark"—with its rock creature, the mother Horta—is an enjoyable presentation of the value of overcoming differences, including those of language, *TNG*'s "Darmok" spends almost the entire episode focusing on the subject in a brilliant recognition of the cultural differences embodied in language differences. Admired actor Paul Winfield holds the screen for most of the episode with Patrick Stewart. *TNG* implies an advance in cultural modesty: Winfield's alien race cannot be understood by the "universal translator" (employed beginning with the original series) because their language is constructed completely of allusions to a culturally defining frame of stories (once again, a kind of metatext). Like the original *Star Trek*, these shows do not always have completely happy endings, and the Winfield character dies. But by the time he does, Picard has learned enough to understand the nature of this kind of communication, and he shares the ancient Earth story of Gilgamesh and Enkidu—two friends—as his new friend passes away. The pleasure of literary consciousness and ethical themes combine in this memorable episode.

As in the original *Star Trek*, more specific social subjects are addressed in *TNG* as well. Ironically, the extremely white character Data often focuses episodes on prejudice: "If you prick me, do I not . . . leak?" he asks in "The Naked Now." In the widely acclaimed second-season episode "The Measure of a Man," with echoes of the Dred Scott case, Data is taken to court over whether he should be considered property, and Guinan makes it clear to Picard that the issue is slavery (Wilcox, "Dating Data"). "Angel One" makes as overt a statement about sexism as the original series' "Let This Be Your Last Battlefield" makes about racism. "Ensign Ro" introduces a representative of the Bajoran species, whose tribulations seem to parallel those of the Palestinians. "The Outcast" raises the question of repression of sexual orientation by having one strange new world repress the heterosexual urge.

There are some problems with the series' subtext; for example, it sometimes seems that in order to survive, a female regular has to be a mother figure in one way or another (Barr; Wilcox, "Shifting Roles"). In the second-season opener, Counselor Troi joins a long line of fictional women in seemingly supernatural-imposed pregnancies, from Rosemary's baby to *Angel*'s Cordelia and beyond. Since this is *Star Trek*, the baby is not demonic but a being of pure life force who wants to explore the crew's existence and then conveniently turns back into a Tinkerbell light and floats away. Whether this is a story about the joy of birth or the acceptance of an unwanted pregnancy is debatable; one can argue that it is both. One might argue that Counselor Troi gets to choose, and she chooses to bear and care for the child; alternatively, one might argue that Troi not only has to take it but also has to like it. In either case, the shift in the opening voice-over, from the line "where no man has gone before" to "where no *one* has gone before"—though a notable effort at change—is not enough in itself to completely alter the *Star Trek* world. But the *Star Trek* world is still more advanced than the world most of its viewers live in.

And *TNG* still makes the stories work by deriving them from characters who seem human (with the possible exception of Wesley Crusher, teen genius). The original series' poker game from "The Corbomite Maneuver" is transformed to a weekly poker game for the officers of *TNG*—again, a sign of their humanity. And in *TNG*'s last episode, "All Good Things . . . ," after a final experience with Q as Greek chorus, the captain joins the game for the first time.

Star Trek: Deep Space Nine

Star Trek: Deep Space Nine (*DS9*) is, like earlier *Trek* series, defined in part by its leader. Respected actor Avery Brooks follows in Patrick Stewart's footsteps in terms of the gravitas he lends to the role of Commander Benjamin Sisko. Brooks was the first African American to take the central role in a *Star Trek* series, and given that, even in the early twenty-first century, minorities are underrepresented, his casting was a continuation of *Star Trek*'s social progressivism. The characters differ in other ways, too: While Picard prefers contemplation with a background of classical music, Sisko tosses a baseball around to help him think. While Picard announces his dislike for children in the pilot, Sisko is a widower with a son, Jake (Cirroc Lofton). Indeed, the series as a whole is more focused on family life. Although *TNG* crew members are like family to one another, on *DS9* there are actual families: Sisko and Jake; Miles O'Brien (Colm Meaney, formerly *TNG* transporter chief, now chief operations officer on *DS9*), his wife Keiko (Rosalind Chao), and their children; the Ferengi Quark (Armin Shimerman) and his nephew Nog (Aron Eisenberg), who becomes Jake's friend and, later, a Starfleet cadet. This subject matter correlates with the very different setting of the series: the original series and *TNG* take place on a starship, but *DS9* takes place on a gigantic space station (Deep Space Nine) near the planet Bajor and a stable wormhole used for transportation. So while the crews on the earlier series could fly away after a short-term conflict, on *DS9* they have to live with trouble.

This series is often described as darker than the first two. The poignantly hesitant rhythms of the theme music by Dennis McCarthy suggest this tone, as do the characters and plots. The Bajorans (introduced by Ensign Ro on *TNG*) have endured occupation by the cruel Cardassians, refugee camps, and resistance; contemporary social parallels are easy to find. Even Commander Sisko and Jake, in the first segment of the pilot, are represented as refugees—from a starship that has been destroyed by the Borg, with orders voiced by Locutus/Picard. *DS9*'s perspective is different: the protagonists are not so much Starfleet elite as people struggling to get by.

Once again, however, the series regulars represent diversity. Former Bajoran resistance fighter Kira Nerys (Nana Visitor) does not fully trust the Federation and the agreement it supports between the Bajorans and the Cardassians, yet she becomes Sisko's second in command. Bar owner Quark gradually shows us some Ferengi values that can be appreciated—not just the amusing, sometimes even sensible, Rules of Acquisition but family loyalty as well. René Auberjonois's Odo takes the place of Data as an extremely different type of person to relate to (Odo is a shape-shifter who spends his downtime in a bucket). And there is Siddig El Fadil's Dr. Julian Bashir, whose ethnicity reminds viewers of contemporary Middle Eastern conflicts; Jadzia Dax (Terry Farrell), a symbiont life-form with a visible humanoid body and a long-lived internal being who has shared bodies with many different people over the centuries (including a friend of Sisko's that he still calls "old man"); and a Klingon—in fact, Worf of *TNG*.

TNG enriched the sense of its fictional world's depth by occasional visits from original series characters—an aged McCoy in the pilot, the long-lived Spock in the fifth season, and Scotty, released from a seventy-five-year-long transporter loop, in the sixth. Here, continuity is established for the first time by regular characters—O'Brien (an occasional character on *TNG*) and Worf (once *TNG* went off the air). Thus *DS9* uses a prime *Star Trek* method (in fact, a prime television method): continuity with difference. Although in later years the characters venture beyond the station, *DS9*'s stew pot of species stays, for much of the series, at home on DS9.

Perhaps in part because it is spatially stationary, some of the series' best episodes explore relationships in time. Indeed, the concept is confronted in the pilot when Sisko encounters an alien race that simply cannot comprehend linear time ("What is this . . . time?"). He explains by means of his own painful memories ("You exist here. It is not linear," they say of his memory of his wife's death) and by means of the human delight in games and the interplay between foreseen consequences and the unknown—specifically, in the form of baseball. Time and emotion also move the plot in "The Visitor," in which Jake as an aged man (Tony Todd) engages with earlier versions of himself and his dead father as he tells the tale of his loss. In "Far beyond the Stars," Avery/Sisko becomes mid-twentieth-century science fiction writer Benny Russell (many other cast members take roles in the twentieth-century story as well), presenting the social problems of the time. Specifically, he writes a story of the future—of Starfleet Commander Benjamin Sisko—and even when he offers to couch it as a "dream," he is told it cannot be published. This suffering is paired with a fierce physical beating when Benny tries to help a young black man (Cirroc Lofton, who also plays Sisko's son), and when Sisko awakes, he wonders which is reality, which is the dream. Both these episodes, like many in *TNG* and others in *DS9*, are clearly metatextual and, as Michele Barrett and Duncan Barrett term it, postmodern (137–41).

While Ben Sisko lives the life of Benny Russell, he is exhorted by a preacher character played by Brock Peters, who also plays Sisko's father. Overtly religious subject matter is another major element of *DS9*. Sisko is not only the commander of the station; he is, in the pilot episode, identified by the Bajorans as the emissary to their prophets—a designation he resists but must grapple with throughout the series. These religious questions, as Barrett and Barrett note (182–94), are entwined with questions of identity—questions that are raised in other contexts too, such as the symbiont-host relationship of the Trill Jadzia Dax. Heroic though it is, *DS9* is much more about doubts and questions than the preceding *Star Treks* were.

Star Trek: Voyager

With *Star Trek: Voyager*, the *Star Trek* series entered the new millennium. In some ways, its captain seems more traditionally certain, secure, and daring; yet *Voyager's* captain represents another step into another new world: the first female lead in a *Star Trek* series. (*Star Trek* thus predicted the course of social progress, with Senator Barack Obama winning the competition for the 2008 Democratic presidential nomination over Senator Hillary Clinton, and a black man becoming leader before a white woman.) There had been a brief appearance of a female *Enterprise* captain in *TNG*'s "Yesterday's Enterprise," but Captain Kathryn

Janeway (Kate Mulgrew) commanded *Voyager* for six years. Like Kirk and Picard, she is in charge of a starship, but the starship *Voyager* has been flung far out of the Alpha quadrant of the galaxy and is trying to return home—a trip estimated to take seventy-five years.

Once again, the series explores moral issues, as in "Death Wish," with the Q character reappearing to ponder euthanasia. Once again, the crew must face interior struggles to embrace those who are different: There is Chakotay (Robert Beltran), a Native American Maquis resistance fighter (a group introduced on *TNG* and *DS9*); he becomes Janeway's second in command, and the crew from his own small vessel joins the Starfleet crew. There is the enthusiastic young ensign Harry Kim (Garrett Wang); there is Janeway's Vulcan friend Tuvok (Tim Russ), the head of security; there is a half-Klingon Maquis with a Latina last name who becomes chief engineer, B'Elanna Torres (Roxann Dawson); there is B'Elanna's eventual husband, an ex-con admiral's son, flyboy Tom Paris (Robert Duncan McNeil); there is, in the first and second season, Kes (Jennifer Lien), a member of the short-lived Ocampan species, whose joyous relationship with her mate, the cheerful Talaxian cook Neelix (Ethan Phillips), gives new meaning to carpe diem; there is the Doctor (Robert Picardo), a holographic physician (like Data, a different sort from the usual biological person); and there is Seven of Nine (Jeri Ryan), the female character who has been individuated from (or is in the process of individuating from) the Borg.

One of the most interesting elements of the series is the relationship between Janeway and Seven of Nine (originally a human girl, Anneka Hansen, who was assimilated by the Borg). Janeway is both mentor and, in some ways, mother to the brilliant, emotionally repressed, statuesque Seven, who is forced to rejoin the human race. Jeri Ryan was not the first *Star Trek* actor to be tightly clad; most of the *TNG* actors had complained, in the first season, about how revealing their costumes were (and costume designer Robert Blackman changed them). But the costuming in this case was so extreme as to cause notably mixed messages in the series' explorations of growth and identity through the character; Seven's forced repatriation also raises questions (indeed, Seven herself—and thus the series—raises those questions) in terms of autonomy (Sobstyl). In the series finale, the mother-mentor Janeway gives her life to save Seven and help the other characters return home. One might be tempted to remark that the first female captain is the only one to die with her series. However, Janeway (that is, the older Janeway) dies because she returns to an earlier point in time and changes the time line in which Seven has died; the series' closing focuses on the living, younger Janeway. The double ending reflects the series' tendency toward double meaning—for good or ill.

Enterprise

In the fall after *Voyager* went off the air, the fifth *Star Trek* series, *Enterprise*, began. A prequel, the series is set in the twenty-second century, before the Earth became a member of the Federation. Perhaps not surprisingly, then, the captain is once again an all-American male (he even has a dog). A Sci-Fi Channel promo conveys something of the series' retro tone: "Experience a future where the Klingons are still bad guys, the women are green ('I'll do anything you want') and the captain gets all the action ('Wouldn't have it any other way')." Captain Jonathan Archer is portrayed by Scott Bakula, who already had a fan base (the Leapers) from his role as the allusive and elusive Samuel Beckett on *Quantum Leap*. In an effort to position the series as emotionally closer to the contemporary viewer, co–executive producers Rick Berman and Brannon Braga eschewed the typical instrumental *Star Trek* theme music—whose symphonic scoring suggests nobility of purpose, while leaving the specifics to be imagined by listeners—and instead presented a pop theme with lyrics (written by Diane Warren). Joss Whedon, for his sci-fi Western *Firefly*, created a theme that the series' fans, known as Browncoats, can (and do) sing aloud; the *Enterprise* theme, however, did not receive a similar fan response. In the DVD pilot commentary, Berman and Braga suggest that viewers may not have liked having a theme with words. The problem may not have been having words per se, but the particular words. To quote from the chorus: "I've got faith (I've got faith) / I've got faith (I've got faith) / Faith of the heart." Further comment seems redundant. If one contrasts the witty language quoted from the original *Star Trek*, one might concede that *Enterprise* suffers from what Dr. Pulaski would have called "replicant fading" (*TNG*: "Up the Long Ladder"). And when Captain Archer has to chide a Vulcan for raising his voice, it seems a cheap triumph for the hero at the expense of the *Star Trek* mythology, of which Vulcan logic and restraint are primary elements.

Nonetheless, the series does, as usual (usual for *Star Trek*, that is), include Asian and black characters and once again grapples with (or at least strokes) the theme of dealing with the Other among us. In this case, there is T'Pol (Jolene Black), a female Vulcan science officer who has apparently taken fashion tips from Seven of Nine. As for Communications Officer Hoshi Sato (Linda Park), fans have complained that she is too timid; however, a case could be made that language scholar Hoshi's attitude is refreshingly human in the land of the heroic. The major enemy, the Suliban, attempt to manipulate time lines, conveying the importance of the unknown future consequences of our actions, which is a primary theme in this prequel series.

Of course, what is to come is important in the world outside the series, too. Although the general consensus is that the last *Trek* series is the weakest, *Star Trek* is far from over. Fans still meet and write, novelists still publish, scholars still ponder, and a new movie came in 2009— a prequel with *Star Trek*'s original Spock (Leonard Nimoy) in its cast, tying the past-future to the future-past. One can only hope that *Star Trek* will always try to reach just beyond what we now have in our grasp.

Supernatural

Alison Peirse

In "The Changing Face of American Television Programs on British Screens," Paul Rixon suggests that a new approach is needed for analyzing the international borders of televisual flow. He suggests that this approach should take place at three interconnecting levels: "at the macro, focusing on the international flow of programs and the changing relationships between national systems, broadcasters and producers; at the meso level (middle), where the focus will be on the schedule, the flow of programs as constructed by particular organizations and broadcasters; and at the last level will be the micro—here there is a need to understand how different textual devices operate within programs and the flow of programs and how the viewer watches, experiences and makes sense of television" (51).

Drawing on Rixon's model, this chapter examines the television series *Supernatural*, first broadcast in the United States on the WB network in September 2005. The series draws heavily from generic tropes of the horror film to provide a universal familiarity to viewers on both sides of the Atlantic and, indeed, globally. Set in small-town America, the series follows the demon-hunting exploits of brothers Sam and Dean Winchester, played by *Gilmore Girls* star Jared Padalecki and *Dawson's Creek* and *Smallville* actor Jensen Ackles, respectively.

Season 1 has a tripartite structure: the brothers search for their missing father, demon hunter John Winchester (Jeffrey Dean Morgan); they hunt the demon Azazel, nicknamed Yellow Eyes, who killed their mother; and they discover that Sam has psychic powers. Season 2 opens with the rediscovered John trading his life for that of the critically ill Dean after a road accident. With John dead, Sam and Dean continue fighting demons on their own, but the central narrative arc revolves around confrontations with Yellow Eyes and his diabolical plans for psychic Sam. However, in "All Hell Breaks Loose Part I" (2.21), Sam is stabbed to death by Jake, another young psychic, and dies in Dean's arms. In "All Hell Breaks Loose Part II" (2.22), Dean sells his soul to the Crossroads Demon to resurrect Sam and kills Azazel. Dean has only twelve months before he is dragged into hell, and season 3 opens with Sam and Dean demon hunting again, while Sam tries to find a way to get Dean out of his devilish predicament.

The diegetic world of *Supernatural* has increased substantially since its inception, and this chapter explores how these worlds are envisaged through the "macro" level of filming in Vancouver, the "miso" level of scheduling and programming of *Supernatural* on the U.K. channel ITV2, and the "micro" level of intertextual reference, horror film homage, and popular culture play. The popularity of *Supernatural* as a cult television text creates a transnational language that moves beyond national boundaries, undercutting specific local cultures and viewing practices.

Although the series is set in the small towns and dusty backroads of America, *Supernatural* is filmed predominantly in Vancouver, British Columbia. In October 2007 the *Vancouver Sun* newspaper ran a long article entitled "They Came from B.C.," examining the importance of fantasy, horror, and science fiction genres for the British Columbia film and television industry. The article suggests that years of filming *The X-Files* in Vancouver's burgeoning "Hollywood North" has created a range of highly skilled production labor, making it attractive to contemporary television program production.

Canada is a lower-cost alternative to America for international television production. In analyzing the increasing decentralization of television and film production, Allen J. Scott points out that there is a "rising tide of de-centralization of film- and TV-shooting activities away from Los Angeles and their execution in other countries, above all, Canada" (193). In September 2007 the following series were among those in production in Vancouver: *Battlestar Galactica, Bionic Woman, The L Word, Reaper, Smallville, Stargate Atlantis,* and *Supernatural* (*Hollywood North Report*). The majority of these shows invite cult status and exemplify Canada's success in international television production. Indeed, all the series listed are screened in the United Kingdom on digital channels such as Sky One, ITV2, E4, and Living TV.

Vancouver's site as a home for cult television has recently been explored by Will Brooker. Focusing on fan pilgrimages, Brooker argues that "while Vancouver may be valued by film and television producers as a generic, anonymous, 'flat' fictional environment, to fan pilgrims who bring their own imaginary maps (based on the fictional geographies of *Smallville*, *The X-Files* and *Battlestar Galactica*), the city is a rich intersection of possible worlds" (423). He writes that Vancouver's Robson Square took the place of Washington, D.C., in *The X-Files* episode "Apocrypha" (3.16); for a *Smallville* fan, Vancouver's public library "is the Metropolis Courthouse . . . and to the fan of *Battlestar Galactica*, who watched Sharon 'Boomer' Valerii and Karl 'Helo' Agathon trek past it on Cylon-occupied Caprica, the Vancouver public library is on another planet entirely" (426–27). For purposes of this chapter, the key to Brooker's argument is the perceived anonymity of Vancouver and its surrounding areas. His comments resonate with the transitory quality of *Supernatural*'s textual preoccupations, where transience and "nowheresville" are built into the very text itself. Despite every episode (except for the pilot) being filmed in and around Vancouver and the city of Burnaby, Dean and Sam are constantly on the road, scouring small-town America for demons and for answers. The specific location of each episode is registered in bold type at the beginning: examples include Toledo, Ohio (1.5); Lawrence, Kansas (1.9); Hibbing, Minnesota (1.15), Fitchburg, Wisconsin, "Population, 20,501" (1.18); Red Lodge, Montana (2.3); Cicero, Indiana (3.2); and Maple Springs, New York (3.5). This accords with Brooker's insight that Vancouver's "streets are considered generic and unrecognizable to a US audience; it can be everywhere—Boston, Sioux City, Washington DC, Metropolis—because, to non-Vancouverites, it looks like nowhere in particular" (427).

The location of Vancouver has become an in-joke within the *Supernatural* text, as evidenced by Sam's comment about the "unusual" weather in Los Angeles: "Does it seem like swimming pool weather to you, Dean? It's practically Canadian" ("Hollywood Babylon," 2.18). The back lots featured in "Hollywood Babylon" have a distinctly gray and overcast air, completely breaking with the popular conception of California as a sunny and colorful space. Similarly, Vancouver's ability to double as middle America is regular reinforced in the dialogue, such as when Dean complains that they never go anywhere exciting. In "Sin City" (3.4), Sam discovers a lead in Ohio, specifically, "Elizabethville . . . a half-dead factory town in the dust belt." Dean bemoans, "There's got to be a demon or two in South Beach." The practical constraints of filming in Canadian weather conditions and within the "perceived anonymity" of Vancouver are thus ably addressed in the text.

In the United States, *Supernatural* first aired on the WB before moving to the CW in season 2, the result of a 2006 merger between the WB and UPN. According to Dawn Ostroff, the CW's president of entertainment, the network's "shows are going to appeal to the 18- to 34-year-olds" (Andreeva). There is a distinct parity between the CW and ITV2, *Supernatural*'s home in the United Kingdom. According to the ITV Web site, "ITV2 continues to capture and retain a fun-loving, brand-conscious, younger audience of 16–34s with a female bias. In terms of audience appeal, ITV2 is a bit like a television version of a glossy celebrity magazine" ("ITV2"). Aside from a brief and ill-fated switch to a late-night slot on ITV1 during season 2, *Supernatural* has been screened on ITV2 since its first season. This suggests a strong presentation and target market "fit" between transatlantic channels.

A review of *Supernatural*'s first season in the U.S. trade paper *Variety* reveals the importance of the reputation of both its network and the programs that preceded it. Brian Lowry states: "The WB enjoyed considerable success with the macabre *Buffy the Vampire Slayer* and *Angel* and fared pretty well with *Smallville* Tuesdays before planting *One Tree Hill* in the post–*Gilmore Girls* timeslot. With new series on ABC, NBC and UPN, the door would seem open if *Supernatural*—really the only new WB show that perfectly dovetails with the netlet's traditional brand—can find the right mix of fright, humor and slowly unfolding mystery." The impact of *Buffy the Vampire Slayer* and *The X-Files* in opening up television networks to horror, science fiction, and fantasy-themed programs should not be underestimated. As Lowry suggests, *Supernatural* combines the generic components of horror television exemplified by *Buffy*, but its unique selling point is Sam and Dean: Ackles and Padalecki are demon-busting visions of loveliness who also possess a Whedonesque penchant for razor-sharp dialogue and pop culture references.

In the United Kingdom's *Observer*, journalist Ian Johns picks up on several of the above points in a discussion of the transnational dimensions of the text. When describing season 3's opening episode for the paper's "Digital Pick of the Day," Johns writes, "Teen-friendly hunks Jensen Ackles and Jared Padalecki return as the ghostbusting brothers in a grimy world in perpetual need of dusting or wiping that's closer to Japanese horror than *Buffy*. . . . Basically, it's beautiful people versus ugly spirits" (4). Indeed, although I firmly stress *Buffy*'s influence on the series, *Supernatural* does overtly display its allegiance to Southeast Asian horror films, particularly the cinematic rendition of Japanese ghost stories exemplified by *Ringu* (1998), *Ju-On* (2000), and *Dark Water* (2002). Asian horror is most explicitly referenced in season 1: episodes are brimming with dead girls with long, dark hair appearing in mirrors and photographs, reaching up through the water of overflowing bathtubs, and crawling around at the edges of the frame. In "Bloody Mary" (1.5), the eponymous Mary appears at the end of the episode climbing out of a shattered mirror. In the pilot, a murderous dead girl with long, black hair and a white dress appears in Sam's rearview mirror as he drives late at night. In "Dead in the Water" (1.3), a malevolent water spirit pulls a grieving man into a sink and drowns him. In "Children Shouldn't Play with Dead Things" (2.4), Matthew watches a home video of his now-dead girlfriend, Angela. As the video plays, an additional image is reflected on the screen: Angela stands behind Matthew, garbed in white clothing and with long, dark hair. Matthew turns and screams, and blood splatters the screen. Through its iconography of the murderous dead girl, an obsession with long hair and watery deaths, and playing around with offscreen space, *Supernatural* draws on Southeast Asian visual tropes of horror. As such, the cultural hybridity and generic intertextuality of *Supernatural* creates a demonstrable pull to international television audiences.

Visually, the series exhibits an obvious predilection for Asian horror, but in terms of *narrative*, episodic structures draw extensively on American horror films, particularly those from the 1960s, 1970s, and 1980s. At the micro level, *Supernatural*'s success can be partially attributed to its popular culture references, exploration of urban legends, and incorporation of horror film tropes. Urban legends are a particularly prominent plot device in *Supernatural*. As noted by executive producer Robert Singer, "In *Supernatural* one thing we try to do is to ground all of this in some sort of legend—something that, if you Googled it, you could find it" (Amatangelo). "Hook Man" (1.7) revolves around a reaper who picks on copulating teens, culminating in a young woman butchered in the bed next to her unsuspecting roommate. The killer writes a message on the bedroom wall for the roommate—"Aren't you glad you didn't turn on the light?"—a narrative act popularized in the teen slasher film

Urban Legend (1998). The series also draws on fairy-tale tropes, culminating in "Bedtime Stories" (3.5), when Grimm's fairy tales are brought to life: a murderous female spirit reenacts "Snow White," "Little Red Riding Hood," and other gruesome tales in the small town of Maple Springs, with disastrous consequences.

"Bugs" (1.8) concerns a new housing development overrun with swarming insects with a taste for human meat. Sam and Dean quickly discover that it is built on sacred ground, mirroring the traditional narrative explanation in both *Poltergeist* (1982) and *The Shining* (1980), where cursed properties are built on Indian burial grounds. Later in the same episode, one of the real estate agents who is staying in one of the new properties decides to take a shower. Naked and alone, she is soon swamped in a deluge of murderous spiders. She crashes out of the shower, blood and glass flying in homage to Alfred Hitchcock's *Psycho* (1960). Similarly, the plot of "The Benders" (1.15) involves an inbred family that kidnaps, tortures, and hunts down innocent people, mirroring films such as *The Hills Have Eyes* (1977) and *The Texas Chainsaw Massacre* (1974).

The denouement of season 1 is a beautifully constructed reworking of two canonized horror films. Having saved John and retrieved the demon-killing Colt revolver, Sam, Dean, and John drive away in the night in Dean's beloved black 1967 Chevy Impala. Creedence Clearwater Revival's "Bad Moon Rising" begins to play, hailing the extradiegetic music of John Landis's *An American Werewolf in London* (1981). Suddenly, a semi appears from the edge of the frame and smashes into them, emulating the "bus stop" sequence in *Cat People* (1942)—a film *An American Werewolf in London* also references. Season 1 concludes with the three main characters left for dead and Dean's beloved car apparently written off. The downbeat, tragic ending with its low lighting concludes the homage to the Landis film.

The transnational quality of the television genre is also revealed in Sam and Dean's knowledge of popular culture. Their quips speak to an intertextual matrix that connects the international viewers of the series, referencing music and a wide variety of cult films and television programs, including the original *Star Trek* series, *Ghostbusters* (1984), *Dawn of the Dead* (1978), and *Star Wars* (1977). In "Skin" (1.6), a double takes over Sam's appearance, thoughts, and memories, causing Dean to ask him if it was "like a Vulcan mind-meld." In "Hook Man" (1.7), Sam uncovers evidence of a killer in the newspaper section of the university library, and Dean commends him: "Nice job there, Dr. Venkman." Another *Ghostbusters* reference occurs in "No Exit" (2.6). When Dean discovers ectoplasm in a electrical socket, he says, "Sam, I think I know what we're dealing with here. It's the Stay-Puffed Marshmallow Man." In "Children Shouldn't Play with Dead Things," Dean asks Sam if the zombie Angela can be killed with a gunshot to the head. Sam reprimands him, "Dude, you've been watching way too many Romero flicks." In "Simon Said" (2.5), Sam and Dean meet Andrew Gallagher, a twenty-three-year-old with psychic abilities like Sam. Andrew tricks Dean into giving him the Impala, and Dean later complains, "He full-on Obi-Wan'ed me. It's mind control, man!" The *Star Wars* motif concludes when Dean and Andrew collude to break into an office and Andrew tells the guards, "These aren't the droids you're looking for."

Sam's psychic abilities are particularly prone to pop culture references. In "Asylum" (1.10), as the brothers creep through an abandoned mental institution, Dean quips, "Let me know if you see any dead people, Haley Joe." A short time later he asks, "Hey Sam, who d'ya think is the hotter psychic? Patricia Arquette, Jennifer Love Hewitt, or you?" Thus, in addition to the film *The Sixth Sense* (1999), he refers to two American TV series playing on U.K. digital channels at the same time as *Supernatural*: *Medium* and *Ghost Whisperer*.

Rock music is an essential textual thread of the series. In "Phantom Traveler" (1.4), the boys decide to impersonate FBI agents. They rent suits, but Sam is not convinced that they will pass as agents. The extradiegetic music is "Paranoid" by Black Sabbath. In "Scarecrow" (1.11), Dean introduces himself in the local café as John Bonham, but the café owner is unconvinced that Dean shares his name with the drummer in Led Zeppelin. References to that band litter the text: in "Bedtime Stories," Sam and Dean present themselves as Detective Plant and Detective Page. Kansas's "Carry on My Wayward Son" is a major aural motif across the seasons, and the lyrics underpin many central plot points: "Carry on my wayward son / There'll be peace when you are done / Lay your weary head to rest / Don't you cry no more." The song encapsulates central familial themes of the show: the brothers' intense but strained relationship, Sam's reluctance to be a hunter, Dean's death wish, the early loss of their mother at the hands of Azazel, and the sons' complex relationship with their emotionally inexpressive, militaristic father.

In addition to savvy scheduling and programming decisions, it can be argued that it is *Supernatural*'s inherently generic nature that creates its cult status. *Supernatural*'s clear adherence to urban legend, the influence of Asian and American horror films, and the overt use of rock music and pop culture quips—all of which are grounded in a post-*Buffy* televisual environment—go some way toward explaining its global popularity and cultish significance.

This Life

Stephen Lacey

It was hard to be indifferent to *This Life*. One writer in the *Daily Mail* stated, "I did not regularly watch *This Life*, but caught the final episode and was appalled at the drugs, booze and, worst of all, simulated sex between homosexuals.... We should complain more often and perhaps our comments would have some weight in preventing such trash being shown" (quoted in McGregor 128). But according to the *Evening Standard*, "*This Life* ... dominate[s] conversation at every smart dinner-party in London" (quoted in McGregor 128). By the time the second season concluded in August 1997, it had become iconic, whatever one's attitude toward its depiction of sex and drugs, and it had reached audiences far beyond London's haute bourgeoisie. Indeed, when the BBC announced that there would be no third season, there were so many complaints that the head of BBC2, Mark Thompson (now director-general of the corporation), was forced to explain the decision in the pages of the *Guardian* newspaper in an unprecedented display of public hand-wringing.

This Life ran for two seasons beginning in March 1996, with a total of thirty-two weekly episodes (eleven in the first season, twenty-one in the second) of forty minutes each. It was made for BBC2 by World Productions, an independent production company. *This Life* was produced by Jane Fallon, and its main writer and originator was Amy Jenkins. Executive producer Tony Garnett, head of World Productions, has been a radical force in British television since the early 1960s. Garnett brokered the deal with the BBC, and his distinctive approach to making television was etched into every aspect of the program.

The way *This Life* came to be commissioned is instructive. According to Garnett, he was approached by the then head of BBC2, Michael

Jackson, who asked him to make a series about and aimed at young people.[1] The central characters would be lawyers, and the program was intended to be "adult" in tone and content, since it would be airing after the 9 P.M. "watershed."[2] The conversation illustrates that broadcasters, even at the BBC, had become intensely concerned with audience profile as well as overall share. (It also indicates how interventionist channel controllers had become.) Jackson's instincts were right, however, and the eventual success of *This Life* was largely the result of the way it was embraced enthusiastically by its audience.

The series concerns a group of friends who met at university, became lawyers, and now live together in a rented house in London. The initial group of housemates consists of Anna (Daniella Nardini), Miles (Jack Davenport), Warren (Jason Hughes), Egg (Andrew Lincoln), and Milly (Amita Dhiri); in season 2, Warren leaves and is replaced by Ferdy (Ramon Tikaram). Beyond them is a wider group of work colleagues, friends, casual acquaintances, sexual partners (gay and straight), and (a few) parents. *This Life* is primarily character rather than plot driven, and although there is no single narrative arc, there are recurring motifs, such as Egg and Milly's long-term but ultimately doomed relationship. If there is a spine to this episodic narrative, it is Anna's on-and-off relationship with Miles and her complicated and contradictory feelings about him. Miles's highly eventful wedding to another woman, Francesca (Rachel Fielding), concludes the second season.[3]

Generically, *This Life*'s multistranded narrative structure is suggestive of soap opera or "soap drama" (Creeber 115), indicating a hybrid of soap, drama, and comedy. The connection with soaps derives from the series' interest in the personal lives of and the relationships among its characters as they go about their everyday business. This involves endless talk, sex (hetero- and homosexual, casual and committed), drug taking, going to the toilet, taking baths, drinking and eating, and even going to work. This, in turn, generates an investment from the audience that is similar to that produced by the continuous serial, with characters' lives running parallel to those of viewers. Like soaps and U.S. series, which became increasingly familiar to U.K. audiences through the 1990s, *This Life* resisted closure: its concluding sequence is a mocking, self-consciously ironic parody of an ending (Miles and Francesca's wedding ends with a fight).

This Life connected to its audience because it was undoubtedly contemporary. For this reason, it was also related to notions of realism that have circulated in British television since the 1960s, in which an engagement with life as it is lived in the here and now is a key element. Garnett was well placed to engage with this tradition, since realism has been a consistent thread in his work, especially a political realism related to depictions of the British working class and socially excluded groups. Garnett's first program as producer was *Cathy Come Home* in 1966, a highly critical and (still) extraordinarily influential exposé of the housing crisis in the midst of affluent Britain; much of his subsequent work has been controversial and provocative from a left-leaning perspective. During most of the 1980s, Garnett worked as an independent producer in Hollywood, where he became convinced of the TV series' potential to deliver not only new, flexible narratives but also open-ended and nondidactic contemporary drama (see Lacey).

The makers of *This Life* aimed to give voice to a distinctive and previously unheard generational consciousness, and this is one reason why Garnett turned to Amy Jenkins, a relatively inexperienced young novelist. It is also why he cast actors who were largely unknown to the general public (Garnett often chooses to use lesser-known actors, believing that familiarity with an actor intervenes between viewer and character). Several cast members have become well known since then—notably, Daniella Nardini and Jack Davenport (the latter familiar from the *Pirates of the Caribbean* films).

The series' twenty-something characters are cut off from both the 1960s of their parents and the 1980s of their teens. (In episode 1, Anna says to Egg, "I'm going to say something really subversive now. The Beatles were crap." Two episodes later, Miles's new Paul Smith jacket is derided by his housemates as being "so '80s.") Sometimes described as "Generation X," this is a generation marked by its cynicism, detachment, and lack of faith in what lies beyond the tangible immediacy of the personal. Jenkins, herself a former law clerk, described the series' intentions in a 2003 interview: "We wanted to reflect that this generation is the first who can't expect to do better than their parents; who can't afford to buy property; who find it very hard to get a job; and who are not threatened by casual drug use."

The world beyond the house is incomprehensible, threatening, and unchangeable. The first line of the first episode is voiced by Warren speaking to his unseen therapist: "Outside is chaos." Egg, in the course of his interview at the law firm (also in the first episode), says, "I don't believe in theories. . . . You can't do anything about the world." The house is a curiously adolescent space in which the responsibilities of the adult world are put on hold. Whenever "adults"—that is, people from an older generation—enter the space, they are either alien outsiders or, like Egg's dad (Paul Copley), in flight from adult responsibilities. Cross-generational relationships, such as Milly's affair with her boss, the middle-aged O'Donnell (David Mallinson), are doomed and destructive.

Part of the realism of the series lies in its depiction of a world in which swearing, nudity, recreational drug use, and casual sex are an accepted part of everyday life. They are not celebrated, denigrated, or exploited symbolically; they are simply there. It was this refusal to condemn or foreground what some reviewers found indecent that provoked a hostile response from the press. Meanwhile, positive reviews celebrated its realistic depiction of contemporary Britain. "While some viewers will doubtless whip up the familiar storm about the language, nudity and explicit sex," argued the *Financial Times,* "others will welcome a drama which, without being coy or aggressive, shows young people behaving as they actually do behave" (McGregor 127). Between the series' first episode and its last, there was a change of governing party in the United Kingdom, and arguments about the series were quick to encompass the new political landscape. "This is Brown-Blair's Britain," wrote the *Guardian.* "Joy tends to be fleeting, and introduced by chemicals and the prospect of Anna" (quoted in McGregor 127).

This Life adopted a groundbreaking (for the time) view of gay identity. The series is notable for not using the stereotypes of campiness or victimhood to represent homosexuality. Its gay characters—particularly Warren and the initially bisexual Ferdy—are allowed an identity beyond the confines of their sexuality. Similarly, neither Milly's nor Ferdy's ethnic background becomes an issue (Amita Dhiri is of Asian descent, and Ramon Tikaram is Fijian). *This Life* marked television's "catching up" with some of the complex realities of mid-1990s Britain, including Egg's attempt to be a "new man" (he gives up his job to become a writer) and Miles's ambivalence about what is expected of him in a post-feminist world of equal opportunity. All the women work, and many of the plotlines revolve around the interaction of the housemates and the workplace.

The characters in *This Life* live in a world where friendship substitutes for family and work is a means of making a living rather than defining one's identity. The program benefited from the success of the U.S. series *Friends,* which provided another take on twenty-somethings living communally and was one of several series from both sides of the Atlantic set among friendship groups (see Creeber 115). (Although it was not an influence on the series, *Friends* was a point of reference for reviewers and possibly the audience.) Like many such series, *This Life* is concerned with the politics of the personal and, in particular, with questions of intimacy—how it is to be won and maintained—which is also, according to sociologist Anthony Giddens, a major contemporary preoccupation. The search for intimacy drives some of the most important plotlines, and the difficulty of finding and holding on to it creates much of the complexity surrounding the characters. The house becomes a space where intimacy is negotiated, resisted, and (less often) embraced, and as viewers, we witness the characters in states of physical and emotional vulnerability.

The problem of intimacy is often foregrounded, especially the intimacy of commitment: "I hate talking," says Anna, "it's so intimate. . . . I just want a fuck." Anna is a pivotal character in this respect, since both intimacy and self-identity are elusive for her. She represents a postfeminist dilemma: fulfillment cannot be found in either of the places where it is supposed to reside—in a relationship or in the workplace. Anna is sexually attractive, highly intelligent, and remorselessly honest and direct, showing behavior that is often considered "male." She drinks, has a repertoire of memorable putdowns, and is capable of sexual ruthlessness. She is both outwardly confident and highly vulnerable, a tension that holds across the two seasons and provides one of the central emotional and narrative threads. True to the series' desire for openness, the tension remains unresolved. Ultimately, the problem for Anna is one of commitment, which may embrace sexual trust and fidelity but is not reducible to them. Commitment is hard to build and demands reciprocity. As in most soap dramas, issues of commitment—how it is obtained, to whom it should be given and on what terms, and, crucially, how it is to be maintained—are vital to *This Life*.

This Life is also distinctive in terms of the way it was filmed, with a restless visual style that aims to match the energy of its narrative. It was shot on digital video, a technology that Garnett had pioneered on British television (much as he had demonstrated the potential of 16mm for television drama in the 1960s). World Productions' caustic hospital series *Cardiac Arrest* was made on Sony digital Betacam, the first on British television to do so. This technology combined the speed and inexpensiveness of video with the visual appeal of film, utilizing flexible and lightweight cameras. The production team of *This Life* was able to get eleven minutes of material a day, noticeably more than the norm. This, in turn, bought the producers a considerable amount of freedom from interference. Georgina Born has noted that with each episode costing just £175,000 to £200,000 ($238,500 to $324,000), this method of filming was touted as a harbinger of the future within the BBC.

The dominant shooting practice was to use natural lighting and a single handheld camera, held as steady as possible, positioned mainly outside the actors' space and cutting into it as necessary. Each scene was shot about ten or twelve times, from different positions and focal lengths, to obtain the maximum amount of footage for the editing process. This shooting system privileged the work of the actors, who were often allowed to play a scene through without interruption (this is one source of the show's freshness and energy). The episode was then created through the editing process, with the production team trying out different versions of each scene, often using innovative and experimental editing strategies (for instance, there are whip pans and jump cuts in abundance). Garnett has said, "We only started to discover the show about halfway through the first series."[4]

This Life eventually attracted passionate and loyal viewers whose commitment has helped ensure its cult status. However, it did not win immediate or huge audiences—indeed, it was not until the longer second season (which was part of the original deal) that *This Life* took off. However, at no point did it reach a mass public (its average audience was a respectable but unremarkable 2.7 million viewers, but the last episode attracted nearer 4 million). The key to its significance can be gleaned from some of the press comments at the time. As the *Daily Express* noted, it was "the program that made BBC2 cool again" (quoted in McGregor 126). *This Life* was successful with the highly desirable audience consisting of affluent young professionals, an audience that is not often drawn to television but is coveted by broadcasters (although it is likely that the actual audience was wider than this). The series helped BBC2 connect to that audience—and change its brand image in the process.

Despite the success of *This Life*, it concluded after two seasons. The BBC was blamed, leading to the howls of outrage and the hasty response noted earlier. In reality, it was Garnett and World Productions that chose not to make a third season, in the face of concerted pressure from Mark Thompson and BBC2. Garnett's and World's view was that nothing more could be done with either the characters or the situation. The clamor for more was eventually met by a one-off episode, *This Life + 10*, which aired on BBC2 at Christmas 2007. In the intervening period, Miles has become filthy rich, and Egg is a successful novelist; Anna is still a lawyer, but increasingly detached and broody. The reunion occurs in Miles's opulent country mansion and is framed by the distancing device of a documentary filmmaker whose subject is Egg. Though much anticipated, *This Life + 10* was a disappointment to critics, although it attracted 3.4 million viewers and a 14 percent audience share. Reviewers measured it against the original and found it wanting (if *This Life + 10* had been a stand-alone drama, it probably would have been better received). As the *Guardian* critic noted, "It's not as much fun as it was. . . . The world has caught up, and overtaken, the show. . . . I just hope this so-called special doesn't cloud the memory of *This Life*, which was groundbreaking telly. Maybe it would have been better to leave Anna, Egg, Miles, Milly and Warren in their graves" (Woollaston 31). Clearly, *This Life + 10* brought the original into relief with a sharpness that was not simply nostalgia but resonated with both personal and cultural experience. *This Life* was undoubtedly a product of its time; yet, if the response of undergraduates in the 2000s is any indication, it refuses (like much of the best television drama) to be bound to it.

Notes

1. Tony Garnett, interview with the author, January 16, 2006.
2. In the United Kingdom, programs transmitted after 9 P.M. are allowed to be considerably more explicit in terms of what they show and how they show it.
3. An episode guide can be found in McGregor.
4. Interview conducted by Lez Cooke, February 29, 2000.

Torchwood

Matt Hills

Cult television sometimes appears to be an accident, consolidated by unpredicted and unpredictable fan audience activity, as was arguably the case for the original *Doctor Who* series (BBC, 1963–1989). And it may occasionally appear to be intended, programmed, and designed as such—a matter of targeting specific fan and niche audiences with material deemed culturally "nonmainstream" or challenging. *Torchwood* (an anagram of *Doctor Who*) can reasonably be described as the latter type of cult TV. It is a *Who* spin-off; its lead character, Captain Jack Harkness (played by John Barrowman), first appeared in the 2005 BBC Wales reimagining of that series. But whereas the cult of *Doctor Who* emerged over time and in response to the show's format, mythology, unusual lead character, and child-adult crossover status, it is hard to view *Torchwood* as anything other than cult by design. It inevitably had a ready-made fan following in the United Kingdom by virtue of its emergence from Russell T. Davies's work on *Doctor Who*; indeed, it can be argued that *Torchwood* was cult TV from the moment of its first preproduction announcement on October 17, 2005. It was promoted and billed as a "sci-fi paranoid thriller . . . for BBC Three . . . announced today by Stuart Murphy, Controller of BBC Three [and] . . . aimed at a post-watershed audience. . . . '[It's] a cop show with a sense of humour. . . . It's dark, wild and sexy, it's *The X-Files* meets *This Life*' [says Davies]" (BBC press release cited in Walker, *Inside the Hub* 12–13).

Linked to the brand identity of one of the BBC's free-view digital channels, *Torchwood* was intertextually connected in this earliest publicity to shows such as "*Casanova . . . Bodies, Conviction* and *Outlaws*, with which [BBC3 had] . . . begun to establish a reputation for cutting-edge British drama" (Walker, *Inside the Hub* 12–13). It was thereby positioned industrially as "high-end" or quality TV, "edgy" in its ambitions. "The multichannel environment has afforded opportunities through new channels aiming only for relatively small audiences in the first instance to try out challenging production ideas. Even established institutions such as the BBC have been able through the new, Freeview, digital provision with its new channels (BBC3 and BBC4) to test the water in respect of drama which might well not have been commissioned for mainstream channels" (Nelson, *State of Play* 76).

Torchwood initially premiered on BBC3 in the United Kingdom, and season 2 premiered on BBC2. Either way, *Torchwood* is contextualized as a minority or niche drama rather than a mainstream (and thus BBC1) show. As a "post-watershed" program, it is designed to be broadcast after 9 P.M., following the long-standing convention in British TV that equates this time slot with material not suitable for children (a pre-watershed edit of *Torchwood* premiered in 2008). It is therefore not merely a spin-off of the family entertainment of *Doctor Who*'s action-adventure telefantasy (Johnson, *Telefantasy*); its cult-by-design status—or, at the very least, its cult by association with *Doctor Who* and its established fan base—supposedly offers a more adult, sophisticated franchise. In the United States, where *Doctor Who* is less widely known, *Torchwood* could not be treated as having a ready-made audience of loyal fans. There, the program was more actively promoted to a niche audience of genre or cult fans. To this end, lead writer Chris Chibnall attended "Comic-Con, courtesy of BBC America, to promote the September launch of *Torchwood* series one in America. . . . I'd been told to expect a convention of 5000 people but, over the four days, I think it was nearer 100,000! It's the largest convention of its kind in the world, and a gathering like no other. The two-hour *Torchwood* panel is packed to the rafters. . . . 6 September 2007: USA. *Torchwood* launches on BBC America, and we're a hit! It's the channel's highest-rated show of all time" (Chibnall 65).

Targeted at genre or cult fans, then, *Torchwood* redeploys familiar tropes. Its lead character is effectively immortal, and it features a rift in space-time through which any number of alien creatures can appear. Its status as both cult and adult transgressive TV is marked in a number of ways, and not just by use of the word *fuck* in the opening moments of episode 1 or the depiction of a character masturbating in episode 2. Its adult content is never simply a matter of breaking sexual or linguistic taboos. As fan commentator Stephen James Walker notes, "raising [the]

... question of the existence, or otherwise, of life after death, *Torchwood* ventures into some very deep religious and philosophical territory, in a way that *Doctor Who* probably never could.... This ... really delivers on the promise of a thought-provoking adult series" (*Inside the Hub* 173).

Unusual for a program that, as telefantasy, deals with extraterrestrials and supernatural forces, *Torchwood* is preoccupied with a materialist, atheistic stance in which there is no life after death; there is just blackness, an everlasting nothingness. This emphasis can no doubt be read in relation to the beliefs of Russell T. Davies, the show's creator, but in any case, it is a rather remarkable element to discover alongside the program's narrative and fantastical format (see Hills, *Fan Cultures* on the focal narrative questions posed by cult TV). Tensions between representing the supernatural (as generic telefantasy) and maintaining a materialist philosophy emerge and are dramatized across the series' run. For instance, "the whole premise of 'Random Shoes' seems to be completely at odds with the usual *Torchwood* doctrine—established in 'Everything Changes' and reinforced in 'They Keep Killing Suzie'— that there is no afterlife, save perhaps for an eternal dark nothingness" (Walker, *Inside the Hub* 184). And the finale of season 1, "End of Days" (written by Chris Chibnall), plays, connotatively at least, somewhat against the established atheism of the program by depicting Captain Jack Harkness as a Christlike figure. Despite such creative tensions between genre and theological concepts, the script for "They Keep Killing Suzie" (1.8; written by Paul Tomalin and Daniel McCulloch, with uncredited input from Davies) explicitly links the series' antireligious positioning with adult sophistication of thought. The character of Suzie Costello (Indira Varma) caustically remarks to Gwen (Eve Myles) that her belief in heaven as a sort of "white light" is just the sort of childish faith that has "never left primary school." Here, any belief in life after death is strongly depicted as a compensatory and consoling value system rather than a grown-up recognition of harsher realities. *Torchwood*'s "rift" may strongly resemble *Buffy*'s "Hellmouth" in narrative terms and possibilities, but whereas the latter is inscribed within religious concepts, the former is stoutly secular.

Torchwood's critical and fan reception has not always validated the show's publicity and industry contextualization as being more "adult" than *Doctor Who*. In particular, noted British TV critic Charlie Brooker, who has written for the left-wing broadsheet the *Guardian* and presented his own BBC digital TV show, *Screen Wipe*, argues: "The trouble with *Who*'s freshly-minted . . . 'sister' serial *Torchwood* . . . is that it's not really clear who it's aimed at. It contains swearing, blood and sex, yet still somehow feels like a children's program. Thirteen-year-olds should love it; anyone else is likely to be more than a little confused. Which isn't to say *Torchwood* is bad. Just bewildering." Brooker alleges that despite the program's inclusion of sex and gore, its telefantasy adventure elements—the high-tech SUV, an invisible entrance to the Hub via a magic paving stone, the Doctor's severed hand preserved in a jar—add a childish aspect to the otherwise adult content, resulting in a bizarre and jarring mixture of tonalities. As Walker observes, a "frequent fan complaint [is] that *Torchwood* has an uneven tone" (*Inside the Hub* 223). Walker does not entirely validate Brooker's point, though, countering with this thoughtful reflection: "Is it really fair to suggest that the series has childish characters and/or storylines? . . . Arguably the only way this criticism makes any sort of sense is if one takes the view that there is something inherently juvenile or childish about TV science-fiction, and that presenting it in an adult context is thus bound to produce an incongruity" (*Inside the Hub* 221–22).

Indeed, there is a sense in which Brooker's critique implies that telefantasy genre elements are connotatively childish, making the compounding of these genre identities with sex and gore "adolescent." Yet despite Walker's laudable reclaiming of the genre, *Torchwood* has itself equated specific religious beliefs—frequently linked to the narratives and fantastical scenarios of supernatural telefantasy—with "primary school" childishness. Thus, rather ironically, the show appears to put forward arguments that are similar to Brooker's criticisms. Arguably, it constructs its adult textual identity at the expense of implicitly putting down the very genre it predominantly inhabits. Part of *Torchwood*'s adult textuality also seems to be premised on including the blood and gore that are visually absent in *Doctor Who*, bringing it very close to TV horror on occasion (Hills, *The Pleasures of Horror*). One example: the spurts of blood that result from a monstrous Weevil attack in "Everything Changes."

Torchwood's adult content is certainly not limited to its showy inclusion of sexual material, such as potential "fuck buddies" (in "Out of Time"), or to its atheistic ambivalence or to its moments of graphic gore. As Davies has pointed out, part of the program's distinctive identity comes not from its depictions of sex but rather from its representations of *sexuality*: "There aren't many series about bisexuals battling aliens underneath Cardiff! . . . That is very distinct. Let's face it, there are a lot of American shows covering ground similar to ours, and the success of *Torchwood* on BBC America has been a bit of a surprise to me because of that. I feared that it might be like taking coals to Newcastle. But the research shows that Jack's sexuality, as well as the fluid sexuality that we have running throughout the show, is a unique feature" (quoted in Cook 55). To an extent, then, it can be argued that *Torchwood*'s cult status reflects not just its position as a telefantasy *Doctor Who* spin-off but also its place as "authored" TV drama, interpretable as part of Russell T. Davies's body of work and hence readable through his culturally progressive and politicized "author function": "Davies has continued to include queer characters . . . with *Doctor Who*, and its subsequent spin-off, *Torchwood*. . . . Davies introduced the character of Captain Jack, a pansexual time-traveller from the 51st century (John Barrowman). . . . Certainly, Davies's contributions to 'gay television' over the last decade . . . have been considerable" (Davis 125).

Whether Captain Jack Harkness is described as "pansexual" or whether a range of Torchwood team members are said to depict "bisexual tension" (Charlie Brooker) or indeed a wholesale queering of fixed categories of sexuality, what emerges is a consistent stress on "fluid sexuality," as Davies codes it in interview. Characters are matter-of-factly depicted as moving between male and female object choices, without this being dramatized as any sort of issue and without narrative punishment or problematization. Ianto Jones (Gareth David-Lloyd), for instance, has a girlfriend who has been partly transformed into a cyberbeing ("Cyberwoman," 1.4) and then later has a relationship with Captain Jack. Toshiko (Naoko Mori) has a fling with an alien who has adopted the female human body as a disguise ("Greeks Bearing Gifts," 1.7) and then falls in love with Owen Harper (Burn Gorman), who is himself depicted seducing a male and female couple in "Everything Changes." Since these developments are presented without any debate or angst, the program seems to naturalize bisexuality as unremarkable or as a given—though *bisexual* is a term that crops up more in commentary than in *Torchwood* itself. The show appears to deliberately refute and deny all cultural nominations—gay, straight, bi—that might otherwise come into play to restrict characters' identities. For this alone, *Torchwood* might merit cult status as a radical and progressive challenge to contemporary ideologies of sexuality.

And note that in the earlier quote from Davies, it is not just "fluid sexuality" that separates *Torchwood* from its cult and telefantasy competitors but also its setting in Wales: "battling aliens underneath Cardiff." Though it can certainly be suggested that *Torchwood* is very knowingly post-*Buffy*—and not just in its casting of James Marsters as Captain John Hart (see Stokes; Walker, *Inside the Hub* 223)—what is interesting about the BBC Wales show is that it simultaneously seeks to co-opt and resemble markers of U.S. quality cult TV as well as reflect and refract its Welsh identity. Its signature look, involving the repeated use of helicopter shots of Cardiff, apes the glossy, high production values of U.S. TV drama, but at the same time, *Torchwood* is geographically and narratively centered on icons of the regenerated Cardiff, such as the Millennium Centre and the Bay area. This duality gives it a "glocal" feel—competing with U.S. TV not by delocalizing its characters and narratives but rather by aestheticizing its urban Cardiff locales and aiming for U.S.-style televisuality (see Caldwell). The result is less mid-Atlantic or transatlantic than bi-Atlantic, indicating a textual hybridity of U.S. TV industry form and Welsh TV industry content that seeks to intertextually link conventions and styles of U.S. genre and cult television with a very much localized agenda. Likewise, the program's U.S.-U.K. duality is structured into its key "high-concept" precursors (*"The X-Files* meets *This Life"*), as well as playing into one of Davies's key dialogue gags in the first story: *"CSI: Cardiff,* I'd like to see that," mutters PC Andy.

As Eric Freedman has noted, in an essay dealing predominantly with *Buffy the Vampire Slayer*: "While setting is commonly underutilised in serial narratives, it is nevertheless an important visual code.... Setting is typically privileged only in the opening montage sequence of any serial program.... Yet rather than ignore setting in favour of character, setting merits further scrutiny as a complex textual code" (163). *Torchwood*'s setting is, by contrast, not at all downplayed or restricted to opening montages. Rather, it is present front and center. Even the Hub set—effectively, the base of team Torchwood—is deliberately designed to include, as its centerpiece, a continuation of the iconic fountain sited in real life outside the Millennium Centre. Although American TV critics reviewing *Torchwood* may mistakenly dub Cardiff a "bleak-looking town" in Wales (Tucker) rather than recognizing it as the nation's capital city, they are unable to wholly neglect the program's setting, which is integral.

This Welsh identity has been prioritized in BBC Wales promotional events, such as "A Celebration of *Torchwood*" hosted at the Millennium Centre in January 2008. This included a special preview in high definition of episode 2.11, "Adrift," written by Chris Chibnall. In interviews, Davies has specifically praised this episode, not by linking it intertextually to cult or U.S. TV precursors but by citing the "golden age" and tradition of quality British TV drama: "Episode 11 is *Play for Today*–good; it's utterly, utterly brilliant. I wish I'd written it myself, and I don't often say that, because I think I'm marvellous! . . . It's very Cardiff, with a strong Welsh cast—it's got Ruth Jones in it . . .—acting their hearts out. It's beautiful, like a little chamber piece" (Bielby 49). In this industry discourse, *Torchwood* is not represented as bi-Atlantic; instead, it is contextualized as "very Cardiff," even as it is articulated with markers of U.K. quality television and the single teleplay. Although these bids for "quality" status may be culturally insecure, they do suggest that *Torchwood*'s very multivocality and hybridity offer further signs of its cult status—intertextually appropriating the norms and narratives of contemporary U.S. cult TV while wearing its Welshness like a badge of honor; jamming together telefantasy genre conventions with "serious" television's focus on materialist, atheistic questions; and radically representing sexuality while offering up "monster of the week" story lines.

Torchwood may well have been cult TV by association with its parent show, *Doctor Who*, before it was even made, let alone broadcast. But given its textual design, it has arguably earned the label of cult TV, using the genre of telefantasy as a way to target fans of previous cult TV shows and to pose existential narrative questions that might be assumed to characterize quality TV. Perhaps the debate over whether *Torchwood* is childish, adolescent, or adult misses the point, which is that, as cult television, it can hybridize, deconstruct, and cross over all these fixed, unhelpful discourses of cultural value.

24

Steven Peacock

If ever (American) television could lay claim to the cultural zeitgeist, then surely *24* would storm the ranks, blow away the opposition, and seize the prize by any means necessary. Ever since its eerily timely arrival on the FOX network in September 2001, this techno-spy thriller has shadowed a nation's spirit, haunted by the omnipresent "war on terror." Creating and courting ever more controversy, *24* pulses with political fear and loathing, gleefully weaving ghoulish tales of global provocation. Many recent films and television series position themselves, in story and style, as manifesting post-9/11 concerns (of the latter, *Lost, Heroes*, and *Rescue Me* come quickly to mind). Most tread carefully, referring to world events through allegory or allusion. Others wear their hearts on their sleeves, earnestly defiant in the face of adversity. But *24* boldly goes it alone, taking matters into its own (gnarled) hands. In Joel Surnow's high-octane TV universe, heartstrings are more likely to be ripped out than tugged. In its no-holds-barred approach, and to paraphrase from another cult classic (*This Is Spinal Tap*), *24* turns it up to 11.

Each season covers twenty-four hours, charting a particularly bad day in the life of the Los Angeles Counter-Terrorist Unit (CTU). Led by the seemingly indestructible Jack Bauer (Kiefer Sutherland), CTU encounters code-red terrorist threats against the U.S. government and citizens alike. These (sometimes literally) heart-stopping events are charged with a litany of crimes against humanity and primed with a top-class armory of (easily located) weapons of mass destruction. With his trusty techno-team to support him, Bauer saves the day (or, indeed, days) by squaring up to nuclear bombs, chemical warfare, presidential assassination attempts, heroin addiction, and the perilous plights of a constantly endangered daughter. To challenge the gruff acumen and gloves-off patriotism of Bauer's squad, 24 plunders the globe to find its "terrorist of the week"; across the seasons, it gathers a rogues' gallery of international villains featuring Russian radicals, Islamic fundamentalists, Mexican desperadoes, and British capitalists. Yet the series is intent on fostering not only the fear of "Others" attacking the homeland but also fear of the lost world of the U.S. government itself. Bringing home J. J. Abrams–style cryptic mysteries and far removed from Aaron Sorkin's rose-tinted White House, the West Wing in 24 is filled with political turncoats and dangerously inept leaders. The most effective of these caricatures of power-hungry decrepitude arrives in later seasons in the form of deposed President Charles Logan (Gregory Itzin). With metronomic beady eyes, a hangdog expression, and a systematically darting tongue, Logan barks and slithers his way out of trouble, sidling up to the bad guys. Bearing an uncanny resemblance to Richard Nixon, Logan's backseat double-dealing constantly endangers the American people. In releasing threats within and without the nation-state, 24 measures and magnifies a climate of collective fear.

As a strangely familiar guiding mantra, repeatedly landing characters and series alike in trouble, 24 is tough on terror and tough on the causes of terror. As has been charted elsewhere by Douglas L. Howard (133–48), unquestioned torture and questionable morality charge the series. From chief villains to chiefs of staff, from bit-part players to Bauer, all are put on the rack at some time in the 24-verse. Often, the series cranks up the cruelty and tests *our* thresholds by first revealing the victims' innocence to the viewer *and then torturing them anyway*. Equally, when a hidden truth *is* forcefully revealed, 24 validates such acts by showing how the end justifies the means. To gain innumerable pieces of vital world-saving information from unspeakably nasty and reticent terrorists, Bauer turns the screw. Sometimes all that is required is for him to repeat his question in a louder, deeper snarl, with a cocked gun held aloft: "Where is the nuclear detonator? . . . WHERE IS THE NUCLEAR DETONATOR?" Yet, when this two-step tactic fails him (and blowing a hole in the perpetrator's kneecap yields nothing but a bloody howl), Bauer must resort to more drastic measures, employing all manner of makeshift medieval implements to get to the truth. Lamp cords, strips of cloth, knives, and knuckles all toil to grind out secret codes, locations, and identities. Back at CTU, the spectral figure of torture specialist Eric Richards (Butch Klein) haunts the halls, repeatedly summoned to work his special kind of dark magic. And yet, as Bauer would undoubtedly and aggressively claim, these methods *get results.* Such a stance sits uncomfortably next to the realities of Abu Ghraib and Guantánamo. In its willful disregard of the Miranda rights and the U.S. Constitution, the series itself is often duplicitous, offering an apologia of current affairs and an augury of possible futures with even more extreme action. It presents a therapeutic fantasy of hard-line defense against the phantoms of terrorism yet positions itself as soothsayer, "telling it how it is." In combining torture and tenets, 24 often rests on a knife's edge.

Some would say that 24 should not exist. As film scholar Jim Leach suggests, the post-9/11 relationship between society and cinema (and, by extension, television) threatens to render such single-hero action-thrillers obsolete (Leach 248–58). After the towers fell, the lore of the lone gunman seemed, on big or small screen, capricious, outmoded, and unneeded. As the world changes, figures like Dirty Harry and Arnold Schwarzenegger (in all his incarnations) do not fit with the cultural consciousness. (This claim is partly contested, or perhaps partly justified, by Sylvester Stallone's recent risible reanimation of his Vietnam veteran in *Rambo.*) Yet Bauer stands as testimony to the continuing popularity of stories that set one man against a faceless enemy. One key distinction between 24 and prior "hard-body" tales of derring-do stems from the series' and the characters' use of communications technology. Although Bauer often goes it alone against the terrorists, he must rely on the trappings of electronic tracking. Never before has a television series so prominently featured the paraphernalia of life led by the microchip; 24 presents a world filled with mobile phones, satellite navigation systems, CCTV, USB, digital networks, and ID databases. Here again, 24 taps directly into the cultural mainframe, exploring the control and paranoia of a computer-driven surveillance society. From the very first images of the series—of a rogue agent tapping a code into a laptop, setting a satellite spinning around the globe—24 declares an interest in the conflation of public and private spheres via electronic surveillance. We are not the only ones watching Bauer save the world.

After six seasons (the seventh was preempted by the writers' strike and Kiefer Sutherland's DUI conviction), the real-time drama has assisted in changing the face of modern television. The impact of its many stylistic innovations matches the intensity of its cultural concerns. The series' distinctive treatment of time—one hour in Bauer's world equals one hour in ours, with the action continuing "behind the veil" of commercial breaks—not only helps ratchet up the tension but also chimes with the incumbent pressures of a twenty-four-hour society. The signature digital clock systematically reappears, accompanied by its doom-laden flinty chimes, to add a death knell to the climactic countdown; equally, it strikes a chord with the constant coverage of rolling television news. Just as CTU repeatedly promises results "within the hour," so do the BBC, CNN, FOX News, and others. Although 24's other celebrated visual flourish—the split screen—draws from graphic novels and previous filmic examples from Suspense (1913) to Timecode (2000), it also finds kinship with twenty-first-century television news reportage. In 24, an imminent terrorist strike causes the screen to splinter into multiple frames, each covering different scenarios taking place in disparate locations held together in time: Bauer racing across the cityscape in his trusty SUV, President Logan hunkered in his bunker, the CTU mole furtively burrowing into encrypted files. In the United Kingdom, on 7/7, Sky News fragmented the screen, training multiple cameras (gunlike) on the various targeted London scenes: the burnt-out wreckage of a bus in Tavistock Square, outside Edgware Road and Liverpool Street tube stations. (Yet it need not be a cataclysmic news event that causes screens to split: BBC News now happily provides a diptych to chart a celebrity wedding.) There are multiple examples of 24's influence on TV fiction, encompassing the good—consider the use of the split screen in Spooks, the bad—such as the hyperdrive pace and visual riffs of Bionic Woman, and the downright meretricious—witness the aping of 24's motifs of multiframe, real-time action in the wildlife documentary Animal 24/7 if you dare.

    The series demands a renegotiation of the oft-cited assumption that TV requires only "casual" viewing practices.[1] Rather than position itself as a throwaway entertainment meriting only glances from an otherwise-occupied viewer, 24 encourages and rewards close attention. Across the split screens, in the continual twists and turns of each season, 24 entreats us to focus on each fleeting glimpse and glance, on decor, trappings, and gestures. It builds and balances moments to allow for many different interpretations of a single action. In doing so, the series shows its acute awareness of modern television viewing practices. The show's structure and style make it enormously satisfying to view "live" in weekly doses: measuring the minutes in real time, creating the bittersweet pleasure of a cliffhanger heralding a seven-day wait until the next installment. Another hugely popular way of getting a 24 fix taps into the DVD box-set culture, as stalwart viewers hungrily consume all twenty-four episodes in one sitting. For a series obsessed with the power of emerging communications technologies, it is fitting that many fans also opt to follow Bauer's exploits over the Internet. Watching the show on DVD or online also permits multiple viewings and a repeated scrutiny of key moments (did Bauer *really* just shoot dead an "innocent" captive in the CTU boardroom?). Thus, 24 is instructive in the ways we watch and talk about television.

In its early incarnations, a seemingly untouchable 24 thrilled in killing off the opposition while breathing new life into mainstream TV. Unable to enjoy the expressive freedom of shows such as *The Sopranos* on HBO and *Queer as Folk* on Showtime, 24 nevertheless pushes the boundaries of network television. The series continues to attest to the possibility of and the need for challenging and innovative material coming from the networks. Further, the form of 24 offers a pathway for TV drama in the future. As Daniel Chamberlain and Scott Ruston suggest, in successfully straddling the stylistic conventions of both film and TV, 24 "deploys and emphasizes both cinematic and videographic techniques" (16). They cite 24's cinematic use of 35mm film stock, as well as its framing for 16:9 wide-screen presentations, on-location shooting, and high budget. At the same time, as noted earlier, 24 is indebted to strategies more normally associated with television: the split-screen, multilayered, graphics-heavy approach akin to TV sports and news coverage, and the real-time clock, indicative of television's fundamental disposition to "liveness" (Chamberlain and Ruston 16–17). At a time when film and television face increasing pressure from ever-more sophisticated online media services and custom-made "webisodes," 24's adept combination of cinematic and televisual signifiers may well provide hope for these "old-school" formats.

Like one of the many sly moles in 24, I have deliberately withheld information about the series' relationship to cult TV. Yet (and happily forgoing the need for Jack to turn the screw) the truth must out. We come to the crux of the matter, taking *crux* to mean both "a difficult problem" and "the essential or deciding point." Just as 24 draws together aspects of television and cinema, the series balances characteristics of "cult" and "quality" programming. Both these categorizing markers of TV are notoriously slippery; both are nevertheless vital terms of inquiry, as recent publications and the appearance of this collection affirm (see McCabe and Akass). Taking the latter label first, criteria for quality television range from "textual self-reflexivity and liberal humanism . . . to the ensemble cast, hybridity of serial and episodic structure, rich narrative complexity and bardic voice noted in such 1980s programs as *Hill Street Blues*, to the wonderfully cinematic qualities of the programs of the late 1990s—like *The West Wing* and *The Sopranos*"; other factors might include "the pedigree of a program's producers . . . and a clear emphasis on realism" (Chamberlain and Ruston 15). A diverting and critically useful game might be to match 24 to many, but not all, of these signifiers of quality TV. (Can 24 align itself with any category that lauds a "clear emphasis on realism"? Do mountain lions live in Los Angeles?)[2]

At the same time, markers of cult programming are equally central to the series' appeal. Despite the label suggesting that it ministers to a niche position, "cult TV" remains a very broad church (again, as the diverse subjects of this book display). In turn, the criteria for culthood can sometimes seem frustratingly wide ranging. Take, for instance, Sara Gwenllian-Jones and Roberta E. Pearson's open-armed assertion that "cult television's imaginary universes support an *inexhaustible range of narrative possibilities*, inviting, supporting and rewarding close textual analysis, interpretation, and inventive reformulations" (xii; emphasis added). They develop a more precise definition by honing in on one aspect of cult TV with which 24 is most closely engaged: "Cult television has become a meta-genre that caters to intense, interpretive audience practices," allowing for "an imaginative involvement with the cult TV narrative that affords fans enormous scope for further interpretation, speculation and invention" (xvi). More so than many other cult TV texts, 24 ignites furious fan-base activity across many media. In the parallel universe of online endeavor, Web sites devoted to 24 (such as 24fans.com and the unusually titled almeidaisgod.com) are charged with busy blogs picking over previous seasons' content and offering prognostications of things to come.

Just as the CTU agents filter through streams of Internet "chatter" to find key information, we can consider "interpretive audience practices" to reveal more of 24. First, the series clearly provides long draughts of "water-cooler" relief, as fans gather to delight in, deduce, and predict characters' ploys and plotlines. (Who is pulling President Logan's strings? Will Jack and Audrey get together again, despite her quasi-comatose state?) Of course, this is not uncommon in the dealings between cult TV and its avid supporters. *Lost* provides an apogee of apoplectic interpretations of this kind (maybe the castaways are in purgatory; maybe it's all a dream). Yet 24 succeeds in pushing past this level of engagement into a much broader cultural arena. To gauge and enter into this phenomenon, simply type "What Would Jack Bauer Do?" into your online search engine. The dizzyingly popular query (often abridged to the acronym WWJBD) has caught the attention of many groups, ranging from individual bloggers (blogs.chron.com) to political forums (rightwingnuthouse.com) to, allegedly, Supreme Court justices.[3] The answers range from the wittily scabrous to earnest comparisons with the Bush administration. Examples of the former include "Don't beg Jack Bauer to shoot you. He will simply shoot your wife. No man tells Jack Bauer what to do"; "Jack Bauer could strangle you with a cordless phone"; and, most fittingly, "When Google can't find something, it asks Jack Bauer for help" (www.fplanque.com). It appears that, in the case of 24, the "intense, interpretive audience practices" extend far beyond the usual framework of the cult TV text.

To end with my own interpretive speculations, 24's cultness looks set to become increasingly crucial to the series' form and survival. In season 6, 24 stumbled. It was rife with hyperbolic drives and literal overkill; whereas previous plots had centered on lethal family feuds, this time it was "personal," as Bauer's father turns up to wreak havoc. We've already had a controlled nuclear explosion over the Mojave Desert (in season 2)—so this time the series started off with a real bang, setting off nukes in populated areas. Despite critical remonstrations about scenes of physical torment in the show, the ante was upped, and nearly everybody got tortured. Moreover, season 6 suffered from half-baked plotlines and narrative convolutions. Having nixed the "Big Bad" two-thirds into the season, the series suddenly changed tack, sending Bauer after his damsel in distress. In turning it up to 11, 24 risked blowing the amps for good. Appropriately, the season closed with Bauer on a hillside, staring into the craggy depths below—a final clunky cliffhanger for a series on the edge. If this dip reduces 24's audience and drops it closer to the outer rim of the current TV landscape, the series' cult status may be further emboldened.

Early signs of season 7 showed not only a concerted effort for renewal and resurgence but also an acknowledgment of the series' response to the "intense audience practices" so central to culthood. The U.K. trailer began with a direct address by Kiefer Sutherland, appealing straight to viewers, promoting "our" importance: "You are the reason we make

24—and for this season we have pulled out all the stops." Reshuffling impacted both the inner and outer workings of the series' world. Extradiegetically, cocreator Joel Surnow left the show after serving as executive producer for the first eight episodes of season 7. Equally, the notion of a candid reappraisal, a redressing of the previous season's failings, continued in the new 24-verse. The action shifted from Los Angeles to Washington; combat fatigues were replaced with freshly laundered shirts. Opening with an extract that appeared to move the series' generic formula closer to that of a legal drama, 24 placed Bauer on trial for his grisly methods (WWJBD?). The series also appeared to be answering online speculation about its strategies, yet the trailer swiftly edited in a clip that openly justifies Bauer's rough justice ("Do whatever is necessary . . . torture him if you want"). Even as CTU was shut down, 24 rebooted the motif of the "mole," this time coming from within the FBI. And a favorite character was brought back from the dead as the season's surprise villain.

In all these ways, the series appears to be acutely aware of cult fans' clamor for an increasingly interactive role. The return of a mole allows a "real-time" online game of "guess who." The shock volte-face of a hero to villainy could be lifted straight from a blog strand ("if you could have any character as Jack's new nemesis . . ."). Elsewhere, the fate of the long-rumored, on-again, off-again film version of 24 seems to rest, ironically, with the success of its latest small-screen season. In removing itself from the "trappings" of television, and unless it is going to be a day-long feature, "24 the movie" must renegotiate some of its signature motifs. The idea of a big-screen version fits with the series' attempts to combine conflicting characteristics: torture and morality, cinematic and videographic, cult and quality programming. For my money, the movie project is more likely to find space as a curio: occupying a cold place in the hearts of TV series fans and dusty shelves in DVD stores, becoming a cult artifact of a very different kind. As 24 constantly reminds us, only time will tell.

Notes

1. As an example of this historical position, in *Visible Fictions*, John Ellis states, "TV does not encourage the same degree of spectator concentration [as cinema]. There is no surrounding darkness, no anonymity of fellow viewers, no large image, no lack of movement amongst the spectators, no *rapt attention*"

(127). This relationship implies that "no extraordinary effort is being invested in the act of looking" (138).

2. See, for instance, David Lavery's cited predilection (in the afterword to Peacock) for "quality television offering richly imaginative, genre-bending, abundantly intertextual teleuniverses with fascinating, inimitable characters and inspired writing" and his enthusiasm for *24*'s tentative relationship with such forms.

3. According to globeandmail.com, Justice Antonin Scalia, as a fan of *24*, recently cited the hot pop-quiz phrase "What Would Jack Bauer Do?" at a legal conference in Ottawa.

The Twilight Zone

Jonathan Malcolm Lampley

In many respects, it may seem odd to find *The Twilight Zone* in a book devoted to cult TV shows. Generally, that phrase suggests programs that failed to find critical or popular success during their initial (usually short-lived) runs; in most cases, these programs are embraced chiefly by relatively small, cultlike bands of devotees and are not recalled by the public at large. *Max Headroom* and *Twin Peaks* exemplify this kind of traditional cult TV show, beloved by faithful fanatics but few others. Yet every now and again, a TV series inspires both a mainstream and a cult following and somehow becomes an immediate signifier to almost anybody raised within the dominant culture. *Star Trek* is the most obvious example of a cult show that has grown into a nigh-universal cultural signifier. Similarly, CBS's *Twilight Zone* is an integral component of American popular culture, with the show's title becoming embedded in the national language as shorthand for the weird or fantastic.

Even if he had never conceived his legendary fantasy-themed anthology, Rod Serling (1924–1975) would still be a significant figure in the history of American television. Born in Syracuse and raised in Binghamton, New York, the young Serling demonstrated traits of imagination and energy early on; his older brother, Robert, recalled, "there was some kind of compulsion in him to do something that nobody else—the ordinary kid—[would] do" (Zicree 4). On the same day he graduated from high school, Serling joined the army, eventually becoming a paratrooper in the Pacific theater during World War II, where he was decorated for wounds sustained in combat. Serling also took up boxing during this period, and his experiences in combat and the ring later provided considerable inspiration for some of his finest writing.

Following military service, Serling enrolled at Antioch College and graduated in 1950. By this time the young veteran had already sold a few radio scripts and married the former Carolyn Kramer, with whom he would have two children. Serling then began writing for television; most of these early efforts were forgettable, and Serling himself later remarked that "style is something you develop by copying the style of someone who writes well.... For a while, you're a cheap imitation. I was a Hemingway imitator. Everything I wrote began, 'It was hot'" (Gerani and Schulman 35).

More than seventy Serling scripts had been televised by early 1955 when "Patterns," his drama about big business, was broadcast live on NBC's *Kraft Television Theater*. Overnight, Serling found himself promoted to the first rank of television writers, winning an Emmy for "Patterns" and then another for "Requiem for a Heavyweight," a 1956 episode of CBS's *Playhouse 90*. During the so-called golden age of television, the networks supported several of these sensitive, literate dramatic anthologies, and the reputations of "teleplaywrights" like Serling symbolized the artistic possibilities the infant medium offered. The heyday of these artists was short-lived, although scribes such as David Chase and J. J. Abrams seem to have recaptured some of their former glory. Yet even the golden age was far from perfect for television writers.

Although he was making a good living and receiving high praise from critics, Rod Serling became increasingly frustrated by network interference. Most television shows were supported by a single sponsor, and these corporations often pressured the networks to change or censor words, ideas, or plot developments that might reflect unfavorably on their products. "Before the script goes before the cameras," Serling observed, "the networks, the sponsors, the ad-agency men censor it so that by the time it's seen on the home screen, all the message has been squeezed out of it" (Gerani and Schulman 36). Examples of such censorship could be as trivial as the elimination of the line "Got a match?" from "Requiem for a Heavyweight" because Ronson lighters sponsored the show, or they could be as serious as the almost total revision of "Noon on Doomsday," a teleplay for *United States Steel Hour* in which a scathing examination of prejudice and bigotry was reduced to inoffensive pabulum (Zicree 14). Eventually, Serling realized that he could write more seriously about the human condition if his realistic themes were clothed in fantastic story lines. It was this realization that led to *The Twilight Zone*.

Although he enjoyed reading pulp magazines such as *Amazing Stories* and *Weird Tales* as a child, Serling had little affinity for science fiction and fantasy prior to *The Twilight Zone*. For example, his script "U.F.O." for a 1954 episode of *Studio One* was particularly weak and offered little evidence that the author had any grasp of the science fiction genre. However, Serling was a quick learner; once he figured out that spaceships would allow him tremendous opportunities to explore the human experience without outside interference, he managed to incorporate them and other sci-fi trappings—robots, time travel, and the like—into the kind of stories he preferred to tell.

Serling's first serious effort at science fiction was "The Time Element," an episode of CBS's *Desilu Playhouse* broadcast on November 24, 1958. William Bendix starred in this tale of a bartender tormented by recurring dreams in which he travels back in time to December 6, 1941, but is unable to prevent the Japanese attack on Pearl Harbor. Critical and popular reaction was so strong that CBS approved a pilot for what Serling called *The Twilight Zone*, a phrase he thought he had made up but later discovered was an obscure aviation term (Zicree 24). On October 2, 1959, CBS broadcast the first episode, called "Where Is Everybody?"—a chilling tale about a man (Earl Holliman) seemingly trapped in a deserted town.

Although far from the show's zenith, the initial offering is significant because it illustrates two crucial elements that define its greatness. The idea of a lone man trapped in a solitary environment became a recurring theme in Serling's teleplays, representing his fascination with the notion of alienation in the modern world. Even more important, "Where Is Everybody?" features the sort of twist ending that became Serling's trademark: Holliman's protagonist is actually an astronaut undergoing an isolation experiment, and his entire experience is merely a hallucination brought on by nearly 500 hours of solitude.

Thirty-six episodes of *The Twilight Zone* were broadcast during the initial 1959–1960 season, most of them written by Rod Serling. In all, Serling would write 92 of the series' 156 installments. During the first season, Serling would craft several classic tales, including "Mr. Denton on Doomsday," in which Dan Duryea portrays a drunken ex-gunslinger restored to his former skill by a magic potion, and "The Lonely," in which Jack Warden plays a murderer condemned to spend decades on a distant asteroid with only a beautiful female robot for company. Serling also contributed what may be the single most memorable *Twilight*

Burgess Meredith in "Time Enough at Last," one of *The Twilight Zone*'s most memorable episodes.

Zone episode of all, "Time Enough at Last," in which Burgess Meredith appears as Henry Bemis, a mild-mannered bank clerk who wants nothing more than to be left alone with his books. Because he happens to be in the bank vault when atomic warfare breaks out, Bemis survives as the last person on Earth. Instead of being chagrined by this fate, Bemis happily settles down to spend the rest of his life reading—only to accidentally break his glasses, leaving him unable to enjoy a world populated by nothing but books. "It's not fair!" the defeated little man complains to his unhearing and now useless companions.

Episodes Serling wrote for later seasons are also highly regarded. In "The Eye of the Beholder" from season 2, Serling offers a tale of a horribly deformed woman in an unnamed totalitarian society who desperately submits to an operation to give herself a normal appearance. The operation fails, and the heavily bandaged woman is revealed to be—by our standards—a stunning beauty (played by Donna Douglas, soon to gain fame as Ellie May on *The Beverly Hillbillies*), and her physicians are terrifying, pig-faced beings. "The Shelter" from season 3 is a fine example of Serling's ability to illustrate the decay of normal society in the wake of abnormal events. When a nuclear attack is announced and one family's bomb shelter is too small to accommodate the neighbors, the former friends start squabbling over who ought to be given sanctuary when the bombs are dropped. Ultimately, a second announcement confirms that the first one was in error, but by that time the damage has been done to the neighborhood's sense of self.

Although the show's creator was incredibly prolific, he couldn't possibly write every episode, so other writers were brought in, most notably science fiction specialists Richard Matheson (1926–), Charles Beaumont (1929–1967), and George Clayton Johnson (1929–). Chief among this triumvirate was Matheson, author of such speculative fiction classics as *I Am Legend* (1954), *The Shrinking Man* (1956), and *Bid Time Return* (also called *Somewhere in Time*, 1975). Generally recognized as the premier American fantasist after H. P. Lovecraft's death and before the rise of Stephen King, Matheson contributed sixteen scripts to *The Twilight Zone*, including "The Invaders" (2.15), a nearly wordless episode in which an old woman (Agnes Moorehead) is terrorized by tiny alien invaders. She manages to destroy her tormentors, but not before one transmits a warning message back to his home planet, which turns out to be Earth, about this dangerous world of giants. Perhaps even more fondly remembered is "Nightmare at 20,000 Feet" (5.3), wherein Captain Kirk–to-be William Shatner plays an airline passenger who can't convince anybody that a gremlin is destroying the plane's wing during a violent storm.

His premature death at age thirty-eight robbed Charles Beaumont of the sort of following Matheson enjoys, but Beaumont actually contributed more *Twilight Zone* scripts than any other writer except Serling himself—a total of twenty-two. Now admired primarily for his short stories, Beaumont also adapted stories by Poe for independent filmmaker Roger Corman and scripted the popular fantasy film *The 7 Faces of Dr. Lao* (1964) for George Pal. Beaumont's most important contribution to *The Twilight Zone* is probably "Living Doll" (5.6), in which Telly Savalas is menaced by "Talky Tina," a deceptively sweet-faced children's toy.

Compared with Matheson and Beaumont, George Clayton Johnson (well regarded for coauthoring the 1967 science fiction novel *Logan's Run* with William F. Nolan and for his contributions to the 1960 Rat Pack film *Ocean's Eleven*) contributed far fewer teleplays to *The Twilight*

Zone—seven in all. However, among that number are two perennial favorites among *Twilight Zone* fans: "Kick the Can" (3.21), in which a mysterious old man offers the fountain of youth in the form of a childhood game, and "A Game of Pool" (3.5), in which billiards hustler Jack Klugman bets his life in a game with a legendary pool shark (Jonathan Winters) who just happens to be dead.

Good writing was certainly an important factor in the show's success, but other elements were significant as well. Many fine performances from both veteran and up-and-coming thespians distinguished *The Twilight Zone*. Among the notable actors who appeared on the show were Robert Redford, Robert Cummings, Roddy McDowall, Carol Burnett, Claude Akins, Patrick Macnee, John Carradine, Anne Francis, Doug McClure, Donald Pleasance, and Burt Reynolds. Equally important was the show's music, which included contributions from veteran composers Bernard Herrmann and Jerry Goldsmith. For season 2, avant-garde composer Marius Constant provided a new theme song, a spooky ditty incorporating electric guitar and bongo drums that arguably is still the most recognizable TV theme song in the world.

For five seasons, *The Twilight Zone* entertained and amazed audiences with tales of horror, fantasy, and whimsy, most of which featured twist endings that underscored the moralistic messages of the show's creator. Although fluctuating ratings frequently brought the series to the brink of cancellation, it continued to garner critical favor, providing CBS with a degree of prestige that justified the show's survival. There were several attempts to make the program more cost-effective, including substituting videotape for film in some episodes and expanding the original thirty-minute running time to a full hour. None of these experiments was particularly successful. As the seasons passed, the show's quality eroded, as did the size of its audience. *The Twilight Zone* was not renewed after season 5 (1963–1964), but it lived on, first in syndication and later on cable and home video.

After *The Twilight Zone* was canceled, Rod Serling kept himself busy as a writer and TV personality, lending his famous face and voice to hundreds of commercials, game shows, and other ventures. Two more science fiction classics bear his mark: the 1968 cinematic adaptation of *Planet of the Apes*, for which he cowrote the screenplay, and *Night Gallery*, another fantasy anthology series that ran on NBC from 1970 to 1973. The energy and imagination that defined Serling as a child endured into middle age, but his youthful vigor did not. Worn out by overwork and decades of heavy smoking—at one point he consumed four packs of cigarettes a day—Serling suffered a series of heart attacks shortly after his fiftieth birthday. In June 1975 Rod Serling died of complications during open-heart surgery.

Serling was gone, but *The Twilight Zone* lived on. Savvy marketing explains much of the show's continued success. Serling's collections of stories from the show were frequently reprinted, and for many years the Gold Key company published a *Twilight Zone* comic book. During the 1980s his wife oversaw publication of a *Twilight Zone* magazine, and in 1983 Steven Spielberg produced *Twilight Zone: The Movie*, an uneasy mixture of comedy and horror that failed to impress either critics or audiences. Today, that production is chiefly remembered because of a tragic accident on the set in which star Vic Morrow and two child actors were killed. As a result, segment director John Landis and others found themselves on trial for involuntary manslaughter (all were acquitted).

In spite of the film's relative failure, CBS decided to revive *The Twilight Zone* in 1985. Initial ratings were promising, but they quickly faded; after two seasons, CBS canceled the show again, although a handful of low-budget episodes were produced later to pad out the package size for syndication purposes. In 2002 UPN launched the show yet again, this time with Forest Whitaker as host, but it lasted only a single season. In spite of the participation of veterans on both sides of the camera and updated versions of original episodes, it appears that only the classic program can stand the test of time. Other fantasy-themed anthologies, including *The Outer Limits, Tales from the Crypt,* and Serling's own *Night Gallery*, have tried to mimic *The Twilight Zone*'s sense of wonder and horror, but none has captured the public's imagination to the same degree. Interestingly, although many science fiction and horror shows have aped the *Twilight Zone* format, few nongenre anthologies have appeared in its wake—a far cry from the days when a plethora of dramatic anthologies filled the airwaves.

Undoubtedly, the irreplaceable factor was Rod Serling himself. With no recurring characters, it was necessary to find a suitable narrator for *The Twilight Zone*, and several notable performers, including Orson Welles, were considered for the job. Finally, Serling reluctantly agreed to narrate the program himself. At first, Serling's narrative comments were delivered offscreen, but eventually he began to appear onscreen as well. Serling's distinctive voice and clipped delivery provided the crucial link to audiences that none of his successors has been able to establish.

As early as 1963 Serling spoofed himself on *The Jack Benny Show*. Since then, hundreds of radio and TV shows have parodied *The Twilight Zone*, including *Saturday Night Live*, *The Simpsons*, *Futurama*, and *Family Guy*. The Dutch rock group Golden Earring had a hit song called "Twilight Zone" in 1982, and the program has been referenced in songs by many other artists, including the Rolling Stones. The very phrase *twilight zone* has entered the cultural lexicon. It is a testament to the brilliance and imagination of Rod Serling that his ideas, image, and voice—both literal and figurative—continue to resonate in the American consciousness long after his passing.

Acknowledgment

The author thanks actor-writer Arthur J. Lundquist for his insights and expertise regarding Rod Serling and his most enduring creation.

Twin Peaks

David Bianculli

Start by throwing down the gauntlet: ABC's *Twin Peaks* is the cult TV show to end all cult TV shows. It resonates more, without reaching too many, than any other. Exclude anthology shows such as *The Twilight Zone* from the mix, and focus on weekly series with linear narratives, and what other program deserves the crown? *Star Trek?* Yes, the original was a cult TV show of the highest order, but with decades of TV and movie offshoots, it's no longer a cult; it's an established, heavyweight religion. *The Prisoner?* It was a brilliantly original vision, and as a model of the self-contained miniseries version of storytelling, it was way ahead of its time, but Patrick McGoohan's bold allegory is all but forgotten forty years later, except by those old enough to have seen it originally.

But if the residual audience and reverence for *The Prisoner* are too small, and for *Star Trek* too big, the one for *Twin Peaks*, like Baby Bear's bed in the Goldilocks story, is just right. Those who have watched and made television since *Twin Peaks* have used it as a touchstone, keeping it alive in memory through a sort of oral-visual history.

Ever since David Lynch and Mark Frost's *Twin Peaks* came and went like a dazzling prime-time comet in 1990–1991, any ambitious TV series with enough originality to be called "quirky" has suffered by comparison, or least suffered the comparisons. From *Northern Exposure* and *Picket Fences* in the years just after *Peaks* peaked to ambitious shows nearly twenty years later, *Twin Peaks* remains the pace car, the record holder, and, at times, an almost mythological case study about narrative lapses and loss of momentum.

This resonance and these comparisons are well earned and are not likely to fade soon. Most TV critics, and I plead guilty here, can't get

Twin Peaks out of their heads. And why should they? When Shaun Cassidy's darkly twisted *American Gothic* premiered in 1995, *Time* described it as *"Twin Peaks* without the sardonic levity" (Tynan and Bellafant). When ABC's brilliant, visually dazzling *Pushing Daisies* premiered a dozen years later, *New York* summarized it as *"Twin Peaks* meets *Waitress"* ("ABC's 'Pushing Daisies'"). Creator Bryan Fuller claims the movie *Amelie* was more of an inspiration, but for those who strive to make original dramatic television and tell their stories in unconventional manners, *Twin Peaks* never seems to be far from the minds of critics, viewers, or the creators themselves.

Joss Whedon, whose superb work on *Buffy the Vampire Slayer*, *Angel*, and *Firefly* makes him one of the most successful and stylish inheritors of the cult TV crown, once picked Kyle MacLachlan's Agent Dale Cooper from *Twin Peaks* as one of his "all-time favorite TV characters," and he continues to credit *Twin Peaks* as "one of the shows I loved the best" (online posting, whedonesque.com). Carlton Cuse and Damon Lindelof, co–executive producers of the cult phenomenon *Lost*, both see *Twin Peaks* as a template for what to avoid as well as what to achieve. "I remember the frustration I felt with *Twin Peaks* as a viewer," Cuse told *USA Today*. "It went from being totally great to totally frustrating, because it just got more and more obtuse. We're really conscious of our show not doing that" (Keveney). Lindelof talked of the dangers of solving too many mysteries as well as solving too few: "Every time we close one door, we have to open up another," he said, "or else we risk falling victim to the *Twin Peaks* curse. Once they told you who killed Laura Palmer, there was no reason to watch that show any more" (Ausiello). Likewise, Tim Kring, creator of NBC's cult show *Heroes*, said that he was wary of revealing too many of his dramatic cards, as he felt *Twin Peaks* had. Although he misremembered the popularity of that series, its quick descent from pop culture fixation to dramatic disappointment was not lost on him or any of his TV-creating contemporaries. "Those of us who remember *Twin Peaks* going from the number one or two or three show on the network to four episodes later being canceled because of revealing who killed Laura Palmer . . . that's a cautionary tale for all of us" (Topel).

Yet that cautionary tale looms so large in the collective imaginations of these imaginative TV writers, it's almost like an urban legend, a narrative boogeyman—an always lurking, always threatening Killer BOB. It's partly because of the attention-getting rise and fall of *Twin Peaks*, and the astonishing speed of its overall trajectory, that it remains so strongly in critical, creative, and collective memory.

Both the ascent and the descent of *Twin Peaks* were due to several significant factors. Phase one, the prelaunch hype, involved getting the word out early about the wonderful weirdness of the David Lynch–Mark Frost telemovie. One of the earliest raves came from the September 1989 issue of *Connoisseur* magazine, in which Howard A. Rodman's article was headlined "The Series That Will Change TV." Once the national TV press got a look, it too responded with lavish and unusually widespread praise. When the series premiered in April 1990, Tom Shales of the *Washington Post* wrote, "For the adventurous explorer in the normally tame wilds of television, *Twin Peaks* is just this side of a godsend." As happened later that year with *The Civil War*, a general and vocal consensus of TV critics actually made a difference. *Twin Peaks*'s two-hour opener drew enough viewers to make it the highest-rated telemovie of the 1989–1990 season. The rest was up to Lynch, Frost, and the others involved in the making of *Twin Peaks*.

Phase two, the viewer and media response to the plots and characters in the early episodes, led to and fed a *Twin Peaks* mania. The "Who Killed Laura Palmer?" story line (examining the mysterious death of the high school beauty, played by Sheryl Lee, who is found washed ashore wrapped in plastic) dominated conversations, and the increasingly paranormal subplots kept viewers involved and guessing in different ways.

After a couple of episodes, the audience leveled off. The viewers who remained, though, were a loyal core, delighting in Lynch's otherworldly dream sequences and playing along at trying to unravel, or at least follow, the various plot threads. The national media, enjoying and propelling the ride, geared up to "Who Shot J. R.?" levels all over again. *Newsweek* and *People* ran elaborate flow charts tracing the characters' intricate relationships, establishing a symbiotic bond between *Twin Peaks* and magazines that would continue throughout 1990. By the end of the year, *Time* had run a cover story on Lynch, and actresses from *Twin Peaks* had graced the covers of *Playboy*, *Rolling Stone*, *TV Guide*, and, fittingly, a photography magazine titled *Exposure*.

After the two-hour premiere and seven one-hour installments, *Twin Peaks* ended its first season with the Palmer murder mystery still unresolved and a cliffhanger ending, as Kyle MacLachlan's Dale Cooper is shot by an unseen assailant. It was, of course, an allusion to the way *Dallas* had ended its season a decade earlier, leading into the summer that begat the "Who Shot J. R.?" silliness. Like *Dallas*, *Twin Peaks* was a hot media topic that summer and was given lots of credit for changing the rules of television. "Tried and true," one network executive said, "is dead and buried" (quoted in Bianculli, *Teleliteracy* 269).

Phase three, the inevitable backlash, was accelerated by several factors. First, the show's momentum as "media darling" was derailed at the Emmy Awards in September, where *Twin Peaks*, nominated for fourteen awards, was snubbed in all but two minor categories, winning only for editing and costume design. Second, the merchandising offshoots went from intriguing to overkill. The demand for cherry pies and *Twin Peaks* memorabilia at the Mar-T Café in North Bend, Washington (the model for the series' Double R Diner), was one thing, and CD releases by *Peaks* composer Angelo Badalamenti and featured singer Julee Cruise were welcome projects. However, the various authorized *Twin Peaks* offshoots piled up too high and may have distracted the show's staff from focusing more energy on the series itself.

The backlash against *Twin Peaks* was spurred most severely, though, by the very folks who had conspired to broadcast the series in the first place: ABC and Lynch-Frost Productions. ABC blew it by moving the series to Saturday night, where it hoped *Twin Peaks* and its lead-in, *China Beach*, would lure audiences back to Saturday night TV and capture the attention of the weekend home-video crowd. Instead, both shows suffered. Many audience members were busy on weekends and unable to be loyal viewers, ultimately frustrating formerly loyal fans who could no longer keep up with the serialized and complicated story lines. Also, the writers frustrated many viewers by stringing out the Laura Palmer story: the killer was revealed eight hours into the show's second season, and the subsequent wrapping up of loose ends turned it into a twenty-hour mystery. Members of the creative team would later plead guilty to losing steam and direction as the realities of weekly TV production made it tougher to match their prior efforts and generate a similarly entrancing story. By the time *Twin Peaks* was finally pulled from the ABC schedule in the middle of the competitive February sweeps period, its audience had shrunk to only 10 percent of the homes watching TV at that hour.

Phase four, the attempted comeback, was a big publicity push generated by the network and production company when *Twin Peaks* returned at the end of March. The episode relaunching the series was even available for preview, the first time this had been the case since the premiere. Unfortunately, it was one of the weakest offerings. The next week's episode, ironically, was excellent, but by then, all hope of a revival had been dashed. *Twin Peaks* limped along through April, then disappeared again until mid-June, when the final two installments were combined into one big finale. It ended with a brilliant, extended sequence directed by Lynch, but most of the audience had already moved on.

In fourteen short months, *Twin Peaks* had washed across the national consciousness, then receded like an ebb tide. "Moving it to Saturday night didn't help," ABC Entertainment president Robert A. Iger said the summer after canceling *Twin Peaks*, but he also suggested that it may have been more effective as a self-contained, seven-episode special. "We tried it as a multiple-season series," he said, "and it just couldn't sustain itself" (quoted in Bianculli, *Teleliteracy* 270).

The following season, at all the commercial networks, "tried and true" was alive (but I wouldn't say it was well). "I don't think," Frost told the *New York Times* just before the series' cancellation, "it changed television one iota" (quoted in Bianculli, *Teleliteracy* 270). But it did. *Twin Peaks* was not for everybody. *Columbo* producer William Link calls it "incredibly overrated" and sneers, "If this is revolutionary television, I'll take vanilla" (quoted in Bianculli, *Teleliteracy* 270–71). Also, the rapid acceptance of its unconventional images and dialogue made it difficult for it to escape its *own* conventions. "How," asks media professor Robert Thompson, "do you parody irony?" (quoted in Bianculli, *Teleliteracy* 271). Yet *Twin Peaks* was unique, and for those making and watching television, it has proved unforgettable.

Lynch directed only a handful of *Twin Peaks* episodes, but all the most resonant set pieces—Cooper's extracting a tiny letter R from under one of Laura's fingernails, his Tibetan rock throwing, the "Red Room" sequences featuring the tiny Man from Another Place (seen early in the series and again in the final episode), and the disturbing death of Laura's look-alike cousin, Madeleine, at the hands of Laura's father Leland Palmer (Ray Wise)—were directed by Lynch. They were also written or cowritten by Frost, who, like Lynch, deserves credit for TV boldness on a very large scale.

Certain elements of *Twin Peaks* caught on quickly and enjoyed a half-life after the series itself had vanished from ABC. These included strange snippets of dialogue: "She's dead; wrapped in plastic." "The owls are not what they seem." "This must be where pies go when they die." "Diane, I'm holding in my hand a small box of chocolate bunnies." "She's filled with secrets." Others consisted of seemingly benign

Front row from left: Shelley Johnson (Mädchen Amick), Norma Jennings (Peggy Lipton), Ed (Everett McGill) and Nadine Hurley (Wendy Robie), and Special Agent Dale Cooper (Kyle MacLachlan) attend Laura Palmer's funeral in *Twin Peaks*.

yet complex images—stacks of doughnuts, a sensuously tied cherry stem, whirring ceiling fans, changing traffic lights—and Badalamenti's alternately eerie and playful music. *Twin Peaks* had an amazingly deep and talented cast, with terrific contributions by MacLachlan as Cooper, Michael Ontkean as Sheriff Harry Truman, Sheryl Lee as both Laura and Madeleine, Sherilyn Fenn as Audrey Horne, Ray Wise as Leland Palmer, Don S. Davis as Major Briggs, Jack Nance as Pete Martell, Piper Laurie as Catherine Martell (and the Japanese mystery man Tojimura), Joan Chen as Josie Packard, Miguel Ferrer as Albert Rosenfeld, and, in smaller roles, David Duchovny as Denise Bryson and Michael J. Anderson as the Man from Another Place. Even the underused regulars, such as Peggy Lipton and Mädchen Amick, shone, and only the pressures of weekly production and a meandering series of plots dragged *Twin Peaks* from its pop culture pedestal.

Had it been a self-contained eight-hour miniseries, with the Laura Palmer murder resolved at the end, *Twin Peaks* would have come and gone quickly, been hailed as utterly brilliant, and left critics and audiences clamoring for more. As it was, *Peaks* lost it way, lapsed dangerously close to self-parody, and was further hurt by the merciless reaction to Lynch's feature-film prequel, 1992's *Twin Peaks: Fire Walk with Me*.

Overall, *Twin Peaks* did as many things right as it did wrong. Ultimately, and regrettably, what it did wrong killed it: *Twin Peaks* dragged on the "Who Killed Laura Palmer?" mystery long past acceptable limits (long before TV viewers had become accustomed to such drawn-out serialized narratives in *Murder One*, *24*, *Lost*, or *Heroes*). After its bold and often brilliant initial season, *Twin Peaks* seemed to care too little about continuity, coherence, and common sense than even its most fervent fans could accept. As the series progressed into a second season, subplots came and went with no rhyme or reason, and although the journey was intriguing to the very end (its very inconclusive end, that is), *Twin Peaks* would end up as a series that was headed nowhere fast, filling up space with digressions and distractions like a college student trying to fake his way through an essay test. The drawn-out chess game with Kenneth Welsh's demonic Windom Earle, for example, makes little sense dramatically—and after a few moves, it makes no sense as an actual chess game either.

But think, for a moment, about what *Twin Peaks* did right. For those who dove in, *Twin Peaks* was as deep a pool as TV had ever provided—not always clear, granted, but deep. *Twin Peaks* tried harder and did more than most weekly series in prime time. It gave as much emphasis to visual images and lighting, and to the musical score and sound effects, as it did to the scripts and performances. Some sequences consist of long, unbroken camera takes; others are subliminal montages, cut together a frame at a time. Several core scenes, such as the rock-throwing experiment from Tibet and the "dancing midget" dream, stretch from one commercial break to the next without changing scenes. Conversely, in the series' final episode, as a doppelganger Laura Palmer runs screaming toward a frightened Cooper, Lynch increases the tension of the scene by inserting single-frame images of the villainous Windom Earle—close-ups alternating from a black-and-white negative image of Earle to a full-color positive image, then to a blending of the two, all shown too briefly for the naked eye to detect. Subliminal spookiness, Lynch style.

In casual conversations and detailed articles, elements of the series were dissected with a fervor that literature professors can both appreciate and envy. Tim Lucas, writing in a little-known journal called *Video Watchdog*, notes, "The first four shots in the pilot episode are all twin images" (36): the twin waterfalls blending into one, two ducks gliding along the lake, a table ornament of two identical dogs, and Josie Packard admiring herself in a mirror. Lucas then makes a lengthy case for the importance of twin imagery in *Twin Peaks*—which, given the importance of the doppelganger concept in the series' final episode, seems positively prescient. Scores of academics have written at length, often brilliantly, about the hidden treasures within *Twin Peaks*, and perhaps the show's most singular claim to cult TV fame is that, before the Internet even existed as a chat-room, fan-gathering place of worship, *Twin Peaks* generated enough interest to warrant and sustain its own fan-based magazine that was launched in 1992 and lasted thirteen years. The magazine's name? *Wrapped in Plastic*. The show's legacy and legend have persisted and, I suspect, will be evident for a long time to come.

Note

This chapter draws on previously published writings on *Twin Peaks* in *Teleliteracy* and *The Dictionary of Teleliteracy*.

Ultraviolet

Stacey Abbott

Every new vampire movie or television series claims to have reinvented vampire mythology, but these changes are usually just minor variations. In the century since Bram Stoker wrote *Dracula*, key examples from literature, film, and television have offered fresh perspectives on the vampire, including F. W. Murnau's *Nosferatu*, Anne Rice's *Interview with the Vampire*, and Kathryn Bigelow's *Near Dark*. In 1998 a British television series appeared whose makers clearly intended to reimagine the vampire genre by modernizing it for contemporary audiences. *Ultraviolet*—the brainchild of writer-director Joe Ahearne,[1] produced by World Productions, and broadcast on Channel 4—sits comfortably between *Buffy the Vampire Slayer* and *Blade*, two highly innovative texts that reworked the vampire genre through the lens of teen television and science fiction, respectively, and subsequently established notable cult followings. *Ultraviolet* is the lesser known of the three, an example of cult TV in its purest sense: a series that was recognized for its quality and innovation by genre fans but largely unrecognized by mainstream audiences. As Matt Hills argues, many "fans tend to view cult as being essentially linked to a minority audience" ("*Star Wars* in Fandom" 179). Consisting of only six episodes, *Ultraviolet* gained cult status almost immediately as genre fans in the United Kingdom and then later in the United States, where it was broadcast on the Sci-Fi Channel, recognized that this show offers not only a distinct vision of a familiar tale but also one that is uniquely British.

Ultraviolet is further positioned as cult by the fact that, at the time it was made, British television was not perceived as a welcoming home for fantasy programs. The BBC's long-running science fiction series *Doc-

tor Who had gone off the air in 1989 and would not come back until 2005, an event that marked a notable change in fantasy genres' position on British television screens.[2] Making a British series about modern-day vampire hunters was a gamble and was far more in keeping with developments in American television in the 1990s, specifically, the cult success of *The X-Files* and *Buffy the Vampire Slayer*.[3] More significantly, the show was an unusual product to emerge from World Productions, known for more realist dramas such as *The Cops* and *This Life* and run by Tony Garnett (producer of Ken Loach's *Cathy Come Home* and *Kes*). Ahearne explains that it was the seeming incompatibility of the vampire genre and British television that influenced his approach to *Ultraviolet*: "I was trying to marry the approach of low-key British naturalism with a basically fantastical premise, partly because I knew that was the only way you'd get it off the ground here. You have to do it seriously" (quoted in Vitaris 35).

This mixture of fantasy with realism is established in the opening credits, which fade in on a close-up of a naked corpse seemingly on a mortuary table and bathed in ultraviolet light. The camera scans the body before settling in extreme close-up on teeth marks on the neck. While the photographic examination of the body maintains a clinical style consistent with police dramas, the haunting music and ultraviolet light give the image an uncanny texture. This mixture of the real and the fantastic is reinforced through the show's understated presentation style, location shooting, scientific rationale, and emotionally restrained performances, marking the series as unique and lending the show its impact. *Ultraviolet* is all the more frightening because it feels plausible, rational, and real.

With echoes of Stoker's 1897 novel, the series returns the vampire to a recognizably up-to-date and modern London and tells its narrative from the point of view of a group of vampire hunters who are funded by the government and use cutting-edge technology, science, and police investigative methods to track down and destroy vampires. The series is clearly indebted to *The X-Files* for its narrative about a government conspiracy, as well as its focus on government agents investigating the supernatural. In his attempt to modernize the genre, Ahearne abandoned the word *vampire*, opting instead for the more scientific label "Code Five"—written with the roman numeral V (for vampire). The series likewise replaces the mythological iconography of the genre—wooden stakes, garlic, sunlight—with their scientific equivalents—carbon-based bullets, the chemical compound allicin, and ultraviolet light. This predates films such as *Blade* and *Underworld*, which would make similar changes to the genre.

As Ahearne explains, "The main idea was to do something about vampires now [as] if vampires really existed. So, if vampires did exist now and they had existed for hundreds of years . . . presumably the government would know about it and they wouldn't be running around with mirrors and garlic and crucifixes and whatever. They'd [sic] be modern weapons" ("Interview"). David Pirie suggests that this approach enables the vampire to be used as a modern metaphor, capturing in each episode a cross section of decidedly modern problems, debates, and social issues. As he explains: "Over six episodes, Ahearne's series features the vampire as bent cop, as parasitic city trader, as pedophile (with a major twist), as fetus, as polluter and finally as treacherous sexual predator once again" (30).

I would argue that *Ultraviolet* not only serves as a metaphor for the anxieties and experience of modern life but also uses the vampire genre to question traditional notions of good and evil in the modern world (see Abbott). It is this moral ambiguity that enables *Ultraviolet*, like other recent cult TV series such as *Angel*, *Alias*, and *Battlestar Galactica*, to disrupt any preconceptions the audience may have about the genre, the characters, and the world in general. For instance, the series is presented from the point of view of the modern vampire hunters, but unlike their iconic predecessor Van Helsing, the investigators are plagued with uncertainties about the righteousness of their vocation.

The leader, Pearse Harman (Philip Quast), is a priest whose faith is shaken, first by his inability to find evidence of God in the existence of evil, and then when he is diagnosed with cancer and the only sure promise of an afterlife comes from a vampire. The team's lead scientist, Dr. Angie Marsh (Susannah Harker), is equally haunted by the loss of her husband and daughter, who "crossed over" and became vampires only to be destroyed by Pearse. She is tormented by a desperate desire to have her family returned to her, knowing that vampires can regenerate, while she silently questions whether Pearse was right to destroy them.

The series raises many of these questions through Mike Colefield (Jack Davenport), a police officer who learns of the existence of vampires when his corrupt partner, Jack (Stephen Moyer), chooses to cross over to evade capture by the police. When Mike confronts Jack in the series' first episode, "Habeas Corpus," Jack challenges the perception that vampires are evil: "Did they tell you I was evil? It's what the church always says, Mike. Women, black, disabled, gay. Now us. Do you like living in the Middle Ages?" Mike is clearly disturbed by Jack's comparison of the vampire hunting squad to the Inquisition. As Mike, who is now a member of the team, unravels the complex and morally ambiguous world of vampires and their hunters, the show questions whether vampires are truly evil or simply another species. Is the indiscriminate hunting of vampires a necessary form of self-defense or a form of genocide? Which is the more dangerous species, vampire or human?

To establish this ambiguity, humans and vampires are shown throughout the series as shadows of each other. The episodes "In Nomine Patris" (1.2), "Sub Judice" (1.3), and "Terra Incognita" (1.5) all focus on the horrors of scientific experimentation carried out by both vampires and humans. In "In Nomine Patris" Mike and Angie find a vampire-run hospital filled with cancer patients who have been exposed to radiation as a means of researching the effects of contamination on the vampires' food supply. Similarly, "Terra Incognita" reveals that the vampires have offered a Brazilian man suffering from sickle-cell anemia a miracle cure in the form of a synthetic blood substitute. In a truly disturbing revelation, however, Angie discovers, when bathing the patient's body in ultraviolet light, that he is covered in bite marks, indicating that the vampires have been tasting him, testing whether the synthetic blood can serve as an acceptable food substitute.

While these examples paint the vampires as cruel and self-serving, "Sub Judice" pays equal attention to humanity's questionable medical interventions. The team discovers that Marion Wainwright, a barrister whose husband apparently died two years earlier but may have crossed over, is pregnant through in vitro fertilization treatment. When she has an ultrasound, however, an empty gestational sac is revealed. Is this a phantom pregnancy or a human-vampire hybrid? The episode exposes the complex issues surrounding scientific intervention in reproduction by depicting the psychological cruelty of the investigative team members, who are prepared to force Marion to have an abortion rather than see the birth of this new life-form — one they perceive to be unnatural and inhuman. Later, when Mike and Vaughn Rice (Idris Elba), the team's military enforcer, discover the vampires' nursery for Marion's baby, Mike asks: "If it was in here now you'd pull the plug, wouldn't you?" To which Vaughn replies, "No. Angie'd kill me. She'd want it for the lab." Vampires and humans are equally capable of cruelty in the name of science.

Humanity's questionable morality is further explored through the lens of pedophilia in the episode "Mea Culpa" (1.4), when a young Catholic schoolboy kills a priest with a knife. While the team assumes that the boy's sudden change in behavior can be explained only by Code V influence, Mike, as a former police officer, knows all too well that these things can happen without any supernatural intervention. Even though it turns out that the boy *has* been infected, humans are still revealed to be the root cause of his actions: he was infected with the Code V strain when he was molested by a human pedophile who acts as a carrier. In an interesting twist, the series finale, "Persona Non Grata" (1.6), reveals that despite their claims otherwise, the vampires are not looking for peace but rather are researching a means of causing a nuclear winter that would destroy a large percentage of humanity and enable the vampires to emerge as the dominant species. Although this revelation seems to suggest that they are monsters, the means of bringing about this apocalypse is of human construction, and the motivation for doing so is entirely within the hands of humanity. As Pearse explains to Mike in "Habeas Corpus," humanity's "capacity for self-destruction [is] growing at an exponential rate." To survive, the vampires must take control of humanity's weaker impulses, and in this, the show addresses humanity's complicity in its own destruction.

The series' focus on moral ambiguity and narrative uncertainty is further illustrated by the manner in which both humans and vampires defend their actions. While the vampire hunters, despite their own uncertainties, regularly assert that their work is necessary for the protection of humanity, the vampires similarly stress that they are only trying to protect themselves from humans. Ahearne claims that he "tried to invent an explanation for everything they could do, so it would be less easy for people to say [that] there is a God and therefore these are evil. They might just be creatures from evolution like the rest of us, but on a different path" (quoted in Vitaris 35). Still, the series goes to great lengths to represent the vampires as decidedly uncanny and abject and, in so doing, undermine any sense of kinship with humanity. Like the vampire hunters, the audience is encouraged to find the vampires disturbing and unsettling to the natural order. In "In Nomine Patris," a vampire runs over a young girl, leaving her paralyzed from the neck down. At the end of the episode, the same vampire "turns" her to save her from a life of pain and torment. She then goes to Mike to convince him that she is better off and has in fact been saved, but as she approaches him, the sequence cuts to a shot of her from behind, and we catch a glimpse of her broken spine, the vertebrae shifting and protruding from her back, creaking with each forward step. This shot emphasizes the abjectness of the vampire body and reminds us that the vampire represents the lifeless body reanimated. Mike is paralyzed by this vision, torn between his sympathy for the girl and the horror of her restoration. In the same episode, a vampire is burned by brief exposure to the sun. Unable to heal itself, it becomes apparent that the vampire will continue to exist eternally in this misshapen and painfully disfigured body. The prospect of eternal life is transformed from dream to nightmare, and the vampire body is revealed to be a site of horror.

The aspect of the series' mythology that truly captures the uncanniness of the vampire body is its lack of a reflection, a convention borrowed from traditional vampire lore but enhanced by the revelation in the opening episode that they cannot be recorded through any form of modern technology (revealed when Mike tries to track a suspect by monitoring the London Underground's surveillance system). Unlike other aspects of the vampire condition, such as their allergy to light and garlic, there is no scientific explanation for this phenomenon. As such, every time the series emphasizes the intangibility of the vampire body through its invisibility, in contrast to its seeming corporeality, the show reminds us that vampires exist outside of our natural world. This does not, however, undermine the ambiguity of the series by suggesting that they are outright monsters; rather, it indicates that they are fundamentally unknowable. Ultimately, the show suggests, it is a matter of faith — in science, religion, love, or friendship — and by the final episode, each of the protagonists has seen his or her faith pushed to its very limits.

Ultraviolet lasted for only one season, and although Ahearne added a coda to the end of the show to create an opening for a second, it was never pursued by either World Productions or Channel 4. Ahearne explains that this was partially because he was the sole writer-director and was therefore too tied up with the first season to develop plans for a second. Additionally, the show was, according to Ahearne, expensive to produce, and the audience figures were not high enough to justify a second season (averaging just 2.5 million viewers). A possible afterlife for *Ultraviolet* briefly presented itself in the form of an American version, and a pilot was commissioned by FOX. This was produced by Howard Gordon (*The X-Files, Angel, 24*) and Chip Johannessen (*Millennium*) and directed by Mark Piznarski (*My So-Called Life*), but the series was never picked up. Gordon's comments about the changes necessary to make the show suit American television unintentionally highlight the essence of what made the original *Ultraviolet* so distinct: "I think at some level the way the story was originally told was understated. . . . The way the stories are told needs to be endowed and in some ways made more emotional" (quoted in "Things to Come" 6). It was, however, precisely this understated presentation style and not the absence of emotion but the *restraint* of intense emotion that reinvigorated the vampire genre and confronted the audience with an emotional array of moral and social issues, making *Ultraviolet* a haunting and uniquely British cult TV experience.

Notes

1. Joe Ahearne originally wrote the treatment and script for the pilot but was eventually commissioned to write and direct all six episodes, lending the series an unusual level of narrative and stylistic coherence. Although the show was scripted episodically, following a team of vampire hunters investigating a different case every week, each episode contributes to an extended narrative arc, building to a near apocalyptic climax.

2. Genre-based shows that appeared on British television subsequent to the success of the revived *Doctor Who* (2005–) include *Torchwood* (2007–), *The Sarah Jane Adventures* (2007–), *Primeval* (2007–), *Dracula* (2006), *Jekyll* (2007), and *Frankenstein* (2007).

3. For further discussion of the position of fantasy TV in Britain, see Johnson, *Telefantasy*; Hill and Calcutt.

Veronica Mars

Sue Turnbull

Creator, writer, and executive producer Rob Thomas *intended* to introduce his teen hero, Veronica Mars (Kristen Bell), with a Chandleresque voice-over when the show premiered on Viacom's UPN in September 2004:

> I'm never getting married. You want an absolute? A sure thing? Well there it is. Veronica Mars, spinster . . . old maid. Carve it in stone. I mean, come on. What's the point? Sure there's that initial primal drive . . . hormonal surge . . . whatever you want to call it. Ride it out. Better yet, ignore it. Sooner or later, the people you love let you down, betray you. And here's where it ends up—fat men, cocktail waitresses, cheap motels on the wrong side of town. And a soon-to-be-ex-spouse wanting a bigger piece of the settlement pie.

These cynical words were supposed to be spoken over a series of elaborate tracking shots depicting neon signs and sexual activities taking place in a cheap motel obviously on the wrong side of town. Cut to Veronica on a stakeout, seated behind the wheel of her sporty black LeBaron and equipped with a flask of coffee; her calculus textbook, in preparation for a test the next day; a camera fitted with a telephoto lens with which to take the "money shot" of the cheating couple; and a pit bull in the backseat, appropriately named Backup.

It's an exquisite noir moment that, happily, is restored on the DVD of season 1. However, if you tuned in to the first episode when it originally aired, you would have started in a very different place, with daylight images of Neptune High School, jogging cheerleaders, and an alternative take on Veronica's fictional world, emphasizing class tension rather than Veronica's disillusionment with love and sex. As Veronica tells us: "This is my school. If you go here, your parents are either millionaires, or your parents work for millionaires. Neptune, California: a town without a middle class. If you're in the second group, you get a job: fast food, movie theatres, mini-marts. Or you could be me. My after-school job means tailing philandering spouses or investigating false injury claims."

Welcome to the genre hybridity of *Veronica Mars*. On the one hand, it's a noirish case-driven mystery show with a prematurely world-weary female private investigator. On the other hand (the one the network wanted Thomas to push), it's a teen coming-of-age melodrama set against a background of haves and have-nots.

Prefaced during the first two seasons with an upbeat title sequence composed of images of the cast, their names superimposed on torn exercise book paper, and accompanied by "cool" contemporary music tracks (an astonishing fourteen in the season 1 pilot), *Veronica Mars* has many of the hallmarks of a teen TV drama, as identified in the collection of essays edited by Glyn Davis and Kay Dickinson. But Thomas was never entirely satisfied with this generic designation, as is apparent in the reimagined titles for season 3, which herald Veronica's move to college. This second title sequence is much more slick and stylishly noir in tone, the original theme music by the Dandy Warhols ("We Used to Be Friends") having been remixed to evoke a more melancholy, downbeat mood.[1]

As a former high school teacher of journalism and the author of five successful teen novels, Thomas seems well qualified to write a teen drama series (see Thomas, *Neptune Noir*). In fact, *Veronica Mars* started out as a teen novel about a boy detective called Keith Mars. However, after a stint writing for *Dawson's Creek* in 1997 and serving as executive producer and writer for the short-lived *Cupid* (starring Jeremy Piven) in 1998, followed by a five-year period when nothing he wrote got picked up at all, Thomas decided to rewrite his boy detective novel as a "spec" TV script. This was around the time that Thomas's favorite teen TV series, *Freaks and Geeks*, got canceled, implying, for him, "the death of small-story television." Thomas's pilot script was based on the following premise: "I see myself as a *Northern Exposure* writer in a *C.S.I.* world, and so when I had that book idea, it occurred to me that it was a way to do a teen show that would be case driven and high incident and yet

Counterclockwise from bottom right: Keith Mars (Enrico Colantoni), Logan Echolls (Jason Dohring), Duncan Kane (Teddy Dunn), Weevil (Francis Capra), Mallory Dent (Sydney Tamiia Poitier), Wallace Fennel (Percy Daggs III), and Veronica Mars (Kristen Bell) from the first season of *Veronica Mars*.

I could still make it a character-driven show, underneath the detective cases and the high concept" (Couch Baron).

Over the next three seasons of *Veronica Mars*, the first two on UPN and the third on the CW (after UPN merged with CBS Corporation and

Warner in September 2006), Thomas persisted with his high-concept show. Although it never attracted high ratings, it did attract critical attention, such as an early *Village Voice* review by Joy Press in 2004, suggesting that *Veronica Mars* might be "the first television drama to attempt a fusion of *Chinatown* and *Heathers*" (Press, "Screen Gems"). Thomas liked this description and quoted it on his Web site (Thomas, "Origins").

Despite network anxiety about the darkness of the series and frequent requests to "lighten" it, UPN agreed to allow Veronica to announce in the pilot episode that she had been raped, with these memorable words: "Want to know how I lost my virginity? So do I." Given that this was the first line Thomas wrote, Veronica's rape was clearly central to his initial high concept for the show (see Thomas, *Neptune Noir* 34). The issue of rape subsequently became a recurring theme across all three seasons (most controversially in season 3),[2] which in common with other long-form drama series, were structured around both seasonal and episodic story arcs.

In season 1, the long-running story arcs include not only Veronica's efforts to find out who drugged and raped her at Shelley Pomeroy's party but also who murdered her best friend, Lilly Kane, daughter of Neptune's software millionaire Jake Kane and brother of Veronica's former boyfriend Duncan (Teddy Dunn), who has broken off their relationship because he fears it may be incestuous.[3] All these events have occurred before we first meet Veronica and are revisited through flashbacks, presented in striking color-coded sequences. A third ongoing story arc involves Veronica's efforts to trace her alcoholic mother Lianne, in a doomed attempt to reunite her family. Other self-contained story arcs involve the specific cases Veronica accepts on behalf of her fellow students and in her capacity as an amateur private eye working for her PI father Keith (Enrico Colantoni), the former sheriff of Neptune who lost his job as a direct result of his (mis)handling of the Kane murder.

Season 2 is similarly structured around a long story arc, this time involving a fatal school bus crash, the investigation of which results in additional details about Veronica's rape after a detour into disturbing revelations about pedophilia involving the mayor of Neptune, former baseball coach Woody Goodman (Steve Guttenberg). Season 3, in contrast, with its setting of Hearst College, is constructed around a number of mini-arcs: one involving a college rapist, another involving the death of the dean of the college, and a third involving the suspected murder of the basketball coach. Episodes 16 through 20 of the somewhat truncated third season are stand-alone episodes, signaling a change in strategy by Thomas, who was faced with likely cancellation due to the show's poor ratings.

Although *Veronica Mars* is certainly case driven, it is also very much about relationships, the most significant of all being that between Veronica and her father. As Joyce Millman points out in her essay "Daddy's Girl": "Parent, child, husband, wife, partner, roommate, best friend—Veronica and Keith play a jumble of roles within their relationship. They are all things to each other, much like lovers or spouses are in the intensely inward-focused first phase of their union" (51–52). Although both Veronica and Keith have a number of romantic relationships during the course of the show, season 3 ends with a significant affirmation of their ongoing devotion. In "The Bitch Is Back" (3.20), Keith sacrifices his chance of reelection as sheriff to protect his daughter, who has stolen some key evidence relating to a top-secret college frat group known as The Castle. Meanwhile, Veronica loyally casts her vote in Keith's favor before walking out onto a wet, windswept Neptune street as the camera pans up and away to the accompaniment of a track by Albert Hammond, ironically entitled "It Never Rains in Southern California."

Although the portrayal of Keith and Veronica's relationship received a Family Television Award in 2006 for "Favorite Father and Daughter," other relationships on the show cast families in a more negative light, whether the family is rich (as in the case of the Echollses and the Kanes) or poor (as in the case of the Hispanic character Eli "Weevil" Navarro, played by Italian actor Francis Capra, whose grandmother is prepared to let him go to jail to protect his older brother in "Credit Where Credit's Due" [1.2]) (Edwards, "On the Low Down" 77).

So-called friends are also revealed to be routinely untrustworthy. Veronica has been dropped by the wealthy 09ers (those who share the 90909 ZIP code) because of her father's loss of status and her split with the affluent Duncan before the start of season 1. The theme sung by the Dandy Warhols, with the lyrics "A long time ago, we used to be friends," thus takes on a specific resonance with regard to Veronica's initial isolation. There are, however, a number of notable exceptions to the fickle friends rule, including Veronica's African American basketball-playing companion Wallace Fennel (Percy Daggs III). When we meet Wallace in episode 1, he is naked and has been gaffer-taped to a flagpole by Weevil and his motorcycle gang the PCHers (derived from their beat on the Pacific Coast Highway). After being rescued by Veronica, Wallace remains a loyal ally throughout the series, providing a moral compass at those moments when Veronica's desire for revenge blurs her vision. This is especially true during the third season, when Wallace fears that Veronica is simply using the smitten Piz (Chris Lowell) to get back at her most recent ex, Logan Echolls (Jason Dohring), with whom Veronica "enjoys" a fraught on-again, off-again relationship over the three seasons.

Smart-mouthed, feisty, and occasionally petty and vindictive, Veronica uses duplicity as her modus operandi. Take the episode "Donut Run" (2.11), in which Veronica pretends to be grief stricken at her very public breakup with Duncan just to throw everyone off track when he kidnaps his baby daughter from her ghastly grandparents and escapes to Australia via Mexico. Veronica's scam includes duping her father, whose reaction when he finds out is one of hurt bewilderment. But Veronica is not alone in her capacity for deceit. There is, as Lynne Edwards has pointed out, a "moral grayness" about life in Neptune, where "nothing is ever clear and nothing is ever final," not unlike another of Edwards's favorite shows, *Buffy the Vampire Slayer*, to which *Veronica Mars* is frequently compared (80). In his response to Edwards's comments, Thomas declared himself both "aware and proud" of the show's "moral grayness," suggesting that it was not easy to get "a titular character on television who so often does as morally ambiguous things as Veronica Mars" (*Neptune Noir* 72).

Perhaps because of its darkness, perhaps because of its lead-in shows and the competition on rival stations, and perhaps because of its location on networks that were not quite right for the show (Thomas, *Neptune Noir* 6), *Veronica Mars* did not do well in the ratings, coming in last in its time slot in season 1. There was, however, a growing critical buzz about the show, particularly among a number of high-profile fans such as author Stephen King, cult movie director Kevin Smith, and *Buffy* creator Joss Whedon, who gave the show a rave in *Entertainment Weekly* (King, "Confessions"). Smith and Whedon went on to appear in cameo roles in the second season of the series: Smith in "Driver Ed" (2.2), and Whedon in "Rat Saw God" (2.6).[4] The buzz was also audible in shopping malls, as Thomas discovered, to his surprise, when he and the cast attended an outing in Seattle during the broadcast of season 1: "We were shocked that, despite our paltry ratings, there was a line stretching the length of the mall" (*Neptune Noir* 82).

Fan interest burgeoned on the Internet, with regular forums on the Television without Pity Web site, as well as dedicated sites such as MarsInvestigations.net and The Neptune Navigator. There was also the usual flurry of fan fiction (Fic from Mars) and a fan-produced blog about the show, Neptune Online. Fan innovations also included a Neptune Pirate Radio site devoted to fan podcasts about the show.

Fans were particularly active when the future of the show appeared to be threatened. On Tuesday, May 9, 2006, as season 2 ended and UPN prepared to morph into the CW, a fan group identifying itself as Cloud-watchers hired a plane to fly between the UPN offices in Los Angeles and the future site of the CW headquarters in Burbank, pulling a banner with the insistent message, "RENEW VERONICA MARS! CW 2006!" This was preceded by the delivery of packages containing *Veronica Mars*–inspired gifts, information about the flight, pairs of binoculars with instructions to the future CW executives to "look to the skies," and an invitation (on watchveronicamars.net) to reconsider the network acronym as standing for Cloud Watchers.

Following the announcement of the show's cancellation at the end of season 3 by CW chief Dawn Ostroff on May 17, 2007, the Bars for Mars fan group campaigned vigorously for a change of network heart, encouraging people to send Mars bar chocolate wrappers to the CW executives. This resulted in an estimated total (as reported on barsformars.com) of 2,040 Mars bars, 4,848 Snickers almond bars, and 510 pounds of marshmallows being sent to the network.

Meanwhile, Thomas went to work constructing a stylish pitch (included with the extras in the season 3 DVD box set) for an updated version of *Veronica Mars*, with Veronica now working as a rookie FBI agent. But it was not to be. Despite dedicated fan support and fast footwork by Thomas, *Veronica Mars* was officially over, having ended on what many people perceived as an unsatisfying and inconclusive note. As Stephanie Zacherek suggests in the online journal *Salon*: "Thomas may have figured that the best way to end *Veronica Mars* was not to end it at all—to leave the show as the unfinished business that it is, to allow his characters to go about their lives as if, somewhere, somehow, on some mythical TV network of the imagination, they would actually continue their existence offscreen. There's nothing so painful as a long goodbye. Maybe the better option is simply not to say goodbye at all."

Witty, fast (with sixty-plus scenes per episode, compared with *Dawson's Creek*'s slower and more talky thirty-five to forty [Thomas, "Favorite"]), at times deeply moving and occasionally frustrating in its overly complex plotting, *Veronica Mars* was the kind of "thick" pop culture text that clearly rewarded the close attention paid to it by its loyal, but finally too small, cult audience. Playing a vital role in attracting that attention and holding it was the remarkable and sustained performance of Kristen Bell as Veronica, a performance to which Joss Whedon paid tribute: "Bell is most remarkable not for what she brings (warmth, intelligence, and big funny) but for what she leaves out. For all the pathos of her arc, she never begs for our affection. There is a distance to her, a hole in the center of Veronica's persona. Bell constantly conveys it without even seeming to be aware of it. It's a star turn with zero pyrotechnics, and apart from the occasionally awkward voice-over, it's a teeny bit flawless" ("Ace of Case"). *Vale* Veronica.

Notes

1. The original track by the Dandy Warhols was from their *Welcome to the Monkey House* album (2003).

2. Space does not permit a long discussion of this controversial plot point, but the portrayal of the Lilith House women and the staging of "fake" rapes were much debated and criticized by fans, a point discussed by Thomas in his interview with Couch Baron on the Television without Pity site.

3. It's a tad convoluted, but Duncan finds out that Veronica's mother has been having a relationship with his father since high school. Doubts about Veronica's paternity are another significant theme in season 1.

4. The title of this episode echoes the title of Thomas's first successful teen novel, *Rats Saw God*.

Wonderfalls

Stan Beeler

Wonderfalls is another shining example of FOX's contribution to the ranks of cult television. Like *Firefly* before it, *Wonderfalls* was developed by a team with an impressive track record of producing critically acclaimed television series. Creators Todd Holland and Bryan Fuller both had substantial experience in television: Holland had worked on *Twin Peaks*, *The Larry Sanders Show*, *Malcolm in the Middle*, and *Felicity*. Fuller got his start with the *Star Trek* franchise—*Deep Space 9* and *Voyager*—but is perhaps most famous for his metaphysical sitcoms *Dead Like Me*, *Heroes*, and *Pushing Daisies*. Tim Minear, who worked in various capacities on cult favorites *Firefly*, *Angel*, and *The X-Files*, served as executive producer and writer on *Wonderfalls*. Despite the credentials of the creative staff, *Wonderfalls* did not achieve the instant ratings success demanded by FOX, and it was abruptly terminated before a full season was broadcast. Like *Angel*, *Firefly*, *Roswell*, and a number of other series considered in this collection, there was an unsuccessful campaign by fans to have *Wonderfalls* moved to another network or renewed.[1] Nevertheless, the series developed an impressively strong following after only four episodes. Rebroadcasts on other networks as well as brisk DVD sales have added to the series' substantial—albeit cult—audience.

Wonderfalls is the story of Jaye Tyler (Caroline Dhavernas), an archetypal Gen-Y slacker who, despite having a degree in philosophy from an Ivy League school (Brown), works a cash register in a cheesy souvenir shop in Niagara Falls, New York.[2] Jaye is a cynical young woman who has no intention of exerting more than the minimum effort required to maintain economic freedom from her overachieving family: her mother Karen (Diana Scarwid), a famous author; her father Darrin (William

Sadler), a physician; her sister Sharon (Katie Finneran), a successful lawyer; and her brother Aaron (Lee Pace), who is finishing a PhD in comparative religion.[3] Jaye's relatively comfortable lifestyle is disrupted one day when a tiny figurine called the Wax Lion talks to her, delivering a cryptic message that eventually causes Jaye to reluctantly break her policy of noninvolvement and help another person.[4] The series is built around Jaye's discomfort at being dragged into the lives of others through the agency of kitschy souvenir figures. She is also quite concerned that she might be going mad.

It is impossible to ascertain all the reasons why a series becomes a cult favorite, but in the broadest definition of the term, a number of criteria can easily be applied to *Wonderfalls*: "In the media, in common usage, and sometimes even in academia 'cult' is often applied to any television program that is considered offbeat or edgy, that draws a niche audience, that has a nostalgic appeal, that is considered emblematic of a particular subculture, or that is considered hip" (Gwenllian-Jones and Pearson ix). *Wonderfalls*, like all of Fuller's metaphysical television shows, can certainly be considered both offbeat and edgy. It deals with aspects of spirituality and sexuality that are not normally discussed on broadcast television. Moreover, nostalgic appeal is woven into the very fabric of the series. Niagara Falls brings with it a host of associations as a once-popular honeymoon destination that has fallen on hard times, and the visual design of the series emphasizes anachronistic objects that are in tune with the ambience of the location. For example, Jaye lives in an Airstream travel trailer that looks like it was retired in 1965, and the various souvenir figures that communicate with her are characteristic of a bygone era. Even the editing style of the series maintains this sense of visual otherness as the wipes between scenes are based on that classic souvenir, the View-Master 3-D Viewer. *Wonderfalls* is so unhip in its constant referencing of nostalgic culture that—like a Quentin Tarantino bowling shirt—it is hip.

Perhaps the most intriguing aspect of *Wonderfalls'* nearly instant transformation from failed series to cult classic is its anomalous attraction of two distinct subcultural niche audiences. Cult television shows—like specialty channels—typically attract a narrow spectrum of available viewers. However, soon after FOX dropped *Wonderfalls*, the entire first season aired in Canada (in 2005) on the Vision Network, a specialty cable channel that focuses on religious programming, and in the United States (also in 2005) on Logo, which is dedicated to gay and lesbian programming. (The series also aired in full on Sky One in the United Kingdom, among other international venues.) The diversity of these two venues gives us some indication that the essence of the show's attraction is not its appeal to a single narrow market group. In fact, it is a testament to its special qualities that *Wonderfalls* managed to develop a cult audience from these two diverse—in fact, often antithetical—demographics. One assumes that Vision picked up the series because of its prominent use of theological musings on the nature of the divine, ethical choice, and free will versus fate, while Logo's interest in the series was probably based on the prominent role of Jaye's sister Sharon, a lesbian who has some difficulty coming out.[5]

Cult television usually develops a loyal following among highly specific audience groups who identify with some aspect of the show. For example, science fiction cult series often attract a high proportion of technically inclined viewers. *Wonderfalls*, with its thematic links to metaphysics as well as its relatively frank representation of a gay lifestyle, immediately tapped into two cult TV–friendly audiences. Unfortunately, although these audiences are often supportive of cult television, they are also relatively far from the mainstream. Perhaps more significantly, network executives (who believe they represent the interests of the mainstream audience) are uncomfortable with programming that attracts the core demographics of the *Wonderfalls* audience.

Wonderfalls was canceled by FOX before midseason, after the episode "Pink Flamingoes" (1.4) was broadcast.[6] In this episode, Sharon Tyler has her first date (offscreen, but just barely) with her lesbian lover Beth (Kari Matchett)—in a scene that is a masterpiece of comic writing. Sharon is reduced to drugging her injured father with painkillers so that she can have some time alone with her new girlfriend. While making out on the couch, Beth disturbs the flow of events with the comment: "I can't imagine how much more stressful things would be for me if I were actually gay." Although Beth apparently moves easily between heterosexual and gay relationships, Sharon is decidedly less comfortable with the concept. When Beth asks Sharon if her bisexual nature is going to be an "issue," Sharon responds, "What? No, it's not an issue. It's a full subscription." Sharon has never had a heterosexual relationship and feels quite threatened by the possibility that Beth might take another male lover in the future. *Wonderfalls* uses humor to deal with serious issues confronting the gay community and is rewarded by the loyalty of its cult audience. Fuller's ability to present this sort of material in a humorous fashion, without appearing to condescend or mock, has won him a great deal of respect and adulation in the gay community.[7]

Many believe that Wonderfalls was canceled because its engagement with gay issues made network executives lose confidence in the series' ability to attract a mainstream audience. Fuller is quite forthright about his problems with network executives concerning the incorporation of gay elements in his television oeuvre.[8] Though comparatively circumspect when discussing why Wonderfalls was canceled, he does confess that FOX's marketing is "heavily geared toward the heavily testosterone set, and I'm just not in that half of the Venn diagram" (Fuller interview on Brilliant but Cancelled).[9]

The twelfth episode of Wonderfalls, entitled "Totem Mole," is perhaps the best example of the series' attraction for those interested in spiritual and ethical matters. The narrative revolves around Jaye's encounter with Native American mysticism. While Jaye, her best friend Mahandra (Tracie Thoms), and Sharon are on an excursion to a reservation, Jaye has an encounter with the spirit of a dead wisewoman. Jaye becomes involved in the search for a new spiritual leader for the tribe in the hope that this may help with her own spiritual problem: unwanted communication with inanimate oracles. A discussion with her brother Aaron makes a direct link between contemporary pop spirituality and more traditional forms:

> AARON: Yeah. Many of the great spiritual leaders didn't realize they had gifts before they were actually called to use them.
> JAYE: Oo, that's good.
> AARON: Saint Paul was a punk until he was blinded by the light. And Gandhi was drinking and whoring it up when he heard the cry of his people.
> JAYE: And Neo was just a big geek until he swallowed that little red pill.

Jaye's reference to a character from the film *The Matrix* is an obvious enticement to the cult audience immersed in fantasy or science fiction tales of enlightenment—a tendency that Jeffrey Sconce characterizes as "a desire to transcend the more brutal and limiting features of our planet" (216).[10]

The second episode broadcast by FOX, "Karma Chameleon," is a clever analysis of the motivations—or lack thereof—of Gen-Y slackers.

In this episode, Jaye is the object of an identity thief, Bianca Knowles (Sarah Drew), who is actually an investigative journalist using Jaye as the subject for an article on disaffected twenty-somethings. Bianca needs to copy Jaye's slacker lifestyle because, she says, "I'm not disaffected. I don't fit the Gen-Y profile. I'm too highly motivated." Bianca calls Jaye the "prototypical Gen-Y-er," representing "a generation of young people who've been blessed with education and opportunity and who don't just fall through the cracks—but jump through." When Bianca finally confesses her true purpose, Jaye is flattered and offers to help with the article. Although the narrative remains, at least on one level, about Jaye's reluctant compliance with the supernatural intervention in her life, it is also a clear psychological analysis of the puzzling phenomenon of apparently unmotivated yet talented young people: "Everything they do is for a single purpose—to avoid engaging with the world around them." Bianca sees Jaye's trailer as a metaphor for her life. It is designed to go someplace but just sits in the trailer park, "never living up to its potential." When Bianca decides to give up her career as a journalist, appropriate Jaye's friends and family, and sink into the comfortable niche Jaye has created for herself, Jaye writes the article for her rival and submits it to a magazine under Bianca's name. Although this could be considered an altruistic act that follows the letter of her oracle's dictum—"Get her words out"—it is, in fact, Jaye's desperate attempt to preserve the womb-like environment she has created for herself. When her family finally reads the published article, still under the impression that it was written by Bianca, they are impressed by the philosophical insight into Jaye's life, completely missing the irony of the role reversal. Jaye has secretly taken on an active role while Bianca has become a slacker, taking credit for someone else's work.

Wonderfalls manages to make relevant commentary on some of the more serious issues of contemporary life while maintaining a light-hearted tone that is particularly attractive to a cult audience. It is often compared to another cult series, *Joan of Arcadia*, but although *Wonderfalls* deals with some of the same issues, it is more hip, humorous, and attractive to a young, style-conscious cult TV audience. This is something of a paradox, as *Joan of Arcadia* managed to last quite a bit longer than *Wonderfalls*. Perhaps this has more to do with the confidence levels of studio executives than the quality of the series.

The mechanism of Jaye's communication with higher powers is particularly suited to modern life. The inanimate objects that communicate with her are persistent and imperious, yet their messages are as cryptic as anything delivered by the Delphic Oracle. The fact that these voices speak to Jaye through the physical presence of items that are, almost by definition, trivial calls into question the whole nature of divine intervention in human life. Jaye does not have the comforting presence of an angel, a pillar of fire, or even a burning bush. Jaye's contact with the divine is completely in keeping with the mundane situation of contemporary humanity.

Notes

1. See www.savewonderfalls.com for a detailed account of the campaign. The site includes a letter from Fuller thanking the fans for their support.
2. Although the diegetic setting for *Wonderfalls* is Niagara Falls, New York, the show was filmed in Niagara Falls, Canada. Cult fans familiar with the geography of the area often comment on this fact.
3. Sadler is well known to cult television audiences as Sheriff Jim Valenti in *Roswell*, and Pace played Ned in *Pushing Daisies*. The rhyming of the names Karen, Darrin, Sharon, and Aaron is deliberate and adds to the sense of kitsch that pervades the series.
4. Each episode of *Wonderfalls* is named after the figure that communicates with Jaye. The first episode is therefore entitled "Wax Lion."
5. It is also possible that Logo was attracted, at least in part, by Fuller's open struggle with Showtime concerning gay aspects of the plotline of *Dead Like Me*.
6. Although "Pink Flamingoes" was the fourth and last episode to appear on FOX (April 1, 2004), it is the second episode on the DVD collection.
7. In the March 26 edition of *Hollywood Reporter*, Jeffrey Epstein hosted a round-table discussion with a number of "television's most influential players—who happen to be openly gay." Fuller was prominently featured in the discussion. He was also interviewed by Sarah Warn on afterellen.com concerning lesbian representation on *Wonderfalls*.
8. Fuller indicates he had originally conceived Clancy Lass (Greg Kean), the father of Georgia (Ellen Muth) on *Dead Like Me*, as a gay man and was dismayed when the character was reconceived as straight. Clancy's sexual orientation was set up in the first season, and Fuller intended this to be an integral component of Georgia's character development:

> Oh yeah, there was an entire episode where (main character) Georgia would find out that her dad was having an affair with one of his male students. And that he was actually gay and about how much more special her life was since her dad was gay and wasn't really meant to procreate. And so what she lost was much more valuable in retrospect. So it was a very poignant and complicated episode. And they changed it, so that he

was sleeping with one of the female students. Which is less specific and less interesting for me, but I was always sort of annoyed by that. I still bear a grudge. (Fuller interview on Brilliant but Cancelled)

One might conjecture that when Fuller left the series after the first season, the distortions of his vision in season 2 contributed to its cancellation.

    9. According to Fuller, "The experience with MGM-TV [while working on *Dead Like Me*] and their lack of professionalism and savvy made it really difficult.... I had arguments where they would tell me that I didn't know what a pretty woman looked like because I'm a gay man. It was the worst type of old boy studio experience you could imagine. They were constantly trying to strong arm me. It was the worst experience of my life" (Fuller interview on Media Village).

    10. Sconce's article "*Star Trek*, Heaven's Gate and Textual Transcendence" is a study of a cult audience—the Heaven's Gate suicide cult—that went far beyond the normal borders of cult engagement with a television series. Although this is a tragic example of excess, it indicates that there is an audience for this sort of spiritualized fiction.

Xena: Warrior Princess

Carolyn Skelton

The iconic image of Xena (Lucy Lawless) resonates beyond the program constructed around her character. With her distinctive leather outfit, swirling brass design on her breastplates, blue eyes, and dark flowing hair, Xena redefined the conventions of action heroes and women warriors. In popular memory, she wields a sword with apparent ease, performs athletic backflips, spins her chakram (her round throwing weapon) with deadly accuracy, and is usually accompanied by a small blond warrior woman. Although *Xena: Warrior Princess* (XWP) appeals to diverse sections of society, it is also renowned for its lesbian following. XWP achieved cult status due to a combination of the imaginative, interactive, and immersive possibilities generated by the adventure-fantasy format, the program's appeal to diverse niche subcultural audiences, and the growing accessibility of globalizing technologies, such as the World Wide Web (see Gwenllian-Jones and Pearson ix, x, xii, xvi). Drawing on this mix, the program created a new myth for the information age. It reworked both pop culture conventions and eighteenth- and nineteenth-century colonial narratives, while incorporating a timely regendering of the action hero. As a consequence, XWP can be distinguished from similar cult programs by its association with female-centered, gender, and sexual transgressions.[1]

At the time XWP was made, it benefited from the many shifts in the U.S. industry that resulted in television shows being designed to attract a cult following. During the late 1980s and 1990s, pressured by industrial changes and developments in globalizing technologies, U.S. television moved away from domination by the networks, which had targeted mainstream audiences. This shift was a consequence of the networks' adaptation to the rise of cable and satellite television channels and the extended interconnectivity that accompanied the fragmentation of free-to-air television and its audiences (Gwenllian-Jones and Pearson xii–xiii; Jancovich and Hunt 37). The targeting of diverse niche audiences brought cult television into the mainstream. As both Gwenllian-Jones and Pearson (xix) and Jancovich and Hunt (41) conclude, cult television is central to the current fragmented state of television and the horizontal connections across media and commercial enterprises.

In the case of XWP, the combined cult and prime-time appeal was enhanced by the program's geographic and culturally fragmented fantasy world, which reflected the impact of accelerated globalization on the television industry. Filmed in New Zealand from 1995 to 2001, XWP was one of the many offshore productions associated with globalization and the deindustrialization of U.S. television in the 1990s (Elmer and Gasher 1–2). It was largely made during the Clinton administration, which encouraged multiculturalism and the international expansion of business (Goldman and Berman 230, 236–38, 243, 245; Klein 13–17, 78–79, 210, 295). XWP's production company, Pacific Renaissance, also benefited from the culmination of New Zealand's neoliberal restructuring, in which overseas business enterprises were welcomed (Cox). Ultimately, XWP became more successful internationally than the parent show, *Hercules: The Legendary Journeys* (*HTLJ*). Of executive producers Rob Tapert and Sam Raimi, the former was the active creative force that drove both the telemovies and the subsequent *HTLJ* and XWP television series. Both programs' first seasons were quickly syndicated in the United States, which, according to XWP director Garth Maxwell, gave the producers more freedom than was available for network shows at the time.

The unique look of XWP was the outcome of negotiations between the New Zealand and U.S. production centers. The coastal location and the greenness of the filmed landscape were constructed as an appealing and, for some, barely believable representation of preindustrial Greece; many scenes also evoked a Gothic medieval Europe. This distinctive fantasy world, admirably suited to a new kind of action hero, was the result of a mixture of design and chance. In the planning stages for the *HTLJ* telemovies, the producers were looking for an offshore location, and by chance, their attention was directed to New Zealand by producer Eric Gruendemann (Investment New Zealand; Rudnick, "Interview with Eric Gruendemann"; Taborn). They decided it was the perfect location for a contemporary, pop culture portrayal of ancient Greece, with the added advantage of having diverse terrain that was easily accessed from the Auckland production center.[2] Also important for this independent production company was the fact that local cast, crew, and resources could be hired at reasonable rates. *HTLJ* had already employed most of the film crew available locally, so *XWP* turned to people with experience working on music videos (Gaines). This was well suited to the program's MTV style of fast-paced editing, mobile cameras, and chaotic and beguiling mixtures of images, characters, and scenarios drawn from a range of ancient and contemporary sources. The producers encouraged local suggestions, contributing to the partial embedding of the production within the New Zealand industry.[3] Although American creative input continued to dominate, this was increasingly supplemented by advice from New Zealand directors, crew, and cast.

The New Zealand location for the program's unique fantasy world inadvertently contributed to the way *XWP* pushed the boundaries of gender and sexuality. When the first-choice British and American actors were unavailable to play Xena in the filming of a trilogy of *HTLJ* episodes, New Zealand actress Lucy Lawless was selected for the part. Her camp, ironic, ambivalently gendered portrayal of the character caught the attention of U.S. studio executives. In the *HTLJ* episode "The Gauntlet" (1.12), she fights aggressively with an Elvis Presley–like sneer, chuckles with menacing pleasure as she brandishes her sword, and crawls battered and muddied through a gauntlet of her rebellious warriors. The studio quickly commissioned Tapert to develop a television series around the character.[4] In addition to Lawless's influence on the show, New Zealand's distance from the Los Angeles production center made it difficult to control the content, resulted in the filming of some boundary-pushing moments that were difficult to edit out.[5]

Although there is evidence of a New Zealand influence on the show and its characters, *XWP* largely reconfigures discourses of gender and sexuality that had been incorporated in previous U.S. and British cult television shows, as well as in wider Hollywood conventions. For instance, the program draws on masculine Hollywood cinematic traditions of buddy bonding, superheroes, and wandering outlaw antiheroes, such as those portrayed by Clint Eastwood. *XWP*'s antecedents can be seen in other cult television female heroines, such as *The Avengers*' Emma Peel and the eponymous heroine of *Wonder Woman*, as well as the female buddy format that attracted a feminist and lesbian cult following for *Cagney and Lacey*. This legacy of assertive heroines was refracted through the appropriation of Eastern mythologies and history. More immediately, the program replaced the masculine muscularity in *HTLJ* with a balletic, Hong Kong style of fighting. This mix of gender and cultural constructions fit well with Lawless's performance, adding a gritty dominatrix edge and an active, earthy physicality to the action-woman legacy.

XWP's innovations in terms of its lead characters' gender and sexuality are further differentiated from its action-woman antecedents by its incorporation of mythical elements similar to those of other fantasy television shows. Xena's sexually ambiguous relationship with her supportive sidekick Gabrielle (Renée O'Connor) is contrasted with Xena's heterosexual attraction to powerful marauding male warriors, highlighting the tension between her conflicting desires. For instance, Gabrielle's promotion of pacifism and compassion is often dramatically contrasted to Xena's flirtatious relationship with Ares (the god of war, played by Kiwi Kevin Smith). Ares had been the young Xena's mentor when she was a carnal, vengeful, predatory warlord out to conquer as many individuals, lands, and communities as possible. In contrast, Gabrielle's development of warrior skills is tempered by her use of strategies such as dialogue and nonviolent negotiation, often to rejuvenate damaged people and communities. She comes into Xena's life in the pilot episode ("Sins of the Past"), at a point when Xena has turned her back on her destructively violent past and is planning to kill herself. Diverted by Gabrielle's entrapment by slave traders, Xena saves her and then reluctantly lets Gabrielle travel with her. Gabrielle encourages, supports, and nurtures Xena's newfound desire to atone for her past and use her warrior skills to help others, often by following the guidance of Eastern mentors.

The combination of online fandom and the program's transgressive rewriting of conventional discourses of gender and sexuality stimulated a unique fan following, which in turn influenced the show. Part of the attraction for feminist and lesbian fans was that Xena and Gabrielle are two traveling warrior women who have no need of male support. Many people found the sexual-romantic "chemistry" between the two women appealing—something that had never before been visible on prime-time television, let alone between lead female characters. The online interest in the "lesbian subtext" resulted in its deliberate but gradual shift to the center of the program (Rudnick, "Interview with Rob Tapert"). According to Maxwell, Lawless "was just so cool with it all," because she knew this differentiated the program from other action shows with heterosexual characters[6] (see also Rudnick, "Interview with Rob Tapert"). However, the sexual ambivalence was precariously balanced by a lack of explicit eroticism, so the program would also appeal to those who preferred a heterosexual heroine or who valued the rare positive portrayal of platonic friendship between women. Consequently, a sizable proportion of fans (known as "shippers" in online fan forums) still prefers to focus on the flirtatious relationship between Xena and Ares.[7]

Along with integrating myth, fantasy, and late-twentieth-century reconfigurations of gender and sexuality, the program's content and style drew attention to other contemporary issues familiar to several audience segments. Although the show's setting is predominantly rural, it incorporates elements derived from an urbanized and conflicted multicultural society, without strongly prescribing a political perspective. In XWP, tensions between destructive imperialism and a humanitarian, Christian-inflected redemption-quest reflect struggles that have accompanied the increasing globalization of economics, culture, technology, and media. The legacy of the old frontier, which was constructed by eighteenth- and nineteenth-century European colonialism, is implied by the way XWP draws on the Western genre and the "heart of darkness" narratives of colonial literature. This is reinforced by the construction of Xena's and Gabrielle's backstories, which indicate they were raised in the peripheral northern colonies of ancient Greece. Prior to meeting, they were outsiders in their home communities—Xena because of her outlaw past, and Gabrielle because she had ambitions of being a traveling "bard" rather than settling for being a farmer's wife. At the same time, the program incorporates elements of transnational digital connectivity, characterized by some as generating a new frontier.[8] The ease with which they travel across the ancient world and between diverse cultures and communities reflects contemporary globalization and multicultural societies. Xena's redemption quest is complicated when she and Gabrielle encounter "foreign" gods, largely of Eastern origin. This includes the monotheistic, fiery, disembodied presence that is the Persian-derived Dahak, and the Christlike Eli (Timothy Omundson), first encountered in ancient India in the episode "Devi" (4.14). Xena also engages with violently imperialistic characters such as Julius Caesar (Karl Urban), who collaborated with and betrayed the young Xena in "Destiny" (2.12). Following this treachery, Xena makes a pact to help the evil shaman Alti (Claire Stansfield) achieve her ambition "to tap into the heart of darkness, at the center of the sheer naked will behind all craving, hatred, and violence [and to] become the face of death itself, capable of destroying not only a person's body but their soul." In return, in "Adventures in the Sin Trade I" (4.1), Alti promises to make Xena the "destroyer of nations" and to help her avenge Caesar's betrayal.

These themes and narratives are portrayed by employing technologies, genres, and contemporary stylistic features that appeal to sophisticated, media-savvy, educated viewers. Such an audience has been associated with the late-twentieth-century expansion of cult television (Jancovich and Hunt 37–39). So, for instance, *XWP* uses the mobile camera style pioneered for the program by U.S. director T. J. Scott. It also includes whiz pans and rushing camera techniques, borrowed from the noncontributing executive producer Sam Raimi. Over the course of *XWP*'s six seasons, computer-generated imaging techniques were increasingly used as they became available at a reasonable price. This contributed to the cinematic and digital reconstruction of the New Zealand landscape.[9] In later seasons, the landscape was constructed to look like mythologized versions of contemporary countries—Japa for Japan, Chin for China, Britannia for Britain, Gaul for France, and a Gothic Amazon territory fictitiously associated with the Russian steppes. As with later fantasy shows, such as *Heroes*, this provides a variety of potential avenues for cult audiences to explore through discussion, creativity, and other forms of interactivity.

The anachronistic mix of ancient mythologies, diverse histories, and contemporary vernacular, plus sexually ambivalent lead characters, multiplied the possibilities for the kind of immersive fan interactivity usually stimulated by cult television (Gwenllian-Jones and Pearson xii; Gwenllian-Jones, "Virtual Reality" 84–86, 90). *XWP*'s cavalier mixture of elements generated some jarring narrative discontinuities and character inconsistencies that fan fiction writers could use selectively, explain, or write out (Lunacy). For instance, several lesbian-alternative fan fiction stories explained in detail why Gabrielle married her childhood betrothed, Perdicus (played by Scott Garrison in "Return of Callisto," 2.5), even though she was really in love with Xena. For some of the girl-power generation, *XWP* provided a new assertive female hero to fuel their exploration of the liberating potential of the World Wide Web. For lesbian subtexters, there was a new collaborative public space to develop explicitly lesbian stories that had so far been glaringly underrepresented on prime-time television (Boese; Armstrong). However, perhaps *XWP*'s relatively low status among fantasy-action programs is in keeping with the tendency for avid fans to see themselves as more discerning and unconventional than the popular audience. Cult television fans can be dismissive of those who are perceived to mimic the conventionally "feminine" characteristics of mainstream television (Jancovich and Hunt 32). However, it should also be noted that the inconsistencies in *XWP*'s content and production are viewed negatively by "discerning" fans (Jancovich and Hunt 38–40).

Nevertheless, although it shares some characteristics with other cult television shows, especially ones in the science fiction and fantasy genre, *XWP* and its fan following distinctively celebrate female warriors who transgress gender and sexual norms. Perhaps because of this, *XWP* never achieved the height of popularity and prime-time status of similar programs, such as *Buffy the Vampire Slayer* or *Lost*. Since *XWP*'s demise, there have been a small number of action-woman shows, such as *Alias*, with a cult following. However, they haven't attracted the same intense lesbian and feminist interest as *XWP* did. Perhaps an exception is *Battlestar Galactica*, whose muscular, gritty, heroic character of Starbuck (Katee Sackhoff) acquired a lesbian following. Furthermore, there is substantial gender equality among *Battlestar Galactica*'s ensemble of characters (Breen). This is in contrast to some other recent science fiction–action programs, such as *Heroes*, which incorporate *XWP*'s action-woman innovations while also reasserting masculine and heterosexual dominance. In spite of this, with the rise of online fan communities, immersive and interactive cult audiences can continue to rework the original texts to be as transgressive as they please.[10]

Notes

1. The program's distinctiveness was evident in my observations of *XWP* viewers, both on- and offline, as well as in my small-scale ethnographic research. I administered a small number of questionnaires, interviews, and focus groups between 2001 and 2003, with respondents in Australia, New Zealand, the United States, and the Netherlands. This material indicates that the action-adventure–fantasy format and the lead characters and their relationships have been major attractions for many viewers.

2. Michael Hurst (*XWP* director and actor, who also played Hercules' sidekick Iolus in *HTLJ*) described *HTLJ* as "ancient Greece without togas and

without columns and pillars" in an interview (interview by the author, Auckland, March 29, 2003). See also Petrie 176–77; Wooley.

3. Garth Maxwell, interview by the author, University of Auckland, July 16, 2003.

4. Michael Hurst, interview by the author, Auckland, March 29, 2003.

5. Maxwell interview.

6. Ibid.

7. See, for instance, the subforum "Shipper Heaven: For Fans of the Ares/Xena Pairing," http://talkingxena.yuku.com.

8. See, for instance, Nakamura (232): "the figuration of cyberspace as the most recent representation of the frontier sets the stage for border skirmishes in the realm of cultural representations of the Other."

9. George Port, interview by the author, West Auckland, July 1, 2003.

10. See, for instance, LiveJournal "bsg_emslash," http://community.livejournal.com/bsg_femslash/.

The X-Files

Mikel J. Koven

With apologies to a certain vampire slayer, *The X-Files* was the American television series that defined the zeitgeist of the 1990s. It was one of the key series contributing to the rise of FOX, making it a viable "fourth network" and directly challenging the oligopoly of ABC, CBS, and NBC. Emerging at the time when "quality TV" (Thompson, *Television's Second Golden Age*) was becoming the norm in the wake of groundbreaking series by the likes of Steven Bochco (*Hill Street Blues* and *L.A. Law*), David E. Kelley (*Picket Fences*), and Joshua Brand and John Falsey (*St. Elsewhere*), *The X-Files* paved the way for television series that balanced stand-alone episodes with multiseason narrative arcs.

The basic premise of the series is fairly simple: FBI Special Agent Dana Scully (Gillian Anderson), a medical doctor whose positivist approach to the world ensures a hefty degree of skepticism, is teamed up with FBI Special Agent Fox "Spooky" Mulder (David Duchovny), an embarrassment to the Bureau for his unshaken belief in the existence of extraterrestrials, the result of witnessing his sister's alien abduction when he was a child. The two agents are assigned to the "X-Files," FBI-speak for those cases that rational science and investigative techniques cannot solve—that is, those involving suspected cases of extraterrestrial encounters and the supernatural.

At its most basic level, *The X-Files* is a typical investigative drama, a long-standing staple of American television. Yet the strange cases that Mulder and Scully investigate have echoes of the (then) less ubiquitous supernatural investigative series such as *Kolchak: The Night Stalker* and science fiction investigative series such as *Project UFO* (created by TV veteran Jack Webb). Whereas *Kolchak* lasted only one season and *Proj-*

ect UFO only two, *The X-Files* lasted a full nine seasons—an unprecedented success for a supernatural–science fiction series.[1] Equally unprecedented, *The X-Files* is the only American television series to date that produced a big-screen version—*The X-Files: Fight the Future* (1998)—while the TV series was still running.

Part of the series' success was how it tapped into pre-millennium paranoia and the collapse of traditional beliefs. The core of the series was the binary opposites of Mulder the believer and Scully the skeptic. The poster on Mulder's office wall—a blurry picture of a flying saucer and the words "I Want to Believe"—expressed the zeitgeist: by the 1990s, what was there to believe in? The other motto of the series, "The Truth Is Out There" (which in most episodes appeared on screen at the end of the opening credits), encapsulated a cultural cry of desperation for meaning. While genre television, as a whole, can be dismissed as mere fantasy, *The X-Files* confronted that dismissal by challenging the very epistemological fabric of our world: If the truth is out there, then where is it? Who has it? I want to believe in God, science, the universe, the U.S. government, and so forth, but how can I when all I see are cover-ups of the truth that is supposedly out there? These two mottoes were picked up by the popular culture nexus, and even those who didn't watch *The X-Files* certainly knew of the series' existence and recognized the names Scully and Mulder and the series' catchphrases. Even Mark Snow's eerie theme music became a synecdoche for all that the series embodied.

Like many of the other series that Robert Thompson identifies as "quality TV" (*Television's Second Golden Age* 14), *The X-Files* was not an immediate success. It finished in the bottom twenty-five of the Nielsen ratings its first season, and although it received an Emmy nomination, it was for Graphic Design and Title Sequence (which it won). Watching that first season again, it comes across as less visually interesting than later seasons. The videographic cinematography looks cheap, and there is a sense that, like other series in both the science fiction and fantasy genres, *The X-Files* would be short-lived. But in that first season, the seeds were sown for the show's later development, particularly the establishment of what series creator Chris Carter calls the "mythology"—the narrative arc that spanned all nine seasons about the reality of extraterrestrial life and the government cover-up of that knowledge orchestrated by the nefarious shadow agency known as the Syndicate.

This mythology was developed throughout all nine seasons of *The*

X-Files; although "myth arc" episodes accounted for only about 20 percent of the first season, by the eighth and ninth seasons, the myth arc dominated the series (43 and 35 percent of episodes, respectively). According to the mythology, an alien life-form has been trying to colonize the Earth, possibly since the dawn of time. The Syndicate, fully aware of this plot, has been negotiating with the alien race to facilitate this colonization through the dissemination of a "black oil" (known as "Purity"), a sentient black ooze that is quickly absorbed and takes over other life-forms, including humans, thereby creating a race of docile slave laborers for the colonists. Although Purity itself first appeared in the mid–season 3 episode "Piper Maru" (3.15), the idea was introduced in the season 1 conclusion, "The Erlenmeyer Flask" (1.24), with the development of "Purity-Control," an alien-human hybridized genetic code that would act as a resistance to Purity. As revealed in *The X-Files: Fight the Future*, released between seasons 5 and 6, Purity is also used to incubate the aliens in human hosts. Eventually, we learn that the alien abduction of Mulder's sister was orchestrated by their father, in connection with the mysterious figure known as the "Cigarette Smoking Man" (William B. Davis), to help in the development of Purity-Control and thereby a vaccine against the black oil.

Although the foregoing description is obviously a gloss on nine years of narrative development and sixty episodes (not including the film), the complexity of *The X-Files* mythology often reached frustrating levels for viewers. As early as season 3, fans were accusing Carter of creating more questions than he was answering in the show (see Parks, "What's Ailing *The X-Files?*"). If the myth arc made up approximately one-third of *The X-Files*' episodes, the remaining two-thirds were stand-alone episodes that did not demand serial viewing. Known as "monster of the week" (or MOTW) episodes, these shows found Mulder and Scully investigating some strange extraterrestrial, paranormal, or cryptozoological phenomena. Truth be told, these were my favorite episodes; like many fans, I got too frustrated trying to keep up with the myth arc, and it was these stand-alone stories that kept me watching. Elsewhere, I have divided these MOTW episodes into two categories, working off the schemata first suggested by Leslie Jones. The first category comprises those MOTW episodes based on existing oral tradition—what I refer to as "Folklore *Files*" (see Koven, "Folklore *Files*"; Koven, *Film, Folklore and Urban Legends*). These episodes feature monsters of oral lore, such as golems ("Kaddish" [4.15]), Jersey devils ("The Jersey Devil" [1.5]), El Chupacabra

("El Mundo Gira" [4.11]), ghosts ("How the Ghosts Stole Christmas" [6.6]), zombies ("Fresh Bones" [2.15]), and lake monsters ("Quagmire" [3.22]), as well as exorcism ("The Calusari" [2.21]), and satanism ("Die Hand Die Verletzt" [2.14]). As I argue, belief in a particular legend is not essential for the legend to work as an effective story; all it must do is raise the *possibility* of truth. Carter himself, in an early interview, describes the series as "fiction that takes place within the realm of extreme possibility" (quoted in Goldstein), thereby making explicit use of similar narratological mechanisms. Although the myth arc itself likewise belongs, in many respects, to much of the contemporary folklore surrounding UFOs and can therefore be seen as a Folklore *File*, these MOTW episodes are more structured and contained (like legend narratives) than the baroque complexity of the myth arc.

The second category comprises MOTW episodes involving what Jones refers to as "generic pop-culture weirdness" (81)—groovy little horror and science fiction short stories, many with a literary pedigree. Stephen King cowrote "Chinga" (5.10), about a possessed doll "like Chucky" (as Mulder puts it), and cyberpunk creator William Gibson offered two episodes—"Kill-Switch" (5.11) and "First Person Shooter" (7.13). Taking a riff from the classic 1950s science fiction story "Who Goes There?" by John W. Campbell, "Ice" (1.8) is about extraterrestrial ice worms that infest an isolated arctic observation post. The season 6 ghost story episode ("How the Ghosts Stole Christmas"), though based at one level on traditional supernatural lore, owes more to the classic Victorian ghost stories of M. R. James, including their evocation of Christmas as a time when ghost stories are traditionally told. Thus, in addition to pilfering their story ideas from contemporary folklore, *The X-Files* writers were equally adept at working within the fantasy literary world. "The Goldberg Variation" (7.6), though narratively referring to the enormous and deadly Rube Goldberg device Mulder and Scully find themselves in, makes a double allusion to pianist Glenn Gould's "Goldberg Variations" on Bach.

These references to both high and low culture—classical music recordings and 1950s pulp science fiction stories—reflect the strong element of "writerliness" *The X-Files* demonstrated (Thompson, *Television's Second Golden Age* 15). The writers had a strong awareness of both high- and low-culture literature and entertainment. This is perhaps best demonstrated in "The Post-Modern Prometheus" (5.5), an episode filmed entirely in black and white with a strong "graphic novel" sensibility. The title of the episode, of course, echoes the subtitle of Mary Shelley's novel, *Frankenstein, or the Modern Prometheus* (1818), and one of the characters is Dr. Polladori (John O'Hurley), named for another of Lord Byron's guests who were present the night Shelley first conceived of *Frankenstein*. But intermingling within this high literary web of allusions are also references to *Jerry Springer* (including a guest appearance by Springer himself) and Cher. Throughout the series, pop cultural references are a constant presence.

Unlike many genre shows today (and each year there seem to be dozens of new ones), which are increasingly serialized, one could "dip into" *The X-Files*—watch an occasional episode and not worry too much about missing the show from one week to the next. *The X-Files* doesn't appear in Thompson's *Television's Second Golden Age*, but it fits the paradigm perfectly. Although the myth arc stretching across nine seasons indicates that the series "had a memory" (Thompson, *Television's Second Golden Age* 14), episodes could be, and were, shown out of sequence—that is, in an order chosen by the network, and not necessarily how Carter envisioned the show progressing. The classic case in point came in early 1997, when *The X-Files* was scheduled to follow FOX's broadcast of the Super Bowl game. Rather than run the next sequential episode—"Never Again" (4.12), a myth-arc episode—the network aired "Leonard Betts" (4.13), a gory MOTW episode, instead. According to the Neilson ratings, "Leonard Betts" was the highest-rated episode of the entire series, largely due to this important place in FOX's schedule. The decision to run an MOTW episode was based primarily on the desire to avoid alienating potential new *X-Files* viewers, who would have been lost if "Never Again" had been screened as planned. The ramifications of this seemingly slight deviation are tremendous: despite the trend toward increasing serialization, at that time, most television episodes could still be screened in practically any order. (Can you imagine if FOX tried that with *24* today?) Syndication, rather than DVD sales of full seasons, was still the norm, and part of the syndication contract enabled affiliates to air the series in whatever order they chose. With one-third of its episodes constituting part of the myth arc, *The X-Files* was a difficult sell to the affiliates, but it was not impossible. Today, most television programs, particularly genre programs, demand that the episodes be screened sequentially, and *The X-Files* was largely responsible for that shift.

In order to experiment with different narrative structures and keep the show fresh and engaging, particularly the MOTW episodes, *The X-Files* often featured a variety of styles and narrative perspectives. For example, in "Jose Chung's *From Outer Space*" (3.20), in a narrative conceit much like Akira Kurosawa's *Rashomon* (1950), no two witnesses interviewed about an alleged alien abduction tell exactly the same story; problematic and untrustworthy narration also plays a major role in "El Mundo Gira." "Bad Blood" (5.12), in which Mulder and Scully have very different views about whether they shot and killed a real vampire, is probably the best of the "untrustworthy narration" episodes. "X-Cops" (7.12) is a pseudo-crossover episode with another FOX series, *Cops*, a fly-on-the-wall documentary series that follows police officers on the job. In this episode, the *Cops* film crew comes across Mulder and Scully investigating a creature that feeds off the fears of residents in East Los Angeles, but the story is filmed as if it is an episode of *Cops* rather than *The X-Files*. "Millennium" (7.4) was an obvious crossover episode with Chris Carter's other FOX series, *Millennium*. In it, Mulder and Scully invite Frank Black (Lance Henricksen), the protagonist from the latter series, to help their investigation. *X-Files* references occasionally cropped up on *Millennium* too. In "Hollywood A.D." (7.19), written and directed by David Duchovny, a film is being made based on the cases of Mulder and Scully (here played by Garry Shandling and Téa Leoni, Duchovny's real-life wife). Having the two characters meet their cinematic doppelgangers is not only a self-referential conceit, reflecting the characters' pop cultural fame, but also a self-reflexive recognition of the show itself as an artificial construct. The episode was perhaps too clever for its own good, and by the seventh season, many fans felt that the show had "jumped the shark." Two years later, in an episode called "Jump the Shark" (9.15), the Lone Gunmen, a trio of conspiracy theorists who occasionally help Mulder and Scully on cases, take center stage.[2] The opening of the episode is a parody of the opening of *Charlie's Angels*, with Byers (Bruce Harwood), Langly (Dean Haglund), and Frohike (Tom Braidwood) standing in for the original *Angels*.

The X-Files developed a remarkable fan following fairly quickly. This is not the place to discuss or define television fandom, but it is worth noting that the development of the study of television fan cultures coincided with the development of, and increased access to, public Internet sites, and that "virtual ethnography" (the study of online fan communities) developed during *The X-Files*' run on television. Three key studies of Internet fan communities focus on *The X-Files* as the subject of fan adoration; all three use different terminology, and it is clear that such terminology is defined by the group itself, not imposed by the researchers. Susan Clerc refers to the DDEB (David Duchovny Estrogen Brigade), the GATB (Gillian Anderson Testosterone Brigade), and the MPPB (Mitch Pileggi Pheromone Brigade) — in other words, those fans whose primary interest in the series is their attraction to one of the lead actors.[3] In a similar vein, Christine Scodari and Jenna Felder refer to a subset of *X-Files* fans as "Shippers" (as in "Relationshippers"), whose primary interest is the developing relationship between Mulder and Scully. Finally, I use the term "X-Philes," a play on words, with *phile* meaning "a lover of something" (Koven, "Have I Got a Monster for You"); self-professed fans use the term to describe themselves on online bulletin boards.

The legacy of *The X-Files* lives on. *The X-Files* made genre television, particularly horror–science fiction television, mainstream (some fans might argue *too* mainstream). Without *The X-Files*, there would have been no proven market for the kinds of supernatural dramas that came later, such as *Buffy the Vampire Slayer* and *Angel*. *The X-Files* was of its time and was in keeping with changes in the way television was produced, maintaining a balance between narrative arcs that reached across the entire series and stand-alone episodes that required neither consistent viewing nor the purchase of complete DVD box sets.[4] The 2008 release of the movie sequel, *The X-Files: I Want to Believe*, did little to excite any additional interest in the series. As of the time of this writing, *The X-Files* are officially closed.

Notes

1. *Kolchak* was preceded by two successful (in terms of viewing figures) television movies: *The Night Stalker* (1972) and *The Night Strangler* (1973). In comparison, *Buffy* lasted for seven seasons, and *Angel* for five.
2. The Lone Gunmen had their own spin-off series on FOX in 2001, titled, appropriately, *The Lone Gunmen*. It lasted only fourteen episodes. The "Jump the Shark" episode was made after the series had been canceled.
3. Mitch Pileggi plays Assistant Director Walter Skinner, Mulder and Scully's boss.
4. The current hit *Supernatural* features much of the writing and directing team of the old *X-Files*, including Kim Manners, David Nutter, and John Shiban, and it is clearly indebted to Chris Carter's brainchild. *Supernatural's* debt to *The X-Files* is perhaps in how the later series balances its two narrative

strategies: in each episode of *Supernatural,* the myth arc is developed in specific scenes, while the Winchester brothers explore a different monster of the week. Such a strategy seems to prevent viewers from becoming too frustrated when they miss an episode, but it encourages them to buy the DVD box sets when they are released.

Appendix
Series by Genre and Nationality

GENRE

Some shows appear in more than one category because of multigenre allegiances.

Action Adventure
Lost (149)
24 (282)

Anthology Drama
Quantum Leap (201)
The Twilight Zone (291)

Comedy
The Daily Show and *The Colbert Report* (77)
The League of Gentlemen (134)
Monty Python's Flying Circus (166)
Mystery Science Theater 3000 (181)

Cop Show, FBI Drama, Police Procedural
Dexter (90)
Life on Mars (142)
Miami Vice (159)
Twin Peaks (299)
The X-Files (337)

Detective
Veronica Mars (314)

Fantasy
Buffy the Vampire Slayer (60)
Twin Peaks (299)

Wonderfalls (322)
Xena: Warrior Princess (329)

Horror
Angel (28)
Buffy the Vampire Slayer (60)
Dark Shadows (84)
Dexter (90)
Supernatural (260)
Ultraviolet (307)
The X-Files (337)

Legal Drama
This Life (268)

News
The Daily Show and *The Colbert Report* (77)

Science Fiction
The Adventures of Brisco County, Jr. (15)
Battlestar Galactica (44)
Blake's 7 (51)
Doctor Who (97)
Farscape (104)
Firefly (111)
Heroes (127)
Lost (149)
Mystery Science Theater 3000 (181)
The Prisoner (189)
Quantum Leap (201)
Red Dwarf (208)
Roswell (214)
Stargate SG-1 (237)
The *Star Trek* Franchise (244)
Torchwood (275)
The Twilight Zone (291)
Ultraviolet (307)
The X-Files (337)

Sitcom
Absolutely Fabulous (7)
The Comeback (68)
The Simpsons (221)
South Park (229)

Spy
Alias (22)
The Avengers (36)
The Prisoner (189)

Teen Comedy and Drama
Buffy the Vampire Slayer (60)
Freaks and Geeks (120)
My So-Called Life (174)
Roswell (214)
Veronica Mars (314)

War
Battlestar Galactica (44)

Western
The Adventures of Brisco County, Jr. (15)
Firefly (111)

NATIONALITY

British
Absolutely Fabulous (7)
The Avengers (36)
Blake's 7 (51)
Doctor Who (97)
The League of Gentlemen (134)
Life on Mars (142)
Monty Python's Flying Circus (166)
The Prisoner (189)
Red Dwarf (208)
This Life (268)
Torchwood (275)
Ultraviolet (307)

American
The Adventures of Brisco County, Jr. (15)
Alias (22)
Angel (28)
Battlestar Galactica (44)
Buffy the Vampire Slayer (60)
The Comeback (68)
The Daily Show and *The Colbert Report* (77)

Dark Shadows (84)
Dexter (90)
Farscape (104)
Firefly (111)
Freaks and Geeks (120)
Heroes (127)
Lost (149)
Miami Vice (159)
My So-Called Life (174)
Mystery Science Theater 3000 (181)
Quantum Leap (201)
Roswell (214)
The Simpsons (221)
South Park (229)
Stargate SG-1 (237)
The *Star Trek* Franchise (244)
Supernatural (260)
24 (282)
The Twilight Zone (291)
Twin Peaks (299)
Veronica Mars (314)
Wonderfalls (322)
Xena: Warrior Princess (329)
The X-Files (337)

TV and Filmography

TELEVISION SHOWS

Shows in bold have chapters of their own in this book. Note that in the text, parenthetical numbers represent the season and episode (e.g., 3.12 denotes season 3, episode 12).

Absolutely Fabulous (BBC, 1992–1996, 2001–2005)
The Addams Family (ABC, 1964–1966)
The Adventures of Brisco County, Jr. (FOX, 1993–1994)
The Agency (CBS, 2001–2003)
Alias (ABC, 2001–2005)
All in the Family (CBS, 1971–1979)
All My Children (ABC, 1970–)
Ally McBeal (FOX, 1997–2002)
American Dreams (NBC, 2002–2005)
American Gothic (CBS, 1995–1996)
Angel (WB, 1999–2004)
Animal 24/7 (BBC, 2006–)
Arrested Development (FOX, 2003–2006)
The Avengers (ITV, 1961–1969)
Babylon 5 (PTEN, 1994–1997; TNT, 1998)
Batman (ABC, 1966–1968)
Battlestar Galactica (Sci-Fi, 2005–2008)
Beavis and Butthead (MTV, 1993–1997)
The Beverly Hillbillies (CBS, 1962–1971)
Beverly Hills 90210 (FOX, 1990–2000)
Bewitched (ABC, 1964–1972)
The Big Valley (ABC, 1965–1969)
Bionic Woman (NBC, 2007)
Blake's 7 (BBC, 1978–1981)
The Boondocks (Cartoon Network, 2005–)
Boston Legal (ABC, 2004–2008)
Buck Rogers in the 25th Century (NBC, 1979–1981)

Buffy the Vampire Slayer (WB, 1997–2001; UPN 2001–2003)
Burn Notice (USA Network, 2007)
Cagney and Lacey (CBS, 1982–1988)
Californication (Showtime, 2007–)
Can't Cook, Won't Cook (BBC, 1995–2000)
Cardiac Arrest (BBC, 1994–1996)
Cathy Come Home (BBC, 1966)
Charlie's Angels (ABC, 1976–1981)
Cheers (NBC, 1982–1993)
China Beach (ABC, 1988–1991)
Chuck (NBC, 2007–)
The Civil War (PBS, 1990)
The Colbert Report (Comedy Central, 2005–)
Columbo (NBC, 1968–2003)
The Comeback (HBO, 2005)
Cops (FOX, 1989–)
The Cosby Show (NBC, 1984–1992)
Cowboy Bebop (Sunrise, 1998–1999)
Criminal Minds (CBS, 2005–)
Crossing Jordan (NBC, 2001–2007)
CSI (CBS, 2000–)
CSI: Miami (CBS, 2002–)
Cupid (ABC, 1998–1999)
Cybill (CBS, 1995–1998)
The Daily Show (Comedy Central, 1996–)
Dallas (CBS, 1978–1991)
Danger Man (CBS, 1960–1961, 1964–1967)
Dark Shadows (ABC, 1966–1971, 1991)
Dawson's Creek (WB, 1998–2003)
Days of Our Lives (NBC, 1965–)
Dead Like Me (Showtime, 2003–2004)
Degrassi Junior High (later *Degrassi High*) (CBC, 1987–1989, 1989–1991)
Desilu Playhouse (CBS, 1958–1960)
Desperate Housewives (ABC, 2004–)
Dexter (Showtime, 2006–)
The District (CBS, 2000–2004)
Doctor Who (BBC TV, 1963–1989; BBC TV and Universal Television, 1996; BBC Wales and CBC, 2005–)
Dracula (CBS, 1973)
The Dukes of Hazzard (CBS, 1979–1985)
Dynasty (ABC, 1981–1989)
EastEnders (BBC, 1985)

Enterprise (UPN, 2001–2005; retitled *Star Trek: Enterprise* in 2003)
ER (NBC, 1994–2009)
Family Guy (FOX, 1999–2002, 2005–)
Family Ties (NBC, 1982–1999)
Farscape (Sci-Fi, 1999–2003)
The Fast Show (BBC, 1994–1997)
Father Knows Best (CBS, 1954–1955; 1958–1960; NBC, 1955–1958)
Father Ted (Channel 4, 1995–1998)
Felicity (WB, 1998–2002)
Firefly (FOX, 2002)
Freaks and Geeks (NBC, 1999–2000)
French and Saunders (BBC, 1987–)
Friends (NBC, 1994–2004)
The Frost Report (BBC, 1966–1967)
Full House (ABC, 1987–1995)
Futurama (FOX, 1999–2003)
Get Smart (NBC, 1965–1966; CBS, 1969–1970)
Ghost Whisperer (CBS, 2005–)
Gilligan's Island (CBS, 1964–1967)
Gilmore Girls (WB, 2000–2006; CW, 2006–2007)
Gossip Girl (CW, 2007–)
Grey's Anatomy (ABC, 2005–)
Growing Pains (ABC, 1985–1992)
Gunsmoke (CBS, 1955–1975)
Happy Days (ABC, 1974–1984)
Heartbeat (ITV, 1991–)
Hercules: The Legendary Journeys (Syndication, 1995–1999)
Heroes (NBC, 2006–)
Hill Street Blues (NBC, 1981–1987)
Homicide (NBC, 1993–1999)
How I Met Your Mother (CBS, 2005–)
Huff (Showtime, 2004–2006)
I Love Lucy (CBS, 1951–1957)
I Spy (NBC, 1965–1968)
In Living Color (FOX, 1990–1994)
Invasion (ABC, 2005–2006)
The Invisible Man (CBS, 1958–1960)
JAG (NBC, 1995–1996; CBS, 1997–2005)
Jericho (CBS, 2006–2008)
Joan of Arcadia (CBS, 2003–2005)
Joanie Loves Chachi (ABC, 1982–1983)
The Jon Stewart Show (MTV, 1993–1995)

Journeyman (NBC, 2007)
Julia (NBC, 1968–1971)
King of the Hill (FOX, 1997–2009)
Kolchak: The Night Stalker (ABC, 1974)
Kraft Television Theater (NBC, 1947–1958, ABC, 1953–1955)
The L Word (Showtime, 2004–2009)
L.A. Law (NBC, 1986–1994)
Laguna Beach (MTV, 2004–2006)
The Larry Sanders Show (HBO, 1992–1998)
Law and Order (NBC, 1990–)
League of Gentlemen (BBC, 1999–2002)
Leave It to Beaver (CBS, 1957–1958; ABC, 1958–1963)
Life on Mars (BBC, 1996–1997)
Life on Mars (ABC, 2008–2009)
Little Britain (BBC, 2003–2006)
Lost (ABC, 2004–2010)
MacGyver (ABC, 1985–1992)
Malcolm in the Middle (FOX, 2000–2006)
The Man from U.N.C.L.E. (NBC, 1964–1968)
Married . . . With Children (FOX, 1987–1997)
The Mary Tyler Moore Show (CBS, 1970–1977)
M*A*S*H (CBS, 1972–1983)
Masterpiece Theatre (PBS, 1971–)
Max Headroom (ABC, 1987–1988)
Medium (NBC, 2005–2009; CBS, 2009–)
Meet the Press (NBC, 1947–)
Melrose Place (FOX, 1992–1999)
Men Behaving Badly (ITV/BBC, 1992–1998)
Miami Vice (NBC, 1984–1989)
Millennium (FOX, 1996–1999)
Mirrorball (BBC, 2000)
Mission: Impossible (CBS, 1966–1973)
Monty Python's Flying Circus (BBC, 1969–1974)
Moonlighting (ABC, 1985–1989)
Murder . . . Most Horrid (BBC, 1991–1999)
Murder One (ABC, 1995–1997)
Murphy Brown (CBS, 1988–1998)
My So-Called Life (ABC, 1994–1995)
Mystery Science Theater 3000 (KTMA, 1988–1989; Comedy Channel, 1989–1991; Comedy Central, 1991–1996; Sci-Fi Channel, 1997–1999)
Nash Bridges (CBS, 1996–2001)
Night Gallery (NBC, 1970–1973)

The Nine (ABC, 2006–2007)
Northern Exposure (CBS, 1990–1995)
Nowhere Man (UPN, 1995–1996)
The OC (FOX, 2003–2007)
The Office (BBC2, 2001–2002)
The Office (NBC, 2005–)
One Tree Hill (WB, 2003–2006; CW, 2006–)
The O'Reilly Factor (FOX News, 1996–)
The Outer Limits (ABC, 1963–1965)
Pee-Wee's Playhouse (CBS, 1986–1990)
Picket Fences (CBS, 1992–1996)
Play for Today (BBC, 1970–1984)
Playhouse 90 (CBS, 1956–1960)
Police Surgeon (ITV, 1960)
Popular (WB, 1999–2001)
The Prisoner (ITV, 1967–1968)
Project UFO (NBC, 1978–1979)
Pushing Daisies (ABC, 2007–2009)
Quantum Leap (NBC, 1989–1993)
Queer as Folk (BBC, 1999–2000)
Queer as Folk (Showtime, 2000–2005)
Real World (MTV, 1992–)
Reaper (CW, 2007–)
Red Dwarf (BBC, 1988–1999)
ReGenesis (Movie Network, 2004–)
Remington Steele (NBC, 1982–1987)
Rescue Me (FX, 2004–)
Ripping Yarns (BBC, 1976–1979)
Roots (ABC, 1977)
Roseanne (ABC, 1988–1997)
Roswell (WB, 1999–2002)
The Saint (Syndicated, 1963–1966; NBC, 1967–1969)
Saturday Night Live (NBC, 1975–)
Saved by the Bell (NBC, 1989–1993)
Screen Wipe (BBC, 2006–)
Secret Agent (CBS, 1964–1965)
Seinfeld (NBC, 1990–1998)
Sex and the City (HBO, 1998–2006)
The Shield (FX, 2002–2008)
The Simpsons (FOX, 1989–)
Six Degrees (ABC, 2006–2007)
Six Feet Under (HBO, 2000–2005)

Smallville (WB, 2001–2006; CW, 2006–)
Softly, Softly: Taskforce (BBC, 1969–1976)
The Sopranos (HBO, 1999–2007)
South Park (Comedy Central, 1997–)
Space: Above and Beyond (FOX, 1995–1996)
Spitting Image (ITV, 1984–1996)
Spooks (BBC, 2002–)
Stargate Atlantis (Sci-Fi, 2004–)
Stargate SG-1 (Sci-Fi, 1997–2007)
Starsky & Hutch (ABC, 1975–1979)
Star Trek (NBC, 1966–1969)
Star Trek: Deep Space Nine (Syndicated, 1992–1999)
Star Trek: The Next Generation (Syndicated, 1987–1994)
Star Trek: Voyager (UPN, 1995–2001)
St. Elsewhere (NBC, 1982–1988)
State of Play (BBC, 2003)
The Strange Case of Dr. Jekyll and Mr. Hyde (CBS, 1968)
Studio One (CBS, 1948–1958)
Supernatural (WB, 2005–2006; CW, 2006–)
Surface (NBC, 2005–2006)
Survivor (CBS, 2000–)
Survivors (BBC, 1975–1977)
The Sweeney (ITV, 1975–1978)
Tales from the Crypt (HBO, 1989–1996)
Talk Soup (now known as *The Soup*) (E!, 1991–2002, 2004–)
Talking Heads (BBC, 1987–1998)
Taxi (ABC, 1978–1982; NBC, 1982–1983)
That '70s Show (FOX, 1998–2006)
That Was the Week That Was (BBC, 1962–1963)
thirtysomething (ABC, 1987–1991)
This Life (BBC, 1996–1997)
Threat Matrix (ABC, 2003–2004)
Three's Company (ABC, 1977–1984)
The Time Tunnel (ABC, 1966–1967)
The Tonight Show with Jay Leno (NBC, 1992–2009)
Torchwood (BBC, 2007–)
The Tracey Ullman Show (FOX, 1987–1990)
24 (FOX, 2001–)
The Twilight Zone (CBS, 1959–1964; 1991)
Twin Peaks (ABC, 1990–1991)
Ugly Betty (ABC, 2006–)
Ultraviolet (BBC, 1998)

The Unit (CBS, 2006–)
United States Steel Hour (ABC, 1953–1955; CBS, 1955–1963)
University Challenge (ITV, 1962–)
Veronica Mars (WB, 2004–2006; CW, 2006–2007)
The Vicar of Dibley (BBC, 1994–2007)
The Waltons (CBS, 1982–1991)
War and Remembrance (ABC, 1988)
Wasteland (ABC, 1999)
Weeds (Showtime, 2005–)
The West Wing (NBC, 1999–2006)
The Wild, Wild West (CBS, 1965–1969)
Will and Grace (NBC, 1998–2006)
The Winds of War (ABC, 1983)
Wonder Woman (ABC, 1976–1978; CBS, 1978–1979)
The Wonder Years (ABC, 1988–1993)
Wonderfalls (FOX, 2004)
Xena: Warrior Princess (Syndication, 1995–2001)
The X-Files (FOX, 1993–2002)

FILMS

Alien (Ridley Scott, 1979)
The Amazing Colossal Man (Bert I. Gordon, 1957)
Amelie (Jean-Pierre Jeunet, 2001)
American Gigolo (Paul Schrader, 1980)
American Pie (Paul Weitz, 1999)
An American Werewolf in London (John Landis, 1981)
Anchorman: The Legend of Ron Burgundy (Adam McKay, 2004)
Armageddon (Michael Bay, 1998)
Army of Darkness (Sam Raimi, 1992)
Attack of the Giant Leeches (Bernard L. Kowalski, 1959)
Blade (Stephen Norrington, 1998)
Blue Velvet (David Lynch, 1986)
Caddyshack (Harold Ramis, 1980)
Cannibal! The Musical (aka *Alfred Packer: The Musical*; Trey Parker, 1996)
Casablanca (Michael Curtiz, 1942)
Casino Royale (Martin Campbell, 2006)
Cat People (Jacques Tourneur, 1942)
Chinatown (Roman Polanski, 1973)
Chitty Chitty Bang Bang (Ken Hughes, 1968)
Dark Star (John Carpenter, 1974)
Dark Water (Hideo Nakata, 2002)
Dawn of the Dead (George A. Romero, 1978)

Dracula's Daughter (Lambert Hillyer, 1936)
Dragonwyck (Joseph L. Mankiewicz, 1946)
Eragon (Stefan Fangmeier, 2006)
Eraserhead (David Lynch, 1977)
Evil Dead (Sam Raimi, 1981)
Evil Dead II (Sam Raimi, 1987)
Forever Young (Steve Miner, 1992)
The 40-Year-Old Virgin (Judd Apatow, 2005)
From Beyond the Grave (Kevin Connor, 1973)
Ghostbusters (Ivan Reitman, 1984)
Goldfinger (Guy Hamilton, 1964)
Hamlet (Franz Peter Wirth, 1961)
Heathers (Michael Lehmann, 1988)
The Hills Have Eyes (Wes Craven, 1977)
House of Dark Shadows (Dan Curtis, 1970)
House of Dracula (Erle C. Kenton, 1945)
I Accuse My Parents (Sam Newfield, 1944)
Independence Day (Roland Emmerich, 1996)
The Jericho Mile (Michael Mann, 1979)
The Jerk (Carl Reiner, 1979)
Ju-On (Takashi Shimizu, 2000)
The Keep (Michael Mann, 1983)
Kes (Ken Loach, 1969)
Knocked Up (Judd Apatow, 2007)
The League of Gentlemen's Apocalypse (Steve Bendelack, 2005)
Logan's Run (Michael Anderson, 1976)
Manhunter (Michael Mann, 1986)
Manos: The Hands of Fate (Harold P. Warren, 1966)
The Matrix (Wachowski Brothers, 1999)
Metropolis (Fritz Lang, 1927)
Mystery Science Theater 3000: The Movie (Jim Mallon, 1996)
Near Dark (Katherine Bigelow, 1987)
Night of Dark Shadows (Dan Curtis, 1971)
Nosferatu (F. W. Murnau, 1922)
Ocean's Eleven (Lewis Milestone, 1960)
On Her Majesty's Secret Service (Peter R. Hunt, 1969)
Pirates of the Caribbean (Gore Verbinski, 2003)
Planet of the Apes (Franklin J. Schaffner, 1968)
Poltergeist (Tobe Hooper, 1982)
Psycho (Alfred Hitchcock, 1960)
Rambo (Sylvester Stallone, 2008)
Rashomon (Akira Kurosawa, 1950)

Rebecca (Alfred Hitchcock, 1940)
Regarding Henry (Mike Nichols, 1991)
Ringu (Hideo Nakata, 1998)
Serenity (Joss Whedon, 2005)
The 7 Faces of Dr. Lao (George Pal, 1964)
The Shining (Stanley Kubrick, 1980)
The Shrinking Man (Jack Arnold, 1956)
Sidehackers (Gus Trikonis, 1969)
The Silence of the Lambs (Jonathan Demme, 1991)
The Simpsons Movie (David Silverman, 2007)
The Sixth Sense (M. Night Shyamalan, 1999)
Somewhere in Time (Jeannot Szwarc, 1975)
South Park—Bigger, Longer, and Uncut (Trey Parker, 1999)
Spider-Man 3 (Sam Raimi, 2007)
Stagecoach (John Ford, 1939)
Stargate: The Ark of Truth (Robert C. Cooper, 2008)
Stargate: Continuum (Martin Wood, 2008)
Star Trek: The Motion Picture (Robert Wise, 1979)
Star Trek: The Wrath of Khan (Nicholas Meyer, 1982)
Star Trek III: The Search for Spock (Leonard Nimoy, 1984)
Star Trek IV: The Voyage Home (Leonard Nimoy, 1986)
Star Wars (George Lucas, 1977)
Superbad (Greg Mottola, 2007)
Suspense (Phillips Smalley and Lois Weber, 1913)
Team America: World Police (Trey Parker, 2004)
Teenage Caveman (Roger Corman, 1958)
Terminator 2 (James Cameron, 1991)
Terminator 3 (Jonathan Mostow, 2003)
The Texas Chainsaw Massacre (Tobe Hooper, 1974)
Thief (Michael Mann, 1981)
This Island Earth (Joseph Newman, 1955)
Timecode (Mike Figgis, 2000)
Tremors (Ron Underwood, 1990)
Trilogy of Terror (Dan Curtis, 1975)
The Truman Show (Peter Weir, 1998)
Tuck Everlasting (Jay Russell, 2002)
The Turn of the Screw (Dan Curtis, 1974)
Twilight Zone—The Movie (Joe Dante, John Landis, George Miller, and Steven Spielberg, 1983)
Twin Peaks: Fire Walk with Me (David Lynch, 1992)
2001: A Space Odyssey (Stanley Kubrick, 1968)
Underworld (Len Wiseman, 2003)

Urban Legend (Jamie Blanks, 1998)
Viva Las Vegas (George Sidney, 1964)
Walk Hard (Jake Kasdan, 2007)
Wall Street (Oliver Stone, 1987)
The Wizard of Oz (Victor Fleming, 1939)
The X-Files: Fight the Future (Rob Bowman, 1998)
The X-Files: I Want to Believe (Chris Carter, 2008)

Works Cited

Abalos, Brenda. "Straightness, Whiteness, and Masculinity: Reflections on *Miami Vice*." *Race and Ideology: Language, Symbolism, and Popular Culture*. Ed. Arthur K. Spears. Detroit: Wayne State UP, 1999. 167–79.
Abbott, Stacey. *Celluloid Vampires: Life after Death in the Modern World*. Austin: U of Texas P, 2007.
Abbott, Stacey, and Simon Brown. "Investigating *Alias*: Secrets and Spies." *Investigating Cult Television Series*. London: I. B. Tauris, 2007.
"ABC's 'Pushing Daisies': Bringing the Dead Back to Life." *New York*, 24 May 2007.
Aitkenhead, D. "What Are You Looking At?" *Guardian*, 19 June 2004, <http://www.guardian.co.uk/film/2004/jun/19/comedy.television>.
Ajaye, Franklyn. *Don't Smoke Dope, Fry Your Hair!* Little David, 1976.
"all_games." *Lost Is a Game.com* <http://www.lostisagame.com/>.
Allen, Robert C., and Annette Hill, eds. *The Television Studies Reader*. London and New York: Routledge, 2004.
Amatangelo, Amy. "A Formula behind the Fright." *Washington Post*, 30 Oct. 2005. <http://community.livejournal.com/sn_daily/8456.html>.
Amy-Chinn, Dee. "Queering the Bitch: Spike, Transgression and Erotic Empowerment." *European Journal of Cultural Studies*. Ed. Dee Amy-Chinn and Milly Williamson. Special Issue 8.3 (2005): 313–28.
Anderson, Brian C. *South Park Conservatives: The Revolt against Liberal Media Bias*. London: Regnery, 2005.
Andreeva, Nellie. "Interview with Dawn Ostroff, President of the CW." *Hollywood Reporter*, 4 Apr. 2007. <http://www.hollywoodreporter.com/hr/content_display/features/interviews_profiles/e3i29278a389c6bdb2f9925897aafa835f2>.
Armstrong, Leila. "The Zeal for Xena: Appropriation, Discursive Elaboration, and Identity Production in Lesbian Fan Fiction." *Whoosh* 25 (Oct. 1998). <http://www.whoosh.org/issue25/arm1a.html>.
Ausiello, Michael. "Can You Give Me a Little . . ." *TV Guide Online*, 8 Nov. 2006. <http://www.tvguide.com/news/little-33281.aspx>.
Bacon-Smith, Camille. *Enterprising Women: Television Fandom and the Creation of Popular Myth*. Philadelphia: U of Philadelphia P, 1992.

Badmington, Neil. "Roswell High: Alien Chic and the In/Human." *Teen TV: Genre, Consumption, Identity*. Ed. Glyn Davis and Kay Dickenson. London: BFI, 2004. 166–75.

Bakhtin, M. M. *Rabelais and His World*. Trans. Helen Iswolsky. Cambridge, Mass: MIT Press, 1968.

Banks, Miranda J. "A Boy for All Planets: *Roswell, Smallville* and the Teen Male Melodrama." *Teen TV: Genre, Consumption, Identity*. Ed. Glyn Davis and Kay Dickenson. London: BFI, 2004. 17–40.

Barr, Marleen S. "The End of *Star Trek: The Next Generation*, the End of *Camelot*—The End of the Tale about Woman as Handmaid to Patriarchy as Superman." *Enterprise Zones: Critical Positions on* Star Trek. Ed. Taylor Harrison et al. Boulder, Colo.: Westview, 1996. 231–43.

Barrett, B. "The Way Back." *DWB #125*. Ed. A. Brown. Brighton: Dream-Watch, 1994.

Barrett, Michele, and Duncan Barrett. *Star Trek: The Human Frontier*. New York: Routledge, 2001.

Battaglio, Steven. "*Heroes* Spinoff Cancelled by NBC." 31 Oct. 2007. <http://www.heroes-tv.com/modules/news/article-4081.html>.

Battis, Jes. *Investigating* Farscape. London: I. B. Tauris, 2007.

———. "My So-Called Queer: Rickie Vasquez and the Performance of Teen Exile." Byers and Lavery 71–90.

Baudrillard, Jean. *Selected Writings*. Stanford, Calif.: Stanford UP, 1988.

Baumgartner, Jody, and Jonathan S. Morris. "The *Daily Show* Effect." *American Politics Research* 34.3 (2006): 341–67.

Baym, Geoffrey. "*The Daily Show*: Discursive Integration and the Reinvention of Political Journalism." *Political Communication* 22.3 (July 2005): 259–76.

———. "Representation and the Politics of Play: Stephen Colbert's *Better Know a District*." *Popular Communication* 24.4 (Oct. 2007): 359–76.

Beaulieu, Trace, Paul Chaplin, Jim Mallon, Kevin Murphy, Michael J. Nelson, and Mary Jo Pehl. *The Mystery Science Theater 3000 Amazing Colossal Episode Guide*. New York: Bantam, 1996.

Beaumont, Chris. *The Adventures of Brisco County, Jr.* (DVD review). *Blogcritics Magazine*, 18 July 2006. <http://blogcritics.org/archives/2006/07/18/084447.php>.

"Before They Were *Lost*." *Lost: The Complete First Season*. Buena Vista Home Entertainment, 2005.

Bell, Barbara. "Holden Caulfield in Doc Martens: *The Catcher in the Rye* and *My So-Called Life*." Byers and Lavery 143–54.

Bernstein, David. "Cast Away." *Chicago Magazine*, August 2007. <http://www.chicagomag.com/Chicago-Magazine/August-2007/Cast-Away/index.php?cp=1&si=0#artanc>.

Bianculli, David. *Dictionary of Teleliteracy*. New York: Continuum, 1996.
———. *Teleliteracy: Taking Television Seriously*. The Television Series. Syracuse, N.Y.: Syracuse UP, 2000.
Bielby, Matt. "Sexy Beasts." *Death Ray* 10 (2008): 40–49.
Bignell, Jonathan, and Andrew O'Day. *Terry Nation*. The Television Series. Manchester: Manchester UP, 2004.
Bishop, Ellen. "Bakhtin, Carnival, and Comedy: The New Grotesque in *Monty Python and the Holy Grail*." *Film Criticism* 15.1 (Fall 1990): 49–64.
Blair, Karin. *Meaning in* Star Trek. New York: Warner, 1977.
"*Blake's 7* Relaunch on Film." BBC Entertainment News, 7 Apr. 2000. <http://news.bbc.co.uk/1/hi/entertainment/705922.stm>.
Bodle, Andy. "Who Dares, Wins." *Guardian*, 23 Mar. 2004. 4.
Boese, Christine. "Spinning off from the Source: Alternative Fan Fiction Changes with the Seasons." *Whoosh* 25 (1998). <http://www.whoosh.org/issue25/boese1.html>.
Booker, M. Keith. *Strange TV: Innovative Television Series from* The Twilight Zone *to* The X-Files. Westport, Conn.: Greenwood, 2002.
Bordwell, David, Janet Staiger, and Kristin Thompson. *The Classical Hollywood Cinema: Film Style and Mode of Production to 1960*. New York: Columbia UP, 1985.
Born, Georgina. *Uncertain Vision: Birt, Dyke and the Reinvention of the BBC*. London: Vintage, 2005.
Bowers, Mary. "Our House, in the Middle of Google's Street." *Guardian*, 10 Apr. 2008.
"Breaking News: *Angel* to End after 5 Seasons." 13 Feb. 2004. <http://movies.ign.com/articles/492/492496p1.html>.
Breen Matthew. "Queers and *Battlestar Galactica*." <http://www.out.com/detail.asp?id=17050>.
Briggs, Asa. *The BBC: The First Fifty Years*. Oxford: Oxford UP, 1985.
Britton, Piers D., and Simon J. Barker. *Reading between Designs: Visual Imagery and the Generation of Meaning in* The Avengers, The Prisoner, *and* Dr. Who. Austin: Texas UP, 2003.
Britton, Wesley. *Spy Television*. Westport, Conn.: Praeger, 2004.
Brook, Vincent. "Myth or Consequences: Ideological Fault Lines in *The Simpsons*." *Leaving Springfield*: The Simpsons *and the Possibility of Oppositional Culture*. Ed. John Alberti. Detroit: Wayne State UP, 2004.
Brooker, Charlie. "Charlie Brooker's Screen Burn." *Guardian*, 28 Oct. 2006. <http://www.guardian.co.uk/media/2006/oct/28/tvandradio.broadcasting>.
Brooker, Will. "Everywhere and Nowhere: Vancouver, Fan Pilgrimage and the Urban Imaginary." *International Journal of Cultural Studies* 10 (2007): 423–44.
Brooks, Peter. *The Melodramatic Imagination: Balzac, Henry James, Melodrama, and the Mode of Excess*. New Haven, Conn.: Yale UP, 1976.

Brown, Peter. "DVD Review: *The Adventures of Brisco County, Jr.* — The Complete Series." *iF Magazine*, 25 July 2006. <http://www.ifmagazine.com/review.asp?article=1312>.

Brown, Simon. "Can't Live With 'Em, Can't Shoot 'Em: *Alias* and the (Thermo)Nuclear Family." Abbott and Brown 87–100.

Brown, Simon, and Stacy Abbott. "Can't Live with 'Em, Can't Shoot 'Em: *Alias* and the (Thermo)Nuclear Family." Abbott and Brown 87–100.

———. "Introduction: 'Serious Spy Stuff': The Cult Pleasures of *Alias*." Abbott and Brown 1–8.

Buchanan, Ginjer. "Who Killed *Firefly?*" Espenson, *Finding Serenity* 47–53.

Burns, Tom. *The BBC: Public Institution and Private World*. New York: Holmes and Meier, 1977.

Buscombe, Ed, ed. *British Television: A Reader*. London: Oxford UP, 2000.

Butler, David. "How to Pilot a TARDIS: Audiences, Science Fiction and the Fantastic in *Doctor Who*." Butler, *Time* 19–42.

———, ed. *Time and Relative Dissertations in Space: Critical Perspectives on Doctor Who*. Manchester: Manchester UP, 2007.

Butler, Judith. *Precarious Life*. London: Verso, 2006.

Buxton, David. *From* The Avengers *to* Miami Vice: *Form and Ideology in Television Series*. Manchester: Manchester UP, 1990.

Byers, Michele, and David Lavery, eds. *Dear Angela: Remembering My So-Called Life*. Lanham, Md.: Lexington Books, 2007.

Caldwell, John Thornton. *Televisuality: Style, Crisis and Authority in American Television*. New Brunswick, N.J.: Rutgers UP, 1995.

Campbell, Bruce. *If Chins Could Kill: Confessions of a B Movie Actor*. Los Angeles: LA Weekly Press, 2002.

Cardwell, Sarah. "The Representation of Youth and the Twenty-Something Serial." Hammond and Mazdon 123–38.

Carrazé, Alain, and Hélène Oswald. *The Prisoner: A Televisionary Masterpiece*. London: Virgin, 1995.

Carter, Bill. *Desperate Networks*. New York: Broadway Books, 2006.

Casey, Bernadette, Neil Casey, Ben Calvert, Liam French, and Justin Lewis. *Television Studies: The Key Concepts*. London: Routledge, 2002.

Chamberlain, Daniel, and Scott Ruston. "24 and Twenty-first Century Quality Television." Peacock 13–24.

Chapman, J. *Inside the TARDIS: The Worlds of Doctor Who*. London: I. B. Tauris, 2006.

———. *Saints & Avengers: British Adventure Series of the 1960s*. London: I. B. Tauris, 2002.

Charles, Craig. "Dwarfing USA." *Red Dwarf*, season 5 DVD. BBC Worldwide Ltd., 2004.

———. "Launching *Red Dwarf*." *Red Dwarf*, season 1, region 2 DVD. BBC Worldwide Ltd., 2002.

———. "The Starbuggers." *Red Dwarf*, season 6, region 2 DVD. BBC Worldwide Ltd., 2005.
Chibnall, Chris. "The Great Escapes." *Torchwood: The Official Magazine* 1 (2008): 64–65.
Christie, Ian, ed. *Gilliam on Gilliam*. London: Faber and Faber, 1999.
Clarke, P. *"This Life."* <www.screenonline.or.uk/tv/id/802194/index.htm>.
Cleese, John, Terry Gilliam, Michael Palin, Eric Idle, Terry Jones, and the Estate of Graham Chapman. *The Pythons: Autobiography by the Pythons*. New York: St. Martin's Press, 2003.
Clemens, Samuel Langhorne. "Puddin'head Wilson." *Century Illustrated Monthly Magazine* 25 (Nov. 1893–Apr. 1894) and 26 (May–Oct. 1894).
Clerc, Susan. "The DDEB, GATB, MPPB and Ratboy: *The X-Files'* Media Fandom, Online and Off." Lavery, Hague, and Cartwright 36–51.
Clifford, Andrew. "Caught in the Act." *New Statesman and Society*, 29 Sept. 1989. 42.
Cockburn, Alexander, and Jeffrey St. Clair. *Whiteout: The CIA, Drugs and the Press* London: Verso, 1998.
Cole, Juan. "Dick Cheney's Least Favorite Show?" Salon.com, 30 May 2007. <http://www.salon.com/opinion/feature/2007/05/30/heroes/>.
Collinson, Gavin. *"Blake's 7:* A Line through the Pattern of Infinity." <http://www.bfi.org.uk/features/tv/100/poll/blakes7.html>.
The Complete Prisoner. Perf. Patrick McGoohan, Leo McKern, Patrick Cargill, Alexis Kanner, Peter Wyngarde, Mary Morris, Colin Gordon. ITC, 1967. DVD. A&E, 2001.
Cook, Benjamin. "Underground Adventures." *Doctor Who Magazine* 391 (2008): 54–58.
Cook, John, and Peter Wright, eds. *British Science Fiction Television*. London: I. B. Tauris, 2006.
Cooke, Lez. *British Television Drama: A History*. London: BFI, 2003.
Coppa, Francesca. "A Brief History of Media Fandom." *Fan Fiction and Fan Communities in the Age of the Internet*. Ed. Karen Hellekson and Kristina Busse. Jefferson, N.C.: McFarland, 2006. 41–59.
Corner, John, ed. *Popular Television in Britain: Studies in Cultural History*. London: BFI, 1991.
Cosgrove, Stuart. "The Zoot Suit and Style Warfare." *Zoot Suits and Second-Hand Dresses*. Ed. Angela McRobbie. Basingstoke: Macmillan, 1989.
Couch Baron. "The Rob Thomas Interview: Part 1." <http://www.televisionwithoutpity.com/articles/contenta2301/>.
Cox, Lloyd. "Trajectories of the Welfare State in New Zealand and Australia 1980–2003." Paper presented at the Conference for the Sociological Association of Aotearoa, New Zealand. <http://saanz.science.org.nz/Cox.doc>.
Craig, Olga. "The Man Who Discovered *Lost*—and Found Himself out of a

Job." *London Daily Telegraph*, 13 Aug. 2005. <http://www.telegraph.co.uk/news/worldnews/northamerica/usa/1496199/The-man-who-discovered-Lost—and-found-himself-out-of-a-job.html>.

Creeber, Glen. *Serial Television: Big Drama on the Small Screen*. London: BFI, 2004.

Crook, James. *Red Dwarf* (1997). <http://www.galactic-guide.com/articles/9R15.html>.

Darrow, Paul. *You're Him, Aren't You? An Autobiography*. Maidenhead: Big Finish Productions, 2006.

Daugherty, A. M. "Just a Girl: Buffy as Icon." *Reading the Vampire Slayer: The Unofficial Critical Companion to* Buffy *and* Angel. Ed. Roz Kaveney. London: I. B. Tauris, 2002. 148–65.

Davies, K. "*Blake's* 7 Merchandise Guide." *The DWB Compendium—The Best of the First 100 Issues*. Ed. G. Leigh. Brighton: DreamWatch, 1993.

Davies, Russell T. *Damaged Goods*. London: Virgin, 1996.

Davis, Glyn. *Queer as Folk*. BFI TV Classics. London: BFI, 2007.

Davis, Glyn, and Kay Dickinson, eds. *Teen TV: Genre, Consumption and Identity*. London: BFI, 2004.

Deaddrop. "Chat Transcript with *Alias* Technical Consultant Rick Orci" (2002). <http://www.deaddrop.us/modulesphp?name=News&file=article&sid=49>.

Deleuze, Gilles. *The Logic of Sense*. Trans. Mark Lester. New York: Columbia UP, 1990. 74–82.

Devlin, William J. "The Philosophical Passion of the Jew: Kyle the Philosopher." *South Park and Philosophy: You Know, I Learned Something Today*. Ed. Robert Arp. Oxford: Blackwell, 2007. 87–94.

Diffrient, David. "*My So-Called Life* in the Balance." Byers and Lavery 181–209.

Dilmore, Kevin. "Of Spies and Survivors." *Amazing Stories* 74.3 (Feb. 2005): 20–24.

Donnelly, Kevin J. "Between Prosaic Functionalism and Sublime Experimentation: *Doctor Who* and Musical Sound Design." Butler, *Time* 190–203.

Douthat, Ross. "Lost and Saved on Television." *First Things: A Monthly Journal of Religion, Culture, & Public Life* (May 2007): 22–26.

Dunn, David Hastings. "*Lost*: Adventures in the American Psyche after the 9/11 Fall." *Defence Studies* 6.3 (2006): 318–21.

Dyson, Jeremy, et al., eds. *The League of Gentlemen: Scripts and That*. London: BBC Books, 2003.

———. *The League of Gentlemen's Book of Precious Things*. London: Prion Books, 2007.

———. *A Local Book for Local People*. London: Fourth Estate, 2000.

Ebert, Roger. Review. *Army of Darkness*. *Chicago Sun-Times*, 19 Feb. 1993.

<http://rogerebert.suntimes.com/apps/pbcs.dll/article?AID=/19930219/REVIEWS/302190301/1023>.

Eco, Umberto. "*Casablanca*: Cult Movies and Intertextual Collage." *Travels in Hyper-Reality*. London: Picador, 1987. 197–211.

Edwards, Lynne. "On the Low Down: How a *Buffy* Fan Fell in Love with *Veronica Mars*." Thomas, *Neptune Noir* 72–81.

Edwards, Tim. *Cultures of Masculinity*. London: Routledge, 2006.

Elfman, Doug. "Tugging on Superman's Cape." *Chicago Sun-Times*, 11 Nov. 2007. <http://www.suntimes.com/entertainment/elfman/644457,SHO-Sunday-elf11.article>.

Ellis, John. *Visible Fictions: Cinema, Television, Video*. London: Routledge, 1982.

Elmer, Greg, and Mike Gasher. "Introduction: Catching up with Runaway Productions." *Contracting Out Hollywood: Runaway Productions and Foreign Location Shooting*. Ed. Greg Elmer and Mike Gasher. Lanham, Md.: Rowan and Littlefield, 2005. 1–18.

"Epilogue." Satellite News: The Official *Mystery Science Theater 3000* Fan Site. <http://www.mst3kinfo.com/history/epilogue.html>.

Epstein, Jeffrey. Round-Table Discussion Including Bryan Fuller in 26 Mar. 2004 *Hollywood Reporter*. <http://www.hollywoodreporter.com/hr/search/article_display.jsp?vnu_content_id=1000473838>.

Erin. "Episode Recap: Fallout." <http://www.televisionwithoutpity.com/Shows/Heroes/Stories/Fallout>.

Erisman, Fred. "*Stagecoach* in Space: The Legacy of *Firefly*." *Extrapolation* 47.2 (2006): 249–58.

Espenson, Jane, ed. *Finding Serenity: Anti-Heroes, Lost Shepherds and Space Hookers in Joss Whedon's Firefly*. Dallas: BenBella Books, 2004.

———. "Introduction." *Finding Serenity*. 1–3.

———. "The Secret to Selling Sci-Fi: Fantasy Land." *New Republic*, 11 Aug. 2007. <https://ssl.tnr.com/p/docsub.mhtml?i=w070806&s=espenson080706>.

Evans, C. "Roaming a Naughty Universe." *Radio Times* (24 Dec. 1977–6 Jan. 1978): 114–17.

Evans, Jeff. *The Penguin TV Companion*. London: Penguin, 2003.

Feuer, Jane. "The Concept of Live Television: Ontology as Ideology." *Regarding Television*. Ed. E. Ann Kaplan. Frederick, Md.: University Publications of America, 1983. 12–21.

"For *Roswell* Writer Ronald D. Moore It's All about the Characters." Interview by Kathie Huddleston. *Science Fiction Weekly* 7.42 (15 Oct. 2001). <http://www.scifi.com/sfw/issue234/interview.html>.

Ford, Sam. "*As the World Turns* in a Convergence Culture." Master's thesis, Massachusetts Institute of Technology, 2007. <http://cms.mit.edu/research/theses/SamFord2007.pdf>.

———. "Externally Located Content." MIT Convergence Culture Consortium Weblog, 23 Aug. 2007. <http://www.convergenceculture.org/weblog/2007/08/externally_located_content.php>.

Forman, Murray. "Freaks, Aliens and the Social Other: Representation's of Student Stratification in U.S. Television's First Post-Columbine Season." *Velvet Light Trap* 53 (Spring 2004): 66–82.

Fox, Julia R., Glory Koloen, and Volkan Sahin. "No Joke: A Comparison of Substance in *The Daily Show with Jon Stewart* and Broadcast Coverage of the 2004 Presidential Election Campaign." *Journal of Broadcasting & Electronic Media* 51.2 (July 2007): 213–27.

Freedman, Eric. "Television, Horror and Everyday Life in *Buffy the Vampire Slayer*." Hammond and Mazdon 159–80.

Frost, David. *An Autobiography: Volume One: From Congregations to Audiences*. London: HarperCollins, 1994.

Frye, Northrop. *Anatomy of Criticism: Four Essays*. Princeton, N.J.: Princeton UP, 1957.

Fuller, Bryan. "Interview." Media Village. <http://www.mediavillage.com/jmentr/2005/06/06/jmer-06-06-05>.

———. "Interview." Brilliant but Cancelled. <http://blogs.brilliantbutcancelled.com/pop_autopsy/2006/12/interview_with_bryan_fuller_1.shtml>.

Gaines, Jonathan. "What You Didn't Know about Xena: A 60-Minute Featurette from the Directors of Season One." Best Buy bonus with the *Xena: Warrior Princess* season 1 DVD set. Davis/Panzer Productions, Evan Geerlings, 2003.

Gardiner, Judith Kegan. "Why Saddam Is Gay: Masculinity Politics in *South Park—Bigger, Longer, and Uncut*." *Quarterly Review of Film and Video* 22.1 (Jan. 2005): 51–62.

Garnett, Tony. "Contexts." *British Television Drama: Past, Present and Future*. Ed. Jonathan Bignell, Stephen Lacey, and M. Madeline Macmurraugh-Kavanagh. Basingstoke: Palgrave, 2000.

———. "Working in the Field." *Looking at Class: Film, Television and the Working Class in Television*. Ed. S. Rowbotham and H Beynon. London: Rivers Oram Press, 2001.

Garron, Barry. "Heroes." *Hollywood Reporter*, 25 Sept. 2006.

"The Genesis of *Lost*." *Lost: The Complete First Season*. Buena Vista Home Entertainment, 2005.

Gerani, Gary, and Paul H. Schulman. *Fantastic Television*. New York: Harmony, 1977.

Gibron, Bill. *Red Dwarf: Series 1–4 and Series 5–8*. DVD Verdict. <http://www.dvdverdict.com/reviews/reddwarf.php>. <http://www.dvdverdict.com/reviews/reddwarfseries58.php>.

Giddens, Anthony. *Modernity and Self-Identity: Self and Society in the Late Modern Age*. Cambridge: Polity Press, 1991.

Gilbert, Mathew. "Lisa Kudrow WAS the 'Comeback' Kid." *Boston Globe Online*, 18 Jan. 2008. <www.highbeam.com/doc/1P2-7969192.html>.
Gilliam, Terry. *Dark Knights and Holy Fools: The Art and Films of Terry Gilliam*. New York: Universe, 1999.
Goffman, Erving. *Interaction Ritual: Essays in Face-to-Face Behavior*. Chicago: Aldine, 1967.
Goldman, Emily O., and Larry Berman. "Engaging the World: First Impressions of the Clinton Foreign Policy Legacy." *The Clinton Legacy*. Ed. Colin Campbell and Bert A. Rockman. New York: Chatham House, 2000. 226–53.
Goldstein, T. J. "Within the Realm of Extreme Possibility: Creator Chris Carter on *The X-Files*." *Cyberspace Vanguard Magazine* 2 (1993). <http://www.skepticfiles.org/skeptic/x-filesj.htm>.
Goodale, Gloria. "Are Women Allowed to Be Funny?" *Christian Science Monitor Online*, 6 Feb. 2007. <www.csmonitor.com/2007/0202/p11s02-algn.html>.
Graham, Allison. "Are You Local?" *Radio Times* 304.3959 (2000): 28–29.
———. "Pick of the Day." *Radio Times* 300.3908 (1999): 90.
Gray, Jonathan. "Imagining America: *The Simpsons* Go Global." *Popular Communication* 5.2 (2007): 129–48.
———. *Watching with* The Simpsons: *Television, Parody, and Intertextuality*. London: Routledge, 2006.
Gregory, Chris. *Be Seeing You . . . Decoding* The Prisoner. Luton, U.K.: Luton UP, 1997.
Gross, Edward. "Man on a Mission." *Cinefantastique* 37.1 (Feb.–Mar. 2005): 34–36.
Gwenllian-Jones, Sara. "The Sex Lives of Cult Television Characters." *Screen* 43.1 (2002): 79–90.
———. "Virtual Reality and Cult Television." Gwenllian-Jones and Pearson 83–96.
———. "Web Wars: Resistance, Online Fandom and Studio Censorship." Jancovich and Lyons 163–77.
Gwenllian-Jones, Sara, and Roberta E. Pearson. "Introduction." Gwenllian-Jones and Pearson ix–xx.
———, eds. *Cult Television*. Minneapolis: U of Minnesota P, 2004.
Hammond, Michael, and Lucy Mazdon, eds. *The Contemporary Television Series*. Edinburgh: Edinburgh UP, 2005.
Hanks, Robert. "*Blake's 7*—BBC1." *Independent*, 15 Jan. 1998.
Haraway, Donna. "Cyborgs and Companion Species." *The Haraway Reader*. Ed. Donna Haraway. New York: Routledge, 2003. 295–320.
Harper, J. S. "Editor's Note: *Quantum Leap* TV Show." *Laboratory Primate Newsletter* 30.4 (Oct. 1991). <http://www.brown.edu/Research/Primate/lpn30-4.html#leap>.

Harris, Cheryl, and Alison Alexander, eds. *Theorizing Fandom: Fans, Subculture and Identity.* Cresskill, N.J.: Hampton Press, 1998.

Havens, Candace. *Joss Whedon: The Genius behind Buffy.* London: Titan Books, 2003.

Heath, Paul. DVD review: *The Adventures of Brisco County, Jr. Hollywood News.* <http://www.thehollywoodnews.com/dvd/the-adventures-of-brisco-county-jnr-06080601.php>.

Helford, Elyce Rae. "'OK, Homeboys, Let's Posse': Gender, Race, Class, and Masculine Anxiety in *Red Dwarf.*" *British Science Fiction Television.* Ed. John Cook and Peter Wright. London: I. B. Tauris, 2006. 240–62.

Henn, Matt, Mark Weinstein, and Sarah Forrest. "Uninterested Youth? Young People's Attitudes towards Party Politics in Britain." *Political Studies* 53.3 (Oct. 2005): 556–78.

"Herc Chats up the Co-Creator of Fall's Best New Series, ABC's LOST!!" *Ain't It Cool News,* 21 Aug. 2004. <http://www.aintitcool.com/node/18187>.

Hewison, Robert. *Monty Python: The Case Against.* New York: Grove Press, 1981.

Hidalgo, Pablo. "A Guy Named Joel: Launching Cinematic Titanic." *StarWars.com.* <http://www.starwars.com/community/news/rocks/f20071109/indexp2.html>.

Hill, Annette, and Ian Calcutt. "Vampire Hunters: The Scheduling and Reception of *Buffy the Vampire Slayer* and *Angel* in the United Kingdom." *Undead TV: Essays on Buffy the Vampire Slayer.* Ed. Elana Levine and Lisa Parks. Durham, N.C.: Duke UP, 2007. 56–73.

Hills, Matt. "Defining Cult TV: Texts, Intertexts and Fan Audiences." *The Television Studies Reader.* Ed. Robert C. Allen and Annette Hill. London: Routledge, 2004. 509–23.

———. "Doctor Who." *Fifty Key Television Programmes.* Ed. Glen Creeber. London: Arnold, 2004. 75–79.

———. *Fan Cultures.* New York: Routledge, 2002.

———. "'Gothic' Body Parts in a 'Postmodern' Body of Work? The Hinchcliffe/Holmes Era of *Doctor Who* (1975–77)." *Intensities: The Journal of Cult Media* 4 (Dec. 2007). <http://intensities.org/Issues/Intensities_Four.htm>.

———. "Media Fandom, Neoreligiosity, and Cult(ural) studies." *Velvet Light Trap* 46 (2000): 73–84.

———. *The Pleasures of Horror.* New York: Continuum, 2005.

———. "*Star Wars* in Fandom, Film Theory, and the Museum: The Cultural Status of the Cult Blockbuster." *Movie Blockbusters.* Ed. Julian Stringer. London and New York: Routledge, 2003.

Hilton, James. *Lost Horizon.* 1933. Reprint, New York: Pocket Books, 1939.

Hitchens, Christopher. "Why Women Aren't Funny." *Vanity Fair Online* (Jan. 2007). <www.vanityfair.com/culture/features/2007/01/hitchens200701>.

Hollywood North Report. <www.hollywoodnorthreport.com>.

Holt, Jennifer. "Vertical Vision: Deregulation, Industrial Economy and Prime-Time Design." Jancovich and Lyons 11–31.

Holzman, Winnie. Untitled essay in booklet accompanying DVD box set. *My So-Called Life: The Complete Series.* DVD. Shout! Media, 2007. 2.

Horton, Andrew S., ed. *Comedy/Cinema/Theory.* Berkeley: U of California P, 1991.

Howard, Douglas L. "'You're Going to Tell Me Everything You Know': Torture and Morality in FOX's *24.*" Peacock 133–48.

Howarth, Chris, and Steve Lyons. *Red Dwarf Program Guide.* 3rd ed. London: Virgin, 2000.

Howe, D., M. Stammers, and S. J. Walker. *Doctor Who—The Handbook: The Fourth Doctor.* London: Virgin, 1992.

Hunt, Leon. *The League of Gentlemen.* BFI TV Classics. London: BFI, 2008.

Hutchings, Peter. "Welcome to Royston Vasey: Grotesque Bodies and the Horror of Comedy in *The League of Gentlemen.*" *Intensities: The Online Journal of Cult Media* 4 (Dec. 2007). <http://intensities.org/Essays/Hutchings.pdf>.

"Interview with Joe Ahearne." *Ultraviolet* Web site. Sept. 2000 <http://www.world-productions.com/wp/content/shows/other/uv/intview1.htm>.

"The Invention of the Motorcycle." <http://www.famous-inventors.com/invention-of-the-motorcycle.html>.

Investment New Zealand. "Hercules: The Legendary Journeys." 5 July 2007. <http://www.investmentnz.govt.nz/section/14261.aspx>.

"ITV2: ITV's Younger Entertainment Channel." 2007. <http://www.itvmedia.co.uk/default.asp?section=105&page=1403>.

Jancovich, Mark, and Nathan Hunt. "The Mainstream Distinction and Cult TV." Gwenllian-Jones and Pearson 27–44.

Jancovich, Mark, Antonio Lazaro-Reboll, Julian Stringer, and Andrew Willis, eds. *Defining Cult Movies.* Manchester: Manchester UP, 2004.

Jancovich, Mark, and James Lyons, eds. *Quality Popular Television.* London: BFI, 2003.

Janeshutz, Trish, and Rob MacGregor. *The Making of Miami Vice.* New York: Ballantine Books, 1986.

Javna, J. *The Best of Science Fiction TV.* New York: Harmony, 1987.

Jenkins, Amy. "Interview" (2003). <http://thislife.tvheaven.com/interview_2.htm>.

Jenkins, Henry. *Convergence Culture: Where Old and New Media Collide.* New York: New York UP, 2006.

———. *Textual Poachers: Television Fans and Participatory Culture.* New York: Routledge, 1992.

———. "Why Mitt Romney Won't Debate a Snowman" (forthcoming).

Jensen, Jeff. "The Bomb Squad." *Entertainment Weekly*, 11 May 2007. <http://www.ew.com/ew/article/0,,20037536,00.html>.

———. "*Heroes* Comes out Swinging." *Entertainment Weekly*, 28 Sept. 2007. <http://www.ew.com/ew/article/0,,20036782_20037403_20057885,00.html>.

———. "'Heroes' Creator Apologizes to Fans." *Entertainment Weekly*, 16 Nov. 2007. <http://www.ew.com/ew/article/0,,20158840,00.html>

———. "The Powers That Be." *Entertainment Weekly*, 10 Nov. 2006. <http://www.ew.com/ew/article/0,,1553770,00.html>.

Jensen, Jeff, and Lynnette Rice. "Last Vamp Standing?" *Entertainment Weekly*, 7 Mar. 2003. <http://www.ew.com/ew/article/0,,427440,00.html>.

Jensen, Jeff, et al. "All about *Lost*." *Entertainment Weekly*. <http://www.ew.com/ew/allabout/0,,20000067,00.html>.

Jewett, Robert, and John Shelton Lawrence. *The American Monomyth*. Garden City, N.Y.: Anchor/Doubleday, 1977.

Johns, Ian. "Digital Pick of the Day: *Supernatural*." *Observer: Television*, 27 Jan. 2008. 4.

Johnson, Catherine. *Telefantasy*. London: BFI, 2005.

Johnson, Howard. *Life before and after Monty Python: The Solo Flights of the Flying Circus*. New York: St. Martin's Press, 1993.

Johnson, Steven. *Interface Culture*. New York: HarperCollins, 1997.

Johnson-Smith, Jan. *American Science Fiction TV: Star Trek, Stargate and Beyond*. London: I. B. Tauris, 2005.

Johnson-Woods, Toni. *Blame Canada! South Park and Contemporary Culture*. London: Continuum, 2007.

Jones, Leslie. "'Last Week We Had an Omen': The Mythological *X-Files*." Lavery, Hague, and Cartwright 77–98.

Jordan, Marion. "Carry On . . . Follow That Stereotype." *British Cinema History*. Ed. James Curran and Vincent Porter. London: Weidenfeld and Nicolson, 1983. 312–28.

Katims, Jason. BBC Cult TV Web site interview (2002). <http://www.bbc.co.uk/cult/roswell/interviews/katims/index.shtml>.

Kaveney, Roz, ed. *Reading the Vampire Slayer: An Unofficial Critical Companion to* Buffy *and* Angel. London: I. B. Tauris, 2002.

Kawin, Bruce. "After Midnight." *The Cult Film Experience: Beyond All Reason*. Ed. J. P. Telotte. Austin: U of Texas P, 1991. 18–25.

Kellner, Douglas. *Media Culture: Cultural Studies, Identity and Politics between the Modern and Postmodern*. New York: Routledge, 1995.

Keveney, Bill. "Island Burns with Mystery." *USA Today*, 23 Feb. 2005.

King, Michael Patrick. Interview. HBO: *The Comeback*. <www.hbo.com/comeback/interviews/michael_patrick_king.html>.

King, Stephen. "Confessions of a TV Slut." *Entertainment Weekly*, 24 Mar. 2006. <http://www.ew.com/ew/article/0,,1176379,00.html>.

———. *The Stand.* 2nd expanded ed. New York: Doubleday, 1990.
Kissell, Rick. "'Knight' Rides Back to Success 'Dexter' Kills in Primetime Ratings." 18 Feb. 2008. <http://www.variety.com/article/VR1117981094.html?categoryid=14&cs=1>.
Klein, Joe. *The Natural: The Misunderstood Presidency of Bill Clinton.* New York: Doubleday, 2002.
Koven, Mikel J. *Film, Folklore and Urban Legends.* Lanham, Md.: Scarecrow Press, 2008.
———. "The Folklore *Files:* In(corp)orating Legends in *The X-Files.*" *The X-Files and Literature: Unweaving the Story, Unraveling the Lie to Find the Truth.* Ed. Sharon Yang. Cambridge: Cambridge Scholars Press, 2007. 91–104.
———. "'Have I Got a Monster for You!' Some Thoughts on the Golem, *The X-Files* and the Jewish Horror Movie." *Folklore* 111.2 (2000): 217–30.
Lacey, Stephen. *Tony Garnett.* Manchester: Manchester UP, 2007.
Langley, Roger. *Patrick McGoohan: Danger Man or Prisoner?* Sheffield: Tomahawk, 2007.
Lavery David. "Afterword." Byers and Lavery 211–16.
———. "Afterword." Peacock 209–12.
Lavery, David, Angela Hague, and Marla Cartwright, eds. *"Deny All Knowledge": Reading the X-Files.* London: Faber and Faber, 1996.
Leach, Jim. "'The World Has Changed': Bond in the 1990s and Beyond?" *The James Bond Phenomenon: A Critical Reader.* Ed. Christoph Lindner. Manchester: Manchester UP, 2003. 248–58.
Lee, Patrick. "What Planet Is Jason Katims From?" (interview). *Science Fiction Weekly*, 27 Mar. 2000. <http://www.scifi.com/sfw/issue153/interview.html>.
Leopold, Todd. "A Milestone for *The Simpsons.*" CNN (2003). <http://www.cnn.com/2003/SHOWBIZ/TV/02/13/simpsons.300/>.
Lewinski, John Scott. "*Mystery Science Theater* Creators Return, with Downloadable Snark." *Wired.* <http://www.wired.com/print/entertainment/hollywood/news/2007/06/mst3k>.
Linford, P. "TV Zone." *Cottage Under Siege* 2. Ed. G. Roberts and N. Corry. London: London Borough of Lewisham Stationery Department, undated.
"The *Lost* Book Club." *Lost: The Complete Third Season.* Buena Vista Home Entertainment, 2007.
Lowry, Brian. "*Supernatural.*" *Variety*, 12 Sept. 2005. <http://www.variety.com/awardcentral_review/VE1117928111.html?nav=reviews07&categoryid=1986&cs=1&p=0>.
Lucas, Tim. "Blood 'n Doughnuts: Notes on *Twin Peaks.*" *Video Watchdog* 2 (1990): 32–49.
Lukacs, Georg. *Writer and Critic and Other Essays.* London: Merlin Press, 1978.

Lunacy. "The History of Xena Fan Fiction on the Internet." *Whoosh* 25 (Oct. 1998). <http://www.whoosh.org/issue25/lunacy1.html>.

Lury, Karen. *British Youth Television: Cynicism and Enchantment.* Oxford: Oxford UP, 2001.

Lyon, J. Shaun. *Back to the Vortex: The Unofficial and Unauthorised Guide to* Doctor Who. Tolworth, U.K.: Telos, 2005.

———. *Back to the Vortex—Second Flight: The Unofficial and Unauthorised Guide to* Doctor Who. Tolworth, U.K.: Telos, 2006.

MacCabe, Colin, and Olivia Stewart, eds. *The BBC and Public Service Broadcasting.* Manchester: Manchester UP, 1986.

Malik, Sarita. *Representing Black Britain: Black and Asian Images on Television.* London: Sage, 2002.

McAllister, G. "*Blake's 7* Ratings Guide." *The DWB Compendium—The Best of the First 100 Issues.* Ed. G. Leigh. Brighton: DreamWatch, 1993.

McCabe, Janet, and Kim Akass, eds. *Quality TV: Contemporary American Television and Beyond.* London: I. B. Tauris, 2007.

McCormack, U. "And All Things Nice . . . ?" *DWB #125.* Ed. A. Brown. Brighton: DreamWatch, 1994.

McGregor, Tom. *This Life: The Companion Guide.* London: BBC Books/Penguin Books, 1997.

McKain, Aaron. "Not Necessarily Not the News: Gatekeeping, Remediation, and *The Daily Show.*" *Journal of American Culture* 28.4 (Dec. 2005): 415–30.

Medina, Victor. "*Alias* May Be Over, but for Fans, the Story Never Ends: Magazines, Books, and Toys Keep the Legend of Sydney Bristow Alive." 31 May 2006. <http://www.associatedcontent.com/article/36527/alias_may_be_over_but_for_fans_the.html>.

Melton, J. Gordon. *The Vampire Book: The Encyclopedia of the Undead.* Detroit: Visible Ink, 1994.

Miller, D. "'3: Servalan' in 'Sutekh the Destroyer.'" *TV Zone Villains Special* 44. London: Visual Imagination, 2002.

Miller, Jeffrey S. *Something Completely Different: British Television and American Culture.* Minneapolis: U of Minnesota P, 2000.

Miller, Toby. *The Avengers.* London: BFI, 1997.

Milligan, Spike, *The Goon Show Scripts.* New York: St. Martin's Press, 1972.

Millman, Joyce. "City of Angel." *Salon.com*, 4 Oct. 1999. <http://dir.salon.com/story/ent/col/mill/1999/10/04/angel/>.

———. "Daddy's Girl." Thomas, *Neptune Noir* 46–57.

———. "The Death of Buffy's Mom." *Salon.com*, 12 Mar. 2001. <http://archive.salon.com/ent/col/mill/2001/03/12/buffy_mom/index.html>.

———. "Lessons in Being Human." *New York Times*, 23 Sept. 2001. <http://query.nytimes.com/gst/fullpage.html?res=9902E6D8153BF930A1575AC0A9679C8B63>.

Mills, Brett. "Comedy Verité: Contemporary Sitcom Form." *Screen* 46.1 (Spring 2004): 63.
———. *Television Sitcom*. London: BFI, 2005.
Mitovich, Matt, and Matt Webb, with Michael Logan. "Heroes Creator Solves Finale's Biggest Mystery." *TV Guide*. <community.tvguide.com/blog-entry/TVGuide-News-Blog/Tv-Guide-News/Heroes-Creator-Solves/800015727>.
Mittell, Jason. "South Park." *The Encyclopedia of Television*. 2nd ed. Ed. Horace Newcomb. London: Fitzroy Dearborn, 2005. 2144.
Morgan, David. *Monty Python Speaks*. London: Fourth Estate, 1999.
Morgan-Russell, Simon. "A Local Shop for Local People: Imbrication and Alienation in British Situation Comedy." *Journal of British Cinema and Television* 4.2 (2007): 322–36.
Muir, J. K. *A History and Critical Analysis of* Blake's 7: *The 1978–1981 British Television Space Adventure*. London: McFarland, 2007.
Mulrine, Anne. "Off to the Flying Circus: Comedy's New Stars Silly-Walk in the Footsteps of Monty Python." *US News and World Report* 124.11 (23 Mar. 1998): 64.
Murphy, Caryn. "'It Only Got Teenage Girls': Narrative Strategies and the Realism of *My So-Called Life*." Byers and Lavery 165–78.
Murray, Susan. "Saving Our So-Called Lives: Girl Fandom, Adolescent Subjectivity, and *My So-Called Life*." Byers and Lavery 35–48.
Nakamura, Lisa. "Race in/for Cyberspace: Identity Tourism and Racial Passing on the Internet." *Reading Digital Culture*. Ed. David Trend. Malden, Mass.: Blackwell, 2001. 226–35.
Neale, Steve, and Frank Krutnik. *Popular Film and Television Comedy*. London: Routledge, 1990.
Nelson, Robin. *State of Play: Contemporary "High-End" TV Drama*. Manchester: Manchester UP, 2007.
———. *TV Drama in Transition: Forms, Values and Cultural Change*. London: Macmillan, 1997.
"New *Leap, Tremors* on Sci Fi." *Sci Fi Wire*. 9 July 2002. <http://www.scifi.com/scifiwire/art-sfc.html?2002–07/09/12.30.sfc>.
Newman, Andrew Adam. "Showtime's New Slogan Speaks the Way It Could Only on Cable." *New York Times*, 3 Sept. 2007. <http://www.nytimes.com/2007/09/03/business/media/03showtime.html>.
Newman, Kim. *Doctor Who*. BFI TV Classics. London: BFI, 2005.
"The 100 Best TV Shows of All Time." *Time*, 13 Aug. 2007. <http://www.time.com/time/specials/2007/completelist/0,,1651341,00.html>.
"An Ordinary Woman." *The United Colors of Cottage under Siege* 3. Ed. G. Roberts and N. Corry. London: London Borough of Lewisham Stationery Department, undated.

Örnebring, Henrik. "Alternate Reality Gaming and Convergence Culture: The Case of *Alias*." *International Journal of Cultural Studies* 10.4 (2007): 445–62.

———. "The Show Must Go On . . . and On: Narrative and Seriality in *Alias*." Abbott and Brown 11–26.

Owen, A. Susan. "Vampires, Postmodernity and Postfeminism: *Buffy the Vampire Slayer*." *Journal of Popular Film and Television* 27.2 (1999): 24–31.

Owen, Rob. "TV Review: New NBC Series Is SUPER." *Pittsburgh Post-Gazette*, 24 Sept. 2006. <http://www.post-gazette.com/pg/06267/723814-237.stm>.

Parisi, Peter. "'Black Bart' Simpson: Appropriation and Revitalization in Commodity Culture." *Journal of Popular Culture* 27.1 (1993): 125–42.

Parks, Jo-Ann. "What's Ailing *The X-Files?*" *Space.com* (2000). <http://www.space.com/sciencefiction/tv/ailing_xfiles_000120.html>.

Parks, Lisa. "Brave New *Buffy*: Rethinking 'TV Violence.'" Jancovich and Lyons 118–33.

The Peabody Awards. Grady College of Journalism and Mass Communication, University of Georgia. <http://128.192.29.189/archives>.

Peacock, Steven, ed. *Reading* 24: *TV against the Clock*. London: I. B. Tauris, 2006.

Petrie, Duncan. *Shot in New Zealand: The Art and Craft of the Kiwi Cinematographer*. Auckland, N.Z.: Random House, 2007.

Pirie, David. "Everyday Vampires." *Sight and Sound* 8.12 (1998): 28–30.

Playden, Zoe-Jane. "What You Are, What's to Come: Feminism, Citizenship and the Divine." Kaveney 32–55.

Poniewozick, James. "Best of 2005: Television." *Time*, 16 Dec. 2005. <http://www.time.com/time/arts/article/0,8599,1141640,00.html>.

Porter, Lynnette, and David Lavery. *Unlocking the Meaning of Lost: An Unauthorized Guide*. Naperville, Ill.: Sourcebooks, 2006.

Porter, Lynnette, David Lavery, and Hillary Robson. *Saving the World: A Guide to Heroes*. Toronto: ECW Press, 2007.

Porter, Noah. "*Farscape*: Gendered Viewer Interpretations in Virtual Community." Unpublished paper, 2005.

Press, Joy. "Screen Gems." *Village Voice*, 30 Nov. 2004. <http://www.villagevoice.com/2004-11-30/art/screen-gems/>.

———. "The Teen Beat." *Village Voice*, 24 Aug. 2004. <http://www.villagevoice.com/2004-08-24/art/the-teen-beat/>.

Punter, David. *The Literature of Terror: A History of Gothic Fiction from 1765 to the Present Day*. London: Longman, 1980.

Pythons. *The Complete Monty Python's Flying Circus: All the Words*. 2 vols. New York: Pantheon Books, 1989.

Rahn, Wendy M., and John E. Transue. "Social Trust and Value Change: The Decline of Social Capital in American Youth, 1976–1995." *Political Psychology* 19.3 (1998): 545–65.

Rakoff, Ian. *Inside the Prisoner: Radical Television and Film in the 1960s.* London: Batsford, 1998.
Read, Nicholas. "Leaping into Controversy on Network TV." *Vancouver Sun,* 16 Nov. 1991.
Reeves-Stevens, Judith, and Garfield Reeves-Stevens. Star Trek: The Next Generation, *The Continuing Mission: A Tenth Anniversary Tribute.* New York: Pocket Books, 1998.
Rixon, Paul. "The Changing Face of American Television Programs on British Screens." Jancovich and Lyons 48–61.
Rodman, Howard A. "The Series That Will Change TV." *Connoisseur,* Sept. 1989.
Roscoe, Jane, and Craig Hight. *Faking It: Mock-Documentary and the Subversion of Factuality.* Manchester: Manchester UP, 2001.
"Roseanne Plans to Produce U.S. Version of British Sitcom." 7 Jan. 1995. <http://query.nytimes.com/gst/fullpage.html?res=990CE7DF103CF934A35752C0A963958260>.
Rosenberg, Howard. "NBC's Forward Move: 'Quantum Leap.'" *St. Petersburg Times,* 27 Dec. 1989. 7D.
Rosenberg, Scott. "Interface This." *Salon.com,* 3 Dec. 1997. <http://archive.salon.com/21st/feature/1997/12/cov_03feature.html>.
Rudnick, Brett. "An Interview with Eric Gruendemann." *Whoosh* 26 (Nov. 1998). <http://www.whoosh.org/issue26/igruend1.html>.
———. "An Interview with Rob Tapert." *Whoosh* 52 (Jan. 2001). <http://www.whoosh.org/issue52/itapert1.html>.
Rutenberg, Jim. "*Buffy,* Moving to UPN, Tries to Be a WB Slayer." *New York Times,* 21 Apr. 2001. <http://query.nytimes.com/gst/fullpage.html?res=9502EEDA1030F932A15757C0A9679C8B63.>
Rutsky, R. L. "Visible Sins, Vicarious Pleasures: Style and Vice in *Miami Vice.*" *SubStance* 17.1 (1988): 77–82.
Sandvoss, Cornel. *Fans: The Mirror of Consumption.* Cambridge: Polity Press, 2005.
Sangster, Jim, and Paul Condon. *TV Heaven.* London: Collins, 2005.
Saxey, Esther. "Staking a Claim: The Series and Its Slash Fiction." Kaveney 187–210.
Schneider, Michael. "NBC Announces Schedule, Shows." *Variety,* 14 May 2007. <http://www.variety.com/article/VR1117964868.html?categoryid=2566&cs=1&query=schneider+nbc+announces>.
———. "Rival Blurbsters Find *Heroes* at NBC." *Variety,* 27 Nov. 2006. <http://www.variety.com/article/VR1117954599.html?categoryid=14&cs=1&query=schneider++rival+blurbsters>.
Schuster, Marc, and Tom Powers. *The Greatest Show in the Galaxy: The Discerning Fan's Guide to* Doctor Who. Jefferson, N.C.: McFarland, 2007.

Schwichtenberg, Cathy. "Sensual Surfaces and Stylistic Excess: The Pleasure and Politics of *Miami Vice*." *Journal of Communication Inquiry* 10 (1986): 45–65.

Scodari, Christine, and Jenna Felder. "Creating a Pocket Universe: 'Shippers,' Fan Fiction, and the *X-Files* Online." *Communication Studies* 51.3 (2000): 238–51.

Sconce, Jeffrey. "*Star Trek*, Heaven's Gate and Textual Transcendence." Gwenllian-Jones and Pearson 199–222.

Scott, Allen J. "The Other Hollywood: The Organizational and Geographic Bases of Television-Program Production." *Media, Culture and Society* 26.2 (2004): 183–205.

Secret Agent aka *Danger Man: The Complete Collection*. Perf. Patrick McGoohan, Richard Wattis, Lionel Murton, Peter Madden. ITC, 1960–1966. DVD. A&E, 2007.

Sellers, Robert. *Cult TV: The Golden Age of ITC*. London: Plexus, 2006.

Shales, Tom. "The Moody Man of *Twin Peaks*." *Washington Post*, 6 Apr. 1990. Sec. C.

Shalit, Ruth. "Nasty Girls." *New Republic* 212.7 (13 Feb. 1995): 42.

Simpson, Paul. *The Rough Guide to Cult TV—The Good, the Bad and the Strangely Compelling*. London: Rough Guides, 2002.

Six of One: The Prisoner Appreciation Society. Granada Ventures. 2 Jan. 2008. <http://www.netreach.net/~sixofone/>.

Skal, David J. *V Is for Vampire: The A to Z Guide to Everything Undead*. New York: Plume, 1996.

Smith, Anthony, ed. *Television: An International History*. Oxford: Oxford UP, 1998.

Smith, Lynn. "The Slicing and Dicing of 'Dexter.'" *Los Angeles Times*, 17 Feb. 2008. <http://www.latimes.com/entertainment/la-ca-dexter17feb17,0, 397916.story>.

Sobstyl, Edrie. "We Who Are Borg, Are We Borg?" *Athena's Daughters: Television's New Women Warriors*. Ed. Frances Early and Kathleen Kennedy. The Television Series. Syracuse, N.Y.: Syracuse UP, 2003. 119–32.

Sontag, Susan. "Notes on Camp." *Against Interpretation*. New York: Farrar, Straus and Giroux, 1964. 275–92.

Spilsbury, Tom. "Letter from the Editor." *Doctor Who Magazine* 392 (2008): 3.

Springer, M. "High School Hell." *Buffy the Vampire Slayer* 3 (Dec. 1999): 12–15.

Stafford, Nikki. "Buffy We Hardly Knew You." *Globe and Mail*, 26 Apr. 2003. Reprinted with permission at <http://www.slayage.com/articles/000058.html>.

Stanley, Alessandra. "Gazing Resolutely into a Mirror (Wink)." *New York Times Online*, 3 June 2005. <www.nytimes.com/2005/06/03/arts/television/03tvwk.html?_r=1&oref=slogin>.

"The Steel Queen." *The United Colors of Cottage under Siege* 3. Ed. G. Roberts and N. Corry. London: London Borough of Lewisham Stationery Department, undated.

Stein, Louisa Ellen. "Subject: Off Topic: Oh My God, US Terrorism! *Roswell* Fans Respond to 11 September." *European Journal of Cultural Studies* 5 (2002): 471–91.

Stelter, Brian. "'Dexter' Gains a Wider Audience." 20 Feb. 2008. <http://tvdecoder.blogs.nytimes.com/2008/02/20/dexter-gains-a-wider-audience/>.

Stevens, Alan, and Fiona Moore. *Liberation: The Unofficial and Unauthorised Guide to* Blake's 7. Tolworth, U.K.: Telos, 2003.

Stewart, James B. *DisneyWar: The Battle for the Magic Kingdom.* New York: Simon and Schuster, 2005.

"Still Flying: An Interview with Joss Whedon." *Firefly: The Official Companion.* Vol. 2. Ed. Abbie Bernstein, Bryan Cairns, Karl Derrick, and Tara Di Lullo. London: Titan Books, 2007. 6–13.

Stokes, Richard. "Like a Kid in a Candy Store." *Torchwood: The Official Magazine* 2 (2008): 64–65.

Susman, Gary. *Entertainment Weekly*, 23 June 2008. <http://popwatch.we.com>.

Sutherland, Sharon, and Sarah Swan. "The Good, the Bad and the Justified: Moral Ambiguity in *Alias*." Abbott and Brown 119–32.

Svetkey, Benjamin. "R.I.P. 'MST3K.'" *Entertainment Weekly*, 15 Dec. 1995. <http://www.ew.com/ew/article/0,,299980,00.html>.

———. "Theater of the Absurdists." *Entertainment Weekly*, 14 June 1996. <http://www.ew.com/ew/article/0,,292974,00.html>.

Taborn, Kym Masera. "Warrior Princess: The Beginning of It All." *Whoosh* 2 (Oct. 1996). <http://www.whoosh.org/issue2/taborn2.html>.

"Things to Come: *Ultraviolet* Lite?" *Star Burst* 257 (2000): 6.

Thomas, Rob. "Favorite Veronica Logan Moments." *Veronica Mars*: The Complete Third Season DVD. Warner Brothers, 2007.

———. "The Origins of *Veronica Mars*." <http://www.robthomasproductions.com/>.

———. *Rats Saw God.* New York: New York: Simon and Schuster, 1996.

Thomas, Rob, ed., with Leah Wilson. *Neptune Noir: Unauthorized Investigations into Veronica Mars.* Dallas: BenBella Books, 2007.

Thompson, Ben. *Sunshine on Putty: The Golden Age of British Comedy from Vic Reeves to* The Office. London: Harper Perennial, 2004.

Thompson, Jeff. *The Television Horrors of Dan Curtis:* Dark Shadows, The Night Stalker, *and Other Productions, 1966–2006.* Jefferson, N.C.: McFarland, 2009.

Thompson, John O. *Monty Python: Complete and Utter Theory of the Grotesque.* London: BFI, 1982.

Thompson, Robert J. *Television's Second Golden Age: From* Hill Street Blues *to* ER. London: Continuum, 1997.

Tircuit, Angela. "*Quantum Leap*—Putting Right What Once Went Wrong, Once Again: A TV Movie in the Works." 26 June 2006. <http://www.associatedcontent.com/article/39572/quantum_leap_putting_right_what_once.html>.
Todorov, Tzvetan. *The Fantastic: A Structural Approach to a Literary Genre*. Ithaca, N.Y.: Cornell UP, 1975.
Topel, Fred. "Tim Kring." CraveOnline.com, 23 Apr. 2007. <http://www.thefreelibrary.com/Heroes+producer,+Tim+Kring.-a01611411708>.
Trimble, Bjo. *Star Trek Concordance*. New York: Ballantine, 1976.
Troup, Gary. *Bad Twin*. New York: Hyperion, 2006.
Tucker, Ken. "Torchwood." *Entertainment Weekly*, 28 Feb. 2008. <http://www.ew.com/ew/article/0,,20180998,00.html>.
Tulloch, John, and Manuel Alvarado. Doctor Who: *The Unfolding Text*. London: Macmillan, 1983.
Tulloch, John, and Henry Jenkins. *Science Fiction Audiences: Watching* Doctor Who *and* Star Trek. New York: Routledge, 1995.
Turner, Chris. *Planet Simpson: How a Cartoon Masterpiece Defined a Generation*. Cambridge, Mass.: Da Capo, 2004.
"*TV Guide* Names the Top Cult Shows Ever." *TV Guide*, 29 June 2007. <http://www.tvguide.com/news/top-cult-shows-40239.aspx>.
Tynan, William, and Ginia Bellafant, "Television: It's a Friendly Fall." *Time*, 11 Sept. 1995. <http://www.time.com/time/magazine/article/0,9171,983410-3,00.html>.
Virilio, Paul. *A Landscape of Events*. Trans. Julie Rose. Cambridge, Mass.: MIT Press, 2000.
Virilio, Paul, and Sylvere Lotringer. *The Accident of Art*. Trans. Michael Taormina. New York: Semiotext(e), 2005.
Vitaris, Paula. "*Ultraviolet*: What You Can't See . . . Can Kill." *Cinefantastique* 34.5 (2002): 34–35, 38–39, 42–43.
Walker, Stephen James. *Inside the Hub: The Unofficial and Unauthorised Guide to* Torchwood *Series*. Tolworth, U.K.: Telos, 2007.
———. *Third Dimension: The Unofficial and Unauthorised Guide to* Doctor Who. Tolworth, U.K.: Telos, 2007.
Walters, Ben. "A Guaranteed Premonition." *Film Quarterly* 61.2 (2007–2008): 66–67.
Weber, Bruce. "Something Completely Nostalgic." *New York Times*, 9 Mar. 1998. E1, E6.
Wheatley, Helen. *Gothic Television*. Manchester: Manchester UP, 2006.
Whedon, Joss. "Ace of Case." *Entertainment Weekly*, 7 Oct. 2005. <http://www.ew.com/ew/article/0,,1114734,00.html.>
———. "*Angel* 100 Featurette." *Angel* season 5 DVD. Beverly Hills, Calif.: Twentieth Century Fox Home Entertainment, 2005.

———. "Into the Black: An Interview with Joss Whedon." *Firefly: The Official Companion*. Vol. 1. Ed. Abbie Bernstein, Bryan Cairns, Karl Derrick, and Tara Di Lullo. London: Titan Books, 2006. 6–13.

———. "Joss Whedon." Interview with Tasha Robinson. *The Onion A.V. Club*, 8 Aug. 2007. <http://www.avclub.com/content/interview/joss_whedon>.

———. Posting to the BronzeBeta. 14 Feb. 2004. <http://www.bronzebeta.com/Archive/Joss/Joss20040214.htm>.

———. "Reality TV." In booklet accompanying DVD box set. *My So-Called Life: The Complete Series*. DVD. Shout! Media. 2007. 5–6.

Whitfield, Stephen E., with Gene Roddenberry. *The Making of* Star Trek. New York: Ballantine, 1968.

Wiggins, Kayla McKinney. "Epic Heroes, Ethical Issues and Time Paradoxes in *Quantum Leap*." *Journal of Popular Film and Television* 21.3 (Fall 1993): 111–20.

Wilcox, Rhonda V. "Dating Data: Miscegenation in *Star Trek: The Next Generation*." *Extrapolation* 34.3 (1993): 265–77. Revised and reprinted in *Enterprise Zones: Critical Positions on* Star Trek. Ed. Taylor Harrison et al. Boulder, Colo.: Westview, 1996. 69–92.

———. "Goldberg, Guinan, and the Celestial Mother in *Star Trek: The Next Generation*." *Mid-Atlantic Almanack* 4 (1995): 18–31.

———. "Shifting Roles and Synthetic Women in *Star Trek: The Next Generation*." *Studies in Popular Culture* 13.2 (1991): 53–65.

———. "Unreal TV." *Thinking Outside the Box: A Contemporary Television Genre Reader*. Ed. Gary R. Edgerton and Brian G. Rose. Lexington: UP of Kentucky, 2005. 201–25.

Wilcox, Rhonda V., and David Lavery, eds. *Fighting the Forces: What's at Stake in* Buffy the Vampire Slayer. Lanham, Md.: Rowman and Littlefield, 2002.

Williams, Raymond. *Television: Technology and Cultural Form*. New York: Schocken Books, 1975.

Williams, Tony. "Authorship Conflict in *The Prisoner*." *Making Television: Authorship and the Production Process*. Ed. Robert J. Thompson and Gary Burns. New York: Praeger, 1990. 65–79.

Wills, Dominic. Jennifer Garner biography (2005). <http://www.tiscali.co.uk/entertainment/film/biographies/jennifer_garner_biog/7>.

Wilmut, Roger. *From Fringe to Flying Circus*. London: Methuen, 1980.

Wolk, Josh. "*Mystery Science Theater 3000* Is Renewed." *Entertainment Weekly*, 5 June 1998. <http://www.ew.com/ew/article/0,,83532,00.html>.

Wood, Tat. *About Time 6, 1985–1989*. Des Moines, Iowa: Mad Norwegian Press, 2007.

Woodman, Brian J. "Escaping Genre's Village: Fluidity and Genre Mixing in Television's *The Prisoner*." *Journal of Popular Culture* 38.5 (2005): 939–56.

Wooley, Charles. "The World of Hercules and Xena." *60 Minutes* (Australia), Channel 9, 11 Apr. 1999.

Woollaston, Sam. "*This Life* Was Groundbreaking TV, but the 10-Year Reunion Proved There Was Nothing to Add." *Guardian*, 3 Mar. 2007.

Wright, John C. "Just Shove Him in the Engine, or the Role of Chivalry in Joss Whedon's *Firefly*." Espenson, *Finding Serenity* 155–68.

Zacherek, Stephanie. "Finale Wrap-up: *Veronica Mars*." *Salon.com*. <http://www.salon.com/ent/tv/review/2007/05/23/veronica_mars/print.html>.

Zicree, Marc Scott. *The Twilight Zone Companion*. 2nd ed. Los Angeles: Silman-James, 1989.

Zoglin, Richard "Cool Cops, Hot Show." *Time,* 16 Sept 1985. <http://www.time.com/time/magazine/article/0,9171,959822,00.html>.

Contributors

Stacey Abbott is senior lecturer in film and television studies at Roehampton University. She is the author of *Angel* and *Celluloid Vampires*, the editor or coeditor of *Reading* Angel: *The TV Spin-off with a Soul* and *Investigating* Alias: *Secrets and Spies*, and the general editor for I. B. Tauris's Investigating Cult TV series.

Dee Amy-Chinn is a lecturer in the Department of Film, Media, and Journalism at the University of Stirling in the United Kingdom. Recent publications include "Good Vampires Don't Suck: Sex, Celibacy, and the Body of Angel" (in *Vampires: Myths and Metaphors of Enduring Evil*); "Queering the Bitch: Spike, Transgression, and Erotic Empowerment" and (with Milly Williamson) "The Vampire Spike in Text and Fandom: Unsettling Oppositions in *Buffy the Vampire Slayer*" (*European Journal of Cultural Studies*); and "'Tis Pity She's a Whore: Postfeminist Prostitution in Joss Whedon's *Firefly*" (*Feminist Media Studies*).

Jes Battis recently received his PhD at Simon Fraser University in Canada. He is the author of *Investigating* Farscape and *Chosen Families in* Buffy the Vampire Slayer *and* Angel. His first novel will be published soon.

Stan Beeler teaches at the University of Northern British Columbia. He has written frequently on science fiction and fantasy television and is the coeditor of books on *Stargate SG-1* and *Charmed*.

David Bianculli is the author of *Teleliteracy* and *The Dictionary of Teleliteracy* and runs the Web site tvworthwatching.com.

Michele Byers teaches at St. Mary's University in Canada and is the editor or coeditor of books on *My So-Called Life*, *Degrassi*, and *CSI*.

Marc Dolan is coordinator of American studies at the Graduate Center of the City University of New York. He is the author of *Modern Lives: A Cultural Re-*

Reading of "The Lost Generation," as well as essays on Herman Melville, *Twin Peaks*, George Pierce Baker, Preston Sturges, and the aesthetics of 1970s punk.

Steven Duckworth recently received his PhD at Brunel University in London, where he now teaches courses in film and television.

Sam Ford is director of customer insights for Peppercom Strategic Communications and a research affiliate with the Convergence Culture Consortium at MIT.

Jonathan Gray is associate professor of media and cultural studies at the University of Wisconsin–Madison. He is the author of *Watching with* The Simpsons: *Television, Parody, and Intertextuality, Television Entertainment,* and the forthcoming *Show Sold Separately: Promos, Spoilers, and Other Media Paratexts.*

Matt Hills is reader in media and cultural studies at Cardiff University and is the author of such books as *Fan Cultures* and *Triumph of a Time Lord.*

Robert Holtzclaw is a professor of English at Middle Tennessee State University, where he teaches courses in film theory, film genre, documentary, and related subjects. He has published articles on film history and literature-to-film adaptations and has written conference papers on a variety of film and television subjects.

Douglas L. Howard is assistant academic chair and associate professor in the English Department at Suffolk County Community College. His publications include articles, essays, and book chapters in *Literature and Theology,* Poppolitics.com, *Chronicle of Higher Education, This Thing of Ours: Investigating* The Sopranos, *The Gothic Other: Racial and Social Constructions in the Literary Imagination* (coeditor and contributor), *Reading* The Sopranos, *Reading* Deadwood, *Reading 24,* and *Milton in Popular Culture.*

Leon Hunt is a senior lecturer in film and TV studies at Brunel University. He is the author of *British Low Culture: From Safari Suits to Sexploitation, Kung Fu Cult Masters: From Bruce Lee to* Crouching Tiger, and *The League of Gentlemen* and is the coeditor of *East Asian Cinemas: Exploring Transnational Connections on Film.*

Jason Jacobs teaches at the University of Queensland in Australia. He is the author of *The Intimate Screen: Early British Television Drama* and *Body Trauma TV.*

Angelina I. Karpovich teaches media at Brunel University. Her recent publications include an essay on *Angela's Ashes* in a collection on *Life on Mars*.

Mikel J. Koven is senior lecturer in film studies at the University of Worcester. He is the author of the books *La Dolce Morte: Vernacular Cinema and the Italian* Giallo *Film* and *Film, Folklore and Urban Legends*.

Stephen Lacey teaches at the University of Glamorgan in Wales. He is the author of *Television Drama: Past, Present and Future* and is one of the founding editors of *Critical Studies in Television*.

Jonathan Malcolm Lampley is assistant professor of English at Dalton State College in Georgia. He is the author of two books, including a forthcoming study of Vincent Price.

Marcia Landy is distinguished professor of English and film studies at the University of Pittsburgh and is the author of more than a dozen books.

David Lavery is professor of English at Middle Tennessee State University. He is the author or editor of volumes on *Twin Peaks, The X-Files, Buffy the Vampire Slayer, The Sopranos, Lost, Deadwood, Seinfeld, My So-Called Life, Heroes, Gilmore Girls,* and *Battlestar Galactica*. He coedits the e-journal *Slayage: The Online International Journal of Buffy Studies* and is one of the founding editors of *Critical Studies in Television: Scholarly Studies of Small Screen Fictions*.

Ian Maull recently completed his studies at Brunel University in London.

Joyce Millman is a television critic whose work has appeared in the *New York Times*, the *Boston Phoenix*, and *Salon.com*. She was a finalist for the Pulitzer Prize in criticism (1989 and 1991) for TV columns written for the *San Francisco Examiner*. She has contributed pop cultural essays to many anthologies, including *Getting Lost* and *Mothers Who Think*, and is the coauthor of *The Great Snape Debate*.

Joanne Morreale teaches communication studies at Northeastern University. She is the editor of *Critiquing the Sitcom*, has written two books on political campaign films and contributed to many anthologies, and has published articles in journals such as *Quarterly Journal of Film and Video, Journal of Popular Film and Television, Iowa Journal of Communication,* and *Television and New Media*.

Angela Ndalianis is head of cinema studies at the University of Melbourne. She has published widely in the areas of contemporary Hollywood cinema; crossovers between films, games, comic books, and theme parks; and media histories. Her books include *Neo-Baroque Aesthetics and Contemporary Entertainment*.

Robin Nelson is professor of theater and TV drama at Manchester Metropolitan University and is the author of numerous publications on the arts and media, including *TV Drama in Transition* and *State of Play: "High End" Contemporary TV Drama*.

Henrik Örnebring is the Axess research fellow in comparative European journalism at the Reuters Institute for the Study of Journalism, University of Oxford. He has published work on *Alias* in the *International Journal of Cultural Studies* and the edited collection *Investigating* Alias: *Secrets and Spies*.

Steven Peacock is lecturer in film at the University of Hertfordshire. He is the editor of *Reading* 24: *TV against the Clock*, the author of numerous articles on small-screen aesthetics, and coeditor of the Television Series published by Manchester University Press.

Alison Peirse lectures in media and popular culture at the University of Hull. Her article "Postfeminism without Limits? *Charmed*, Horror and Sartorial Style," was recently published in *Investigating* Charmed: *The Magic Power of Television*.

Bartley Porter is a corporate communication specialist and has written extensively for a variety of newspaper, academic, popular culture, and business publications.

Lynnette Porter is associate professor of humanities and communications at Embry-Riddle Aeronautical University in Daytona Beach, Florida, and is the author or coauthor of books on *The Lord of the Rings, Lost, Heroes,* and *Battlestar Galactica*.

Carolyn Skelton recently completed her PhD at the University of Auckland. She has taught film, television and media studies, cultural studies, and gender studies at universities in Sydney and Auckland. Her writing has appeared in *Media Studies in Aotearoa/New Zealand* and *Critical Studies in Television*.

Nikki Stafford is the author of several television guides, including the *Finding Lost* series of books, the best-selling *Bite Me! An Unofficial Guide to the World of* Buffy the Vampire Slayer, *Once Bitten: An Unofficial Guide to the World of* Angel, and *Lucy Lawless and Reneé O'Connor: Warrior Stars of* Xena. She blogs regularly about television at Nik at Nite (www.nikkistafford.blogspot.com).

Jon Stratton is professor of cultural studies at Curtin University of Technology, Perth. His published works include a chapter on *Australian Idol* in *Sonic Synergies: Music, Identity, Technology and Community*. His most recent books are *Australian Rock: Essays on Popular Music* and *Jewish Identity in Western Pop Culture: The Holocaust and Trauma through Modernity*.

J. P. Telotte is a professor of film and media in the School of Literature, Communication, and Culture at Georgia Tech. He is the author of more than 100 articles on film, television, and literature and coeditor of the journal *Post Script*. His most recent books are *The Essential Science Fiction Television Reader* and *The Mouse Machine: Disney and Technology*.

Sue Turnbull is associate professor in the Media Studies program at La Trobe University in Melbourne, Australia, and is coeditor of a forthcoming collection on *Veronica Mars*. She also reviews crime fiction for the *Sydney Morning Herald* and is a co-convener of Sisters in Crime Australia.

Rhonda V. Wilcox is professor of English at Gordon College and the author of *Why Buffy Matters: The Art of* Buffy the Vampire Slayer.

Milly Williamson is senior lecturer in film and television at Brunel University in London and author of *The Lure of the Vampire: Gender, Fiction and Fandom from Bram Stoker to* Buffy and a forthcoming book on celebrity. With Dee Amy-Chinn she coedited "The Vampire Spike in Text and Fandom," a special issue of the *European Journal of Cultural Studies*.

Index

Abbott, Stacey, 23–24, 26
ABC, 2, 22, 40, 44, 53, 85, 149, 155–56, 158, 175–79, 263, 299–300, 302–3, 337
Abrams, J. J., 2, 4, 6, 22–23, 25, 149–51, 155, 157, 244, 283, 292
Absolutely Fabulous (series), 3, 5–14
Abu Ghraib, 128, 284
accidents, 111–17. See also *Firefly*
Ackles, Jensen, 260, 263
Adams, Douglas, 209
Addams Family, The (series), 16
adult content, 276, 278
Adventures of Brisco County, Jr., The (series), 2, 15–21, 155
African Americans, 33, 94, 161–62, 204, 246, 250–51, 254, 318
Agency, The (series), 24
Ahearne, Joe, 3, 307–13
AIDS, 33
Albright, Madeline, 78
Alias (series), 2, 22–27, 149, 155, 309, 335
Alien (movie), 209
alienation, 63, 293
aliens, 47, 104–5, 110, 237–38, 241, 246, 249, 278, 280, 339
allegory, 33, 127, 157, 189, 194, 196, 199, 282, 299
Alliance, the, 113, 115–18, 238. See also *Firefly*
All in the Family (series), 182
All My Children (series), 84
Ally McBeal (series), 14, 257
al-Qaeda, 24

Alvarado, Manuel, 98–99
Amazing Colossal Man, The (movie), 186–87
ambiguity, 41, 55, 63, 91, 309–12
Amelie (movie), 300
American Dreams (series), 124
American Gigolo (movie), 163–64
American Gothic (series), 300
American Pie (movie), 121
American Werewolf in London, An (movie), 265
Amicus Studios, 139–40
Amy-Chinn, Dee, 63
anachronisms, 18, 43, 323, 334
Anchorman: The Legend of Ron Burgundy (movie), 121
ancient Greece, 331, 333, 335
Anderson, Gillian, 337, 343
Anderson, Richard Dean, 239–40
Angel, 1–2, 5, 28–35, 88, 155, 263, 343
Angel: After the Fall, 35
Animal 24/7 (series), 285
antagonists, 25–26, 31, 42, 53, 105–6, 198, 209
antiheroes, 91, 331
AOL Time Warner, 66
Apatow, Judd, 2, 120–21
apocalypse/the apocalyptic, 6, 51, 56, 127, 134, 140, 196, 199, 208, 211, 311, 313
Armageddon (movie), 23
Army of Darkness (movie), 20
Arrested Development (series), 14
Art Deco, 163–64
Asian horror, 264

atheism, 277
Attack of the Giant Leeches (movie), 186
Australia, 104, 226, 239, 335
Avengers, The (series), 3, 36–43, 167, 331

Babylon 5 (series), 54, 238
backstories, 23–24, 26–27, 31, 38, 53, 91, 216, 242, 333
Bad Robot, 155, 158
Bad Twin, 156. See also *Lost*
BAFTA (British Academy of Film and Television Awards), 12
Baker, Tom, 99
Bakhtin, M. M., 167
Bakula, Scott, 201–3, 205–7, 258
Barr, Roseanne, 12
Barrowman, John, 275, 279
Batman, 86, 131
Battis, Jes, 180
Battlestar Galactica (series), 3, 5, 44–50, 127, 129, 182, 206, 215, 238, 261–62, 309, 335
Baudrillard, Jean, 164, 196
Bay Harbor Butcher, 94. See also *Dexter*
BBC, 7, 10–12, 14, 51–52, 54, 57–59, 83, 97, 99, 101–2, 140–42, 147–48, 166–70, 172, 208–9, 211–13, 219, 268–69, 273–76, 278–80, 285, 307–8
BBC America, 276, 279
BBC2, 83, 136, 138, 141, 170, 172, 202, 208, 268, 273–74, 276
BBC3, 136, 275–76
BBC Wales, 97, 101–2, 142, 275, 280
Beaumont, Charles, 17, 295
Beavis and Butthead (series), 188, 231
Behr, Jason, 215
Bellisario, Don, 206
Bennett, Alan, 135
Benz, Julie, 32, 92
"Better Know a District," 79. See also *Colbert Report, The*
Beverly Hillbillies, The (series), 295, 349
Beverly Hills 90210 (series), 121, 177–78

Bewitched (series), 216
Bianculli, David, 2
Bigelow, Katherine, 307
Big Valley, The (series), 150
Billboard, 164
Bionic Woman (series), 206, 261, 285
bisexuality, 279
Black, Claudia, 104, 110, 239, 243
Blade (movie), 307, 309
Blair, Tony, 223–24, 271
Blake's 7 (series), 3–4, 51–59
blood and gore, 278
Blue Velvet (movie), 2
B-movies, 17, 21, 188
Boam, Jeffrey, 15
Bochco, Steven, 337
body switching, 109
Boondocks, The (series), 228
Bordwell, David, 150
Boreanaz, David, 28, 35, 61
Borg, the 251, 255, 257. See also *Star Trek: The Next Generation*
Boston Legal (series), 16
Boucher, Chris, 52–53, 59
Bourke-White, Margaret, 37
Bowie, David, 146, 148
Brand, Joshua and John Falsey, 337
Braun, Lloyd, 149–50, 156–57
Bridges, Beau, 239
"Brilliant but Cancelled," 4, 325, 328
Brit-grit, 136
British cinema, 168
British Columbia, 261
Britishness/Englishness, 36, 42, 210
Brooker, Will, 262, 277–79
Brooks, James L., 225
Browder, Ben, 104, 110, 239, 243
Brown, James, 159
Browncoats, 118, 258. See also *Firefly*
Buck Rogers in the 25th Century (series), 52
budgets, 12, 20, 38–39, 51–52, 58, 88–89, 131, 181, 184, 208, 286, 297
Buffy the Vampire Slayer (series), 1–2, 25, 28, 54, 60–67, 88, 125, 176, 263, 280, 300, 308, 319, 335, 343

Bundy, Ted, 231
Burn Notice (series), 189
Bush, George H. W., 224–26, 288
Bush, George W., 5, 33, 79, 127, 129, 225

Caddyshack (movie), 122
Cagney and Lacey (series), 332
Californication (series), 90
camp, 4, 10, 57
Campbell, Bruce, 15, 17–18, 20
Canada, 40, 179, 221, 261, 323, 327
cancellation (of television shows), 15–16, 34, 57–58, 69, 112, 126, 176, 178, 181–82, 186–87, 190, 202, 225, 244, 296, 303, 318, 320, 328
Cannibal! The Musical (movie), 229
Can't Cook, Won't Cook (television show), 208
Cardiac Arrest (series), 272
Cardiff, Wales, 103, 279–81
caricatures, 9, 122–24, 210, 226, 283
carnivalesque, the, 167, 231
Carpenter, Charisma, 31, 61
Carry On films, 168
Carter, Chris, 2, 220, 338–43. See also *X-Files, The*
Carter, Samantha, 239
Casablanca (movie), 111
Casablanca, Morocco, 160
Casino Royale (movie), 191
catchphrases, 4, 17, 73, 138, 141, 144, 182, 225, 338
Cathy Come Home (series), 270, 308
Cat People (movie), 265
CBC, 83
CBS, 66–67, 95–96, 190, 195, 291–93, 296–97, 316, 337
CDs, 58, 202, 227, 302
Central America, 160
Chabon, Michael, 224
Chandler, Raymond/Chandleresque, 29, 314
Channel 4 (UK), 132, 307, 312
Chapman, Graham, 166
Charles, Craig, 210–11, 213

Charlie Rose Show, The (television show), 235
Charlie's Angels (series), 342
Chase, Chevy, 83
Chase, David, 195, 292
Cheers, 73
chemistry, 332
Cheney, Dick, 128–29, 225
China Beach (series), 302
Chinatown (movie), 317
Chitty Chitty Bang Bang (movie), 137
Christlike, 277, 333
Christmas specials, 134, 138–39
Chuck (series), 123
CIA, 22–24
cinematic, the, 139, 184, 187, 264, 286–87, 289, 296, 331, 334, 342
cinematography, 170, 182, 217, 338
Civil War, The (miniseries), 301
Cixous, Hélène, 235
Cleese, John, 166, 170–72
Cleveland, Carol, 166
cliffhangers, 53, 58, 128–29, 133, 285, 288, 301
Clinton, Bill, 78, 205, 330
Clinton, Hillary, 78, 231, 256
Clooney, George, 231
closure, 25–26, 58, 65, 143, 146, 169, 269
Cloverfield (movie), 158
codes, 25, 61, 235, 279, 283
Colbert, Stephen, 3, 5, 77–83
Colbert Nation, 81–82
Colbert Report, The (television show), 3, 5, 77, 79–83, 228
Cold War, 189, 246
Collinson, Phil, 51, 53–54, 104
colonialism, 55, 333
colonial literature, 333
Columbine massacre, 62–63, 219
Columbo (series), 303
Comeback, The (series), 68–76
Comedy Central, 12, 77, 81, 83, 181, 186, 229–30
comedy verité, 68
comic books, 82–83, 86, 131

Comic-Con, 34–35, 276
Comic Relief (charity), 10, 13
comic relief, 72, 132
Company, the, 128–29. See also *Heroes* (series)
conspiracy theories, 5, 206
convergence culture, 80, 83, 123
Cops (television show), 308, 342
Cops, The (series), 308
Corman, Roger, 295
Cosby Show, The (series), 222
Cowboy Bebop (series), 113
CTU (Counter Terrorism Unit), 282, 285–87, 289. See also *24*
Curtis, Dan, 84–87, 89
Cylons, 5, 45–50, 127, 262
   Final Five Cylons, 49
   See also *Battlestar Galactica*

Daily Show, The (television show), 3, 5, 77–83, 128, 222, 228, 233
dark comedy, 135
Darkly Dreaming Dexter, 90
Dark Shadows (series), 3, 83–89
Dark Star (movie), 209
Dark Water (movie), 264
Davies, Russell T., 3, 6, 102, 275, 277–81. See also *Doctor Who*; *Torchwood*
Dawkins, Richard, 231
Dawson's Creek (series), 179, 260, 315
Days of Our Lives (series), 84
DDEB (David Duchovny Estrogen Brigade), 343. See also *X-Files, The*
Dead Like Me (series), 90, 327–28
Degrassi High (series), 177–78
Degrassi Junior High (series), 177
demographics, 5, 66, 72, 98, 175, 235, 324
demons, 31, 33, 261–62
Desilu Playhouse (television show), 293
Desperate Housewives (series), 150, 156
Dexter, 3, 5, 90–96
Dharma Initiative, 157. See also *Lost*
Dhavernas, Caroline, 322
Dickens, Charles, 140, 157, 168

direct address, 169, 288
Disch, Thomas M., 159
Disney Television, 121, 155–56
District, The (series), 16
Doctor Who (series), 3, 6, 51–52, 54, 58, 97–103, 142–43, 209, 212, 275–79, 281, 313
Doctor Who Appreciation Society, 97, 102
Doctor Who Magazine, 97, 102–3
Dohring, Jason, 316, 319
Dollhouse (series), 1
Dracula (series; 1973), 87
Dracula (series; 2006), 313
Dracula (Stoker's novel), 307
Dracula, 6, 88
Dracula's Daughter (movie), 88
Dragonwyck (movie), 85
dreams, 28, 106–7, 120, 123–24, 177, 216, 293
Dr. No (movie), 193
drugs, drug use, 90, 160, 191, 268, 270–71
Duchovny, David, 304, 337, 342–43
Duckworth, Steven, 4
Dukes of Hazzard, The (series), 206
DVD, 4, 6, 17, 25–26, 30, 43, 49–50, 69, 87, 103, 113, 120–21, 155, 173, 177, 179, 187, 202, 211–13, 215, 227, 237, 239–40, 258, 285–86, 289, 314, 320, 322, 327, 341, 343–44
DVD box sets, 285
DVD extras, 49, 103
Dynasty (series), 150, 160
Dyson, Jeremy, 3, 135–36, 140–41. See also *League of Gentlemen, The*
dystopia/dystopian, 52–53, 56, 245

Earth, 5, 23, 34, 49, 101, 216, 220, 238, 241, 253, 258, 294–95, 339
EastEnders (series), 97
Eastwood, Clint, 331
Eccleston, Christopher, 100
EC Comics, 138
Eco, Umberto, 141

écriture feminine, 235
Edinburgh Festival, 136
Edlund, Ben, 34
Eick, David, 3, 44, 50
Elba, Idris, 310
Ellison, Harlan, 245
Emmerich, Roland, 237
Emmy awards, 12, 16, 24, 26, 65, 69, 78–79, 90, 160, 181, 202, 208, 211, 233, 248, 292, 302, 338
Empire Films, 168
ensembles, 128, 217, 250, 287, 335
Enterprise (series), 207, 245, 258–59
Enterprise, the USS, 108, 244–45, 248–51, 298. See also *Star Trek*
Entertainment Weekly, 60, 71, 73, 129, 132, 319
epic, 19, 104, 110, 131, 170, 204, 240
Equality Now, 60
ER (series), 100, 121
Eragon (movie), 187
Eraserhead (movie), 2
Espenson, Jane, 50, 113
Europe, 40, 95, 162–63, 165, 171, 330, 333
evil, 24, 29, 31, 22, 34, 94, 128, 186, 196, 309
Evil Dead films, 16, 20
Evil Dead video games, 21
Extras (series), 212

face, concept of, 69–70
Facebook, 214, 218–19
facework, 69
family, 8, 22–24, 31–33, 61, 85–86, 110, 118, 126, 166, 211, 216–19, 222–25, 254–55, 271, 317
family drama, 22, 24, 175, 203, 223
Family Guy (series), 130, 228, 298
family relationships, 22
Family Ties (series), 105, 107, 222
fan bases, 287
fan fiction, 49, 65, 110, 206, 242, 244, 320, 334
fantastic, the, 4, 308
fantasy, 16, 65, 86, 89, 97–100, 143, 147, 149–50, 168, 177–78, 202, 233, 237, 245, 261, 263, 284, 291, 293, 295–97, 307–8, 313, 325, 329–35, 338, 340
Farscape (series), 3, 104–10, 238–39, 243
fashion, 7–8, 10–13, 26, 41, 161–63, 165, 230, 259
Fast Show, The (television show), 136, 141
Father Knows Best (series), 222
Father Ted (series), 211
FBI, the, 96, 214, 266, 289, 320, 337
Feig, Paul, 120
Felicity (series), 22–23, 149, 179
Fiennes, Ralph, 40
Fillion, Nathan, 114
film noir, 29, 243, 251, 314–15
Financial Times, 271
Firefly (series), 1–2, 33, 54, 109, 111–19, 258, 300, 322
flashbacks, 12, 32, 116, 127, 152–54, 317
flash-forwards, 152–53
Fleming, Ian, 189
flexi-narrative, 53, 143
Ford Granada, 142. See also *Life on Mars*
Forever Young (movie), 23
40-Year-Old Virgin, The (movie), 121
FOX, 1–2, 5, 16–17, 33, 112, 179, 214, 222, 225, 229, 282, 312, 322–25, 327, 337, 341–43
FOX Family Channel, 120
FOX News, 79, 225, 285
France, 11–12, 99, 195, 334
Franco, James, 121
Franzen, Jonathan, 223–24
Freaks and Geeks (series), 2, 120–26
French and Saunders (series), 7
Frid, Jonathan, 85, 88
Friday night programming, 1, 16, 112
Friends (series), 75, 160, 272
From Beyond the Grave (series), 139
Frost, Mark, 301–3

Frost Report, The (television show), 167
Frye, Northrup, 168
Fuller, Bryan, 2, 300, 322–25, 327–28
Fury, David, 155
Fuselage, the, 155, 158
Futurama (series), 298

Garber, Victor, 23
Garner, Jennifer, 23–24
Garnett, Tony, 268, 279, 272–74, 308
GATB (Gillian Anderson Testosterone Brigade), 343. See also *X-Files, The*
Gatiss, Mark, 3, 103, 135, 139–41. See also *League of Gentlemen, The*
gay and lesbian programming, 323–24
gay characters, 271
Geller, Sarah Michelle, 28, 60, 62
gender, 45–46, 64, 60, 64, 76, 82, 96, 162, 167, 172, 204, 239, 329, 331–33, 335
Generation X, 270
genre, 3–4, 12, 15–16, 23, 28–29, 33, 36, 39, 41, 51–53, 57, 61, 65, 68, 80, 97, 99–101, 112, 139, 141, 159, 161–62, 168, 189–91, 203, 209, 211, 214–16, 219, 223, 230, 239, 251, 261, 265, 276–78, 280–81, 287, 290, 293, 297, 307–9, 313, 315, 333–35, 338, 341, 343
genre hybridity, 4, 112, 315
Gere, Richard, 162
Germany, 19, 56, 173
Get Smart (series), 206
Ghostbusters (movie), 265–66
Ghost Whisperer (series), 266
Gibson, Mel, 231
Giddens, Anthony, 272
Gilliam, Terry, 166, 169, 232
Gilligan's Island (series), 181
Gilmore Girls (series), 260, 263
Glassner, Jonathan, 237
Glenister, Philip, 143–44
globalization, 5, 330, 333
Goffman, Erving, 69
Goldberg, Rube, 340
Goldberg, Whoopi, 246, 251

Golden Globe Awards, 24, 202
Goldfinger (movie), 38, 195
Goldsmith, Jerry, 296
Google, 83, 264, 288
Goon Show, The (television show), 168
Gordon, Howard, 312
Gossip Girl (series), 16
Gothic, the, 62, 83–85, 87, 98, 134, 140, 330, 334
Grade, Lew, 190, 193
Graham, Matthew, 142, 145
"Grand Non-narrative, 58
Grant, Rob, 209–13
graphic novels, 29, 130, 137, 285, 340
Gray, Jonathan, 223, 227
"Green Screen Challenge," 81. See also *Colbert Report, The*
Grey's Anatomy (series), 2
Groening, Matt, 2, 222–23, 227
grotesque, the, 134–35, 138, 141, 167–68, 171, 234
Growing Pains (series), 222
Grunberg, Greg, 23, 128
Guantánamo, 284
Guardian, The, 102, 196, 268, 271, 277
Gunsmoke (series), 18
Gwenllian-Jones, Sara, 3, 6, 25, 160, 208, 240, 242, 287, 323, 329–30, 334

Hall, Michael C., 91, 93
Hamlet (television show), 186
Hannigan, Alyson, 61
Happy Days (series), 124–25
Haraway, Donna, 108
Hawking, Stephen, 208, 223
HBO, 5, 33, 68, 84, 90–91, 230, 286, 295
HBO comedies, 68
Head, Anthony Stewart, 61
Heartbeat (series), 142–43, 148
Heathers (movie), 317
Heaven's Gate cult, 328
Hellmouth, 60–61, 277
Henson, Brian, 104
Hercules: The Legendary Journeys (series), 16, 21, 330, 335

Heroes (series), 3, 6, 15, 27, 127–33, 207, 282, 300, 305, 322, 334–35
heroes, 15, 18, 48, 52, 55, 125, 128–29, 131, 194, 331
Heroes: Origins, 132–33
Herrman, Bernard, 296
Hills, Matt, 2–3, 25, 58, 97–98, 147, 161, 193, 199, 277, 278, 307
Hills Have Eyes, The (movie), 265
Hill Street Blues (series), 150, 159, 337
Hilton, Paris, 13, 231
Hitchcock, Alfred, 85, 168, 265
Hitchens, Christopher, 78
Hitchhiker's Guide to the Galaxy, 209
Hodgson, Joel, 183, 185, 187
Holland, Todd, 322
Hollywood, 17, 26, 31, 95, 123, 130, 133, 150, 201, 225, 230, 261–62, 270, 327, 331, 342
Holzman, Winnie, 175
Homicide (series), 150
homosexuality, 10, 204, 271
Hopkins, Anthony, 96
Horrocks, Jane, 7
horror, 20, 24, 28, 61, 86–89, 134–35, 138–39, 141, 187, 202, 223–24, 234, 241, 260–61, 263–65, 267, 278, 296–97, 312, 340, 343
horror film, 20, 89, 135, 139, 141, 186, 202, 260–61, 264–65, 267
horror television, 87, 263, 278
House of Dark Shadows (series), 86
House of Dracula (series), 88
Howard, Douglas L., 283
How I Met Your Mother (series), 121
Hub, the, 278, 280. See also *Torchwood*
Huff (series), 90
Hugo Boss, 163
Hulk, the, 131
hyperdiegesis, 3, 25, 57, 147
hyperreal, 164, 196

I Accuse My Parents (movie), 186
Ice Truck Killer, the, 92. See also *Dexter*
iconic, the, 10, 30, 38, 100–101, 137, 189, 194, 226, 231, 268, 280, 309, 329
iconography, 36, 264, 308
Idle, Eric, 166, 170
Iger, Robert C., 303
I Love Lucy (series), 68, 182
immersive, the, 82–83, 134, 141, 329, 334–35
Independence Day (movie), 237
Independent Television Authority, 167
Indiana Jones, 6
In Living Color (television show), 222
Interface Culture (Johnson), 188
intertexuality, 4, 39, 65, 121, 144, 191, 216, 232, 241–42, 261, 265, 275, 280–81, 290
Invasion (series), 149
Invisible Man, The (movie), 36
Iraq war, 48, 87
Ireland, 226
Iron Curtain, the, 42
I Spy (series), 189
ITV, 36, 51, 83, 167, 261, 263
ITV2, 261, 263

JAG (series), 16
Japan/Japanese, 26, 128, 132, 173, 264, 293, 304, 334
Jekyll (series), 313
Jenkins, Amy, 268, 270
Jenkins, Henry, 58, 80, 73, 103, 123, 244
Jensen, Jeff, 33, 129, 131, 133
Jericho (series), 127, 182
Jericho Mile, The (movie), 162
Jerk, The (movie), 123
Joanie Loves Chachi (series), 28
Joan of Arcadia (series), 326
Johnson, Don, 161
Johnson, Steven, 188
jokes, 17–18, 68, 82–83, 123, 126, 135, 138–39, 184
Jon Stewart Show, The (television show), 78
Jordan, Tony, 148
journalism, 80–81, 315

Journeyman (series), 203
Judge, Christopher, 239
jumping the shark, 139, 342–43
Ju-On (movie), 264

Kafka, Franz, 194, 199
Katims, Jason, 214–15, 219
Kawin, Bruce, 5, 118
Keep, The (movie), 162
Kelley, David E., 151, 157, 337
Kennedy, John Fitzgerald, 89, 205
Keystone Cops, 144
King, Michael Patrick, 68
King, Stephen, 151, 156
King of the Hill (series), 228
kitchen sink films, 136
Klingons, 105, 250, 257–58. See also *Star Trek*
Knocked Up (movie), 121
Kolchak: The Night Stalker (series), 337, 343
Kraft Television Theater (television show), 292
Kring, Tim, 3, 6, 128–29, 131–33, 300
Kripke, Eric, 2
KTMA, 181
Kubrick, Stanley, 168
Kudos, 142
Kudrow, Lisa, 68–70, 75

Lacan, Jacques, 165
laddism, 10
Laguna Beach (series), 121
Landis, John, 265, 297
Lang, Fritz, 39
language, 4–5, 96, 105, 144, 167–68, 171, 182, 218, 221, 230, 247–48, 252–53, 258–59, 261, 271, 291
Larry Sanders Show, The (series), 322
laugh tracks, 68
Lavery, David, 66, 133, 150, 156
Law and Order (series), 159
Lawless, Lucy, 50, 329, 331–33
lawyers, 33, 269
League of Gentlemen, The (television show), 3, 6, 134–41, 212

League of Gentlemen's Apocalypse, The (movie), 134
Leave It to Beaver (series), 223
Lecter, Hannibal, 96, 162
Leno, Jay, 74
Life in Hell (comic), 222. See also *Simpsons, The*
Life on Mars (series), 2, 6, 142–48
Lindelof, Damon, 3, 150–51, 156–57, 300
Lindsay, Jeff, 90, 96
Little Britain (television show), 141
liveness, 68, 169, 286
Loach, Ken, 308
local, the, 135, 137–38. See also *League of Gentlemen, The*
Loeb, Jeph, 131
London, England 7, 135, 138, 162, 196, 265, 285, 308, 312
Lone Gunmen, the, 343. See also *X-Files, The*
Lopez, Jennifer, 231
Los Angeles, California, 29, 33, 61, 88, 128, 261, 282, 289, 331, 342
Lost (series), 2–3, 6, 15, 19, 27, 48, 50, 127, 129–31, 149–58, 201, 244, 282, 287, 300, 305, 335
Lovecraft, H. P., 86, 295
Lucas, George, 6
Lucas, Tim, 306
L Word, The (series), 90, 261
Lynch, David, 2, 299, 301–3, 305

MacGyver (series), 237, 240
MacLachlan, Kyle, 300–301, 304
Macnee, Patrick, 36–40, 296
mainstream TV, 1–2, 6, 11, 21, 24, 34, 57, 98, 102, 118, 121, 141, 149, 160, 182, 222, 276, 324–25, 329, 335, 343
Malcolm in the Middle (series), 322
Manchester, England, 143, 145–46
Man from U.N.C.L.E., The (series), 42, 189, 304
Manhunter (movie), 162
Mankiewicz, Joseph L., 85

Mann, Michael, 159–60, 162
Manners, Kelly A., 30
Manners, Kim, 343
Manos, James, 3, 90
Manos: The Hands of Fate (movie), 186
Markstein, George, 197–98
Married . . . With Children (series), 222
Marsters, James, 31, 61, 280
mass audiences, 66, 98
Masterpiece Theatre (television show), 167
Matheson, Richard, 88, 295
Matrix, The (movie), 189, 325
Max Headroom (series), 291
McCaffrey, Anne, 108
McGoohan, Patrick, 189–92, 194–99, 299
McKern, Leo, 193, 196, 198–99
Mead, Margaret, 37
Medium (series), 266
Meet the Press (television show), 81
melodrama, 2, 61–62, 216–18, 315
Melrose Place (series), 16
Memphis, 104
Men Behaving Badly (series), 10, 211
Meredith, Burgess, 294
meta-genre, 3, 287
metatextual, 4, 65, 242, 251–53, 256
Metropolis (movie), 39
Metropolis (*Smallville*), 262
MGM, 237, 328
Miami, Florida, 91, 94, 160–61, 163–64
Miami Vice (series), 3, 159–65
military science fiction, 238
Millennium (movie), 342
Millennium Centre (Cardiff, Wales), 280
Millennium Falcon, 108
Milligan, Spike, 168
Millman, Joyce, 28–29, 318
Mills, Brett, 68, 135
Mirrorball (movie), 13
Mission: Impossible (series), 41, 191
mobisodes, 156
mock epic, 170

Moffatt, Stephen, 6
"Monkey's Paw, The," 140
monotheism, 333
"monster of the week," 281, 339, 344
Monty Python's Flying Circus (television show), 3, 134–35, 141, 166–73, 232
Moonlighting (series), 41
Moore, Ronald D., 3, 44, 46, 48–50
moral ambiguity, 63, 65, 91, 309, 311
Moyer, Stephen, 309
MPPB (Mitch Pileggi Pheromone Brigade), 343. See also *X-Files, The*
MTV, 78, 83, 159–60, 172, 164–65, 176, 179, 331
Muppets, 34
Murder . . . Most Horrid (series), 7
Murder One (series), 305
Murdoch, Rupert, 225
Murnau, F. W., 307
Murphy Brown (series), 16
My So-Called Life (series), 174–80, 215, 312
Mystery Science Theater: The Movie (movie), 356
Mystery Science Theater 3000 (series), 4, 181–88
mythology, 16, 19, 23, 28, 131, 215–16, 238, 241, 258, 275, 307, 312, 338–39

narcissism, 210, 234, 236
narrative, 1, 3, 5, 8, 14, 23, 25–27, 40–41, 49, 53, 56–58, 61, 75, 92, 94–95, 99–100, 106, 112, 115, 134, 139, 141, 143–46, 150–54, 156–58, 159, 161, 178, 185, 193–94, 198–99, 217–18, 231–34, 239–42, 261, 264, 269–70, 272, 278–81, 287, 297, 299, 305, 308, 311, 313, 325–26, 329, 333–34, 337–43
narrative arcs, 56, 143m 178, 261, 269, 313, 337–38, 343
narrative time, 153
Nash Bridges (series), 15, 151, 201

Nation, Terry, 51
naturalistic science fiction, 46
Naylor, Grant, 209–10, 212–13
NBC, 77, 87, 120, 127, 130, 132–33, 156, 186, 201–3, 263, 292, 296, 300, 337
Neale, Steve, 169
Near Dark (movie), 307
Nelson, Robin, 143
Neptune Noir, 315, 317, 319. See also *Veronica Mars*
News Corporation, 222, 224–25, 227
news parody, 77, 83
New York City, 6, 88, 96, 128–30, 161
New Zealand, 104, 330–31, 335
Niagara Falls, 322–23, 327. See also *Wonderfalls*
niche audiences, 97, 275–76, 323, 330
Nicholson, Jack, 138
Nielsen ratings, 160, 214, 221, 227, 338
Night Gallery, 297
nightmares, 138, 194, 295, 312
Night of the Living Dead, 243
Nimoy, Leonard, 248, 259
Nine, The (series), 127
9/11, 24, 44–45, 127, 157, 282, 284
Nixon, Richard, 283
Northern Exposure (series), 299, 315
Nosferatu (movie), 307
nostalgia, 4, 41, 89, 102, 104, 124–26, 140, 172, 274
Nowhere Man (movie), 189

Obama, Barack, 5, 256
O'Bannon, Rockne, 3, 104
Observer, The, 263
OC, The (series), 123
Oceanic 815, 152, 157. See also *Lost*
Ocean's Eleven (movie), 295
O'Connor, Renée, 332
Office, The (series), 70, 75, 139
Oka, Masi, 128, 132
Olmos, Edward James, 45, 47, 50, 160–61
O'Neillisms, 241–42. See also *Stargate SG-1*

One Tree Hill (series), 179, 263
On Her Majesty's Secret Service (movie), 40
Onion, The, 77, 83
Onion AV Club, The, 34
opening credit sequence, 30, 96, 223, 338
Operation Iraqi Freedom, 128
Operation *Life* Support, 178
O'Reilly, Bill, 231
Orwell, George, 194, 199
Ostroff, Dawn, 263, 320
otherness, 62, 101, 118, 323
Outer Limits, The (television show), 297
outsider status, 61–62, 70, 120–21, 123, 219, 250, 271, 333

Padalecki, Jared, 260, 263
Pal, George, 295
Palin, Michael, 166, 169–71
Panettiere, Hayden, 328
pansexuality, 279
Parker, Trey, 2, 229–33, 235
parody, 7–77, 79–83, 226, 242, 269, 303, 305, 342
PBS, 57, 99, 232
Peabody Awards, 181, 252
Peacock, Steven, 3
Pearson, Roberta, 3, 6, 25, 160, 208, 240, 242, 287, 323, 329–30, 334
Peckinpah, Sam, 168, 172
Pee-Wee's Playhouse (television show), 182
Pemberton, Steve, 3, 135, 137, 139–40. See also *League of Gentlemen, The*
Petersen, William, 151
Pharaoh, Ashley, 148
Picket Fences (series), 299, 337
Piper, Billie, 100
Pirates of the Caribbean (movie), 270
Pittsburgh, Pa., 174
Planet of the Apes (movie), 296
platforms, 5
Play for Today (series), 281
Playhouse 90 (movie), 292

Poe, Edgar Allan, 86
Police Surgeon (series), 36
politics, 54, 77, 80–81, 93, 124, 164, 184, 236, 272
Poltergeist (movie), 265
polymorphous perversity/sexuality, 63–65
pop culture phenomenon, 127
pop music, 217
Popular (series), 176, 179
popular culture, 10, 18–19, 37, 43, 69, 77, 151, 174, 184, 188, 226, 231, 235, 261, 264–65, 291, 338
Porter, Lynnette, 131, 133, 150, 152, 156
postmodern, 11, 36, 105, 142, 164–65, 188–89, 196–97, 200, 232
presidential election, 5
Prime Directive, 249. See also *Star Trek*
Prisoner, The (series), 3, 6, 36, 189–200, 299
   Rover, the, 196
   Village, the, 190–99
progressive politics, 124, 225
Project Quantum Leap, 202. See also *Quantum Leap*
Project UFO (series), 337
protagonists, 10, 25, 42, 52, 54–55, 62, 85, 107, 144, 192, 255, 293, 312, 342
Proust, Marcel, 181
Psycho (movie), 265
Pudd'nhead Wilson (Twain), 19
puppets, 107, 109–10, 191, 212
Pushing Daisies (series), 300, 322, 327

Q (Bond character), 26
quality television, 46, 276, 281, 297, 290, 337, 338
Quantum Leap (series), 3, 201–7, 258
Queer as Folk (series), 90, 286
Quinto, Zachary, 129

race, 110, 238, 249
Radio Times, 136, 139
Raimi, Sam, 20–21, 330, 334
Raimi, Ted, 21

Rambo (movie), 284
Rashomon (movie), 342
ratings, 1–2, 16, 25, 28, 33, 44, 57, 71, 73, 85–86, 95, 97–98, 102, 132, 136, 156, 160, 176–77, 186, 202, 213–14, 216, 221, 227, 242, 296–97, 317–19, 322, 338, 341
raw footage, 70
reality television, 68–70, 75
Real World (television show), 176
Reaper (series), 261
Reavers, 115–16, 119. See also *Firefly*
Rebecca (movie), 85
reboots, 25, 191, 238, 289
Red Dwarf (series), 3, 208–13
Regarding Henry (movie), 23
ReGenesis (series), 27
Remington Steele (movie), 41
replicants, 237
Rescue Me (series), 282
Reservoir Dogs (movie), 96
Rifkin, Ron, 23
rift, the, 276–77. See also *Torchwood*
Rigg, Diana, 38–40
Ringu (movie), 264
Ripping Yarns (series), 140
Rixon, Paul, 260
Robin Hood, 55, 114
Roddenberry, Gene, 242, 244–45, 248–51
Rogen, Seth, 121, 125
Romeo and Juliet (movie), 215–16
Romero, George A., 243, 266
Room and Bored, 68, 70–71, 73. See also *Comeback, The*
Roots (miniseries), 251
Roseanne (series), 12
Roswell (series), 179, 214–20, 322, 327
Roswell, New Mexico, 215–16
Roswell High novels, 219
Royston Vasey, 134–37. See also *League of Gentlemen, The*
Russell, Kurt, 240

Sackhoff, Katee, 46, 335
Saint, The (series), 36, 167, 190

Sale, Tim, 131
satire, 10, 38, 77–78, 168, 226, 232
Saturday evening timeslot, 302–3
Saturday Night Live (series), 77, 83, 127, 213, 298
Saunders, Jennifer, 7, 11–13
Saved by the Bell (series), 121
"Save the cheerleader, save the world," 127, 129. See also *Heroes* (series)
Scalia, Justice Antonin, 290
Schiavo, Terri, 233
Schrader, Paul, 162
Schwartz, Josh, 123
Schwarzenegger, Arnold, 224
science fiction, 15–16, 19, 23–24, 43, 46, 51, 54, 58, 87, 99, 107–8, 110, 112, 127, 149, 159, 186, 189, 202, 208, 212, 214–16, 219, 237–39, 242, 245, 248, 256, 261, 263, 293, 295–97, 307, 324–25, 335, 337–38, 340, 343
Sci-Fi Channel, 44, 58, 110, 127, 181, 187, 237, 239, 258, 307
Scooby Gang, 31, 62–63. See also *Buffy the Vampire Slayer*
Screen Wipe (series), 278
Scrimm, Angus, 24
season/series finales, 18, 31–32, 34–35, 56, 131–33, 202, 257, 277, 303, 311
Seattle, Wash., 319
Secret Agent (series), 190–91, 197–99
Segel, Jason, 121–22
Seinfeld (series), 182
self-reflexivity, 242, 287, 342
Sellers, Peter, 168
Senior Partners, 29, 31. See also *Angel*
Serenity (movie), 111–12, 118
Serenity (spaceship), 113–18. See also *Firefly*
seriality, 4–5, 25–26, 53, 65, 82, 84, 87–88, 92, 135, 143, 150, 157, 167, 215, 217, 231, 237, 240–43, 269, 278, 280, 287, 302, 305, 339, 341
serial killers, 5, 90–94, 96, 135, 162, 231

serial narrative, 143, 240, 280
Serling, Rod, 245, 291–98
7 Faces of Dr. Lao, The (movie), 295
Sex and the City (series), 13
SF, 108, 215
Shakespeare, William, 168, 178, 216, 242, 245, 250
Shanks, Michael, 239
Shatner, William, 244, 248–49
Shearsmith, Reece, 3, 135, 137–40. See also *League of Gentlemen, The*
Shield, The (series), 90
Shining, The (movie), 151, 265
"shippers," 333, 336, 343
shocking comedy, 235
Showtime, 5, 90, 95–96, 237, 286, 327
Shrinking Man, The (movie), 295
Sidehackers (series), 186
Silence of Lambs, The (movie), 96, 252
Silverman, Sarah, 75
Simm, John, 143–44
Simpsons, The (series), 2, 6, 125, 221–28, 231–32, 235, 240–41, 298
Simpsons Game, 227
Simpsons Movie, The (movie), 221
Singer, Bryan, 44
situation comedy, 7, 10–13, 68–70, 72–73, 75, 121, 134, 170–71, 211, 213, 216, 222–23, 225, 230
Six Degrees (series), 127
Six Feet Under (series), 91–92
Sixth Sense, The (movie), 266
Sky News, 285
Sky One, 227, 261, 324
slasher films, 264
slash fiction, 65
small-town America, 226, 260, 262
Smallville (series), 131, 179, 260–63
Smith, Kevin, 319
soap operas, 28, 82–85, 87–88, 134, 160, 269, 272
Softly, Softly: Taskforce (series), 52
Solo, Napoleon, 191, 193
Somewhere in Time (movie), 295
Sopranos, The (series), 90, 182, 195, 287
Sorkin, Aaron, 283

soul, the, 4, 29–31, 64, 75, 159, 182, 245, 261, 334
sound effects, 168, 305
Southern California, 60, 177
South Park (series), 2, 6, 17, 222, 229–36
South Park—Bigger, Longer, and Uncut (movie), 235
Space: Above and Beyond (series), 238
Spamalot (musical), 173
Spider-Man movies, 21, 121, 131
Spielberg, Steven, 6, 297
Spike, 31, 34, 57, 61, 63–65. See also *Buffy the Vampire Slayer*
Spitting Image (television show), 83, 210, 213
split screen, 285
Spooks (series), 285
Springer, Jerry, 341
Springfield, 221, 223–24, 227. See also *Simpsons, The*
Stafford, Nikki, 179
Stagecoach (movie), 112, 118
Stallone, Sylvester, 284
Stand The (miniseries), 151, 155–56, 158
stand-alone episodes, 6, 318, 337, 339, 343
Stargate Atlantis (series), 237, 240, 242, 261
Stargate: Continuum (series), 238
Stargate SG-1 (series), 6, 50, 237–43
Stargate Universe (series), 237
Stargate: The Ark of Truth (series), 237
Starsky & Hutch (series), 161, 163
Star Trek (series), 3, 6, 47, 84, 86, 96, 100, 105, 113, 160, 186, 215, 237–38, 241–42, 244–59, 265, 291, 299, 322, 328
Star Trek: Deep Space Nine (series), 245, 254–56
Star Trek IV: The Voyage Home (movie), 244
Star Trek: The Motion Picture (movie), 244
Star Trek: The Next Generation (series), 96, 245–46, 250–54

Star Trek: The Wrath of Khan (movie), 244
Star Trek III: The Search for Spock (movie), 244
Star Trek: Voyager (series), 256–58, 322
Star Wars (movie), 44, 49, 54–55, 58, 113, 123, 265–66, 307
State of Play (miniseries), 276
St. Elsewhere (series), 337
Stewart, Jon, 3, 61, 77–80, 82, 222, 228
Stewart, Patrick, 208, 250, 253–54
Stockwell, Dean, 202–3
Stone, Matt, 2, 222–33
Stoppard, Tom, 252
story arcs, 19, 26, 47, 53, 64, 104, 137, 143, 206, 240, 317
Straczynski, J. Michael, 54
straight man, 73
Strange Case of Dr. Jekyll and Mr. Hyde, The (movie), 87
Streisand, Barbra, 231
string theory, 202
Studio One (television show), 293
subtext, 4, 65, 79, 253, 332, 334
suicide, 57, 62, 328
Sunnydale, 29, 60–61. See also *Buffy the Vampire Slayer*
Superbad (movie), 121
Superman, 131
Supernatural (series), 2, 6, 260–67, 343–44
supernatural, the, 24–25, 29, 37, 43, 60–62, 84–85, 88, 100, 151, 253, 277–78, 311, 326, 337–38, 340, 343–44
Surface (series), 149
Surnow, Joel, 282, 289
surveillance society, 284
Survivor (television show), 15, 51, 156
Suspense (television show), 285
Sweeney, The (series), 143–44
syndication, 43, 66, 87, 120, 229, 296–97

Tales from the Crypt (television show), 141, 297
Talking Heads (television show), 135

Talk Soup (television show), 188
Tappert, Rob, 21
Tapping, Amanda, 239
Tarantino, Quentin, 23, 134
Tartikoff, Brandon, 159–60, 162
Taxi (series), 70, 73
Team America: World Police (movie), 231
technology, 38, 42, 48, 108, 196, 218, 238, 240, 272, 284, 308, 312, 333
"Tek Janson Adventures," 79. See also *Colbert Report, The*
telefantasy, 276–79, 281
Television Act of 1954, 167
television production, 170, 242, 261–62
Tennant, David, 6, 97, 103
Terminator: Sarah Connor Chronicles (series), 1
test-cards, 147–48. See also *Life on Mars*
Texas Chainsaw Massacre, The (movie), 265
That '70s Show (series), 124
That Was the Week That Was (television show), 167
Thief (movie), 162
thirtysomething (series), 174
This Island Earth (movie), 187
This is Spinal Tap (movie), 282
This Life (series), 268–74, 275, 280, 308
This Life + 10 (series), 274
Thomas, Philip Michael, 161
Thomas, Rob, 2, 314–15, 317–21
Thompson, Robert, 303, 337–38, 340–41
"Threatdown, The," 79. See also *Colbert Report, The*
Three's Company (series), 73
Thurman, Uma, 40
Timecode (series), 285
time travel, 20, 32, 142, 144, 147, 202–3, 279
Time Tunnel, The (series), 203
"Tip of the Hat/Wag of the Finger," 79. See also *Colbert Report, The*
Todorov, Tzvetan, 100
tone, 30, 58, 148, 231, 269, 326
Tonight Show with Jay Leno, The (television show), 233
Torchwood (series), 3, 6, 143, 275–81, 313
Torres, Gina, 114
torture, 5, 29, 48, 61, 64, 85, 107, 129, 265, 283–84, 288–89
Touchstone, 156
Tracey Ullman Show, The (television show), 222, 227
transgression/the transgressive, 54, 169–71, 276, 329, 332, 335
"Treehouse of Horror," 224. See also *Simpsons, The*
Truman Show, The (movie), 189
Tuck Everlasting (movie), 149
Tulloch, John, 98–99, 103
Turn of Screw, The (movie), 86
TV Guide, 65, 182, 201, 301
Twain, Mark, 19
24 (series), 1, 4–5, 24, 129, 151, 282–90, 305, 312
Twilight Zone (television show), 3, 6, 245, 291–98
Twilight Zone: The Movie (movie), 297
Twin Peaks (series), 2, 11, 136, 150, 189, 291, 299–6, 322
Twin Peaks: Fire Walk with Me (movie), 305

UFOs, 337–38, 340
Ugly Betty (series), 130
Ultraviolet (series), 3, 307–13
uncanny, the, 99–100, 103
Underworld (movie), 309
United Kingdom, 3, 6, 11–12, 37, 40, 54, 57, 97, 99, 102, 166, 226, 239, 261, 263, 271, 274–76, 285, 307
United States Steel Hour (television show), 292
University Challenge (television show), 208
upfronts, 70
UPN, 33, 35, 66–67, 213, 263, 297, 314, 316–17, 320

Urban Legend (movie), 265
urban legends, 264, 267, 300
USA Network, 159
utopias, 116, 124, 245

vampire genre, the, 307, 309, 313
vampire hunters, 308–11, 313
vampires, 29, 60, 63, 86, 88, 177, 308–12
Vancouver, Canada, 237, 261–63
Van Helsing, 60, 87, 309
Von Daniken, Erich, 238
Variety, 112, 187, 263
Veronica Mars (series), 2, 176, 314–21
Vicar of Dibley, The (series), 7
video games, 16, 21, 27, 153, 156–57
Vietnam/Vietnam War, 89, 162, 195, 223, 246
vigilante justice, 91–92, 95–96. See also *Dexter*
villains, 24, 37, 39, 42–43, 53, 54, 128, 185, 191, 240, 283
villains as heroes, 52
violence, 51, 63–64, 93, 128, 334
Virilio, Paul, 111, 113, 117–18
visual icons, 36, 101
visual jokes, 70, 139
Viva Las Vegas (movie), 18
Vulcan, 246, 248, 250, 257–59. See also *Star Trek*

Wales, 194, 197, 280
Walk Hard (movie), 121
Wall Street (movie), 251
Waltons, The (series), 225
War and Remembrance (miniseries), 84
war on terror, 127–28, 282
Wasteland (series), 151
watershed (on UK television), 269, 276
WB, the, 28, 33–35, 62–63, 66–67, 87, 176, 179, 214, 260, 263
webisodes, 47, 49, 286
Weeds (series), 90
"Weekend Update," 83
werewolves, 61, 86
West, Mae, 18
Western, the, 15, 17–19, 43, 112, 258, 333

West Wing, The (series), 283, 287
Whedon, Joss, 1–2, 4, 28–30, 33–35, 54, 60, 62–63, 65, 109, 112, 118, 134, 177, 179, 258, 263, 300, 319, 321
"Who Killed Laura Palmer?" 300, 305. See also *Twin Peaks*
Wiccans, 61, 63
Wicker Man, The (movie), 141
Wii, 234
Wikipedia, 81, 158
Wilcox, Rhonda V., 66
Will and Grace (series), 13
Williamson, Kevin, 151
Winds of War, The (miniseries), 84
Wise, Ray, 304
Wizard of Oz, The (movie), 243
Wolf, Dick, 159
Wolfram and Hart, 29, 31, 33–34. See also *Angel*
woman warriors, 25
Wonderfalls (series), 3, 322–27
Wonder Woman (series), 37, 331
Wonder Years, The (series), 124
World of Warcraft (series), 233
wormholes, 105–6, 237, 242–43, 254
Wrapped in Plastic, 306
writers' strike, 5–6, 74, 78, 95, 133, 284
WWJBD (What Would Jack Bauer Do?), 288–89. See also *24*

Xena: Warrior Princess (series), 3, 17, 21, 329–36
X-Files, The (series), 1–2, 6, 16, 25, 41–42, 87, 100, 150, 160, 215, 220, 237, 241, 262–63, 275, 280, 308, 312, 322, 337–44
X-Files: Fight the Future, The (movie), 338–39
X-Files: I Want to Believe, The (movie), 343
X-Philes, 343. See also *X-Files, The*

YouTube, 80–81

Zacherek, Stephanie, 320
zeitgeist, 90, 127, 282, 337–38